ACCA

Paper P2 INT/UK

Corporate Reporting

Study Text

British Library Cataloguing-in-Publication Data

A catalogue record for this book is available from the British Library.

Published by:
Kaplan Publishing UK
Unit 2 The Business Centre
Molly Millars Lane
Wokingham
Berkshire
RG41 2QZ

ISBN: 978-1-78415-816-3

Acknowledgements

This Product includes propriety content of the International Accounting Standards Board which is overseen by the IFRS Foundation, and is used with the express permission of the IFRS Foundation under licence.

Contents

chapter

ntroduction

Paper Introduction

This document references IFRS® Standards and IAS® Standards, which are authored by the International Accounting Standards Board (the Board), and published in the 2016 IFRS Standards Red Book.

How to Use the Materials

The nature of the P2 Corporate Reporting exam, is that of a 'pillar topic'. This means that students will need a good understanding of the basics of accounting as covered initially in F3 and then in F7.

The ACCA website www.accaglobal.com includes a useful FAQ section. Within this section the examiner recommends:

> *'It is important that students have done some pre-course work such as attempting as homework a past F7 exam as appropriate revision before starting work on P2. This message applies equally to students who have attempted and passed F7 and to those who have gained an exemption from F7'.*
>
> *P2 examiner – ACCA website*

These Kaplan Publishing learning materials have been carefully designed to make your learning experience as easy as possible and to give you the best chances of success in your examinations.

The product range contains a number of features to help you in the study process. They include:

(1) Detailed study guide and syllabus objectives

(2) Description of the examination

(3) Study skills and revision guidance

(4) Study text

(5) Question practice

The sections on the study guide, the syllabus objectives, the examination and study skills should all be read before you commence your studies. They are designed to familiarise you with the nature and content of the examination and give you tips on how to best approach your learning.

The **study text** comprises the main learning materials and gives guidance as to the importance of topics and where other related resources can be found. Each chapter includes:

- The **learning objectives** contained in each chapter, which have been carefully mapped to the examining body's own syllabus learning objectives or outcomes. You should use these to check you have a clear understanding of all the topics on which you might be assessed in the examination.

- The **chapter diagram** provides a visual reference for the content in the chapter, giving an overview of the topics and how they link together.
- The **content** for each topic area commences with a brief explanation or definition to put the topic into context before covering the topic in detail. You should follow your studying of the content with a review of the illustration/s. These are worked examples which will help you to understand better how to apply the content for the topic.
- **Test your understanding** sections provide an opportunity to assess your understanding of the key topics by applying what you have learned to short questions. Answers can be found at the back of each chapter.
- **Summary diagrams** complete each chapter to show the important links between topics and the overall content of the paper. These diagrams should be used to check that you have covered and understood the core topics before moving on.
- **Question practice** is provided through this text.

Quality and accuracy are of the utmost importance to us so if you spot an error in any of our products, please send an email to mykaplanreporting@kaplan.com with full details, or follow the link to the feedback form in MyKaplan.

Our Quality Coordinator will work with our technical team to verify the error and take action to ensure it is corrected in future editions.

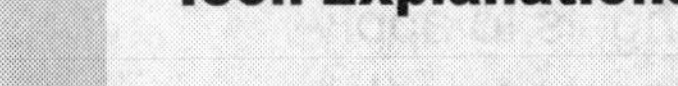

Icon Explanations

Definition – Key definitions that you will need to learn from the core content.

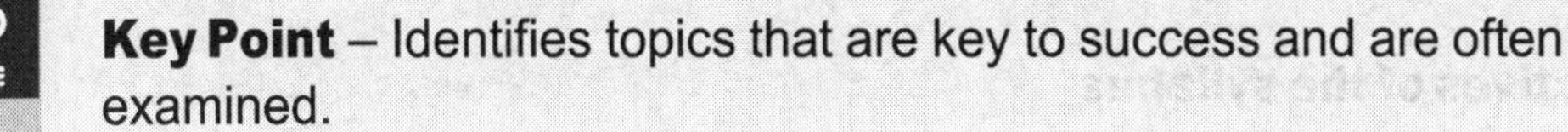

Key Point – Identifies topics that are key to success and are often examined.

New – Identifies topics that are brand new in papers that build on, and therefore also contain, learning covered in earlier papers.

Test Your Understanding – Exercises for you to complete to ensure that you have understood the topics just learned.

Illustration – Worked examples help you understand the core content better.

Tricky topic – When reviewing these areas care should be taken and all illustrations and test your understanding exercises should be completed to ensure that the topic is understood.

Tutorial note – Included to explain some of the technical points in more detail.

Footsteps – Helpful tutor tips.

On-line subscribers

Our on-line resources are designed to increase the flexibility of your learning materials and provide you with immediate feedback on how your studies are progressing.

If you are subscribed to our on-line resources you will find:

(1) On-line referenceware: reproduces your Study Text on-line, giving you anytime, anywhere access.

(2) On-line testing: provides you with additional on-line objective testing so you can practice what you have learned further.

(3) On-line performance management: immediate access to your on-line testing results. Review your performance by key topics and chart your achievement through the course relative to your peer group.

Ask your local customer services staff if you are not already a subscriber and wish to join.

Paper introduction

Paper background

The aim of ACCA Paper P2 (INT), Corporate Reporting, is to apply knowledge and skills and to exercise professional judgement in the application and evaluation of financial reporting principles and practices in a range of business contexts and situations.

Objectives of the syllabus

- Discuss the professional and ethical duties of the accountant
- Evaluate the financial reporting framework
- Advise on and report the financial performance of entities
- Prepare the financial statements of groups of entities in accordance with relevant accounting standards
- Explain reporting issues relating to specialised entities
- Discuss the implications of changes in accounting regulation on financial reporting
- Appraise the financial performance and position of entities
- Evaluate current developments.

Core areas of the syllabus

- The professional and ethical duty of the accountant
- The financial reporting framework
- Reporting the financial performance of entities
- Financial statements of groups of entities
- Specialised entities
- Implications of changes in accounting regulation on financial reporting
- The appraisal of financial performance and position of entities
- Current developments.

Approach to INT and UK syllabus elements

Both the International and UK P2 syllabus apply the principles of International Financial Reporting Standards.

The international syllabus has been used as the basis of the text.

UK syllabus students are also required to outline and discuss the differences between the IFRS for SMEs® Standard and UK accounting standards. They must also have a knowledge of some of the requirements of the Companies Act. The examinable differences are covered in chapter 25 of this text.

Syllabus objectives

We have reproduced the ACCA's syllabus below, showing where the objectives are explored within this book. Within the chapters, we have broken down the extensive information found in the syllabus into easily digestible and relevant sections, called Content Objectives. These correspond to the objectives at the beginning of each chapter.

Syllabus learning objective/Chapter

A THE PROFESSIONAL AND ETHICAL DUTIES OF THE ACCOUNTANT

1 Professional behaviour and compliance with accounting standards

(a) Appraise and discuss the ethical and professional issues in advising on corporate reporting.[3] **Ch. 2**

(b) Assess the relevance and importance of ethical and professional issues in complying with accounting standards.[3] **Ch. 2**

2 Ethical requirements of corporate reporting and the consequences of unethical behaviour

(a) Appraise the potential ethical implications of professional and managerial decisions in the preparation of corporate reports.[3] **Ch. 2**

(b) Assess the consequences of not upholding ethical principles in the preparation of corporate reports.[3] **Ch. 2**

3 Social responsibility

(a) Discuss the increased demand for transparency in corporate reports, and the emergence of non-financial reporting standards.[3] **Ch. 17**

(b) Discuss the progress towards a framework for integrated reporting.[3] **Ch. 17**

B THE FINANCIAL REPORTING FRAMEWORK

1 The applications, strengths and weaknesses of an accounting framework

(a) Evaluate the valuation models adopted by standard setters.[3] **Ch. 1**

(b) Discuss the use of an accounting framework in underpinning the production of accounting standards.[3] **Ch. 1**

(c) Assess the success of such a framework in introducing rigorous and consistent accounting standards.[3] **Ch. 1**

2 Critical evaluation of principles and practices

(a) Identify the relationship between accounting theory and practice.[2] **Ch. 1**

(b) Critically evaluate accounting principles and practices used in corporate reporting.[3] **Ch. 1**

C REPORTING THE FINANCIAL PERFORMANCE OF ENTITIES

1 Performance reporting

(a) Prepare reports relating to corporate performance for external stakeholders.[3] **Ch. 3**

(b) Discuss and apply the criteria that must be met before an entity can apply the revenue recognition model to a contract.[3] **Ch. 4**

(c) Discuss and apply the five step model which relates to revenue earned from a contract with a customer.[3] **Ch. 4**

2 Non-current assets

(a) Apply and discuss the timing of the recognition of non-current assets and the determination of their carrying amounts including impairment and revaluations.[3] **Ch. 5**

(b) Apply and discuss the treatment of non-current assets held for sale.[3] **Ch. 5**

(c) Apply and discuss the accounting treatment of investment properties including classification, recognition and measurement issues.[3] **Ch. 5**

(d) Apply and discuss the accounting treatment of intangible assets including the criteria for recognition and measurement subsequent to acquisition and classification.[3] **Ch. 5**

3 Financial instruments

(a) Apply and discuss the recognition and derecognition of financial assets and financial liabilities.[2] **Ch. 11**

(b) Apply and discuss the classification of financial assets and financial liabilities and their measurement.[2] **Ch. 11**

(c) Apply and discuss the treatment of gains and losses arising on financial assets and financial liabilities.[2] **Ch. 11**

(d) Apply and discuss the treatment of the expected loss impairment model.[2] **Ch. 11**

(e) Account for derivative financial instruments, and simple embedded derivatives.[2] **Ch. 11**

(f) Outline the principles of hedge accounting and account for fair value hedges and cash flow hedges including hedge effectiveness.[2] **Ch. 11**

4 Leases

(a) Apply and discuss the accounting for leases by lessees including the measurement of the right of use asset and liability.[3] **Ch. 7**

(b) Apply and discuss the accounting for leases by lessors.[3] **Ch. 7**

(c) Apply and discuss the circumstances where there may be re-measurement of the lease liability.[3] **Ch. 7**

(d) Apply and discuss the reasons behind the separation of the components of a lease contract into lease and non-lease elements.[3] **Ch. 7**

(e) Discuss the recognition exemptions under the current leasing standard.[3] **Ch. 7**

(f) Account for and discuss sale and leaseback transactions.[3] **Ch. 7**

5 Segment reporting

(a) Determine the nature and extent of reportable segments.[3] **Ch. 13**

(b) Specify and discuss the nature of segment information to be disclosed.[3] **Ch. 13**

6 Employee benefits

(a) Apply and discuss the accounting treatment of short term and long term employee benefits and defined contribution and defined benefit plans. [3] **Ch. 8**

(b) Account for gains and losses on settlements and curtailments.[2] **Ch. 8**

(c) Account for the 'Asset Ceiling' test and the reporting of actuarial gains and losses.[2] **Ch. 8**

7 Income taxes

(a) Apply and discuss the recognition and measurement of deferred tax liabilities and deferred tax assets.[3] **Ch. 12**

(b) Determine the recognition of tax expense or income and its inclusion in the financial statements.[3] **Ch. 12**

8 Provisions, contingencies, events after the reporting date

(a) Apply and discuss the recognition, derecognition and measurement of provisions, contingent liabilities and contingent assets including environmental provisions and restructuring provisions.[3] **Ch. 10**

(b) Apply and discuss the accounting for events after the reporting date.[3] **Ch. 10**

(c) Determine and report going concern issues arising after the reporting date.[3] **Ch. 10**

9 Related parties

(a) Determine the parties considered to be related to an entity.[3] **Ch. 14**

(b) Identify the implications of related party relationships and the need for disclosure.[3] **Ch. 14**

10 Share-based payment

(a) Apply and discuss the recognition and measurement criteria for share-based payment transactions.[3] **Ch. 9**

(b) Account for modifications, cancellations and settlements of share-based payment transactions.[2] **Ch. 9**

11 Reporting requirements of small and medium-sized entities (SMEs)

(a) Discuss the accounting treatments not allowable under the SMEs Standard including the revaluation model for certain assets.[3] **Ch. 16**

(b) Discuss and apply the simplifications introduced by the SMEs Standard including accounting for goodwill and intangible assets, financial instruments, defined benefit schemes, exchange differences and associates and joint ventures.[3] **Ch. 16**

D FINANCIAL STATEMENTS OF GROUPS OF ENTITIES

1 Group accounting including statements of cash flow

(a) Apply the method of accounting for business combinations, including complex group structures.[3] **Chs. 19, 20 and 21**

(b) Apply the principles in determining the cost of a business combination.[3] **Chs. 19, 20 and 21**

(c) Apply the recognition and measurement criteria for identifiable acquired assets and liabilities and goodwill including step acquisitions.[3] **Chs. 19 and 21**

(d) Apply and discuss the criteria used to identify a subsidiary and an associate.[3] **Ch. 19**

(e) Determine and apply appropriate procedures to be used in preparing group financial statements.[3] **Chs. 19 – 23**

(f) Identify and outline the circumstances in which a group is required to prepare consolidated financial statements; the circumstances when a group may claim an exemption from the preparation of consolidated financial statements, and why directors may not wish to consolidate a subsidiary and where this is permitted.[2] **Ch. 19**

(g) Apply the equity method of accounting for associates.[3] **Ch. 19**

(h) Outline and apply the key definitions and accounting methods which relate to interests in joint arrangements.[3] **Ch. 19**

(i) Prepare and discuss group statements of cash flows.[3] **Ch. 24**

2 Continuing and discontinued interests

(a) Prepare group financial statements where activities have been discontinued, or have been acquired or disposed in the period.[3] **Ch. 21**

(b) Apply and discuss the treatment of a subsidiary which has been acquired exclusively with a view to subsequent disposal.[3] **Ch. 21**

3 Changes in group structures

(a) Discuss the reasons behind a group reorganisation.[3] **Ch. 23**

(b) Evaluate and assess the principal terms of a proposed group reorganisation.[3] **Ch. 23**

4 Foreign transactions and entities

(a) Outline and apply the translation of foreign currency amounts and transactions into the functional currency and the presentational currency.[3] **Ch. 22**

(b) Account for the consolidation of foreign operations and their disposal.[2] **Ch. 22**

E SPECIALISED ENTITIES AND SPECIALISED TRANSACTIONS

1 Financial reporting in specialised, not-for-profit and public sector entities

(a) Apply knowledge from the syllabus to straightforward transactions and events arising in specialised, not-for-profit, and public sector entities.[3] **Chs. 5 and 16**

2 Entity reconstructions

(a) Identify when an entity may no longer be viewed as a going concern or uncertainty exists surrounding the going concern status.[2] **Ch. 16**

(b) Identify and outline the circumstances in which a reconstruction would be an appropriate alternative to a company liquidation.[2] **Ch. 16**

(c) Outline the appropriate accounting treatment required relating to reconstructions.[2] **Ch. 16**

F IMPLICATIONS OF CHANGES IN ACCOUNTING REGULATION ON FINANCIAL REPORTING

1 The effect of changes in accounting standards on accounting systems

(a) Apply and discuss the accounting implications of the first time adoption of a body of new accounting standards.[3] **Ch. 15**

2 Proposed changes to accounting standards

(a) Identify the issues and deficiencies which have led to a proposed change to an accounting standard.[2] **Ch. 15**

G THE APPRAISAL OF FINANCIAL PERFORMANCE AND POSITION OF ENTITIES

1 The creation of suitable accounting policies

(a) Develop accounting policies for an entity which meets the entity's reporting requirements.[3] **Ch. 3**

(b) Identify accounting treatments adopted in financial statements and assess their suitability and acceptability.[3] **Ch. 3**

2 Analysis and interpretation of financial information and measurement of performance

(a) Select and calculate relevant indicators of financial and non-financial performance.[3] **Ch. 3**

(b) Identify and evaluate significant features and issues in financial statements.[3] **Ch. 3**

(c) Highlight inconsistencies in financial information through analysis and application of knowledge.[3] **Ch. 3**

(d) Make inferences from the analysis of information taking into account the limitation of the information, the analytical methods used and the business environment in which the entity operates.[3] **Ch. 3**

H CURRENT DEVELOPMENTS

1 Environmental and social reporting

(a) Appraise the impact of environmental, social, and ethical factors on performance measurement.[3] **Ch. 3 and 17**

(b) Evaluate current reporting requirements in the area, including the development of integrated reporting.[3] **Ch. 17**

(c) Discuss why entities might include disclosures relating to the environment and society.[3] **Ch. 17**

2 Convergence between national and international reporting standards

(a) Evaluate the implications of worldwide convergence with International Financial Reporting Standards.[3] **Ch. 15**

(b) Discuss the influence of national regulators on international financial reporting.[2] **Ch. 15**

3 Current reporting issues

(a) Discuss current issues in corporate reporting, including

- recent IFRS® Standards
- practice and regulatory issues
- proposed changes to IFRS and IAS® Standards
- problems with extant standards.[3] **Ch. 18 and throughout**

The superscript numbers in square brackets indicate the intellectual depth at which the subject area could be assessed within the examination. Level 1 (knowledge and comprehension) broadly equates with the Knowledge module, Level 2 (application and analysis) with the Skills module and Level 3 (synthesis and evaluation) to the Professional level. However, lower level skills can continue to be assessed as you progress through each module and level.

The examination

Examination format

The syllabus is assessed by a three-hour fifteen minute paper-based examination. It examines professional competences within the corporate reporting environment.

Students will be examined on concepts, theories and principles and on their ability to question and comment on proposed accounting treatments.

Students should be capable of relating professional issues to relevant concepts and practical situations. The evaluation of alternative accounting practices and the identification and prioritisation of issues will be a key element of the paper. Professional and ethical judgement will need to be exercised, together with the integration of technical knowledge when addressing corporate reporting issues in a business context.

Global issues will be addressed via the current issues questions on the paper. Students will be required to adopt either a stakeholder or an external focus in answering questions and to demonstrate personal skills such as problem solving, dealing with information and decision making.

The paper also deals with specific professional knowledge appropriate to the preparation and presentation of consolidated and other financial statements from accounting data, to conform with accounting standards.

Section A will consist of one scenario based question worth 50 marks. It will deal with the preparation of consolidated financial statements including group statements of cash flows and with issues in financial reporting.

Students will be required to answer two out of three questions in Section B, which will normally comprise two questions which will be scenario or case-study based and one essay question which may have some computational element. Section B could deal with any aspects of the syllabus.

UK syllabus students will sit an exam that is identical in format to the International syllabus exam. The Examiner has indicated that the differences from the INT paper will account for no more than 20% of the UK paper. The differences examined may be included within one or more questions in the examination paper.

	Number of marks
Section A	
Compulsory question	50
Section B	
Two from three 25-mark questions	50
	___
Total time allowed: 3 hours and 15 minutes	100

Note that, in common with other ACCA Professional level papers, there will be a total of four professional marks available to candidates in each P2 examination paper. In the case of P2, the professional marks will be only available in section B, with two marks allocated to each of the three optional questions, with candidates required to attempt any two of those questions.

Study skills and revision guidance

This section aims to give guidance on how to study for your ACCA exams and to give ideas on how to improve your existing study techniques.

Preparing to study

Set your objectives

Before starting to study decide what you want to achieve – the type of pass you wish to obtain. This will decide the level of commitment and time you need to dedicate to your studies.

Devise a study plan

Determine which times of the week you will study.

Split these times into sessions of at least one hour for study of new material. Any shorter periods could be used for revision or practice.

Put the times you plan to study onto a study plan for the weeks from now until the exam and set yourself targets for each period of study – in your sessions make sure you cover the course, course assignments and revision.

If you are studying for more than one paper at a time, try to vary your subjects as this can help you to keep interested and see subjects as part of wider knowledge.

When working through your course, compare your progress with your plan and, if necessary, re-plan your work (perhaps including extra sessions) or, if you are ahead, do some extra revision/practice questions.

Effective studying

Active reading

You are not expected to learn the text by rote, rather, you must understand what you are reading and be able to use it to pass the exam and develop good practice. A good technique to use is SQ3Rs – Survey, Question, Read, Recall, Review:

(1) **Survey the chapter** – look at the headings and read the introduction, summary and objectives, so as to get an overview of what the chapter deals with.

(2) **Question** – whilst undertaking the survey, ask yourself the questions that you hope the chapter will answer for you.

(3) **Read** through the chapter thoroughly, answering the questions and making sure you can meet the objectives. Attempt the exercises and activities in the text, and work through all the examples.

(4) **Recall** – at the end of each section and at the end of the chapter, try to recall the main ideas of the section/chapter without referring to the text. This is best done after a short break of a couple of minutes after the reading stage.

(5) **Review** – check that your recall notes are correct.

You may also find it helpful to re-read the chapter to try to see the topic(s) it deals with as a whole.

Note-taking

Taking notes is a useful way of learning, but do not simply copy out the text. The notes must:

- be in your own words
- be concise
- cover the key points
- be well-organised
- be modified as you study further chapters in this text or in related ones.

Trying to summarise a chapter without referring to the text can be a useful way of determining which areas you know and which you don't.

Three ways of taking notes:

Summarise the key points of a chapter.

Make linear notes – a list of headings, divided up with subheadings listing the key points. If you use linear notes, you can use different colours to highlight key points and keep topic areas together. Use plenty of space to make your notes easy to use.

Try a diagrammatic form – the most common of which is a mind-map. To make a mind-map, put the main heading in the centre of the paper and put a circle around it. Then draw short lines radiating from this to the main sub-headings, which again have circles around them. Then continue the process from the sub-headings to sub-sub-headings, advantages, disadvantages, etc.

Highlighting and underlining – you may find it useful to underline or highlight key points in your study text, but do be selective. You may also wish to make notes in the margins.

Revision

The best approach to revision is to revise the course as you work through it. Also try to leave four to six weeks before the exam for final revision. Make sure you cover the whole syllabus and pay special attention to those areas where your knowledge is weak. Here are some recommendations:

Read through the text and your notes again and condense your notes into key phrases. It may help to put key revision points onto index cards to look at when you have a few minutes to spare.

Review any assignments you have completed and look at where you lost marks – put more work into those areas where you were weak.

Practise exam standard questions under timed conditions. If you are short of time, list the points that you would cover in your answer and then read the model answer, but do try to complete at least a few questions under exam conditions.

Also practise producing answer plans and comparing them to the model answer.

If you are stuck on a topic find somebody (a tutor) to explain it to you.

Read good newspapers and professional journals, especially ACCA's Student Accountant – this can give you an advantage in the exam.

Ensure you know the structure of the exam – how many questions and of what type you will be expected to answer. During your revision attempt all the different styles of questions you may be asked.

Further reading

The P2 examining team have frequently stated the need for students to read widely.

You may find the following additional reading helpful:

'A student's guide to preparing financial statements' by Sally Baker

'A student's guide to group accounts' by Tom Clendon.

'A student's guide to International Financial Reporting Standards' by Clare Finch.

You can also find technical articles in Student Accountant magazine, as well as elsewhere on the ACCA website.

Please be aware that ACCA update their list of examinable documents annually. You should refer to this before undertaking any further reading.

Technical update

This text has been updated to reflect Examinable Documents September 2016 to June 2017 issued by ACCA.

chapter

1

Frameworks

Chapter learning objectives

Upon completion of this chapter you will be able to:

- evaluate the valuation models adopted by standard setters
- discuss the use of an accounting framework in underpinning the production of accounting standards
- assess the success of such a framework in introducing rigorous and consistent accounting standards
- identify the relationship between accounting theory and practice
- critically evaluate accounting principles and practices used in corporate reporting

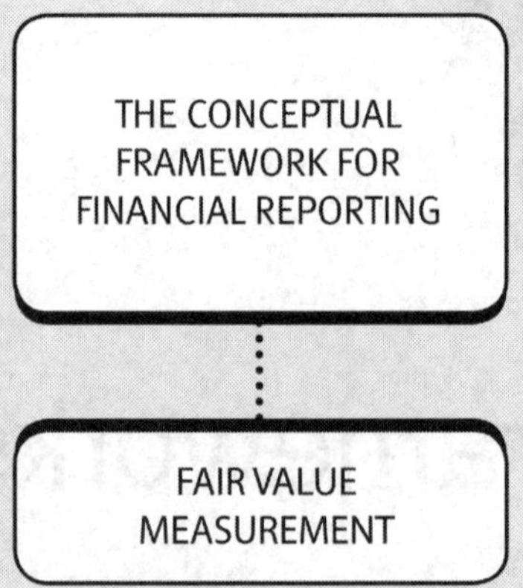

1 Conceptual Framework for Financial Reporting

Introduction: the need for a conceptual framework

A conceptual framework is a set of theoretical principles and concepts that underlie the preparation and presentation of financial statements.

If no conceptual framework existed, then it is more likely that accounting standards would be produced on a haphazard basis as particular issues and circumstances arose. These accounting standards might be inconsistent with one another, or perhaps even contradictory.

A strong conceptual framework therefore means that there is a set of principles in place from which all future accounting standards draw. It also acts as a reference point for the preparers of financial statements if there is no adequate accounting standard governing the types of transactions that an entity enters into (this will be extremely rare).

This section of the text considers the contents of the Conceptual Framework for Financial Reporting ('the Framework') in more detail.

The purpose of the Framework

The purpose of the Framework is:

(a) to assist the International Accounting Standards Board (the Board) when developing new standards

(b) to help national standard setters develop new standards

(c) to provide guidance on issues not covered by IFRS Standards

(d) to assist auditors.

The objective of financial reporting

The Framework says that the objective of financial reporting is to provide information to existing and potential investors, lenders and other creditors which helps them when making decisions about providing resources to the reporting entity.

Underlying assumption

The Framework identifies **going concern** as the underlying assumption governing the preparation of financial statements.

The going concern basis assumes that the entity will not liquidate or curtail the scale of its operations.

Qualitative characteristics of useful financial information

The Framework identifies types of information that are useful to the users of financial statements.

It identifies two fundamental qualitative characteristics of useful financial information:

(1) **Relevance**

Information is relevant if it will impact decisions made by its users.

- Relevant information has predictive value or confirmatory value to a user
- Relevance is supported by materiality considerations:
  - Information is regarded as material if its omission or misstatement could influence the decisions made by users of that information
  - An omission or mis-statement could be material due to its size or nature
  - Materiality is an entity-specific consideration and so the Framework does not specify a minimum threshold.

(2) **Faithful representation**

For financial information to be faithfully presented, it must be:

- complete
- neutral
- free from error.

Therefore, it must comprise information necessary for a proper understanding, it must be without bias or manipulation and clearly described.

In addition to the two fundamental qualitative characteristics, there are four enhancing qualitative characteristics of useful financial information. These should be maximised when possible:

(1) **Comparability**

Information is more useful if it can be compared with similar information about other entities, or even the same entity over different time periods.

Consistency of presentation helps to achieve comparability of financial information. Permitting different accounting treatments for similar items is likely to reduce comparability.

(2) **Verifiability**

The Framework explains that verifiability means '**that different, knowledgeable and independent observers could reach consensus, although not necessarily complete agreement, that a particular presentation of an item or items is a faithful representation**' (Framework, para QC26).

Verifiability of financial information provides assurance to users regarding its credibility and reliability.

(3) **Timeliness**

Information should be made available to users within a timescale which is likely to influence their decisions. Older information is less useful.

(4) **Understandability**

Information should be presented clearly and concisely.

Prudence

Older versions of the Framework referred to the importance of the concept of prudence.

Being prudent means exercising caution. In corporate reporting, this is often interpreted as meaning that entities should not overstate their assets or understate their liabilities.

The Board removed prudence from the Framework because they thought it was inconsistent with neutrality. This is because reducing assets in one period is likely to lead to the over-statement of financial performance in the next period.

However, as discussed later in this chapter, the Board are considering reintroducing into the Framework an explicit reference to prudence.

The cost constraint

It is important that the costs incurred in reporting financial information are justified by the benefits that the information brings to its users.

The elements of financial statements

The financial effects of a transaction can be grouped into broad classes, known as the elements.

According to the Framework, there are five elements of financial statements:

Assets – resources controlled by an entity from a past event that will lead to a probable inflow of economic benefits.

Liabilities – obligations of an entity arising from a past event that will lead to a probable outflow of economic resources.

Equity – the residual net assets of an entity after deducting its liabilities.

Incomes – increases in economic benefits during the accounting period.

Expenses – decreases in economic benefits during the accounting period.

Recognition of the elements of financial statements

The Framework says that an item should be recognised in the financial statements if:

- it meets the definition of an element
- it is probable that future economic benefits will flow to or from the entity
- the item can be measured reliably.

Measurement of the elements of financial statements

Measurement is the process of determining the amount at which the elements should be recognised and carried at in the statement of financial position and the statement of profit or loss and other comprehensive income.

The Framework identifies four possible measurement bases:

Historical cost

Assets are recorded at the amount paid to acquire them.

Liabilities are recorded at the value of the proceeds received, or at the amount expected to be paid to satisfy the liability.

Current cost

Assets are carried at their current purchase price.

Liabilities are carried at the amount currently required to settle them.

Realisable value

Assets are carried at the amount that would be received in an orderly disposal.

Liabilities are carried at the amount to be paid to satisfy them in the normal course of business.

Present value

Assets are carried at the present value of the future cash flows that the item will generate.

Liabilities are carried at the present value of the future cash outflows required to settle them.

Current issues: Materiality

The following Practice Statement is an examinable document for P2.

ED 2015/8: IFRS Practice Statement – Application of Materiality in Financial Statements

Materiality as a concept is used widely in financial reporting. The purpose of this Practice Statement is to help management when applying the concept of materiality to the production of financial statements. The key contents are summarised below.

Defining materiality and the users

Something is material if its omission or mis-statement would influence the economic decisions of users.

Deciding on whether an item is material is judgemental. Management must therefore consider the users of the financial statements.

The primary users, according to the Framework, are investors, lenders and other creditors. It can be assumed that the users have reasonable business knowledge. The purpose of financial reporting is to enable these users to make decisions about providing resources to the reporting entity.

Quantitative and qualitative thresholds

Materiality is often determined quantitatively (e.g. as a percentage of assets). However, materiality should also be considered qualitatively. For example, misleading or incomplete disclosure notes may omit or obscure information and therefore affect the users' interpretation of the financial statements.

Some items can be material for other reasons, such as:

- Items that trigger non-compliance with laws and regulations, or loan covenants
- Transactions that might be key to future operations (even if immaterial in the current year).

Presentation and disclosure

Management should consider not just whether an item is included in the financial statements but also how it is presented. Management should use judgement to determine the appropriate level of aggregation, as well as the level of prominence it attains. Examples include:

- Deciding what line items to present separately on the face of the primary financial statements
- Deciding on the level of detail to be provided in both current year and prior year disclosure notes.

Materiality and practicality

Entities are able to adopt certain procedures that reduce the time and cost of preparing financial statements without causing material errors. Examples include:

- Capitalising capital expenditure only if it exceeds a certain threshold
- Selecting a monetary unit, such as $1,000, and rounding to this unit when producing financial statements.

These choices should be regularly reviewed to ensure that they are not leading to a material error, or a material loss of detail.

Errors

It is best practice to correct all errors identified, whether material or not. However, the correction of immaterial errors may involve undue cost or create delays in publishing the financial statements. In such instances, management should consider how pervasive an error is – e.g. an error recording purchases would potentially also impact cost of sales, payables, and inventory.

Material mis-statements identified before the authorisation of the financial statements must be corrected no matter how costly.

If a material error relates to a prior period then it is adjusted retrospectively (in accordance with IAS 8 Accounting Policies, Changes in Accounting Estimates and Errors).

Intentional errors

Sometimes management may choose not to comply with a requirement within an IFRS Standard because the impact is immaterial. For example, management may choose not to discount a liability to present value because the discounted and un-discounted values are so similar.

The Practice Statement notes that this is different from management using an inappropriate discount rate so as to minimise the value of the liability. In this case, management is clearly trying to achieve a particular presentation in the financial statements, and so this must therefore be material.

Current issues: The Framework

The following exposure draft is an examinable document for P2.

ED/2015/3: Conceptual Framework for Financial Reporting

The Board has identified weaknesses in the existing Framework:

- Important areas are not covered. For example, the existing Framework provides very little guidance on the presentation and disclosure of financial information.
- Some aspects of the existing Framework are out of date and fail to reflect the current thinking of the Board, such as the guidance on the recognition of assets and liabilities.
- Some guidance is unclear, such as how to deal with measurement uncertainties.

The exposure draft proposes amendments to the Framework that will address these weaknesses as well as a number of other areas.

Objectives and qualitative characteristics

In the exposure draft, the Board proposes to amend the Framework in order to:

- emphasise the importance of being able to assess management's **stewardship** of an entity's resources
- reintroduce the concept of prudence (the exercise of caution when making judgements) and to stress its importance in relation to the faithful representation of financial information
- make an explicit statement that a faithful representation reports the economic substance of a transaction rather than its legal form.

The reporting entity

The exposure draft proposes a definition of the reporting entity as one that produces financial statements.

The exposure draft states that consolidated financial statements are those where the boundary of the reporting entity is based on both direct and indirect control. The Board believes that consolidated financial statements are more useful than individual financial statements.

Definitions of assets and liabilities

The exposure draft proposes the following definitions:

- An asset is '**a present economic resource controlled by the entity as a result of past events**' (ED/2015/3, para 4.5).
- A liability is '**a present obligation of the entity to transfer an economic resource as a result of past events'** (ED/2015/3, para 4.24).
- An 'economic resource' is **'a right that has the potential of producing economic benefits'** (ED/2015/3, para 4.4).

These differ from current definitions of assets and liabilities, which state that inflows or outflows of economic benefits should be probable.

Recognition

The exposure draft proposes recognition criteria for the elements that are centred on the qualitative characteristics of useful financial information. It is proposed that an element would be recognised if recognition provides:

- relevant information about the element
- a faithful representation of the element
- benefits to the users of the financial information that outweighs the cost of preparation.

Derecognition

The existing Framework does not address derecognition.

The exposure draft addresses this. It provides guidance to ensure an entity provides a faithful representation of assets or liabilities retained after the transaction and the changes in an entity's net assets that result from the transaction.

Measurement

The exposure draft outlines two broad ways of measuring the elements:

- Historical cost
- Current value

The exposure draft proposes guidance on the factors to consider when selecting a measurement basis.

Presentation and disclosure

The existing Framework does not provide enough guidance on presentation and disclosure.

The exposure draft states the importance of effective communication. It notes that financial information should be well structured and not obscured by unnecessary detail.

In terms of the presentation of financial performance, the exposure draft states that profit or loss is the primary source of information. As such, there is a rebuttable presumption that incomes and expenses will be recorded in profit or loss. The exposure draft proposes that incomes and expenses should only be recognised outside of profit or loss in other comprehensive income if:

- the entity holds assets or liabilities at current value and components of the value change would not arise if the asset or liability was held at historical cost, and
- excluding the item from profit or loss enhances the relevance of financial information.

The exposure draft also proposes a rebuttable presumption that incomes and expenses included in other comprehensive income will be recycled to profit or loss in the future.

Test your understanding 1 – Framework

In September 2010, the Board issued the Conceptual Framework for Financial Reporting 2010 ('the Framework'). Nonetheless, proposals to restart work on the Framework quickly achieved a lot of support. This led to the release of a discussion paper in 2013 and an exposure draft in 2015 that outlined further potential changes to the Framework. These discussions clearly highlight the importance of the Framework to the users and producers of International Financial Reporting Standards.

Required:

How does the Framework define the elements relating to financial position, and why might these definitions be criticised?

2 IFRS 13 Fair Value Measurement

Introduction

The objective of IFRS 13 is to provide a single source of guidance for fair value measurement where it is required by a reporting standard, rather than it being spread throughout several reporting standards.

Many accounting standards require or allow items to be measured at fair value. Some examples from your prior studies include:

- IAS 16 Property, Plant and Equipment, which allows entities to measure property, plant and equipment at fair value
- IFRS 3 Business Combinations, which requires the identifiable net assets of a subsidiary to be measured at fair value at the acquisition date.

Scope

IFRS 13 does not apply to:

- share-based payment transactions (IFRS 2 Share-based Payments)
- leases (IFRS 16 Leases).

The definition of fair value

Fair value is defined as **'the price that would be received to sell an asset or paid to transfer a liability in an orderly transaction between market participants at the measurement date'** (IFRS 13, para 9).

Market participants are knowledgeable, third parties. When pricing an asset or a liability, they would take into account:

- Condition
- Location
- Restrictions on use.

It should be assumed that market participants are not forced into transactions (i.e. they are not suffering from cash flow shortages).

IFRS 13 notes that there are various approaches to determining the fair value of an asset or liability:

- Market approaches (valuations based on recent sales prices)
- Cost approaches (valuations based on replacement cost)
- Income approaches (valuations based on financial forecasts).

Whatever approach is taken, the aim is always the same – to estimate the price that would be transferred in a transaction with a market participant.

The price

Fair value is a market-based measurement, not one that is entity specific. As such, when determining the price at which an asset would be sold (or the price paid to transfer a liability), observable data from active markets should be used where possible.

An **active market** is a market where transactions for the asset or liability occur frequently.

IFRS 13 classifies inputs into valuation techniques into three levels.

- **Level 1** inputs are quoted prices for identical assets in active markets.
- **Level 2** inputs are observable prices that are not level 1 inputs. This may include:
  - Quoted prices for similar assets in active markets
  - Quoted prices for identical assets in less active markets
  - Observable inputs that are not prices (such as interest rates).

- **Level 3** inputs are unobservable. This could include cash or profit forecasts using an entity's own data.

  A significant adjustment to a level 2 input would lead to it being categorised as a level 3 input.

Priority is given to level 1 inputs. The lowest priority is given to level 3 inputs.

Inputs to determine fair value

IFRS 13 gives the following examples of inputs used to determine fair value:

	Asset	**Example**
Level 1	Equity shares in a listed entity	Unadjusted quoted prices in an active market.
Level 2	Building held and used	Price per square metre for the building from observable market data, such as observed transactions for similar buildings in similar locations.
Level 3	Cash-generating unit	Profit or cash flow forecast using own data.

Test you understanding 2 – Baklava

Baklava has an investment property that is measured at fair value. This property is rented out on short-term leases.

The directors wish to fair value the property by estimating the present value of the net cash flows that the property will generate for Baklava. They argue that this best reflects the way in which the building will generate economic benefits for Baklava.

The building is unique, although there have been many sales of similar buildings in the local area.

Required:

Discuss whether the valuation technique suggested by the directors complies with International Financial Reporting Standards.

Markets

The price received when an asset is sold (or paid when a liability is transferred) may differ depending on the specific market where the transaction occurs.

Principal market

IFRS 13 says that fair value should be measured by reference to the **principal market**.

The principal market is the market with the greatest activity for the asset or liability being measured.

The entity must be able to access the principal market at the measurement date. This means that the principal market for the same asset can differ between entities.

Most advantageous market

If there is no principal market, then fair value is measured by reference to prices in the most advantageous market.

The most advantageous market is the one that maximises the net amount received from selling an asset (or minimises the amount paid to transfer a liability).

Transaction costs (such as legal and broker fees) will play a role in deciding which market is most advantageous. However, fair value is not adjusted for transaction costs because they are a characteristic of the market, rather than the asset.

Test your understanding 3 – Markets

An asset is sold in two different active markets at different prices. An entity enters into transactions in both markets and can access the price in those markets for the asset at the measurement date as follows:

	Market 1	**Market 2**
	$	$
Price	26	25
Transaction costs	(3)	(1)
Transport costs	(2)	(2)
Net price received	21	22

What is the fair value of the asset if:

(a) **market 1 is the principal market for the asset?**

(b) **no principal market can be determined?**

Non-financial assets

What is a non-financial asset?

The difference between financial and non-financial assets is covered in detail in Chapter 11. Financial assets include:

- Contractual rights to receive cash (such as receivables)
- Investments in equity shares.

Non-financial assets include:

- Property, plant and equipment
- Intangible assets.

The fair value of a non-financial asset

IFRS 13 says that the fair value of a non-financial asset should be based on its **highest and best use**.

The highest and best use of an asset is the use that a market participant would adopt in order to maximise its value.

The current use of a non-financial asset can be assumed to be the highest and best use, unless evidence exists to the contrary.

The highest and best use should take into account uses that are:

- Physically possible
- Legally permissible
- Financially feasible.

IFRS 13 says a use can be legally permissible even if it is not legally approved.

Test you understanding 4 – Five Quarters

Five Quarters has purchased 100% of the ordinary shares of Three Halves and is trying to determine the fair value of the net assets at the acquisition date.

Three Halves owns land that is currently developed for industrial use. The fair value of the land if used in a manufacturing operation is $5 million.

Many nearby plots of land have been developed for residential use (as high-rise apartment buildings). The land owned by Three Halves does not have planning permission for residential use, although permission has been granted for similar plots of land. The fair value of Three Halves' land as a vacant site for residential development is $6 million. However, transformation costs of $0.3 million would need to be incurred to get the land into this condition.

Required:

How should the fair value of the land be determined?

Disclosures

Disclosures should provide information that enables users of financial statements to evaluate the inputs and methods used to determine how fair value measurements have been arrived at.

The level in the three-tier valuation hierarchy should be disclosed, together with supporting details of valuation methods and inputs used where appropriate. As would be expected, more detailed information is required where there is significant use of level-three inputs to arrive at a fair value measurement to enable users of financial statements to understand how such fair values have been arrived at.

Disclosure should also be made when there is a change of valuation technique to measure an asset or liability. This will include any change in the level of inputs used to determine fair value of particular assets and/or liabilities.

Chapter summary

The Framework

- Underpins accounting standards
- Fundamental qualitative characteristics of useful information are:
  - Relevance
  - Faithful representation
- Defines the elements of financial statements

↓

IFRS 13 Fair Value Measurement

- Provides single source of guidance where fair value measurement is required
- Fair value hierarchy – 3 levels

Test your understanding answers

Test your understanding 1 – Framework

The Framework (para 4.4) provides the following definitions:

- **'An asset is a resource controlled by the entity as a result of past events and from which future economic benefits are expected to flow to the entity.**
- **A liability is a present obligation of the entity arising from past events, the settlement of which is expected to result in an outflow from the entity of resources embodying economic benefits.**
- **Equity is the residual interest in the assets of the entity after deducting all its liabilities.'**

The following criticisms could be made of these definitions:

- The definitions are inconsistently applied across the range of IFRS and IAS Standards
- The concept of 'control' is not clearly defined and can prove difficult to apply
- There is a lack of guidance about the meaning of an 'economic resource'
- The notion of 'expectation' is vague. Does it refer to the probability of an inflow/outflow or to a mathematical 'expected value'?
- The definitions do not offer enough guidance as to the difference between liabilities and equity. Further guidance here would benefit users, particularly when applying these concepts to financial instruments.

Test you understanding 2 – Baklava

The directors' estimate of the future net cash flows that the building will generate is a level 3 input. IFRS 13 gives lowest priority to level 3 inputs. These should not be used if a level 1 or level 2 input exists.

Observable data about the recent sales prices of similar properties is a level 2 input. The fair value of the building should therefore be based on these prices, with adjustments made as necessary to reflect the specific location and condition of Baklava's building.

Test your understanding 3 – Markets

(a) If Market 1 is the principal market then the fair value would be measured using the price that would be received in that market less transport costs. The fair value would therefore be $24 ($26 – $2). Transaction costs are ignored as they are not a characteristic of the asset.

(b) If neither market is the principal market for the asset then the fair value would be measured in the most advantageous market. The most advantageous market is the market that maximises the net amount received from the sale.

The net amount received in Market 2 ($22) is higher than the net amount received in Market 1 ($21). Market 2 is therefore the most advantageous market. This results in a fair value measurement of $23 ($25 – $2). IFRS 13 specifies that transaction costs play a role when determining which market is most advantageous but that they are not factored into the fair value measurement itself.

Test you understanding 4 – Five Quarters

Land is a non-financial asset. IFRS 13 says that the fair value of a non-financial asset should be based on its highest and best use. This is presumed to be its current use, unless evidence exists to the contrary.

The current use of the asset would suggest a fair value of $5 million.

However, there is evidence that market participants would be interested in developing the land for residential use.

Residential use of the land is not legally prohibited. Similar plots of land have been granted planning permission, so it is likely that this particular plot of land will also be granted planning permission.

If used for residential purposes, the fair value of the land would be $5.7 million ($6m – $0.3m).

It would seem that the land's highest and best use is for residential development. Its fair value is therefore $5.7 million.

chapter

2

The professional and ethical duty of the accountant

Chapter learning objectives

Upon completion of this chapter you will be able to:

- appraise and discuss the ethical and professional issues in advising on corporate reporting
- assess the relevance and importance of ethical and professional issues in complying with accounting standards
- appraise the potential ethical implications of professional and managerial decisions in the preparation of corporate reports
- assess the consequences of not upholding ethical principles in the preparation of corporate reports.

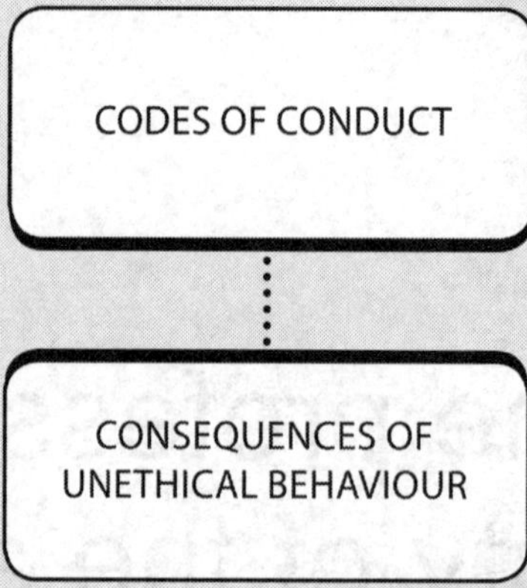

1 Introduction

Accounting and ethics

A number of user groups rely on the financial statements to make economic decisions. It is important that these users are not misled.

However, the ethical beliefs of individual accountants may be too simplistic when dealing with real-life, complex ethical dilemmas. The study of ethics is therefore vital so that accountants develop the skills that will help them to decide on the right course of action.

2 Approaches to accounting and ethics

Rules and principles

Some national accounting standards are primarily rules based. In other words, they provide extensive and detailed guidance about the accounting treatment of particular transactions.

This approach is sometimes criticised for nurturing a 'rule-book mentality'. In fact, complying with the letter of the law rather than the spirit of the accounting standard may prevent transactions from being faithfully represented.

International Financial Reporting Standards are often principles based, albeit with some detailed rules in place to eliminate uncertainties and to increase comparability.

Such principles-based approaches to accounting create ethical challenges because of the professional judgement that accountants are required to exercise. An understanding of ethical principles, such as those contained in the ACCA ethical code, is therefore essential.

3 Ethical codes

The ACCA ethical code

The ACCA requires its members to adhere to a code of professional ethics. This provides a set of moral guidelines for professional accountants.

The fundamental principles of this code are:

(a) **Integrity** – to be straightforward and honest in all professional and business relationships.

(b) **Objectivity** – to not allow bias, conflict of interest or undue influence of others to override professional or business judgments.

(c) **Professional Competence and Due Care** – to maintain professional knowledge and skill at the level required to ensure that a client or employer receives competent professional services based on current developments in practice, legislation and techniques and act diligently and in accordance with applicable technical and professional standards.

(d) **Confidentiality** – to respect the confidentiality of information acquired as a result of professional and business relationships and, therefore, not disclose any such information to third parties without proper and specific authority, unless there is a legal or professional right or duty to disclose, nor use the information for the personal advantage of the professional accountant or third parties.

(e) **Professional behaviour** – to comply with relevant laws and regulations and avoid any action that discredits the profession.

Some of the elements of the ethical code are now considered in more detail.

Integrity

Acting with integrity involves being honest and straight-forward. Any attempt to conceal or hide transactions, either through omitting them or through inadequate or confusing disclosure, demonstrates a lack of integrity.

Later in this text, you will learn that forms of non-financial reporting are becoming increasingly important. Many entities prepare reports that detail their relationship with, and impact on, society and the environment. These issues could be combined in an integrated report. Such reports are voluntary. However, it could be argued that withholding information from users about a company's social and environmental impact lacks integrity. Moreover, failing to report issues about long-term sustainability may be just as misleading as incorrect information within the historical financial statements.

Objectivity

There are many times when an accountant might find that they have an incentive to represent the performance or position of a company in a particular way:

- **Profit related bonuses:** An accountant might be motivated to maximise profit in the current period in order to achieve their bonus. Alternatively, if current period targets have been met, an accountant might be motivated to shift profits into the next reporting period.
- **Financing:** An entity is more likely to be given a loan if it has valuable assets on which the loan can be secured. An incentive may therefore exist for the accountants to over-state assets on the statement of financial position.
- **Achieving a listing:** A company that is being listed on a stock exchange will want to maximise the amount that it receives from investors. Therefore, there may be an incentive for the accountants to over-state the assets and profits of a company before it lists.

Financial statements should faithfully represent the transactions that have occurred. The ethical code encourages accountants to not let bias or outside influence impact their judgements.

Areas of judgement in financial statements

One of the reasons why objectivity is such an important part of the ACCA ethical code is that accounting standards frequently involve the use of judgement. Bias would therefore have a direct impact on the financial statements produced. Some examples of the judgements required by IFRS Standards are presented below:

- Many standards permit assets or liabilities to be held at fair value. IFRS 13 Fair Value Measurement defines fair value as 'the price that would be received to sell an asset or paid to transfer a liability in an orderly transaction between market participants at the measurement date'. IFRS 13 stresses the importance of level 1 inputs – quoted prices for identical assets and liabilities in active markets – but, in the absence of these, allows more judgemental measures to be used.
- IAS 16 Property, Plant and Equipment states that entities should depreciate assets over their estimated useful life. By over-stating an asset's useful economic life, depreciation is charged more slowly to profit or loss.
- IAS 36 Impairment of Assets says that the recoverable amount of an asset is the higher of the fair value less costs to sell and the value in use. Both of these figures involve judgements about events that will happen in the future and are therefore open to manipulation.
- IFRS 2 Share-Based Payment requires entities to estimate the expense of an equity-settled share-based payment scheme based on the number of options expected to vest. By under-estimating the number of options expected to vest, profit in the short-term might be maximised.
- IAS 37 Provisions, Contingent Liabilities and Contingent Assets states that provisions should recorded at the best estimate of the expenditure to be incurred. Using lower than expected estimates will reduce the value of a provision and therefore maximise current year profits.

Unless an accountant understands and adheres to the code of ethics, then manipulation of these (and other) standards is likely. The financial statements would therefore not faithfully represent the performance and position of the entity and the users may be misled into making incorrect economic decisions.

Professional competence and due care

As you will be aware from your studies, new accounting standards are frequently issued and older standards are often updated or withdrawn. This means that accounting knowledge becomes out-of-date very quickly.

In order to comply with the code of ethics, accountants have a responsibility to ensure that they are aware of changes to accounting standards. This is often referred to as CPD (Continuing Professional Development).

CPD involves:

- Reading technical articles
- Attending seminars or presentations
- Attending training courses

Without up-to-date technical knowledge, it is unlikely that an accountant can produce financial statements that comply with IFRS Standards. Material errors within financial statements will mislead the users.

4 The impact of ethical and unethical behaviour

Consequences of unethical behaviour

The journals and magazines of professional institutes regularly include details of professional disciplinary proceedings brought against individual members who were believed to have fallen short of the ethical standards expected of them.

The consequences of unethical behaviour in deliberately presenting incorrect financial information are severe. Many accountants have been fined or jailed for not fulfilling their professional duties.

The consequences for individuals include:

- Fines
- The loss of professional reputation
- Being prevented from acting as a director or officer of a public company in the future
- The possibility of being expelled by a professional accountancy body
- A prison sentence.

Ethics and the profit motive

It is commonly argued that the primary objective of a company is to maximise the wealth of its shareholders. Acting ethically might be seen to contradict this objective. For example, whilst it may be ethical to incur costs associated with looking after the environment, such costs reduce profits.

However, in modern society, companies are considered to be corporate citizens within society. Corporate social responsibility is increasingly important to investors and other stakeholders. It can attract 'green' investors, ethical consumers and employees and so in turn have a positive impact on financial results. Thus, it could be argued that the performance and sustainability of a company may not be maximised unless it behaves in an ethical manner.

Test your understanding 1 – Cookie

The directors of Cookie are very confident about the quality of the products that the company sells. Historically, the level of complaints received about product quality has been low. However, when calculating their warranty provision, they have over-estimated the number of items that will be returned as faulty. The directors believe that this is acceptable because it is important for financial statements to exhibit prudence.

Required:

Discuss the ethical issues raised by the treatment of the warranty provision.

Chapter summary

Codes of ethics

The principles in the ACCA Code of Ethics and Conduct are:

- Integrity
- Objectivity
- Professional competence and due care
- Confidentiality
- Professional behaviour

Consequences of unethical behaviour

The consequences of failing to act ethically are many and can be severe. They include:

- Prison sentence
- Fines or repayments of amounts taken fraudulently
- Loss of professional reputation
- Being prevented from acting in the same capacity in the future
- Investigation by professional accountancy body

Test your understanding answers

Test your understanding 1 – Cookie

Financial statements are important to a range of user groups, such as shareholders, banks, employees and suppliers. Prudence is important because over-stated assets or under-stated liabilities could mislead potential or current investors. However, excessive cautiousness means that the financial performance and position of an entity is not faithfully represented.

A faithful representation is often presumed to have been provided if accounting standards have been complied with. It would appear that the directors are not calculating the provision in line with the requirements of IAS 37, which requires provisions to be recognised at the 'best estimate' of the expenditure to be incurred. This may mean that profit is understated in the current period and then over-stated in subsequent periods.

Professional ethics is a vital part of the accountancy profession and ACCA members are bound by its Code of Ethics and Conduct. This sets out the importance of the fundamental principles of confidentiality, objectivity, professional behaviour, integrity, and professional competence and due care.

Integrity is defined as being honest and straight-forward. Over-estimating a provision in order to shift profits from one period to another demonstrates a lack of integrity.

If the provision is being over-stated in order to achieve bonus targets or profit expectations in the next financial period, then this demonstrates a lack of objectivity.

If the directors are unaware of the requirements of IAS 37, then they may not be sufficiently competent.

Financial statements should faithfully represent the transactions that have occurred. Compliance with the ethical code thus encourages accountants to ensure that they are technically capable and sufficiently independent to comply with the requirements of IFRS Standards.

Test your understanding answers

Test your understanding 1 – Cust

Financial statements are important to a range of user groups, such as shareholders, banks, employees and suppliers. Prudence is important because over-stated assets or under-stated liabilities could mislead potential or current investors. However, excessive cautiousness means that the financial performance and position of an entity is not faithfully represented.

A faithful representation is often presumed to have been provided if accounting standards have been complied with. It would appear that the directors are not calculating the provision in line with the requirements of IAS 37, which requires provisions to be recognised at the 'best estimate' of the expenditure to be incurred. This may mean that profit is understated in the current period and then over-stated in subsequent periods.

Professional ethics is a vital part of the accountancy profession and ACCA members are bound by its Code of Ethics and Conduct. This sets out the importance of the fundamental principles of confidentiality, objectivity, professional behaviour, integrity, and professional competence and due care.

Integrity is defined as being honest and straight-forward. Over-estimating a provision in order to shift profits from one period to another demonstrates a lack of integrity.

If the provision is being over-stated in order to achieve bonus targets or profit expectations in the next financial period, then this demonstrates a lack of objectivity.

If the directors are unaware of the requirements of IAS 37, then they may not be sufficiently competent.

Financial statements should faithfully represent the transactions that have occurred. Compliance with the ethical code thus encourages accountants to ensure that they are technically capable and sufficiently independent to comply with the requirements of IFRS Standards.

chapter

3

Performance reporting and performance appraisal

Chapter learning objectives

Upon completion of this chapter you will be able to:

- prepare reports relating to corporate performance for external stakeholders
- select and calculate relevant indicators of financial and non-financial performance
- Identify and evaluate significant features and issues in financial statements

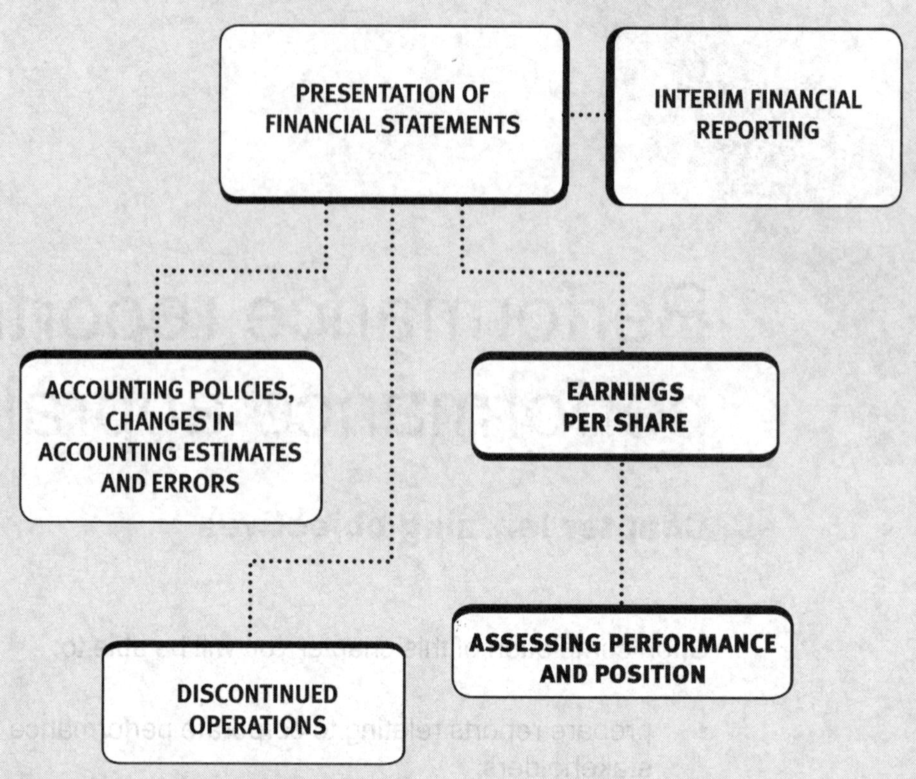

1 IAS 1 Presentation of Financial Statements

Components of financial statements

According to IAS 1 Presentation of Financial Statements, a complete set of financial statements has the following components:

- a statement of financial position
- a statement of profit or loss and other comprehensive income (or statement of profit or loss with a separate statement of other comprehensive income)
- a statement of changes in equity
- a statement of cash flows (discussed in a later chapter)
- accounting policies note and other explanatory notes
- a statement of financial position at the beginning of the earliest comparative period when an entity applies an accounting policy retrospectively or corrects an error retrospectively.

Other reports and statements in the annual report (such as a financial review, an environmental report or a social report) are outside the scope of IAS 1.

Statement of financial position

IAS 1 says that an entity must classify an asset as current on the statement of financial position if:

- it is realised or consumed during the entity's normal trading cycle, or
- it is held for trading, or
- it will be realised within 12 months of the reporting date.

All other assets are classified as non-current.

IAS 1 says that an entity must classify a liability as current on the statement of financial position if:

- it is settled during the entity's normal trading cycle, or
- it is held for trading, or
- it will be settled within 12 months of the reporting date.

All other liabilities are classified as non-current.

Statement of profit or loss and other comprehensive income

IAS 1 provides the following definitions:

Other comprehensive income (OCI) are incomes and expenses recognised outside of profit or loss, as required by particular IFRS Standards.

Total comprehensive income (TCI) is the total of the entity's profit or loss and other comprehensive income for the period.

IAS 1 requires that OCI is classified into two groups as follows:

- items that might be reclassified (or recycled) to profit or loss in subsequent accounting periods:
  - foreign exchange gains and losses arising on translation of a foreign operation (IAS 21)
  - effective parts of cash flow hedging arrangements (IFRS 9)
  - Remeasurement of investments in debt instruments that are classified as fair value through OCI (IFRS 9)

- items that will not be reclassified (or recycled) to profit or loss in subsequent accounting periods:
  - changes in revaluation surplus (IAS 16 & IAS 38)
  - remeasurement components on defined benefit plans (IAS 19)
  - remeasurement of investments in equity instruments that are classified as fair value through OCI (IFRS 9)

Entities can prepare one combined statement showing profit or loss for the year and OCI. Alternatively, an entity can prepare a statement of profit or loss and a separate statement of OCI. If the latter option is chosen, the statement of OCI should begin with profit or loss for the year so that there is no duplication or confusion as to which items are included within each statement.

Format one: statement of profit or loss and other comprehensive income

For illustration, one of the recommended formats from the implementation guidance in IAS 1 is as follows:

XYZ Group – Statement of profit or loss and other comprehensive income for the year ended 31 December 20X3

	$000
Revenue	X
Cost of sales	(X)
Gross profit	X
Other operating income	X
Distribution costs	(X)
Administrative expenses	(X)
Other operating expenses	(X)
Profit from operations	X
Finance costs	(X)
Share of profit of associates	X
Profit before tax	X
Income tax expense	(X)
Profit or loss for the period	X

Other comprehensive income

Items that will not be reclassified to profit or loss:	
Gains on property revaluation	X
Remeasurement or actuarial gains and losses on defined benefit pension plans	(X)
Remeasurement of equity investments designated to be accounted for through OCI	X
Income tax relating to items that will not be reclassified	(X)
Total – items that will not be reclassified to profit or loss net of tax:	**X**
Items that may be reclassified subsequently to profit or loss:	
Cash flow hedges	X
Exchange differences on translating foreign operations	X
Income tax relating to items that may be reclassified	(X)
Total – items that may be reclassified to profit or loss net of tax:	**X**
Total – other comprehensive income net of tax for the year	**X**
Total comprehensive income for the year	**X**

Profit attributable to:	$000
Owners of the parent	X
Non-controlling interest	X
	X

Total comprehensive income attributable to:	
Owners of the parent	X
Non-controlling interest	X
	X

Other comprehensive income and related tax

IAS 1 requires an entity to disclose income tax relating to each component of OCI. This may be achieved by either:

- disclosing each component of OCI net of any related tax effect, or
- disclosing OCI before related tax effects with one amount shown for tax (as shown in the above examples).

The purpose of this is to provide users with tax information relating to these components, as they often have tax rates different from those applied to profit or loss.

Statement of changes in equity

IAS 1 requires all changes in equity arising from transactions with owners in their capacity as owners to be presented separately from non-owner changes in equity. This would include:

- Issues of shares
- Dividends.

Total comprehensive income is shown in aggregate only for the purposes of reconciling opening to closing equity.

XYZ Group – Statement of changes in equity for the year ended 31 December 20X3

	Equity capt'l	Ret'd earng's	Transl'n of for'gn operations	Financial assets thru' OCI	Cash flow hdg's	Reval'n surplus	Total
	$000	$000	$000	$000	$000	$000	$000
Balance at 1 Jan 20X3	X	X	(X)	X	X	–	X
Changes in accounting policy	–	X	–	–	–	–	X
Restated balance	X	X	X	X	X	X	X
Changes in equity for 20X3							
Dividends	–	(X)	–	–	–	–	(X)
Issue of equity capital	X	–	–	–	–	–	X
Total comprehensive income for year	–	X	X	X	X	X	X
Transfer to retained earnings	–	X	–	–	–	(X)	–
Balance at 31 December 20X3	X	X	X	X	X	X	X

In addition to these columns, there should be columns headed:

(a) Non-controlling interest

(b) Total equity

A comparative statement for the prior period must also be published.

General features of financial statements

Going concern

Once management have assessed that there are no material uncertainties as to the ability of an entity to continue for the foreseeable future, the financial statements should be prepared on the assumption that the entity will in fact continue. In other words, the financial statements will be prepared on a going concern basis.

Accruals basis of accounting

The accruals basis of accounting means that transactions and events are recognised when they occur, not when cash is received or paid for them.

Consistency of presentation

The presentation and classification of items in the financial statements should be retained from one period to the next unless:

- it is clear that a change will result in a more appropriate presentation, or
- a change is required by an IFRS or IAS Standard.

Materiality and aggregation

An item is material if its omission or misstatement could influence the economic decisions of users taken on the basis of the financial statements. This could be based on the size or nature of an omission or misstatement.

When assessing materiality, entities should consider the characteristics of the users of its financial statements. It can be assumed that these users have a knowledge of business and accounting.

To aid user understanding, financial statements should show material classes of items separately.

Immaterial items may be aggregated with amounts of a similar nature, as long as this does not reduce understandability.

Offsetting

IAS 1 says that assets and liabilities, and income and expenses, should only be offset when required or permitted by an IFRS standard.

Comparative information

Comparative information for the previous period should be disclosed.

Disclosures

Disclosure note presentation

IAS 1 says that entities must present their disclosure notes in a systematic order. This might mean:

- Giving prominence to the most relevant areas
- Grouping items measured in similar ways, such as assets held at fair value
- Following the order in which items are presented in the statement of profit or loss and the statement of financial position.

Compliance with IFRS Standards

Entities should make an explicit and unreserved statement that their financial statements comply with IFRS Standards.

Accounting policies

Entities must produce an accounting policies disclosure note that details:

- the measurement basis (or bases) used in preparing the financial statements (e.g. historical cost, fair value, etc)
- each significant accounting policy.

Sources of uncertainty

An entity should disclose information about the key sources of estimation uncertainty that may cause a material adjustment to assets and liabilities within the next year, e.g. key assumptions about the future.

Reclassification adjustments

Reclassification adjustments are amounts 'recycled' from other comprehensive income to profit or loss.

IAS 1 requires that reclassification adjustments are disclosed, either on the face of the statement of profit or loss and other comprehensive income or in the notes.

Dividends

Distributions to equity holders are disclosed in the statement of changes.

This requirement is in line with separate disclosure of owner and non-owner changes in equity discussed earlier.

Problems with IAS 1

The accounting treatment and guidance with respect to other comprehensive income (OCI) has been criticised in recent years. Some of these criticisms are as follows:

- There is no consistent basis across IFRS Standards for determining when a gain or loss is recognised in profit or loss and when it is recognised in OCI. This often means that the OCI is not fully understood by the users of the financial statements.
- Many users ignore OCI, since the gains and losses reported there are not related to the operating flows of an entity. As a result, material losses presented in OCI may not be given the attention that they require.
- The notion of recycling gains and losses from OCI is unclear, particularly with regards to which items are recycled and when. Moreover this recycling results in profits or losses being recorded in a different period from the change in the related asset or liability, thus contradicting the Conceptual Framework's definition of incomes and expenses.
- There are differences between IFRS Standards and US GAAP in respect of OCI. This reduces the comparability of profit-based performance measures.

Current issues: liabilities

The following exposure draft is an examinable document for P2.

ED/2015/1: Classification of Liabilities

The Board proposes to amend IAS 1 to clarify that the classification of a liability as current or non-current is based on rights as at the reporting date.

2 IFRS 5 Non-current Assets Held for Sale and Discontinued Operations

Discontinued operations

IFRS 5 Non-current Assets Held for Sale and Discontinued Operations says that a discontinued operation is a component of an entity that has been sold, or which is classified as held for sale, and which is:

- a separate line of business (either in terms of operations or location)
- part of a plan to dispose of a separate line of business, or
- a subsidiary acquired solely for the purpose of resale.

An operation is held for sale if its carrying amount will not be recovered principally by continuing use. To be classified as held for sale (and therefore to be a discontinued operation) at the reporting date, it must meet the following criteria.

- The operation is available for sale immediately in its current condition.
- The sale is highly probable and is expected to be completed within one year.
- Management is committed to the sale.
- The operation is being actively marketed.
- The operation is being offered for sale at a reasonable price in relation to its current fair value.
- It is unlikely that the plan will change or be withdrawn.

Presentation

Users of the financial statements are more interested in future profits than past profits. They are able to make a better assessment of future profits if they are informed about operations that have been discontinued during the period.

IFRS 5 requires information about discontinued operations to be presented in the financial statements.

- A single amount should be presented on the face of the statement of profit or loss and other comprehensive income that is comprised of:
  - the total of the post-tax profit or loss of discontinued operations
  - the post-tax gain or loss on the measurement to fair value less costs to sell or on the disposal of the discontinued operation.
- An analysis of the single amount described above should be provided. This can be presented on the face of the statement of profit or loss and other comprehensive income or in the notes to the financial statements.
- If a decision to sell an operation is taken after the year-end but before the accounts are approved, this is treated as a non-adjusting event after the reporting date and disclosed in the notes. The operation does not qualify as a discontinued operation at the reporting date and separate presentation is not appropriate.
- In the comparative figures the operations are also shown as discontinued (even though they were not classified as such at the end of the previous year).

Example presentation

Statement of profit or loss (showing discontinued operations as a single amount, with analysis in the notes)

	20X2	20X1
	$m	$m
Revenue	100	90
Operating expenses	(60)	(65)
Profit from operations	40	25
Finance cost	(20)	(10)
Profit before tax	20	15
Income tax expense	(6)	(7)
Profit from continuing operations	14	8
Discontinued operations		
Loss from discontinued operations*	(25)	(1)
Profit/(loss) for the year	(11)	7

The entity did not recognise any components of other comprehensive income in the periods presented.

* The analysis of this loss would be given in a note to the accounts.

Illustration – Discontinued operations

The Portugal group of companies has a financial year-end of 30 June 20X4. The financial statements were authorised three months later. The group is disposing of many of its subsidiaries, each of which is a separate major line of business or geographical area.

- A subsidiary, England, was sold on 1 January 20X4.
- On 1 January 20X4, an announcement was made that there were advanced negotiations to sell subsidiary Switzerland and that, subject to regulatory approval, this was expected to be completed by 31 October 20X4.

- The board has also decided to sell a subsidiary called France. Agents have been appointed to find a suitable buyer but none have yet emerged. The agent's advice is that potential buyers are deterred by the expected price that Portugal hopes to achieve.
- On 10 July 20X4, an announcement was made that another subsidiary, Croatia, was for sale. It was sold on 10 September 20X4.

Required:

Explain whether each of these subsidiaries meets the definition of a 'discontinued operation' as defined by IFRS 5.

Solution

England has been sold during the year. It is a discontinued operation per IFRS 5.

Switzerland is a discontinued operation per IFRS 5. There is clear intention to sell, and the sale is highly probable within 12 months.

France is not a discontinued operation per IFRS 5. It does not seem that France is being offered for sale at a reasonable price in relation to its current fair value. The sale does not seem to be highly probable within 12 months.

Croatia is not a discontinued operation per IFRS 5. The conditions for classification as held for sale were not met until after the year end.

3 IAS 8 Accounting Policies, Changes in Accounting Estimates and Errors

Policies, estimates and errors

Accounting policies

Accounting policies are the principles and rules applied by an entity which specify how transactions are reflected in the financial statements.

Where a standard exists in respect of a transaction, the accounting policy is determined by applying that standard.

Where there is no applicable standard or interpretation, management must use its judgement to develop and apply an accounting policy. The accounting policy selected must result in information that is relevant and reliable. Management should refer to :

- standards dealing with similar and related issues
- the Framework.

Provided they do not conflict with the sources above, management may also consider:

- pronouncements from other standard-setting bodies, as long as they use a similar conceptual framework
- other accepted industry practices.

Changes in accounting policies

An entity should only change its accounting policies if required by a standard, or if it results in more reliable and relevant information.

New accounting standards normally include transitional arrangements on how to deal with any resulting changes in accounting policy.

If there are no transitional arrangements, changes in accounting policy should be applied **retrospectively**. The entity adjusts the opening balance of each affected component of equity, and the comparative figures are presented as if the new policy had always been applied.

Where a change is applied retrospectively, IAS 1 revised requires an entity to include in its financial statements a statement of financial position at the beginning of the earliest comparative period. In practice this will result in 3 statements of financial position

- at the reporting date
- at the start of the current reporting period
- at the start of the previous reporting period.

Changes in accounting estimates

Making estimates is an essential part of the preparation of financial statements. For example, preparers have to estimate allowances for financial assets, inventory obsolescence and the useful lives of property, plant and equipment.

A change in an accounting estimate is **not** a change in accounting policy.

According to IAS 8, a change in accounting estimate must be recognised **prospectively** by including it in the statement of profit or loss and other comprehensive income for the current period and any future periods that are also affected.

Prior period errors

Prior period errors are mis-statements and omissions in the financial statements of prior periods as a result of not using reliable information that should have been available.

IAS 8 says that material prior period errors should be corrected **retrospectively** in the first set of financial statements authorised for issue after their discovery. Opening balances of equity, and the comparative figures, should be adjusted to correct the error.

IAS 1 also requires that where a prior period error is corrected retrospectively, a statement of financial position is provided at the beginning of the earliest comparative period.

Problems with IAS 8

It has been argued that the requirements of IAS 8 to adjust prior period errors retrospectively may lead to earnings management. By adjusting prior period errors through opening reserves, the impact is never shown within a current period statement of profit or loss.

4 IAS 33 Earnings per Share

Earnings per share

Scope

IAS 33 Earnings per Share applies to listed entities. If private entities choose to disclose an earnings per share figure, it must have been calculated in accordance with IAS 33.

The basic calculation

The actual earnings per share (EPS) for the period is called the **basic EPS** and is calculated as:

$$\frac{\text{Profit or loss for the period attributable to equity shareholders}}{\text{Weighted average number of ordinary shares outstanding in the period}}$$

Profit for the period must be reduced (or a loss for the period must be increased) for any irredeemable preference dividends paid during the period.

If an entity prepares consolidated financial statements, then EPS will be based on the consolidated profit for the period attributable to the equity shareholders of the parent company (i.e. total consolidated profit less the profit attributable to the non-controlling interest).

The weighted average number of shares takes into account the timing of share issues during the year.

Illustration – Basic EPS

An entity issued 200,000 shares at full market price on 1 July 20X8.

Relevant information

	20X8	**20X7**
Profit attributable to the ordinary shareholders for the year ending 31 Dec	$550,000	$460,000
Number of ordinary shares in issue at 31 Dec	1,000,000	800,000

Required:

Calculate basic EPS for the years ended 31 December 20X7 and 20X8.

Solution

Calculation of earnings per share

20X7 = $460,000/800,000 = 57.5c

20X8 = $550,000/900,000 (W1) = 61.1c

(W1) **Weighted average number of shares in 20X8**

800,000 × 6/12 =	400,000
1,000,000 × 6/12 =	500,000
	900,000

Since the additional 200,000 shares were issued at full market price but have only contributed finance for half a year, a weighted average number of shares must be calculated. The earnings figure is not adjusted.

Bonus issues

If an entity makes a bonus issue of shares then share capital increases. However, no cash has been received and therefore there is no impact on earnings. This means that a bonus issue reduces EPS.

For the purpose of calculating basic EPS, the bonus issue shares are treated as if they have always been in issue. The easiest way to do this is multiply the number of shares outstanding before the bonus issue by the bonus fraction.

The bonus fraction is calculated as follows:

$$\frac{\text{Number of shares after bonus issue}}{\text{Number of shares before bonus issue}}$$

EPS for the comparative period must be restated. The easiest way to achieve this is to multiply the EPS figure from the prior year's financial statements by the inverse of the bonus fraction.

Illustration – Bonus issue

An entity made a bonus issue of one new share for every five existing shares held on 1 July 20X8.

Relevant information

	20X8	**20X7**
Profit attributable to the ordinary shareholders for the year ending 31 Dec	\$550,000	\$460,000
Number of ordinary shares in issue at 31 Dec	1,200,000	1,000,000

Required:

(a) **Calculate basic EPS for the year ended 31 December 20X8.**

(b) **Calculate the prior year comparative EPS figure as it would appear in the financial statements for the year ended 31 December 20X8.**

Solution

(a) EPS = \$550,000/1,200,000 (W1) = 45.8c

(W1) **Weighted average number of shares**

1,000,000 × 6/12 × 6/5 (W2)	600,000
1,200,000 × 6/12	600,000
Weighted average number of shares	1,200,000

(W2) **Bonus fraction**

It was a one for five bonus issue.

A shareholder who had five shares before the bonus issue would have six shares after the bonus issue.

The bonus fraction is therefore 6/5.

(b) EPS in the financial statements for the year ended 31 December 20X7 would have been 46.0c ($460,000/1,000,000).

This is re-stated in the financial statements for the year ended 31 December 20X8 by multiplying it by the inverse of the bonus fraction.

The restated comparative is therefore 38.3c (46.0c × 5/6).

Rights issues

A rights issue of shares is normally made at less than the full market price. A rights issue therefore combines the characteristics of an issue at full market price with those of a bonus issue.

As already seen, the easiest way to deal with the bonus element is to calculate the bonus fraction and to apply this to all shares outstanding before the rights issue.

The bonus fraction for a rights issue is calculated as follows:

$$\frac{\text{Market price per share before rights issue}}{\text{Theoretical market price per share after the rights issue}}$$

EPS for the comparative period must be restated. The easiest way to achieve this is to multiply the EPS figure from the prior year's financial statements by the inverse of the bonus fraction.

Illustration – Rights issue

An entity issued one new share for every two existing shares at $1.50 per share on 1 July 20X8. The pre-issue market price was $3.00 per share.

Relevant information

	20X8	**20X7**
Profit attributable to the ordinary shareholders for the year ending 31 Dec	$550,000	$460,000
Number of ordinary shares in issue at 31 Dec	1,200,000	800,000

Required:

(a) **Calculate basic EPS for the year ended 31 December 20X8.**

(b) **Calculate the prior year comparative EPS figure as it would appear in the financial statements for the year ended 31 December 20X8.**

Solution

(a) EPS = $550,000/1,080,000 (W1) = 50.9c

(W1) **Weighted average number of shares**

800,000 × 6/12 × 3.00/2.50 (W2)	480,000
1,200,000 × 6/12	600,000
Weighted average number of shares	1,080,000

(W2) **Bonus fraction**

The bonus fraction is calculated as:

Share price before rights issue/Theoretical share price after rights issue.

The bonus fraction is $3.00/$2.50 (W3).

(W3) **Theoretical share price after rights issue**

	No. shares	Price per share	Market capitalisation
		$	$
Before rights issue	800,000	3.00	2,400,000
Rights issue	400,000	1.50	600,000
	1,200,000		3,000,000

The theoretical price per share after the rights issue is $2.50 ($3,000,000/1,200,000).

(b) EPS in the financial statements for the year ended 31 December 20X7 would have been 57.5c ($460,000/800,000).

This is restated in the financial statements for the year ended 31 December 20X8 by multiplying it by the inverse of the bonus fraction.

The restated comparative is therefore 47.9c (57.5c × 2.50/3.00).

Diluted earnings per share

Many companies issue convertible instruments, options and warrants that entitle their holders to purchase shares in the future at below the market price. When these shares are eventually issued, the interests of the original shareholders will be diluted. The dilution occurs because these shares will have been issued at below market price.

The Examiner has indicated that diluted earnings per share will not be examined in detail. However, students should have awareness of the topic as summarised below:

- Shares and other instruments that may dilute the interests of the existing shareholders are called potential ordinary shares.

- Examples of potential ordinary shares include:
  - debt and other instruments, including preference shares, that are convertible into ordinary shares
  - share warrants and options (instruments that give the holder the right to purchase ordinary shares)
  - employee plans that allow employees to receive ordinary shares as part of their remuneration and other share purchase plans
  - contingently issuable shares (i.e. shares issuable if certain conditions are met).
- Where there are dilutive potential ordinary shares in issue, the diluted EPS must be disclosed as well as the basic EPS. This provides relevant information to current and potential investors.
- When calculating diluted EPS, the profit used in the basic EPS calculation is adjusted for any expenses that would no longer be paid if the convertible instrument were converted into shares, e.g. preference dividends, loan interest.
- When calculating diluted EPS, the weighted average number of shares used in the basic EPS calculation is adjusted for the conversion of the potential ordinary shares.

Presentation

An entity should present basic and diluted earnings per share on the face of the statement of profit or loss and other comprehensive income for each class of ordinary shares that has a different right to share in the net profit for the period. IAS 33 notes the following:

- An entity should present basic and diluted earnings per share with equal prominence for all periods presented
- If an entity has discontinued operations, it should also present basic and diluted EPS from continuing operations
- Basic and diluted losses per share, if applicable, must be disclosed.

Disclosure

An entity should disclose the following.

- The earnings used for basic and diluted EPS. These earnings should be reconciled to the net profit or loss for the period.
- The weighted average number of ordinary shares used to calculate basic and diluted EPS. The two averages should be reconciled to each other.

EPS as a performance measure

The EPS figure is used to compute the major stock market indicator of performance, the Price/Earnings ratio (P/E ratio). Rightly or wrongly, the stock market places great emphasis on the earnings per share figure and the P/E ratio. IAS 33 sets out a standard method of calculating EPS, which enhances the comparability of the figure.

However, EPS has limited usefulness as a performance measure:

- An entity's earnings are affected by its choice of accounting policies. Therefore, it may not always be appropriate to compare the EPS of different companies.
- EPS does not take account of inflation. Apparent growth in earnings may not be true growth.
- EPS does not provide predictive value. High earnings and growth in earnings may be achieved at the expense of investment, which would have generated increased earnings in the future.
- In theory, diluted EPS serves as a warning to equity shareholders that the return on their investment may fall in future periods. However, diluted EPS as currently required by IAS 33 is not intended to be forward-looking but is an additional past performance measure. Diluted EPS is based on current earnings, not forecast earnings. Therefore, diluted EPS is only of limited use as a prediction of future EPS.
- EPS is a measure of profitability. Profitability is only one aspect of performance. Concentration on earnings per share and 'the bottom line' arguably detracts from other important aspects of an entity's affairs, such as cash flow and stewardship of assets.

5 IAS 34 Interim Financial Reporting

Interim reporting

Interim financial reports are prepared for a period shorter than a full financial year. Entities may be required to prepare interim financial reports under local law or listing regulations.

IAS 34 does not require the preparation of interim reports, but sets out the principles that should be followed if they are prepared and specifies their minimum content. An interim financial report should include, as a minimum, the following components:

- condensed statement of financial position as at the end of the current interim period, with a comparative statement of financial position as at the end of the previous financial year
- condensed statement of profit or loss and other comprehensive income for the current interim period and cumulatively for the current financial year to date (if, for example the entity reports quarterly), with comparatives for the interim periods (current and year to date) of the preceding financial year
- condensed statement showing changes in equity. This statement should show changes in equity cumulatively for the current year with comparatives for the corresponding period of the preceding financial year
- condensed statement of cash flows cumulatively for the year to date, with a comparative statement to the same date in the previous year
- selected explanatory notes
- basic and diluted EPS should be presented on the face of interim statements of profit or loss and other comprehensive income for those entities within the scope of IAS 33.

6 Assessing financial performance and position

Ratio analysis

In your previous studies, you will have learned a number of ratios that can be used to interpret an entity's financial statements.

A selection of the key ratios are provided below:

Profitability

Gross profit margin:

$$\frac{\text{Gross profit}}{\text{Revenue}} \times 100\%$$

An increase in gross profit margin may be a result of:

- higher selling prices
- lower purchase prices (perhaps resulting from bulk-buy discounts)
- a change in the sales mix.

Operating profit margin:

$$\frac{\text{Operating profit}}{\text{Revenue}} \times 100\%$$

Operating profit margin is affected by more factors than gross profit margin. Many operating costs are fixed and therefore do not necessarily increase or decrease with revenue. This means that operating profit margin may be more volatile year-on-year than gross profit margin.

Be aware that many operating costs, such as depreciation and impairment losses, are heavily reliant on management judgement. This may hinder the ability to compare the operating profit margin of one company with another company.

Return on capital employed (ROCE):

$$\frac{\text{Operating profit}}{\text{Capital employed}} \times 100\%$$

Capital employed is equity plus interest bearing finance.

ROCE is a measure of how efficiently an entity is using its resources. It should be compared to:

- previous years' figures
- the target ROCE
- the ROCE of competitors
- the cost of borrowing.

Liquidity and working capital

Current ratio:

$$\frac{\text{Current assets}}{\text{Current liabilities}} : 1$$

The current ratio measures whether an entity has sufficient current assets to meet its short-term obligations. The higher the ratio, the more financially secure the entity is. However, if the ratio is too high then it may suggest inefficiencies in working capital management.

Inventory turnover period:

$$\frac{\text{Inventories}}{\text{Cost of sales}} \times 365 \text{ days}$$

A high inventory turnover period may suggest:

- lack of demand for the entity's goods
- poor inventory control.

Receivables collection period:

$$\frac{\text{Trade receivables}}{\text{Credit sales}} \times 365 \text{ days}$$

An increase in the receivables collection period may suggest a lack of credit control, which could lead to irrecoverable debts.

Payables payment period:

$$\frac{\text{Trade payables}}{\text{Credit purchases}} \times 365 \text{ days}$$

This represents the credit period taken by the company from its suppliers. A long credit period can be a good sign because it is a free source of finance. However, if an entity is taking too long to pay its suppliers then there is a risk that credit facilities could be reduced or withdrawn.

Long-term financial stability

Gearing:

$$\frac{\text{Debt}}{\text{Equity}} \quad \text{or} \quad \frac{\text{Debt}}{\text{Debt + equity}}$$

Gearing indicates the risk attached to the entity's finance. Highly geared entities have a greater risk of insolvency.

Interest cover:

$$\frac{\text{Operating profit}}{\text{Finance costs}}$$

Interest cover indicates the ability of an entity to pay interest out of the profits generated. A low interest cover suggests that an entity may have difficulty financing its debts if profits fall.

Investor ratios

P/E ratio:

$$\frac{\text{Current share price}}{\text{EPS}}$$

The P/E ratio represents the market's view of the future prospects of an entity's shares. A high P/E ratio suggests that growth is expected.

Limitations of financial information and its analysis

Limitations of financial information

Ratio analysis generally relies on the published financial statements of an entity. However, many user groups have become increasingly aware of the limitations of traditional financial reporting.

- Preparing financial statements involves a substantial degree of classification and aggregation. There is always a risk that essential information will either not be given sufficient prominence or will be lost completely.
- Financial statements focus on the financial effects of transactions and other events and do not focus to any significant extent on their non-financial effects or on non-financial information in general.
- Published financial statements provide information that is largely historical. They do not reflect future events or transactions, nor do they anticipate the impact of potential changes to an entity. This means that it is not always possible to use them to predict future performance.
- There is often a time interval of several months between the year-end and the publication of the financial statements. Most financial information is out of date by the time it is actually published.

Limitations of financial analysis

Ratio analysis is a useful means of identifying significant relationships between different figures, but it also has many limitations.

- Profit is highly dependent on the accounting policies and estimates adopted by an entity.
- Many businesses produce financial statements to a date on which there are relatively low amounts of trading activity. As a result the items on a statement of financial position are not typical of the items throughout the reporting period.
- Ratios based on historical costs do not give a true picture of trends from year to year. An apparent increase in profit may not be a 'true' increase, because of the effects of inflation.
- Comparing the financial statements of similar businesses can be misleading for a number of reasons, including the effect of size differences and of operating in different markets.
- There are particular problems in comparing the financial statements of similar businesses that operate in different countries. There can be significant differences in accounting policies, terminology and presentation.

Impact of accounting policies and choices

Accounting policies can significantly affect the view presented by financial statements, and the ratios computed by reference to them, without affecting a business's core ability to generate profits and cash.

The potential impact of accounting policies is especially important where:

- accounting standards permit a choice between a cost model or a fair value model
- judgement is needed in making accounting estimates, such as with depreciation and provisions
- there is no relevant accounting standard (although this is now extremely rare).

The impact of accounting policy choices on the financial statements will be highlighted throughout this text.

Non-financial performance measures

Ratio analysis and other interpretation techniques based on the financial statements cannot measure all aspects of performance. As a result, non-financial performance measures are becoming increasingly important to management, the shareholders and other interested parties external to an entity.

Examples of non-financial performance measures are:

- the number of instances of environmental spillage per year
- the reduction in CO_2 emissions during the year
- the amount of waste (kg) arising from packaging on each $1,000 of products
- employee turnover
- training time per employee
- lost time injury frequency rate (relating to employees).

You will learn more about types of non-financial reporting later in this text.

7 Chapter summary

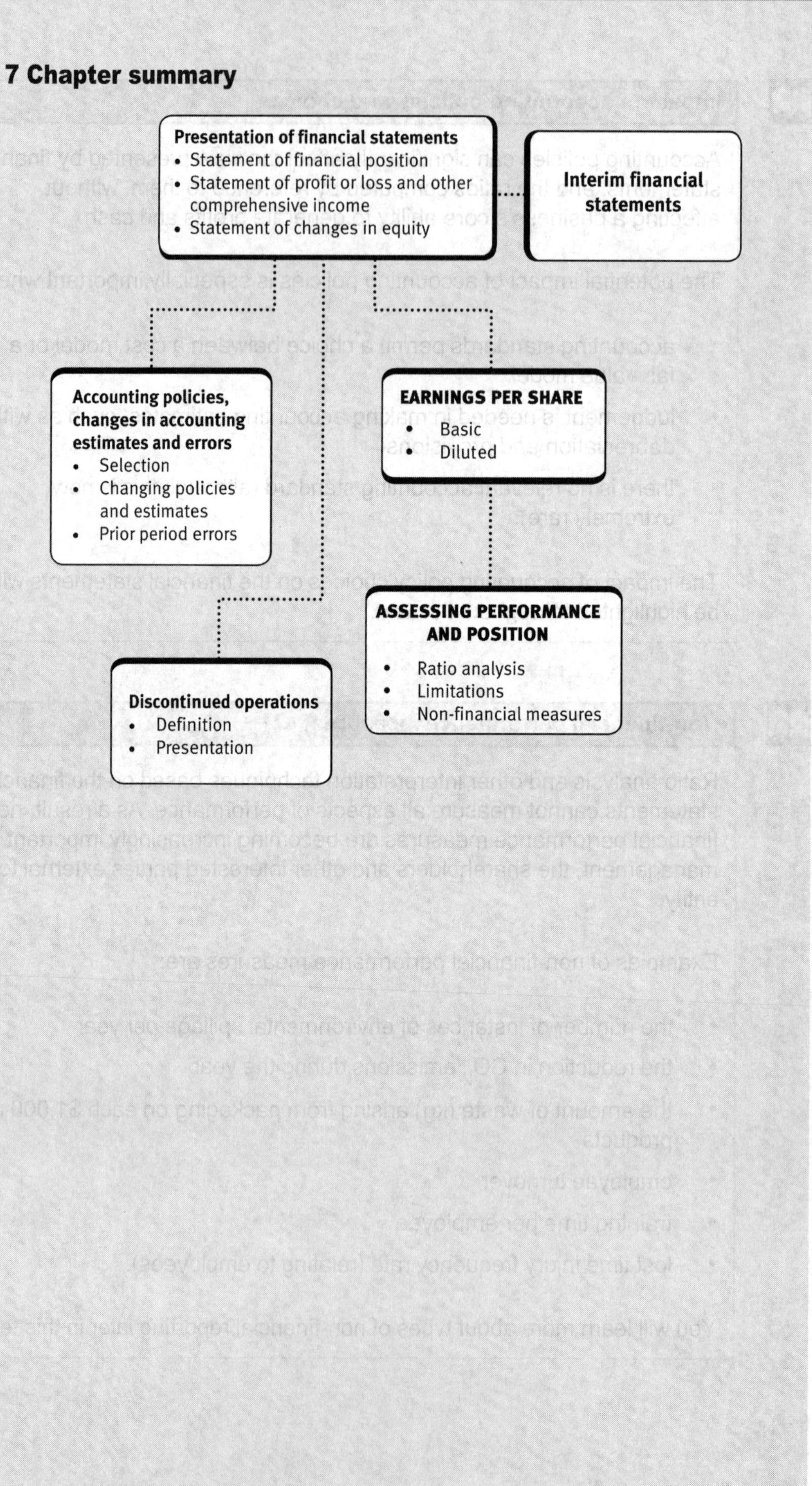
Presentation of financial statements
• Statement of financial position
• Statement of profit or loss and other comprehensive income
• Statement of changes in equity
Interim financial statements
Accounting policies, changes in accounting estimates and errors
• Selection
• Changing policies and estimates
• Prior period errors
EARNINGS PER SHARE
• Basic
• Diluted
ASSESSING PERFORMANCE AND POSITION
• Ratio analysis
• Limitations
• Non-financial measures
Discontinued operations
• Definition
• Presentation

chapter

4

Revenue

Chapter learning objectives

- discuss and apply the five-step model which relates to revenue earned from a contract with a customer
- discuss and apply the criteria that must be met before an entity can apply the revenue recognition model to that contract.

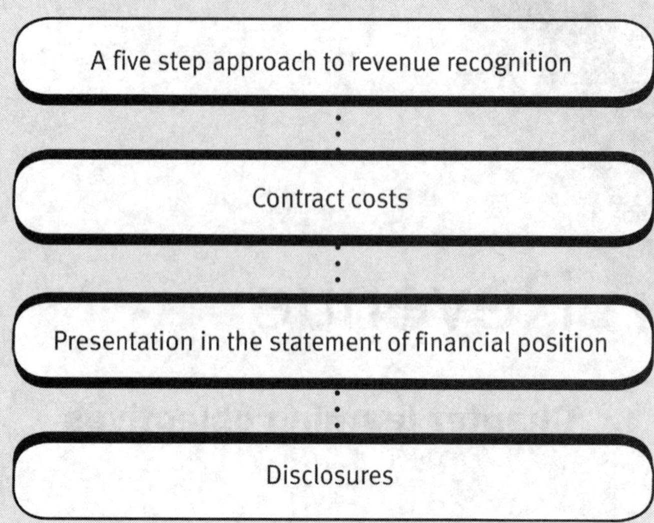

1 Revenue from contracts with customers (IFRS 15)

Revenue is income arising in the course of an entity's ordinary activities.

- 'Ordinary activities' means normal trading or operating activities.
- 'Revenue' presented in the statement of profit or loss should not include items such as proceeds from the sale of non-current assets or sales tax.

2 Revenue recognition

A five step process

IFRS 15 Revenue from Contracts with Customers (para IN7) says that an entity recognises revenue by applying the following five steps:

(1) **'Identify the contract**

(2) **Identify the separate performance obligations within a contract**

(3) **Determine the transaction price**

(4) **Allocate the transaction price to the performance obligations in the contract**

(5) **Recognise revenue when (or as) a performance obligation is satisfied.'**

These five steps will be considered in more detail. However, the following illustration may help you to gain an understanding of the basic principles of the IFRS 15 revenue recognition model.

Illustration 1 – The five steps

On 1 December 20X1, Wade receives an order from a customer for a computer as well as 12 months' of technical support. Wade delivers the computer (and transfers its legal title) to the customer on the same day.

The customer paid $420 upfront. If sold individually, the selling price of the computer is $300 and the selling price of the technical support is $120.

Required:

Apply the 5 stages of revenue recognition, per IFRS 15, to determine how much revenue Wade should recognise in the year ended 31 December 20X1.

Solution

Step 1 - Identify the contract

There is an agreement between Wade and its customer for the provision of goods and services.

Step 2 - Identify the separate performance obligations within a contract

There are two performance obligations (promises) within the contract:

- The supply of a computer
- The supply of technical support.

Step 3 - Determine the transaction price

The total transaction price is $420.

Step 4 - Allocate the transaction price to the performance obligations in the contract

Based on standalone selling prices, $300 should be allocated to the sale of the computer and $120 should be allocated to the technical support.

Step 5 – Recognise revenue when (or as) a performance obligation is satisfied

Control over the computer has been passed to the customer so the full revenue of $300 allocated to the supply of the computer should be recognised on 1 December 20X1.

The technical support is provided over time, so the revenue allocated to this should be recognised over time. In the year ended 31 December 20X1, revenue of $10 (1/12 × $120) should be recognised from the provision of technical support.

The five steps of revenue recognition will now be considered in more detail.

Step 1: Identify the contract

IFRS 15 says that a contract is an agreement between two parties that creates rights and obligations. A contract does not need to be written.

An entity can only account for revenue from a contract if it meets the following criteria:

- the parties have approved the contract and each party's rights can be identified
- payment terms can be identified
- the contract has commercial substance
- it is probable that the entity will be paid.

The contract

Aluna has a year end of 31 December 20X1.

On 30 September 20X1, Aluna signed a contract with a customer to provide them with an asset on 31 December 20X1. Control over the asset passed to the customer on 31 December 20X1. The customer will pay $1m on 30 June 20X2.

By 31 December 20X1, as a result of changes in the economic climate, Aluna did not believe it was probable that it would collect the consideration that it was entitled to. Therefore, the contract cannot be accounted for and no revenue should be recognised.

Step 2: Identifying the separate performance obligations within a contract

Performance obligations are promises to transfer distinct goods or services to a customer.

Some contracts contain more than one performance obligation. For example:

- An entity may enter into a contract with a customer to sell a car, which includes one year's free servicing and maintenance.
- An entity might enter into a contract with a customer to provide 5 lectures, as well as to provide a textbook on the first day of the course.

The distinct performance obligations within a contract must be identified. If goods or services are regularly sold separately then the supply of each is likely to form a distinct performance obligation if included within the same contract.

Warranties

Most of the time, a warranty is assurance that a product will function as intended. If this is the case, then the warranty will be accounted for in accordance with IAS 37 Provisions, Contingent Liabilities and Contingent Assets.

If the customer has the option to purchase the warranty separately, then it should be treated as a distinct performance obligation. This means that a portion of the transaction price must be allocated to it.

Principal versus agent considerations

An entity must decide the nature of each performance obligation. IFRS 15 (para B34) says this might be:

- **'to provide the specified goods or service itself (i.e. it is the principal), or**
- **to arrange for another party to provide the goods or service (i.e. it is an agent)'.**

If an entity is an agent, then revenue is recognised based on the fee or commission it is entitled to.

Step 3: Determining the transaction price

IFRS 15 defines the transaction price as the amount of consideration the entity expects in exchange for satisfying a performance obligation. Sales tax is excluded.

When determining the transaction price, the following must be considered:

- variable consideration
- significant financing components
- non-cash consideration
- consideration payable to a customer.

Variable consideration

If a contract includes variable consideration then an entity must estimate the amount it will be entitled to.

IFRS 15 says that this estimate **'can only be included in the transaction price if it is highly probable that a significant reversal in the amount of cumulative revenue recognised will not occur when the uncertainty is resolved'** (IFRS 15, para 56).

Test your understanding 1 – Bristow

On 1 December 20X1, Bristow provides a service to a customer for the next 12 months. The consideration is $12 million. Bristow is entitled to an extra $3 million if, after twelve months, the number of mistakes made falls below a certain threshold.

Required:

Discuss the accounting treatment of the above in Bristow's financial statements for the year ended 31 December 20X1 if:

(a) **Bristow has experience of providing identical services in the past and it is highly probable that the number of mistakes made will fall below the acceptable threshold.**

(b) **Bristow has no experience of providing this service and is unsure if the number of mistakes made will fall below the threshold.**

Refunds

If a product is sold with a right to return it then the consideration is variable. The entity must estimate the variable consideration and decide whether or not to include it in the transaction price.

The refund liability should equal the consideration received (or receivable) that the entity does not expect to be entitled to.

Illustration: Refunds

Nardone enters into 50 contracts with customers. Each contract includes the sale of one product for $1,000. The cost to Nardone of each product is $400. Cash is received upfront and control of the product transfers on delivery. Customers can return the product within 30 days to receive a full refund. Nardone can sell the returned products at a profit.

Nardone has significant experience in estimating returns for this product. It estimates that 48 products will not be returned.

Required:

How should the above transaction be accounted for?

Solution

The fact that the customer can return the product means that the consideration is variable.

Using an expected value method, the estimated variable consideration is $48,000 (48 products × $1,000). The variable consideration should be included in the transaction price because, based on Nardone's experience, it is highly probable that a significant reversal in the cumulative amount of revenue recognised ($48,000) will not occur.

Therefore, revenue of $48,000 and a refund liability of $2,000 ($1,000 × 2 products expected to be returned) should be recognised.

Nardone will derecognise the inventory transferred to its customers. However, it should recognise an asset of $800 (2 products × $400), as well as a corresponding credit to cost of sales, for its right to recover products from customers on settling the refund liability.

Financing

In determining the transaction price, an entity must consider if the timing of payments provides the customer or the entity with a financing benefit.

If there is a financing component, then the consideration receivable needs to be discounted to present value using the rate at which the customer borrows money.

Indications of a financing component

IFRS 15 provides the following indications of a significant financing component:

- the difference between the amount of promised consideration and the cash selling price of the promised goods or services
- the length of time between the transfer of the promised goods or services to the customer and the payment date.

Test your understanding 2 – Rudd

Rudd enters into a contract with a customer to sell equipment on 31 December 20X1. Control of the equipment transfers to the customer on that date. The price stated in the contract is $1m and is due on 31 December 20X3.

Market rates of interest available to this particular customer are 10%.

Required:

Explain how this transaction should be accounted for in the financial statements of Rudd for the year ended 31 December 20X1.

Non-cash consideration

Any non-cash consideration is measured at fair value.

If the fair value of non-cash consideration cannot be estimated reliably then the transaction is measured using the stand-alone selling price of the good or services promised to the customer.

Test your understanding 3 – Dan and Stan

Dan sells a good to Stan. Control over the good is transferred on 1 January 20X1. The consideration received by Dan is 1,000 shares in Stan with a fair value of $4 each. By 31 December 20X1, the shares in Stan have a fair value of $5 each.

Required:

How much revenue should be recognised from this transaction in the financial statements of Dan for the year ended 31 December 20X1?

Consideration payable to a customer

If consideration is paid to a customer in exchange for a distinct good or service, then it should be accounted for as a purchase transaction.

Assuming that the consideration paid to a customer is not in exchange for a distinct good or service, an entity should account for it as a reduction of the transaction price.

Test your understanding 4 – Golden Gate

Golden Gate enters into a contract with a major chain of retail stores. The customer commits to buy at least $20m of products over the next 12 months. The terms of the contract require Golden Gate to make a payment of $1m to compensate the customer for changes that it will need to make to its retail stores to accommodate the products.

By the 31 December 20X1, Golden Gate has transferred products with a sales value of $4m to the customer.

Required

How much revenue should be recognised by Golden Gate in the year ended 31 December 20X1?

Step 4: Allocate the transaction price

The total transaction price should be allocated to each performance obligation in proportion to stand-alone selling prices.

The best evidence of a stand-alone selling price is the observable price when the good or service is sold separately.

If a stand-alone selling price is not directly observable then it must be estimated. Observable inputs should be maximised whenever possible.

If a customer is offered a discount for purchasing a bundle of goods and services, then the discount should be allocated across all performance obligations within the contract in proportion to their stand-alone selling prices (unless observable evidence suggests that this would be inaccurate).

Test your understanding 5 – Shred

Shred sells a machine and one year's free technical support for $100,000. The sale of the machine and the provision of technical support have been identified as separate performance obligations. Shred usually sells the machine for $95,000 but it has not yet started selling technical support for this machine as a stand-alone product. Other support services offered by Shred attract a mark-up of 50%. It is expected that the technical support will cost Shred $20,000.

Required:

How much of the transaction price should be allocated to the machine and how much should be allocated to the technical support?

Step 5: Recognise revenue

Revenue is recognised when (or as) the entity satisfies a performance obligation by transferring a promised good or service to a customer.

An entity must determine at contract inception whether it satisfies the performance obligation over time or satisfies the performance obligation at a point in time.

IFRS 15 (para 35) states that an entity satisfies a performance obligation over time if one of the following criteria is met:

(a) **'the customer simultaneously receives and consumes the benefits provided by the entity's performance as the entity performs**

(b) **the entity's performance creates or enhances an asset (for example, work in progress) that the customer controls as the asset is created or enhanced, or**

(c) **the entity's performance does not create an asset with an alternative use to the entity and the entity has an enforceable right to payment for performance completed to date'.**

If a performance obligation is satisfied over time, then revenue is recognised over time based on progress towards the satisfaction of that performance obligation.

Test your understanding 6 – Evans

On 1 January 20X1, Evans enters into a contract with a customer to provide monthly payroll services. Evans charges $120,000 per year.

Required:

What is the accounting treatment of the above in the financial statements of Evans for the year ended 30 June 20X1?

Test your understanding 7 – Crawford

On 31 March 20X1, Crawford enters into a contract to construct a specialised factory for a customer. The customer paid an upfront deposit which is only refundable if Crawford fails to complete construction in line with the contract. The remainder of the price is payable when the customer takes possession of the factory. If the customer defaults on the contract before completion of the factory, Crawford only has the right to retain the deposit.

Required:

Should Crawford recognise revenue from the above transaction over time or at a point in time?

Methods of measuring progress towards satisfaction of a performance obligation include:

- output methods (such as surveys of performance, or time elapsed)
- input methods (such as costs incurred as a proportion of total expected costs).

If progress cannot be reliably measured then revenue can only be recognised up to the recoverable costs incurred.

Test your understanding 8 – Baker

On 1 January 20X1, Baker enters into a contract with a customer to construct a specialised building for consideration of $2m plus a bonus of $0.4m if the building is completed within 18 months. Estimated costs to construct the building are $1.5m. If the contract is terminated by the customer, Baker can demand payment for the costs incurred to date plus a mark-up of 30%. On 1 January 20X1, as a result of factors outside of its control, such as the weather and regulatory approval, Baker is not sure whether the bonus will be achieved.

At 31 December 20X1, Baker is still unsure whether the bonus target will be met. Baker decides to measure progress towards completion based on costs incurred. Costs incurred on the contract to date are $1.0m.

Required:

How should Baker account for this transaction in the year ended 31 December 20X1?

If a performance obligation is not satisfied over time then it is satisfied at a point in time. The entity must determine the point in time at which a customer obtains control of a promised asset.

An entity controls an asset if it can direct its use and obtain most of its remaining benefits. Control also includes the ability to prevent other entities from obtaining benefits from an asset.

IFRS 15 (para 38) provides the following indicators of the transfer of control:

- **'The entity has a present right to payment for the asset**
- **The customer has legal title to the asset**
- **The entity has transferred physical possession of the asset**
- **The customer has the significant risks and rewards of ownership of the asset**
- **The customer has accepted the asset'.**

Test your understanding 9 – Clarence

On 31 December 20X1, Clarence delivered the January edition of a magazine (with a total sales value of $100,000) to a supermarket chain. Legal title remains with Clarence until the supermarket sells a magazine to the end consumer. The supermarket will start selling the magazines to its customers on 1 January 20X2. Any magazines that remain unsold by the supermarket on 31 January 20X2 are returned to Clarence.

The supermarket will be invoiced by Clarence in February 20X2 based on the difference between the number of issues they received and the number of issues that they return.

Required:

Should Clarence recognise revenue from the above transaction in the year ended 31 December 20X1?

3 Contract costs

IFRS 15 says that the following costs must be capitalised:

- The costs of obtaining a contract. This must exclude costs that would have been incurred regardless of whether the contract was obtained or not (such as some legal fees, or the costs of travelling to a tender).
- The costs of fulfilling a contract if they do not fall within the scope of another standard (such as IAS 2 Inventories) and the entity expects them to be recovered.

The capitalised costs of obtaining and fulfilling a contract will be amortised to the statement of profit or loss as revenue is recognised.

4 Presentation on the statement of financial position

When an entity has recognised revenue before it has received consideration, then it should recognise either:

- a receivable if the right to the consideration is unconditional, or
- a contract asset.

An entity has an unconditional right to receive consideration if only the passage of time is required before payment is due.

A contract liability should be recognised if the entity has received consideration (or has an unconditional right to receive consideration) before the related revenue has been recognised.

5 Other issues

Revenue disclosures

IFRS 15 requires an entity to disclose:

- revenue recognised from contracts with customers
- contract balances and assets recognised from costs incurred obtaining or fulfilling contracts
- significant judgements used, and any changes in judgements.

IFRS 15 and judgement

Management judgement is required throughout all five steps of revenue recognition. For example:

- Contracts with customers do not need to be in writing but may arise through customary business practice. An entity must therefore ascertain whether it has a constructive obligation to deliver a good or service to a customer.
- A contract can only be accounted for if it is probable that the entity will collect the consideration that it is entitled to. Whether benefits are probable is, ultimately, a judgement.
- The entity must identify distinct performance obligations in a contract. However, past performance may give rise to expectations in a customer that goods or services not specified in the contract will be transferred. The identification of distinct performance obligations thus relies on management judgement about both contract terms, and the impact of the entity's past behaviour on customer expectations.
- Variable consideration should be included in the transaction price if it is highly probable that a significant reversal in the amount of cumulative revenue recognised to date will not occur. This may involve making judgements about whether performance related targets will be met.
- The transaction price must be allocated to distinct performance obligations, based on observable, standalone selling prices. However, estimation techniques must be used if observable prices are not available.
- If a performance obligation is satisfied over time, revenue is recognised based on progress towards the completion of the performance obligation. There are various ways to measure completion, using either input or output methods, and the entity must determine which one most faithfully represents the transaction.
- If a performance obligation is satisfied at a point in time, the entity must use judgement to ascertain the date at which control of the asset passes to the customer.

These judgements increase the risk that the management of an entity could manipulate its profits. Adherence to the ACCA ethical code is, therefore, vital.

6 Chapter summary

A five step approach to revenue recognition
(1) Identify the contract
(2) Identify the performance obligations
(3) Determine the transaction price
(4) Allocate the transaction price
(5) Recognise revenue

Contract costs
- Capitalise the costs of fulfilling the contract

Presentation in the statement of financial position
- Contract assets
- Contract liabilities

Disclosures

Test your understanding answers

Test your understanding 1 – Bristow

The $12 million consideration is fixed. The $3 million consideration that is dependent on the number of mistakes made is variable.

Bristow must estimate the variable consideration. It could use an expected value or a most likely amount. Since there are only two outcomes, $0 or $3 million, then a most likely amount would better predict the entitled consideration.

(a) Bristow expects to hit the target. Using a most likely amount, the variable consideration would be valued at $3 million.

Bristow must then decide whether to include the estimate of variable consideration in the transaction price.

Based on past experience, it seems highly probable that a significant reversal in revenue recognised would not occur. This means that the transaction price is $15 million ($12m + $3m).

As a service, it is likely that the performance obligation would be satisfied over time. The revenue recognised in the year ended 31 December 20X1 would therefore be $1.25 million ($15m × 1/12).

(b) Depending on the estimated likelihood of hitting the target, the variable consideration would either be estimated to be $0 or $3 million.

Whatever the amount, the estimated variable consideration cannot be included in the transaction price because it is not highly probable that a significant reversal in revenue would not occur. This is because Bristow has no experience of providing this service. Therefore, the transaction price is $12 million.

As a service, it is likely that the performance obligation would be satisfied over time. The revenue recognised in the year ended 31 December 20X1 would be $1 million ($12m × 1/12).

Test your understanding 2 – Rudd

Due to the length of time between the transfer of control of the asset and the payment date, this contract includes a significant financing component.

The consideration must be adjusted for the impact of the financing transaction. A discount rate should be used that reflects the characteristics of the customer i.e. 10%.

Revenue should be recognised when the performance obligation is satisfied.

As such revenue, and a corresponding receivable, should be recognised at \$826,446 (\$1m × $1/1.10^2$) on 31 December 20X1.

The receivable is subsequently accounted for in accordance with IFRS 9 Financial Instruments.

Test your understanding 3 – Dan and Stan

The contract contains a single performance obligation.

Consideration for the transaction is non-cash. Non-cash consideration is measured at fair value.

Revenue should be recognised at \$4,000 (1,000 shares × \$4) on 1 January 20X1.

Any subsequent change in the fair value of the shares received is not recognised within revenue but instead accounted for in accordance with IFRS 9 Financial Instruments.

Test your understanding 4 – Golden Gate

The payment made to the customer is not in exchange for a distinct good or service. Therefore, the \$1m paid to the customer must be treated as a reduction in the transaction price.

The total transaction price is essentially being reduced by 5% (\$1m/ \$20m). Therefore, Golden Gate reduces the price allocated to each good by 5% as it is transferred.

By 31 December 20X1, Golden Gate should have recognised revenue of \$3.8m (\$4m × 95%).

Test your understanding 5 – Shred

The selling price of the machine is $95,000 based on observable evidence.

There is no observable selling price for the technical support. Therefore, the stand-alone selling price needs to be estimated.

A residual approach would attribute $5,000 ($100,000 – $95,000) to the technical support. However, this does not approximate the stand-alone selling price of similar services (which normally make a profit).

A better approach for estimating the selling price of the support would be an expected cost plus a margin (or mark-up) approach. Based on this, the selling price of the service would be $30,000 ($20,000 × 150%).

The total of standalone selling prices of the machine and support is $125,000 ($95,000 + $30,000). However, total consideration receivable is only $100,000. This means that the customer is receiving a discount for purchasing a bundle of goods and services of 20% ($25,000/$125,000).

IFRS 15 assumes that discounts relate to all performance obligations within a contract, unless evidence exists to the contrary.

The transaction price allocated to the machine is $76,000 ($95,000 × 80%).

The transaction price allocated to the technical support is $24,000 ($30,000 × 80%).

The revenue will be recognised when (or as) the performance obligations are satisfied.

Test your understanding 6 – Evans

The payroll services are a single performance obligation.

This performance obligation is satisfied over time because the customer simultaneously receives and consumes the benefits of the payroll processing. This is evidenced by the fact that the payroll services would not need to be re-performed if the customer changed its payroll service provider.

Evans must therefore recognise revenue from the service over time. In the year ended 30 June 20X1, they would recognise revenue of $60,000 (6/12 × $120,000).

Test your understanding 7 – Crawford

In assessing whether revenue is recorded over time, it is important to note that the factory under construction is specialised. Therefore, the asset being created has no alternative use to the entity.

However, Crawford only has an enforceable right to the deposit received and therefore does not have a right to payment for work completed to date.

Consequently, Crawford must account for the sale of the unit as a performance obligation satisfied at a point in time, rather than over time. Revenue will most likely be recognised when the customer takes possession of the factory (although a detailed assessment should be made of the date when the customer assumes control).

Test your understanding 8 – Baker

Constructing the building is a single performance obligation.

The bonus is variable consideration. Whatever its estimated value, it must be excluded from the transaction price because it is not highly probable that a significant reversal in the amount of cumulative revenue recognised will not occur.

The construction of the building should be accounted for as an obligation settled over time. This is because the building has no alternative uses for Baker, and because payment can be enforced for the work completed to date.

Baker should recognise revenue based on progress towards satisfaction of the construction of the building. Using costs incurred, the performance obligation is 2/3 ($1.0m/$1.5m) complete. Accordingly, the revenue and costs recognised at the end of the year are as follows:

	$m
Revenue ($2m × 2/3)	1.3
Costs ($1.5m × 2/3)	(1.0)
Gross profit	0.3

Test your understanding 9 – Clarence

The performance obligation is not satisfied over time because the supermarket does not simultaneously receive and benefit from the asset. Clarence therefore satisfies the performance obligation at a point in time and will recognise revenue when it transfers control over the assets to the supermarket.

The fact that the supermarket has physical possession of the magazines at 31 December 20X1 is an indicator that control has passed. Also, Clarence will invoice the supermarket for any issues that are stolen and so the supermarket does bear some of the risks of ownership.

However, as at 31 December 20X1, legal title of the magazines has not passed to the supermarket. Moreover, Clarence has no right to receive payment until the supermarket sells the magazines to the end consumer. Finally, Clarence will be sent any unsold issues and so bears significant risks of ownership (such as the risk of obsolescence).

All things considered, it would seem that control of the magazines has not passed from Clarence to the supermarket chain. Therefore, Clarence should not recognise revenue from this contract in its financial statements for the year ended 31 December 20X1.

chapter

5

Non-current assets, agriculture and inventories

Chapter learning objectives

Upon completion of this chapter you will be able to:

- apply and discuss the timing of the recognition of non-current assets and the determination of their carrying amounts including impairment and revaluations
- apply and discuss the treatment of non-current assets held for sale
- apply and discuss the accounting treatment of investment properties including classification, recognition and measurement issues
- apply and discuss the accounting treatment of intangible assets including the criteria for recognition and measurement subsequent to acquisition and classification
- apply and discuss the accounting treatment of inventories.

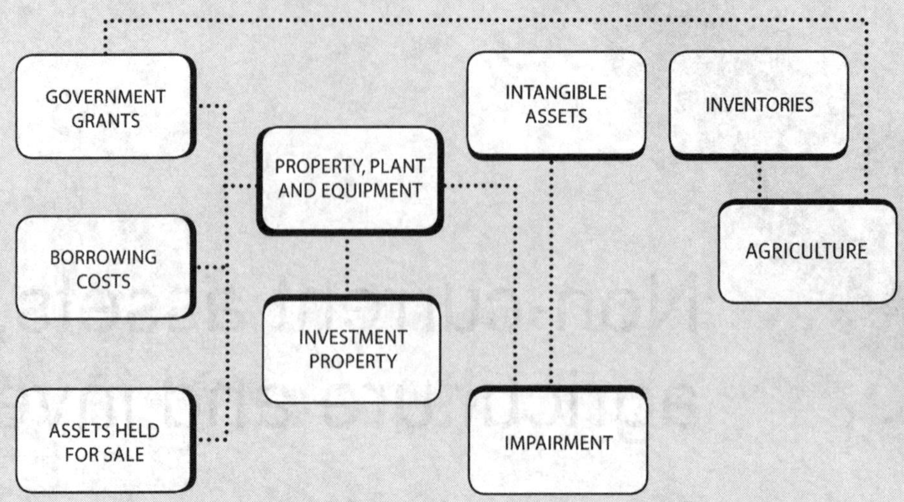

1 Property, plant and equipment

IAS 16 Property, plant and equipment: Initial recognition

Definition

IAS 16 defines property, plant and equipment as tangible items that:

- **'are held for use in the production or supply of goods or services, for rental to others, or for administrative purposes**
- **are expected to be used during more than one period'** (IAS 16, para 6).

Tangible items have physical substance and can be touched.

Initial recognition

An item of property, plant and equipment should be recognised as an asset when:

- it is probable that the asset's future economic benefits will flow to the entity
- the cost of the asset can be measured reliably.

Property, plant and equipment should initially be measured at its cost. According to IAS 16, this comprises:

- the purchase price
- costs that are directly attributable to bringing the asset to the necessary location and condition
- the estimated costs of dismantling and removing the asset, including any site restoration costs. This might apply where, for example, an entity has to recognise a provision for the cost of decommissioning an oil rig or a nuclear power station.

IAS 16 says that the following costs should **never** be capitalised:

- administration and general overheads
- abnormal costs (repairs, wastage, idle time)
- costs incurred after the asset is physically ready for use (unless these costs increase the economic benefits the asset brings)
- costs incurred in the initial operating period (such as initial operating losses and any further costs incurred before a machine is used at its full capacity)
- costs of opening a new facility, introducing a new product (including advertising and promotional costs) and conducting business in a new location or with a new class of customer (including training costs)
- costs of relocating/reorganising an entity's operations.

Measurement after initial recognition

IAS 16 allows a choice between:

- the cost model
- the revaluation model.

Under the **cost model**, property, plant and equipment is held at cost less any accumulated depreciation.

Under the **revaluation model**, property, plant and equipment is carried at fair value less any subsequent accumulated depreciation.

If the revaluation model is adopted, then IAS 16 provides the following rules:

- Revaluations must be made with 'sufficient regularity' to ensure that the carrying amount does not differ materially from the fair value at each reporting date.
- If an item is revalued, the entire class of assets to which the item belongs must be revalued.
- If a revaluation increases the value of an asset, the increase is presented as other comprehensive income (and disclosed as an item that will not be recycled to profit or loss in subsequent periods) and held in a 'revaluation surplus' within other components of equity.
- If a revaluation decreases the value of the asset, the decrease should be recognised immediately in profit or loss, unless there is a revaluation reserve representing a surplus on the same asset.

Depreciation

All assets with a finite useful life must be depreciated. Depreciation is charged to the statement of profit or loss, unless it is included in the carrying amount of another asset.

IAS 16 says that depreciation must be allocated on a systematic basis, reflecting the pattern in which the asset's future economic benefits are expected to be consumed. Depreciation methods based on the revenue generated by an activity are not appropriate. This is because revenue reflects many factors, such as inflation, sales prices and sales volumes, rather than the economic consumption of an asset. In practice, many entities depreciate property, plant and equipment on a straight line basis over its estimated useful economic life.

Depreciation begins when the asset is available for use and continues until the asset is derecognised, even if it is idle.

The residual value and the useful life of an asset should be reviewed at least at each financial year-end and revised if necessary. Depreciation methods should also be reviewed at least annually. Any adjustments are accounted for as a change in accounting estimate (under IAS 8 Accounting Policies, Changes in Accounting Estimates and Errors), rather than as a change in accounting policy. This means that they are reflected in the current and future statements of profit or loss and other comprehensive income.

Illustration: Change in depreciation estimates

An asset was purchased for $100,000 on 1 January 20X5 and straight line depreciation of $20,000 per annum was charged (five year life, no residual value). A general review of asset lives was undertaken and the remaining useful life of this asset as at 1 January 20X7 was deemed to be eight years.

Required:

What is the annual depreciation charge for 20X7 and subsequent years?

Solution

Carrying amount as at 1 January 20X7 (3/5 × $100,000)	$60,000
Remaining useful life as at 1 January 20X7	8 years
Annual depreciation charge ($60,000/8 years)	$7,500

Depreciation of separate components

Certain large assets are in fact a collection of smaller assets, each with a different cost and useful life. For example, an aeroplane consists of an airframe (which may last for 40 years or so) plus engines, radar equipment, seats, etc. all of which have a relatively short life. Instead of calculating depreciation on the aeroplane as a whole, depreciation is charged on each component (airframe, engines, etc.).

For example, an entity buys a ship for $12m. The ship as a whole should last for 25 years. The engines, however, will need replacing after 7 years. The cost price of $12m included about $1.4m in respect of the engines.

The annual depreciation charge will be $624,000 made up as follows:

Engines: $1.4m over seven years = $200,000 pa, plus

The rest of the ship: $10.6m over 25 years = $424,000 pa.

Derecognition

IAS 16 says that an asset should be derecognised when disposal occurs, or if no further economic benefits are expected from the asset's use or disposal.

- The gain or loss on derecognition of an asset is the difference between the net disposal proceeds, if any, and the carrying amount of the item.
- When a revalued asset is disposed of, any revaluation surplus may be transferred directly to retained earnings, or it may be left in the revaluation surplus within other components of equity.

Test your understanding 1 – Cap

Cap bought a building on 1 January 20X1. The purchase price was $2.9m, associated legal fees were $0.1m and general administrative costs allocated to the purchase were $0.2m. Cap also paid sales tax of $0.5m, which was recovered from the tax authorities. The building was attributed a useful economic life of 50 years. It was revalued to $4.6m on 31 December 20X4 and was sold for $5m on 31 December 20X5.

Cap purchased a machine on 1 January 20X3 for $100,000 and attributed it with a useful life of 10 years. On 1 January 20X5, Cap reduced the estimated remaining useful life to 4 years.

Required:

Explain how the above items of property, plant and equipment would have been accounted for in all relevant reporting periods up until 31 December 20X5.

The impact on the financial statements

IAS 16 Property, Plant and Equipment permits entities to use a cost model or a revaluation model. This choice will have a big impact on the financial statements.

Example

Entities A and B are identical in all respects, except for their accounting policy for property, plant and equipment.

Both entities purchased an asset four years ago for $200,000. This was deemed to have a useful economic life of 10 years. Its fair value at the start of the current reporting period was $350,000.

Entity A uses the cost model. The current year depreciation charge on the asset is $20,000 ($200,000/10). The carrying amount of the asset in the statement of financial position at the year end is $120,000 (6/10 × $200,000).

Entity B uses the revaluation model. The asset was revalued at the start of the year by $210,000 ($350,000 – (7/10 × $200,000)). The depreciation charge on the asset in the current year is $50,000 ($350,000/7). The asset has a carrying amount in the statement of financial position of $300,000 ($350,000 – $50,000).

Extracts from the financial statements of both entities are provided below:

Statement of profit or loss

	A	**B**
	$000	$000
Revenue	220	220
Operating costs	(180)	(210)
Profit from operations	40	10

Statement of financial position

	A	B
	$000	$000
Share capital	50	50
Retained earnings	90	60
Other components of equity	–	210
Total equity	140	320
Borrowings	100	100
Total equity and liabilities	240	420
Operating profit margin	18.2%	4.5%
Return on capital employed	16.7%	2.4%
Gearing (debt/debt + equity)	41.7%	23.8%

Entity B's upwards revaluation has increased equity in the statement of financial position. This reduces its ROCE, making entity B appear less efficient than entity A. However it also means that entity B's gearing is lower than entity A's, making it seem like a less risky investment.

Disclosure requirements

Disclosures required by IAS 16 include:

- the measurement bases used
- depreciation methods, useful lives and depreciation rates
- a reconciliation of the carrying amount at the beginning and end of the period

If items of property, plant and equipment are stated at revalued amounts, information about the revaluation should also be disclosed.

2 Government grants

IAS 20 Government grants: Definitions

IAS 20 Accounting for Government Grants and Disclosure of Government Assistance defines the following terms:

Government grants are transfers of resources to an entity in return for past or future compliance with certain conditions. They exclude assistance that cannot be valued and normal trade with governments.

Government assistance is government action designed to provide an economic benefit to a specific entity. It does not include indirect help such as infrastructure development.

General principles

Recognition

IAS 20 says that government grants should not be recognised until the conditions for receipt have been complied with and there is reasonable assurance that the grant will be received.

Grants should be matched with the expenditure towards which they are intended to contribute in the statement of profit or loss:

- Income grants given to subsidise expenditure should be matched to the related costs.
- Income grants given to help achieve a non-financial goal (such as job creation) should be matched to the costs incurred to meet that goal.

Grants related to assets

Grants for purchases of non-current assets should be recognised over the expected useful lives of the related assets. IAS 20 provides two acceptable accounting policies for this:

- deduct the grant from the cost of the asset and depreciate the net cost
- treat the grant as deferred income and release to profit or loss over the life of the asset.

Repayments and other issues

Repayments

A government grant that becomes repayable is accounted for as a revision of an accounting estimate.

(a) Income-based grants

Firstly, debit the repayment to any liability for deferred income. Any excess repayment must be charged to profits immediately.

(b) Capital-based grants deducted from cost

Increase the cost of the asset with the repayment. This will also increase the amount of depreciation that should have been charged in the past. This should be recognised and charged immediately.

(c) Capital-based grants treated as deferred income

Firstly, debit the repayment to any liability for deferred income. Any excess repayment must be charged against profits immediately.

Government assistance

As implied in the definition set out above, government assistance helps businesses through loan guarantees, loans at a low rate of interest, advice, procurement policies and similar methods. It is not possible to place reliable values on these forms of assistance, so they are not recognised.

Illustration – Government grants

On 1 June 20X1, Clock received written confirmation from a local government agency that it would receive a $1m grant towards the purchase price of a new office building. The grant becomes receivable on the date that Clock transfers the $10m purchase price to the vendor.

On 1 October 20X1 Clock paid $10m in cash for its new office building, which is estimated to have a useful life of 50 years. By 1 December 20X1, the building was ready for use. Clock received the government grant on 1 January 20X2.

Required:

Discuss the possible accounting treatments of the above in the financial statements of Clock for the year ended 31 December 20X1.

Solution

Government grants should be recognised when there is reasonable assurance that:

- The entity will comply with any conditions attached, and
- It is reasonably certain that the grant will be received.

The only condition attached to the grant is the purchase of the new building. Therefore, the grant should be accounted for on 1 October 20X1.

A receivable will be recognised for the $1m due from the local government. Clock could then choose to either:

(a) Reduce the cost of the building by $1m

In this case, the building will have a cost of $9m ($10m – $1m). This will be depreciated over its useful life of 50 years. The depreciation charge in profit or loss for the year ended 31 December 20X1 will be $15,000 (($9m/50 years) × 1/12) and the building will have a carrying value of $8,985,000 ($9m – $15,000) as at 31 December 20X1.

(b) Recognise deferred income of $1m.

In this case, the building is recognised at its cost of $10m. This will be depreciated over its useful life of 50 years. The depreciation charge in profit or loss for the year ended 31 December 20X1 will be $16,667 (($10m/50 years) × 1/12) and the building will have a carrying value of $9,983,333 ($10m – $16,667) as at 31 December 20X1.

The deferred income will be amortised to profit or loss over the building's useful economic life. Therefore, income of $1,667 (($1m/50) × 1/12) will be recorded in profit or loss for the year ended 31 December 20X1. The carrying value of the deferred income balance within liabilities on the statement of financial position will be $998,333 ($1m – $1,667) as at 31 December 20X1.

Disclosure requirements

IAS 20 requires the following disclosures:

- the accounting policy and presentation methods adopted
- the nature of government grants recognised in the financial statements
- unfulfilled conditions relating to government grants that have been recognised.

3 Borrowing costs

IAS 23 Borrowing costs

Borrowing costs are defined as **'interest and other costs that an entity incurs in connection with the borrowing of funds'** (IAS 23, para 5).

Borrowing costs should be capitalised if they relate to the acquisition, construction or production of a **qualifying asset**. IAS 23 defines a qualifying asset as one that takes a substantial period of time to get ready for its intended use or sale.

Capitalisation period

Borrowing costs should only be capitalised while construction is in progress.

IAS 23 stipulates that:

- Capitalisation of borrowing costs should commence when all of the following apply:
  - expenditure for the asset is being incurred
  - borrowing costs are being incurred
  - activities that are necessary to get the asset ready for use are in progress.
- Capitalisation of borrowing costs should cease when substantially all the activities that are necessary to get the asset ready for use are complete.
- Capitalisation of borrowing costs should be suspended during extended periods in which active development is interrupted.

Borrowing costs eligible for capitalisation

Where a loan is taken out specifically to finance the construction of an asset, IAS 23 says that the amount to be capitalised is the interest payable on that loan less income earned on the temporary investment of the borrowings.

If construction of a qualifying asset is financed from an entity's general borrowings, the borrowing costs eligible to be capitalised are determined by applying the weighted average general borrowings rate to the expenditure incurred on the asset.

IAS 23 is silent on how to arrive at the expenditure on the asset, but it would be reasonable to calculate it as the weighted average carrying amount of the asset during the period, including finance costs previously capitalised.

Illustration – Borrowing costs

On 1 January 20X1, Hi-Rise obtained planning permission to build a new office building. Construction commenced on 1 March 20X1. To help fund the cost of this building, a loan for $5m was taken out from the bank on 1 April 20X1. The interest rate on the loan was 10% per annum.

Construction of the building ceased during the month of July due to an unexpected shortage of labour and materials.

By 31 December 20X1, the building was not complete. Costs incurred to date were $12m (excluding interest on the loan).

Required:

Discuss the accounting treatment of the above in the financial statements of Hi-Rise for the year ended 31 December 20X1.

Solution

An entity must capitalise borrowing costs that are directly attributable to the production of a qualifying asset. The new office building is a qualifying asset because it takes a substantial period of time to get ready for its intended use.

Hi-Rise should start capitalising borrowing costs when all of the following conditions have been met:

- It incurs expenditure on the asset – 1 March 20X1.

- It incurs borrowing costs – 1 April 20X1.
- It undertakes activities necessary to prepare the asset for intended use – 1 January 20X1.

Capitalisation of borrowing costs should therefore commence on 1 April 20X1. Capitalisation of borrowing costs ceases for the month of July because active development was suspended. In total, 8 months' worth of borrowing costs should be capitalised in the year ended 31 December 20X1.

The total borrowing costs to be capitalised are $333,333 ($5m × 10% × 8/12). These will be added to the cost of the building, giving a carrying amount of $12,333,333 as at 31 December 20X1. The building is not ready for use, so no depreciation is charged.

Disclosure requirements

IAS 23 requires the following disclosures:

- the value of borrowing costs capitalised during the period
- the capitalisation rate.

4 Investment property

IAS 40 Investment property: Definitions

IAS 40 Investment Property relates to **'property (land or buildings) held (by the owner or by the lessee as a right-of-use asset) to earn rentals or for capital appreciation or both'** (IAS 40, para 5).

Examples of investment property are:

- land held for capital appreciation
- land held for undecided future use
- buildings leased out under an operating lease
- vacant buildings held to be leased out under an operating lease.

The following are **not** investment property:

- property held for use in the production or supply of goods or services or for administrative purposes (IAS 16 Property, Plant and Equipment applies)
- property held for sale in the ordinary course of business or in the process of construction of development for such sale (IAS 2 Inventories applies)
- property being constructed or developed on behalf of third parties (IFRS 15 Revenue from Contracts with Customers applies)
- owner-occupied property (IAS 16 applies)
- property that is being constructed or developed for use as an investment property (IAS 16 currently applies until the property is ready for use, at which time IAS 40 starts to apply)
- property leased to another entity under a finance lease (IFRS 16 Leases applies).

Measurement

On recognition, investment property shall be recognised at cost.

After recognition an entity may choose either:

- the cost model
- the fair value model.

The policy chosen must be applied to all investment properties.

If the cost model is chosen, investment properties are held at cost less accumulated depreciation. No revaluations are permitted.

Change from one model to the other is permitted only if this results in a more appropriate presentation. IAS 40 notes that this is highly unlikely for a change from the fair value model to the cost model.

The fair value model

Under the fair value model, the entity remeasures its investment properties to fair value each year. No depreciation is charged.

All gains and losses on revaluation are reported in the statement of profit or loss.

If, in exceptional circumstances, it is impossible to measure the fair value of an individual investment property reliably then the cost model should be adopted.

Transfers

Transfers to or from investment property can only be made if there is a change of use. There are several possible situations in which this might occur and the accounting treatment for each is set out below:

Transfer from investment property to owner-occupied property

Use the fair value at the date of the change for subsequent accounting under IAS 16.

Transfer from investment property to inventory

Use the fair value at the date of the change for subsequent accounting under IAS 2 Inventories.

Transfer from owner-occupied property to investment property to be carried at fair value

Normal accounting under IAS 16 (cost less depreciation) will have been applied up to the date of the change. On adopting fair value, there is normally an increase in value. This is recognised as other comprehensive income and credited to the revaluation surplus in equity in accordance with IAS 16. If the fair valuation causes a decrease in value, then it should be charged to profits.

Transfer from inventories to investment property to be carried at fair value

Any change in the carrying amount caused by the transfer should be recognised in profit or loss.

Illustration: Investment property

Lavender owns a property, which it rents out to some of its employees. The property was purchased for $30 million on 1 January 20X2 and had a useful life of 30 years at that date. On 1 January 20X7 it had a market value of $50 million and its remaining useful life remained unchanged. Management wish to measure properties at fair value where this is allowed by accounting standards.

Required:

How should the property be treated in the financial statements of Lavender for the year ended 31 December 20X7.

Solution

Property that is rented out to employees is deemed to be owner-occupied and therefore cannot be classified as investment property.

Management wish to measure the property at fair value, so Lavender adopts the fair value model in IAS 16 Property, Plant and Equipment, depreciating the asset over its useful life and recognising the revaluation gain in other comprehensive income.

Before the revaluation, the building had a carrying amount of $25m ($30m × 25/30). The building would have been revalued to $50m on 1 January 20X7, with a gain of $25m ($50m – $25m) recognised in other comprehensive income.

The building would then be depreciated over its remaining useful life of 25 years (30 – 5), giving a depreciation charge of $2m ($50m/25) in the year ended 31 December 20X7. The carrying amount of the asset as at 31 December 20X7 is $48m ($50m – $2m).

Illustration – ABC

ABC owns a building that it used as its head office. On 1 January 20X1, the building, which was measured under the cost model, had a carrying amount of $500,000. On this date, when the fair value of the building was $600,000, ABC vacated the premises. However, the directors decided to keep the building in order to rent it out to tenants and to potentially benefit from increases in property prices. ABC measures investment properties at fair value. On 31 December 20X1, the property has a fair value of $625,000.

Required:

Discuss the accounting treatment of the building in the financial statements of ABC for the year ended 31 December 20X1.

Solution

When the building was owner-occupied, it was an item of property plant and equipment. From 1 January 20X1, the property was held to earn rental income and for capital appreciation so it should be reclassified as investment property.

Per IAS 40, if owner occupied property becomes investment property that will be carried at fair value, then a revaluation needs to occur under IAS 16 at the date of the change in use.

The building must be revalued from $500,000 to $600,000 under IAS 16. This means that the gain of $100,000 ($600,000 – $500,000) will be recorded in other comprehensive income and held in a revaluation reserve within equity.

Investment properties measured at fair value must be revalued each year end, with the gain or loss recorded in profit or loss. At year end, the building will therefore be revalued to $625,000 with a gain of $25,000 ($625,000 – $600,000) recorded in profit or loss.

Investment properties held at fair value are not depreciated.

Impact on financial statements

Assume that two separate entities, A and B, both buy an identical building for $10m on 1 January 20X1 and classify them as investment properties. Each building is expected to have a useful life of 50 years. By 31 December 20X1, the fair value of each building is $11m.

Entity A measures investment properties using the cost model. Entity B measures investment properties at fair value.

Extracts from the financial statements of the two entities are provided below:

Statement of financial position

	Entity A	Entity B
	$m	$m
Investment properties	9.8	11.0

Statement of profit or loss

	Entity A	Entity B
	$m	$m
Depreciation	(0.2)	–
Gain on investment properties	–	1.0

Assuming no other differences between the two entities, entity B will report higher profits and therefore higher earnings per share than entity A. Entity B will also show higher equity in its statement of financial position, so its gearing will reduce.

As this example shows, the fact that IAS 40 permits a choice in accounting policy could be argued to reduce the comparability of financial information.

Disclosure requirements

In respect of investment properties, IAS 40 says that an entity must disclose:

- whether the cost or fair value model is used
- amounts recognised in profit or loss for the period
- a reconciliation between the carrying amounts of investment property at the beginning and end of the period.

5 Intangible assets

Definition and recognition criteria

An **intangible asset** is defined as **'an identifiable non-monetary asset without physical substance'** (IAS 38, para 8).

An entity should recognise an intangible asset should be recognised if all the following criteria are met.

- The asset is identifiable
- The asset is controlled by the entity
- The asset will generate future economic benefits for the entity
- The cost of the asset can be measured reliably.

An intangible asset is identifiable if it:

- **'is separable (capable of being separated and sold, transferred, licensed, rented, or exchanged, either individually or as part of a package), or**
- **it arises from contractual or other legal rights, regardless of whether those rights are transferable or separable from the entity or from other rights and obligations'** (IAS 38, para 12).

If an intangible asset does not meet the recognition criteria, expenditure should be charged to the statement of profit or loss as it is incurred. Once the expenditure has been so charged, it cannot be capitalised at a later date.

Examples of intangible assets

Examples of intangible assets include:

- goodwill acquired in a business combination
- computer software
- patents
- copyrights
- motion picture films
- customer list
- mortgage servicing rights
- licences
- import quotas
- franchises
- customer and supplier relationships
- marketing rights.

Please note that the accounting treatment of goodwill arising on a business combination is dealt with in IFRS 3 Business Combinations rather than IAS 38 Intangible Assets.

Meeting the recognition criteria

(a) **Identifiability**

Intangible assets such as customer relationships cannot be separated from goodwill unless they:

- arise as a result of a legal right, if there are ongoing supply contracts, for example
- are separable, i.e. can be sold separately. This is unlikely unless there are legal contracts in existence, in which case they fall under the previous bullet point.

(b) **Control**

The knowledge that the staff have is an asset. It can be possible for the entity to control this knowledge. Patents, copyrights and restraint-of-trade agreements will give the entity legal rights to the future economic benefits and prevent other people from obtaining them. Therefore copyrights and patents can be capitalised.

(c) **Probable future economic benefits**

An intangible asset can generate future economic benefits in two ways. Owning a brand name can boost revenues, while owning the patent for a production process may help to reduce production costs. Either way, the entity's profits will be increased.

When an entity assesses the probability of future economic benefits, the assessment must be based on reasonable and supportable assumptions about conditions that will exist over the life of the asset.

(d) **Reliable measurement**

If the asset is acquired separately then this is straightforward. For example, the purchase price of a franchise should be capitalised, along with all the related legal and professional costs.

However, the cost of **internally generated intangible assets** cannot be distinguished from the cost of the entity's day-to-day operations. Therefore, internally generated intangible assets are not recognised on the statement of financial position unless they relate to research and development activity (see later in this chapter).

Measurement

Initial recognition

When an intangible asset is initially recognised, it is measured at cost.

Subsequent recognition

After recognition, an entity must choose either the cost model or the revaluation model for each class of intangible asset.

- The cost model measures the asset at cost less accumulated amortisation and impairment.
- The revaluation model measures the asset at fair value less accumulated amortisation and impairment.

The revaluation model

The revaluation model can only be adopted if fair value can be determined by reference to an **active market**. An active market is one where the products are homogenous, there are willing buyers and sellers to be found at all times, and prices are available to the public.

Active markets for intangible assets are rare. They may exist for assets such as:

- milk quotas
- European Union fishing quotas
- stock exchange seats.

Active markets are unlikely to exist for brands, newspaper mastheads, music and film publishing rights, patents or trademarks.

Revaluations should be made with sufficient regularity such that the carrying amount does not differ materially from actual fair value at the reporting date.

Revaluation gains and losses are accounted for in the same way as revaluation gains and losses of tangible assets held in accordance with IAS 16 Property, Plant and Equipment.

Amortisation

An entity must assess whether the useful life of an intangible asset is finite or indefinite.

- An asset with a finite useful life must be amortised on a systematic basis over that life. Normally the straight-line method with a zero residual value should be used. Amortisation starts when the asset is available for use.
- An asset has an indefinite useful life when there is no foreseeable limit to the period over which the asset is expected to generate net cash inflows. It should not be amortised, but be subject to an annual impairment review.

Test your understanding 2 – Innovate

Ten years ago, Innovate developed a new game called 'Our Sports'. This game sold over 10 million copies around the world and was extremely profitable. Due to its popularity, Innovate release a new game in the Our Sports series every year. The games continue to be best-sellers.

The directors have produced cash flow projections for the Our Sports series over the next five years. Based on these projections, they have prudently valued the Our Sports brand at $20 million and wish to recognise this in the statement of financial position as at 30 September 20X3.

On 30 September 20X3, Innovate also paid $1 million for the rights to the 'Pets & Me' videogame series after the original developer went into administration.

Required:

Discuss the accounting treatment of the above in the financial statements of Innovate for the year ended 30 September 20X3.

Research and development expenditure

Research is defined as **'original and planned investigation undertaken with the prospect of gaining new scientific or technical knowledge and understanding'** (IAS 38, para 8).

Research expenditure cannot be recognised as an intangible asset. (although tangible assets used in research should be recognised as plant and equipment).

Development is defined as **'the application of research findings or other knowledge to a plan or design for the production of new or substantially improved materials, devices, products, processes, systems or services before the start of commercial production or use'** (IAS 38, para 8).

IAS 38 says that development expenditure should only be recognised as an intangible asset if the entity can demonstrate that:

- the project is technically feasible
- the entity intends to complete the intangible asset, and then use it or sell it
- the intangible asset will generate future economic benefits
- it has adequate resources to complete the project
- it can reliably measure the expenditure on the project.

Test your understanding 3 – Scone

During the year ended 31 December 20X1, Scone spent $2 million on researching and developing a new product. The entity has recognised all $2 million as an intangible asset. A breakdown of the expenditure is provided below:

	$m
Research into materials	0.5
Market research	0.4
Employee training	0.2
Development activities	0.9

The expenditure on development activities was incurred evenly over the year. It was not until 1 May 20X1 that market research indicated that the product was likely to be profitable. At the reporting date, the product development was not yet complete.

Required:

Discuss the correct accounting treatment of the research and development expenditure in the year ended 31 December 20X1.

Disclosure requirements

IAS 38 states that an entity must disclose:

- The amount of research and development expenditure expensed in the period
- The amortisation methods used
- For intangible assets assessed as having an indefinite useful life, the reasons supporting that assessment
- The date of any revaluations, if applicable, as well as the methods and assumptions used
- A reconciliation of the carrying amount of intangibles at the beginning and end of the reporting period.

6 Impairment of assets (IAS 36)

Definition

Impairment is a reduction in the recoverable amount of an asset or cash-generating unit below its carrying amount.

IAS 36 Impairment of Assets says that an entity should carry out an impairment review at least annually if:

- an intangible asset is not being amortised because it has an indefinite useful life
- goodwill has arisen on a business combination.

Otherwise, an impairment review is required only where there is an indication that impairment may have occurred.

Indications of impairment

IAS 36 lists the following indications that an asset is impaired:

- **External sources of information:**
  - unexpected decreases in an asset's market value
  - significant adverse changes have taken place, or are about to take place, in the technological, market, economic or legal environment
  - increased interest rates have decreased an asset's recoverable amount
  - the entity's net assets are measured at more than its market capitalisation.
- **Internal sources of information:**
  - evidence of obsolescence or damage
  - there is, or is about to be, a material reduction in usage of an asset
  - evidence that the economic performance of an asset has been, or will be, worse than expected.

Calculating an impairment loss

An impairment occurs if the carrying amount of an asset is greater than its recoverable amount.

The **recoverable amount** is the higher of fair value less costs to sell and value in use.

Fair value is defined in IFRS 13 as the price received when selling an asset in an orderly transaction between market participants at the measurement date.

Costs to sell are incremental costs directly attributable to the disposal of an asset.

Value in use is the present value of future cash flows from using an asset, including its eventual disposal.

Carrying out an impairment test

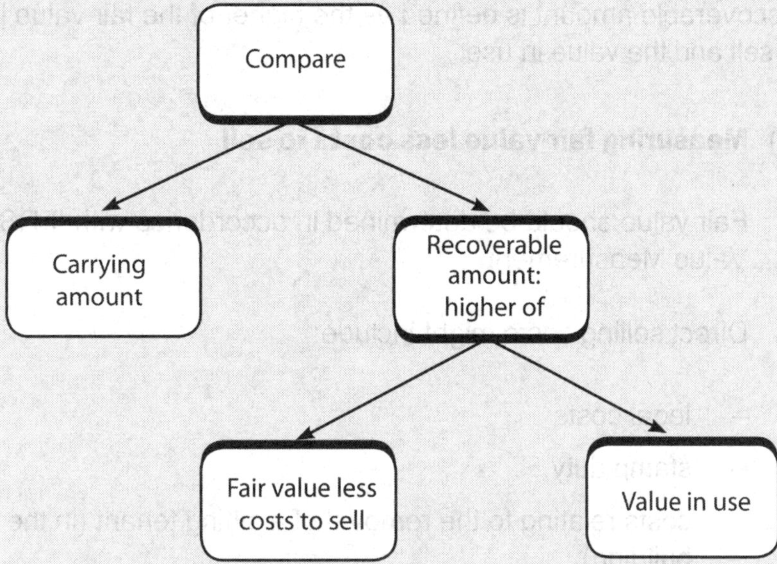

If fair value less costs to sell is higher than the carrying amount, there is no impairment and no need to calculate value in use.

Illustration: Impairment of item of plant

An item of plant is included in the financial statements at a carrying amount of $350,000. The present value of the future cash flows from continuing to operate the plant is $320,000. The plant could be sold for net proceeds of $275,000.

Required:

Is the item of plant impaired and, if so, by how much?

Solution

The recoverable amount is the greater of the fair value less costs to sell and the value in use. The fair value less costs to sell (net selling price) is $275,000 and the value in use is $320,000. The recoverable amount is therefore $320,000.

To determine whether the plant is impaired, the carrying amount is compared to the recoverable amount. The carrying amount of $350,000 is greater than the recoverable amount, so the asset must be written down to its recoverable amount. The impairment loss is $30,000 ($350,000 – $320,000).

Measurement of recoverable amount

Recoverable amount is defined as the higher of the fair value less costs to sell and the value in use.

(a) **Measuring fair value less costs to sell**

Fair value should be determined in accordance with IFRS 13 Fair Value Measurement.

Direct selling costs might include:

- legal costs
- stamp duty
- costs relating to the removal of a sitting tenant (in the case of a building).

Redundancy and reorganisation costs (e.g. following the sale of a business) are not direct selling costs.

(b) **Measuring value in use**

Value in use is calculated by estimating future cash inflows and outflows from the use of the asset and its ultimate disposal, and applying a suitable discount rate to these cash flows.

With regards to estimates of cash flows, IAS 36 stipulates that:

- The cash flow projections should be based on reasonable assumptions and the most recent budgets and forecasts
- The cash flow projections should relate to the asset's current condition and should exclude expenditure to improve or enhance it
- For periods in excess of five years, management should extrapolate from earlier budgets using a steady, declining or zero growth rate
- Management should assess the accuracy of their budgets by investigating the reasons for any differences between forecast and actual cash flows.

The discount rate should reflect:

– **'the time value of money, and**
– **the risks specific to the asset for which the future cash flow estimates have not been adjusted'** (IAS 36, para 55).

Recognising impairment losses in the financial statements

An impairment loss is normally charged immediately in the statement of profit or loss and other comprehensive income.

- If the asset has previously been revalued upwards, the impairment is recognised as a component of other comprehensive income and is debited to the revaluation reserve until the surplus relating to that asset has been reduced to nil. The remainder of the impairment loss is recognised in profit or loss.
- The recoverable (impaired) amount of the asset is then depreciated/amortised over its remaining useful life.

Test your understanding 4 – Impaired asset

On 31 December 20X1, an entity noticed that one of its items of plant and machinery is often left idle. On this date, the asset had a carrying amount of $500,000 and a fair value of $325,000. The estimated costs required to dispose of the asset are $25,000.

If the asset is not sold, the entity estimates that it would generate cash inflows of $200,000 in each of the next two years. The discount rate that reflects the risks specific to this asset is 10%.

Required:

(a) **Discuss the accounting treatment of the above in the financial statements for the year ended 31 December 20X1.**

(b) **How would the answer to part (a) be different if there was a balance of $10,000 in other components of equity relating to the prior revaluation of this specific asset?**

Cash-generating units

It is not usually possible to identify cash flows relating to particular assets. For example, a factory production line is made up of many individual machines, but the revenues are earned by the production line as a whole. This means that value in use must be calculated (and the impairment review performed) for groups of assets, rather than individual assets.

These groups of assets are called cash-generating units (CGUs).

Cash-generating units are segments of the business whose income streams are largely independent of each other.

- In practice they are likely to mirror the strategic business units used for monitoring the performance of the business.
- It could also include a subsidiary or associate within a corporate group structure.

Test your understanding 5 – Cash generating units

An entity has three stages of production:

- A – growing and felling trees
- B – creating parts of wooden furniture
- C – assembling the parts from B into finished goods.

The output of A is timber that is partly transferred to B and partly sold in an external market. If A did not exist, B could buy its timber from the market. The output of B has no external market and is transferred to C at an internal transfer price. C sells the finished product in an external market and the sales revenue achieved by C is not affected by the fact that the three stages of production are all performed by the entity.

Required:

Identify the cash-generating unit(s).

Allocating assets to cash-generating units

The carrying amount of a cash-generating unit includes the carrying amount of assets that can be attributed to the cash-generating unit and will generate the future cash inflows used in determining the cash-generating unit's value in use.

There are two problem areas:

- Corporate assets: assets that are used by several cash-generating units (e.g. a head office building or a research centre). They do not generate their own cash inflows, so do not themselves qualify as cash-generating units.
- Goodwill, which does not generate cash flows independently of other assets and often relates to a whole business.

Corporate assets and goodwill should be allocated to cash-generating units on a reasonable and consistent basis. A cash-generating unit to which goodwill has been allocated must be tested for impairment annually.

Allocation of an impairment to the unit's assets

If an impairment loss arises in respect of a cash-generating unit, IAS 36 requires that it is allocated among the assets in the following order:

- goodwill
- other assets in proportion to their carrying amount.

However, the carrying amount of an asset cannot be reduced below the highest of:

- fair value less costs to sell
- value in use
- nil.

Illustration 1 – Impairment allocation within CGU

Tinud has identified an impairment loss of $41m for one of its cash-generating units. The carrying amount of the unit's net assets was $150m, whereas the unit's recoverable amount was only $109m. The draft values of the net assets of the unit are as follows:

	$m
Goodwill	13
Property	20
Machinery	49
Vehicles	35
Patents	14
Net monetary assets	19
	150

The net selling price of the unit's assets were insignificant except for the property, which had a market value of $35m. The net monetary assets will be realised in full.

Required:

How is the impairment loss allocated to the assets within the cash-generating unit?

Solution

Firstly, the impairment loss is allocated to the goodwill, reducing its carrying amount to nil.

The impairment loss cannot be set against the property because its net selling price is greater than its carrying amount.

Likewise, the impairment loss cannot be set against the net monetary assets (receivables, cash, etc.) because they will be realised in full.

The balance of the impairment loss of $28 million ($41m – $13m) is apportioned between the remaining assets in proportion to their carrying amounts. So, for example, the impairment allocated to the machinery is $14 million ((49/(49 + 35 + 14)) × 28m)

The table below shows how the impairment will be allocated.

	Draft values	Impairment loss	Revised value
	$m	$m	$m
Goodwill	13	(13)	–
Property	20	–	20
Machinery	49	(14)	35
Vehicles	35	(10)	25
Patents	14	(4)	10
Net monetary assets	19	–	19
	150	(41)	109

Test your understanding 6 – Factory explosion

There was an explosion in a factory. The carrying amounts of its assets were as follows:

	$000
Goodwill	100
Patents	200
Machines	300
Computers	500
Buildings	1,500
	2,600

The factory operates as a cash-generating unit. An impairment review reveals a net selling price of $1.2 million for the factory and value in use of $1.95 million. Half of the machines have been blown to pieces but the other half can be sold for at least their carrying amount. The patents have been superseded and are now considered worthless.

Required:

Discuss, with calculations, how any impairment loss will be accounted for.

Impairment if reasonable allocation is not possible

If no reasonable allocation of corporate assets or goodwill is possible, then a group of cash-generating units must be tested for impairment together in a two-stage process.

Example

An entity acquires a business comprising three cash-generating units, D, E and F, but there is no reasonable way of allocating goodwill to them. After three years, the carrying amount and the recoverable amount of the net assets in the cash-generating units and the purchased goodwill are as follows:

	D	E	F	Goodwill	Total
	$000	$000	$000	$000	$000
Carrying amount	240	360	420	150	1,170
Recoverable amount	300	420	360		1,080

Step 1: Review the individual units for impairment.

F is impaired. A loss of $60,000 is recognised and its carrying amount is reduced to $360,000.

Step 2: Compare the carrying amount of the business as a whole, including the goodwill, with its recoverable amount.

The total carrying amount of the business is now $1,110,000 ($1,170,000 – $60,000). A further impairment loss of $30,000 must then be recognised in respect of the goodwill ($1,110,000 – $1,080,000).

Reversal of an impairment loss

The calculation of impairment losses is based on predictions of what may happen in the future. Sometimes, actual events turn out to be better than predicted. If this happens, the recoverable amount is re-calculated and the previous write-down is reversed.

- Impaired assets should be reviewed at each reporting date to see whether there are indications that the impairment has reversed.
- A reversal of an impairment loss is recognised immediately as income in profit or loss. If the original impairment was charged against the revaluation surplus, it is recognised as other comprehensive income and credited to the revaluation reserve.
- The reversal must not take the value of the asset above the amount it would have been if the original impairment had never been recorded. The depreciation that would have been charged in the meantime must be taken into account.
- The depreciation charge for future periods should be revised to reflect the changed carrying amount.

An impairment loss recognised for goodwill cannot be reversed in a subsequent period.

Impairment reversals

Indicators of an impairment reversal

External indicators of an impairment reversal are:

- Increases in the asset's market value
- Favourable changes in the technological, market, economic or legal environment
- Decreases in interest rates.

Internal indicators of an impairment reversal are:

- Favourable changes in the use of the asset
- Improvements in the asset's economic performance.

Impairment reversals and cash-generating unit

If the reversal relates to a cash-generating unit, the reversal is allocated to assets other than goodwill on a pro rata basis. The carrying amount of an asset must not be increased above the lower of:

- its recoverable amount (if determinable)
- the carrying amount that would have been determined (net of amortisation or depreciation) had no impairment loss been recognised for the asset in prior periods.

The amount that would otherwise have been allocated to the asset is allocated pro rata to the other assets of the unit, except for goodwill.

Impairment reversals and goodwill

Impairment losses relating to goodwill can never be reversed. The reason for this is that once purchased goodwill has become impaired, any subsequent increase in its recoverable amount is likely to be an increase in internally generated goodwill, rather than a reversal of the impairment loss recognised for the original purchased goodwill. Internally generated goodwill cannot be recognised.

Test your understanding 7 – Boxer

Boxer purchased a non-current asset on 1 January 20X1 at a cost of $30,000. At that date, the asset had an estimated useful life of ten years. Boxer does not revalue this type of asset, but accounts for it on the basis of depreciated historical cost. At 31 December 20X2, the asset was subject to an impairment review and had a recoverable amount of $16,000.

At 31 December 20X5, the circumstances which caused the original impairment to be recognised have reversed and are no longer applicable, with the result that recoverable amount is now $40,000.

Required:

Explain, with supporting computations, the impact on the financial statements of the two impairment reviews.

Test your understanding 8 – CGUs and impairment reversals

On 31 December 20X2, an impairment review was conducted on a cash generating unit and the results were as follows:

Asset	Carrying amount pre-impairment	Impairment	Carrying amount post-impairment
	$000	$000	$000
Goodwill	100	(100)	Nil
Property, plant and equipment	300	(120)	180
	400	(220)	180

The property, plant and equipment was originally purchased for $400,000 on 1 January 20X1 and was attributed a useful economic life of 8 years.

At 31 December 20X3, the circumstances which caused the original impairment have reversed and are no longer applicable. The recoverable amount of the cash generating unit is now $420,000.

Required:

Explain, with supporting computations, the impact of the impairment reversal on the financial statements for the year ended 31 December 20X3.

Disclosure requirements

IAS 36 requires disclosure of the following:

- losses recognised during the period
- reversals recognised during the period

For each material loss or reversal:

- the amount of loss or reversal and the events causing it
- the recoverable amount of the asset (or cash generating unit)
- whether the recoverable amount is the fair value less costs to sell or value in use
- the level of fair value hierarchy (per IFRS 13) used in determining fair value less costs to sell

- the discount rate(s) used.

7 Non-current assets held for sale (IFRS 5)

IFRS 5 Non-current Assets Held for Sale and Discontinued Operations says that a non-current asset or disposal group should be classified as 'held for sale' if its carrying amount will be recovered primarily through a sale transaction rather than through continuing use.

A **disposal group** is a group of assets (and possibly liabilities) that the entity intends to dispose of in a single transaction.

Classification as 'held for sale'

IFRS 5 requires the following conditions to be met before an asset or disposal group can be classified as 'held for sale':

- The item is available for immediate sale in its present condition.
- The sale is highly probable.
- Management is committed to a plan to sell the item.
- An active programme to locate a buyer has been initiated.
- The item is being actively marketed at a reasonable price in relation to its current fair value.
- The sale is expected to be completed within one year from the date of classification.
- It is unlikely that the plan will change significantly or be withdrawn.

Assets that are to be abandoned or wound down gradually cannot be classified as held for sale because their carrying amounts will not be recovered principally through a sale transaction.

Test your understanding 9 – Hyssop

Hyssop is preparing its financial statements for the year ended 31 December 20X7.

(a) On 1 December 20X7, the entity became committed to a plan to sell a surplus office property and has already found a potential buyer. On 15 December 20X7 a survey was carried out and it was discovered that the building had dry rot and substantial remedial work would be necessary. The buyer is prepared to wait for the work to be carried out, but the property will not be sold until the problem has been rectified. This is not expected to occur until summer 20X8.

Required:

Can the property be classified as 'held for sale'?

(b) A subsidiary entity, B, is for sale at a price of $3 million. There has been some interest from prospective buyers but no sale as of yet. One buyer has made an offer of $2 million but the Directors of Hyssop rejected the offer. The Directors have just received advice from their accountants that the fair value of the business is $2.5 million. They have decided not to reduce the sale price of B at the moment.

Required:

Can the subsidiary be classified as 'held for sale'?

Measurement of assets and disposal groups held for sale

Items classified as held for sale should, according to IFRS 5, be measured at the lower of their carrying amount and fair value less costs to sell.

- Where fair value less costs to sell is lower than carrying amount, the item is written down and the write down is treated as an impairment loss.
- If a non-current asset is measured using a revaluation model and it meets the criteria to be classified as being held for sale, it should be revalued to fair value immediately before it is classified as held for sale. It is then revalued again at the lower of the carrying amount and the fair value less costs to sell. The difference is the selling costs and these should be charged against profits in the period.
- When a disposal group is being written down to fair value less costs to sell, the impairment loss reduces the carrying amount of assets in the order prescribed by IAS 36
  - Impairments are firstly allocated to goodwill and then to other assets on a pro-rata basis.
- A gain can be recognised for any subsequent increase in fair value less costs to sell, but not in excess of the cumulative impairment loss that has already been recognised, either when the assets were written down to fair value less costs to sell or previously under IAS 36.

An asset held for sale is not depreciated, even if it is still being used by the entity.

Test your understanding 10 – AB

On 1 January 20X1, AB acquires a building for $200,000 with an expected life of 50 years. On 31 December 20X4 AB puts the building up for immediate sale. Costs to sell the building are estimated at $10,000.

Required

Outline the accounting treatment of the above if the building had a fair value at 31 December 20X4 of:

(a) **$220,000**

(b) **$110,000.**

Test your understanding 11 – Nash

Nash purchased a building for its own use on 1 January 20X1 for $1m and attributed it a 50 year useful economic life. Nash uses the revaluation model to account for buildings.

On 31 December 20X2, this building was revalued to $1.2m.

On 31 December 20X3, the building met the criteria to be classified as held for sale. Its fair value was deemed to be $1.1m and the costs necessary to sell the building were estimated to be $50,000.

Nash does not make a reserves transfer in respect of excess depreciation.

Required:

Discuss the accounting treatment of the above.

Presentation in the statement of financial position

IFRS 5 states that assets classified as held for sale should be presented separately from other assets in the statement of financial position.

The liabilities of a disposal group classified as held for sale should be presented separately from other liabilities in the statement of financial position.

The major classes of assets and liabilities classified as held for sale must be separately disclosed either on the face of the statement of financial position or in the notes.

Where an asset or disposal group is classified as held for sale after the reporting date, but before the issue of the financial statements, details should be disclosed in the notes (this is a non-adjusting event after the reporting period).

Illustration – Presentation

Statement of financial position (showing non-current assets held for sale)

	20X2	**20X1**
	$m	$m
ASSETS		
Non-current assets		
Property, plant and equipment	X	X
Goodwill	X	X
Financial assets	X	X
	X	X
Current assets		
Inventories	X	X
Trade receivables	X	X
Cash and cash equivalents	X	
Non-current assets classified as held for sale	X	X
	X	X
Total assets	X	X

Changes to a plan of sale

If a sale does not take place within one year, IFRS 5 says that an asset (or disposal group) can still be classified as held for sale if:

- the delay has been caused by events or circumstances beyond the entity's control
- there is sufficient evidence that the entity is still committed to the sale.

If the criteria for 'held for sale' are no longer met, then the entity must cease to classify the assets or disposal group as held for sale. The assets or disposal group must be measured at the lower of:

- **'its carrying amount before it was classified as held for sale adjusted for any depreciation, amortisation or revaluations that would have been recognised had it not been classified as held for sale**
- **its recoverable amount at the date of the subsequent decision not to sell'** (IFRS 5, para 27).

Any adjustment required is recognised in profit or loss as a gain or loss from continuing operations.

Disclosure requirements

In the period in which a non-current asset or disposal group has been classified as held for sale, or sold, IFRS 5 says that the entity must disclose:

- a description of the non-current asset (or disposal group)
- a description of the facts and circumstances of the sale or expected sale
- any impairment losses or reversals recognised.

8 Agriculture (IAS 41)

Definitions

IAS 41 Agriculture applies to biological assets and to agricultural produce at the point of harvest.

Definitions

A biological asset is **'a living plant or animal'** (IAS 41, para 5).

Agricultural produce is **'the harvested product of the entity's biological assets'** (IAS 41, para 5).

Harvest is **'the detachment of produce from a biological asset or the cessation of a biological asset's life processes'** (IAS 41, para 5).

Application of IAS 41 definitions

A farmer buys a dairy calf.	The calf is a biological asset.
The calf grows into a mature cow.	Growth is a type of biological transformation.
The farmer milks the cow.	The milk has been harvested. Milk is agricultural produce.

Biological assets

Recognition criteria

A biological asset should be recognised if:

- it is probable that future economic benefits will flow to the entity from the asset
- the cost or fair value of the asset can be reliably measured
- the entity controls the asset.

Initial recognition

Biological assets are initially measured at fair value less estimated costs to sell.

Gains and losses may arise in profit or loss when a biological asset is first recognised. For example:

- A loss can arise because estimated selling costs are deducted from fair value.
- A gain can arise when a new biological asset (such as a lamb or a calf) is born.

Subsequent measurement

At each reporting date, biological assets are revalued to fair value less costs to sell.

Gains and losses arising from changes in fair value are recognised in profit or loss for the period in which they arise.

Biological assets are presented separately on the face of the statement of financial position within non-current assets.

Physical changes and price changes

The fair value of a biological asset may change because of its age, or because prices in the market have changed.

IAS 41 recommends separate disclosure of physical and price changes because this information is likely to be of interest to users of the financial statements. However, this disclosure is not mandatory.

Inability to measure fair value

IAS 41 presumes that the fair value of biological assets should be capable of being measured reliably.

If market prices are not readily available then the biological asset should be measured at cost less accumulated depreciation and accumulated impairment losses.

Once the asset's fair value can be measured reliably, it should be remeasured to fair value less costs to sell.

Test your understanding 12 – Cows

On 1 January 20X1, a farmer had a herd of 100 cows, all of which were 2 years old. At this date, the fair value less point of sale costs of the herd was $10,000. On 1 July 20X1, the farmer purchased 20 cows (each two and half years old) for $60 each.

As at 31 December 20X1, three year old cows sell at market for $90 each.

Market auctioneers have charged a sales levy of 2% for many years.

Required:

Discuss the accounting treatment of the above in the financial statements for the year ended 31 December 20X1.

Agricultural produce

At the date of harvest, agricultural produce should be recognised and measured at fair value less estimated costs to sell.

Gains and losses on initial recognition are included in profit or loss (operating profit) for the period.

After produce has been harvested, it becomes an item of inventory. Therefore, IAS 41 ceases to apply. The initial measurement value at the point of harvest is the deemed 'cost' for the purpose of IAS 2 Inventories, which is applied from then onwards.

Assets outside of the scope of IAS 41

IAS 41 does not apply to intangible assets (such as production quotas), bearer plants, or to land related to agricultural activity.

- In accordance with IAS 38, intangible assets are measured at cost less amortisation or fair value less amortisation.
- Bearer plants are used to produce agricultural produce for more than one period. Examples include grape vines or tea bushes. Bearer plants are accounted for in accordance with IAS 16 Property, Plant and Equipment.
  - However, any unharvested produce growing on a bearer plant, such as grapes on a grape vine, is a biological asset and so is accounted for in accordance with IAS 41.
- Land is not a biological asset. It is treated as a tangible non-current asset and accounted for under IAS 16 Property, Plant and Equipment.
  - When valuing a forest, for example, the trees must be accounted for separately from the land that they grow on.

Test your understanding 13 – GoodWine

GoodWine is a company that grows and harvests grapes. Grape vines, which produce a new harvest of grapes each year, are typically replaced every 30 years. Harvested grapes are sold to wine producers. With regards to property, plant and equipment, GoodWine accounts for land using the revaluation model and all other classes of assets using the cost model.

On 30 June 20X1, its grape vines had a carrying amount of $300,000 and a remaining useful life of 20 years. The grapes on the vines, which are generally harvested in August each year, had a fair value of $500,000. The land used for growing the grape vines had a fair value of $2m.

On 30 June 20X2, grapes with a fair value of $100,000 were harvested early due to unusual weather conditions. The grapes left on the grape vines had a fair value of $520,000. The land had a fair value of $2.1m.

All selling costs are negligible and should be ignored.

Required:

Discuss the accounting treatment of the above in the financial statements of GoodWine for the year ended 30 June 20X2.

Agriculture and government grants

If a government grant relates to a biological asset measured at its cost less accumulated depreciation and accumulated impairment losses, it is accounted for under IAS 20 Accounting for Government Grants.

If a government grant relates to biological assets measured at fair value less costs to sell, then it is accounted for under IAS 41 Agriculture as follows:

- An **unconditional** government grant related to a biological asset measured at its fair value less costs to sell shall be recognised in profit or loss when it becomes receivable.
- A **conditional** government grant related to a biological asset measured at its fair value less costs to sell, shall be recognised in profit or loss when the conditions attaching to the government grant are met.

Disclosure requirements

IAS 41 says that an entity must disclose:

- The aggregate gain or loss arising during the period on the initial recognition of biological assets and agricultural produce and from the changes in fair value less costs to sell of biological assets
- A description of each group of biological assets
- The methods and significant assumptions used when determining fair value
- A reconciliation of the carrying amounts of biological assets between the beginning and the end of the reporting period.

9 Inventories

IAS 2 Inventories

Inventories are **'measured at the lower of cost and net realisable value'** (IAS 2, para 9).

Cost

Cost, according to IAS 2, includes all purchase costs, conversion costs and other costs incurred in bringing the inventories to their present condition and location.

- Purchase costs include the purchase price (less discounts and rebates), import duties, irrecoverable taxes, transport and handling costs and any other directly attributable costs.
- Conversion costs include all direct costs of conversion (materials, labour, expenses, etc), and a proportion of the fixed and variable production overheads. The allocation of fixed production overheads must be based on the normal level of activity.
- Abnormal wastage, storage costs, administration costs and selling costs must be excluded from the valuation and charged as expenses in the period in which they are incurred.

IAS 2 Inventories allows three methods of arriving at cost:

- actual unit cost
- first-in, first-out (FIFO)
- weighted average cost (AVCO).

Actual unit cost must be used where items of inventory are not ordinarily interchangeable.

Net realisable value (NRV)

NRV is defined by IAS 2 as the expected selling price of the inventory less the estimated costs of completion and sale.

Disclosure requirements

Entities should disclose:

- their accounting policy and cost formulae
- the total carrying amount of inventories by category
- details of inventories carried at net realisable value.

Illustration – Valuation of inventories

An entity has the following items of inventory.

(a) Materials costing $12,000 bought for processing and assembly for a profitable special order. Since buying these items, the cost price has fallen to $10,000.

(b) Equipment constructed for a customer for an agreed price of $18,000. This has recently been completed at a cost of $16,800. It has now been discovered that, in order to meet certain regulations, conversion with an extra cost of $4,200 will be required. The customer has accepted partial responsibility and agreed to meet half the extra cost.

Required:

In accordance with IAS 2 Inventories, at what amount should the above items be valued?

Solution

(a) Inventory is valued at the lower of cost or net realisable value, not the lower of cost or replacement cost. Since the materials will be processed before sale there is no reason to believe that net realisable value will be below cost. Therefore the inventory should be valued at its cost of $12,000.

(b) The net realisable value is $15,900 (contract price $18,000 – constructor's share of modification cost $2,100). The net realisable value is below the cost price. Therefore the inventory should be held at $15,900.

10 Chapter summary

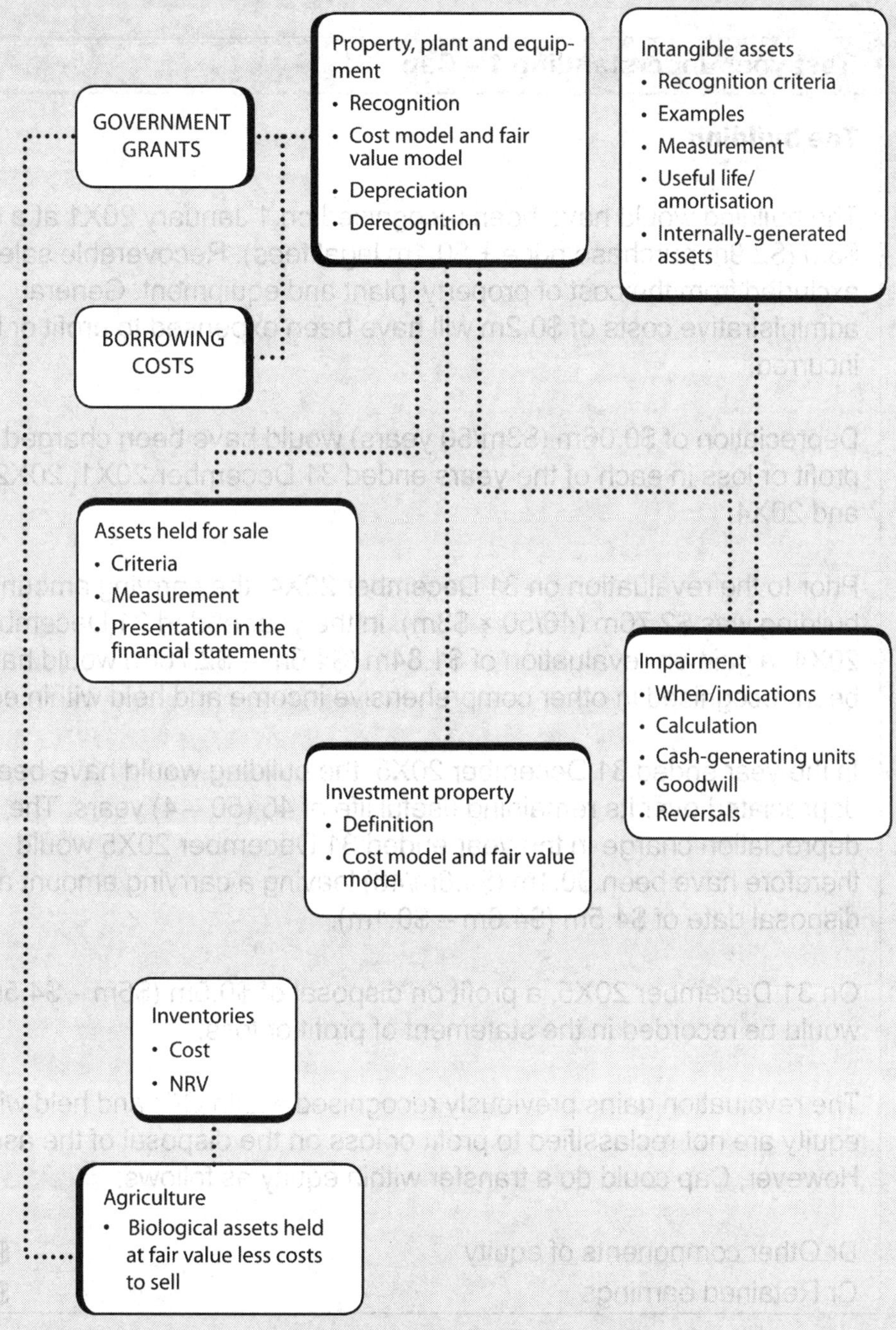

Test your understanding answers

Test your understanding 1 – Cap

The building

The building would have been recognised on 1 January 20X1 at a cost of $3m ($2.9m purchase price + $0.1m legal fees). Recoverable sales tax is excluded from the cost of property, plant and equipment. General administrative costs of $0.2m will have been expensed to profit or loss as incurred.

Depreciation of $0.06m ($3m/50 years) would have been charged to profit or loss in each of the years ended 31 December 20X1, 20X2, 20X3 and 20X4.

Prior to the revaluation on 31 December 20X4, the carrying amount of the building was $2.76m (46/50 × $3m). In the year ended 31 December 20X4, a gain on revaluation of $1.84m ($4.6m – $2.76m) would have been recognised in other comprehensive income and held within equity.

In the year ended 31 December 20X5, the building would have been depreciated over its remaining useful life of 46 (50 – 4) years. The depreciation charge in the year ended 31 December 20X5 would therefore have been $0.1m ($4.6m/46) leaving a carrying amount at the disposal date of $4.5m ($4.6m – $0.1m).

On 31 December 20X5, a profit on disposal of $0.5m ($5m – $4.5m) would be recorded in the statement of profit or loss.

The revaluation gains previously recognised within OCI and held within equity are not reclassified to profit or loss on the disposal of the asset. However, Cap could do a transfer within equity as follows:

Dr Other components of equity	$1.84m
Cr Retained earnings	$1.84m

The machine

The machine would be recognised on 1 January 20X3 at $100,000 and depreciated over 10 years. Depreciation of $10,000 ($100,000/10) will be charged in the years ended 31 December 20X3 and December 20X4.

On 1 January 20X5, Cap changes its estimate of the machine's useful economic life. This is a change in accounting estimate and therefore dealt with prospectively. The carrying amount of the asset at the date of the estimate change is $80,000 (8/10 × $100,000). This remaining carrying amount will be written off over the revised life of 4 years. This means that the depreciation charge is $20,000 ($80,000/4) in the year ended 31 December 20X5.

Test your understanding 2 – Innovate

According to IAS 38, an intangible asset can be recognised if:

- it is probable that expected future economic benefits attributable to the asset will flow to the entity
- the cost of the asset can be measured reliably.

Cash flow projections suggest that the Our Sports brand will lead to future economic benefits. However, the asset has been internally generated and therefore the cost of the asset cannot be measured reliably. This means that the Our Sports brand cannot be recognised in the financial statements.

The Pets & Me brand has been purchased for $1 million. Therefore, its cost can be measured reliably. An intangible asset should be recognised in respect of the Pets & Me brand at its cost of $1 million.

In subsequent periods, the Pets & Me brand will be amortised over its expected useful economic life.

Test your understanding 3 – Scone

Expenditure on research, market research and employee training cannot be capitalised and so must be written off to profit or loss.

In relation to development activities, $0.3 million (4/12 × $0.9m) was incurred before the product was known to be commercially viable. This amount must also be written off to profit or loss.

In total, $1.4 million ($0.5m + $0.4m + $0.2m + $0.3m) must be written off from intangible assets to profit or loss:

Dr Profit or loss	$1.4m
Cr Intangible assets	$1.4m

The intangible asset recognised on the statement of financial position will be $0.6 million ($2m – $1.4m). No amortisation will be charged because the product is not yet complete.

Test your understanding 4 – Impaired asset

(a) The value in use is calculated as the present value of the asset's future cash inflows and outflows.

	$000
Cash flow Year 1 (200 × 0.909)	182
Cash flow Year 2 (200 × 0.826)	165
	347

The recoverable amount is the higher of the fair value less costs to sell of $300,000 ($325,000 – $25,000) and the value in use of $347,000.

The carrying amount of the asset of $500,000 exceeds the recoverable amount of $347,000. Therefore, the asset is impaired and must be written down by $153,000 ($500,000 – $347,000). This impairment loss would be charged to the statement of profit or loss.

Dr Profit or loss	$153,000
Cr PPE	$153,000

(b) The asset must still be written down by $153,000. However, $10,000 of this would be recognised in other comprehensive income and the remaining $143,000 ($153,000 – $10,000) would be charged to profit or loss.

Dr Profit or loss	$143,000
Dr Other comprehensive income	$10,000
Cr PPE	$153,000

Test your understanding 5 – Cash generating units

A forms a cash-generating unit and its cash inflows should be based on the market price for its output. B and C together form one cash-generating unit because there is no market available for the output of B. In calculating the cash outflows of the cash-generating unit B + C, the timber received by B from A should be priced by reference to the market, not any internal transfer price.

Test your understanding 6 – Factory explosion

The patents have been superseded and have a recoverable amount of $nil. They therefore should be written down to $nil and an impairment loss of $200,000 must be charged to profit or loss.

Half of the machines have been blown to pieces. Therefore, half of the carrying value of the machines should be written off. An impairment loss of $150,000 will be charged to profit or loss.

The recoverable amount of the other assets cannot be determined so therefore they must be tested for impairment as part of their cash generating unit.

The carrying value of the CGU after the impairment of the patents and machines is $2,250,000 (see working below), whereas the recoverable amount is $1,950,000. A further impairment of $300,000 is therefore required.

This is firstly allocated to goodwill and then to other assets on a pro-rata basis. No further impairment should be allocated to the machines as these have already been written down to their recoverable amount.

Allocation of impairment loss to CGU

	Draft	Impairment	Revised
	$000	$000	$000
Goodwill	100	(100)	Nil
Patents	nil	–	Nil
Machines	150	–	150
Computers	500	(50)	450
Buildings	1,500	(150)	1,350
	2,250	(300)	1,950

The total impairment charged to profit or loss is $650,000 ($200,000 + $150,000 + $300,000).

Test your understanding 7 – Boxer

Year ended 31 December 20X2

	$
Asset carrying amount ($30,000 × 8/10)	24,000
Recoverable amount	16,000
Impairment loss	8,000

The asset is written down to $16,000 and the loss of $8,000 is charged to profit or loss. The depreciation charge per annum in future periods will be $2,000 ($16,000 × 1/8).

Year ended 31 December 20X5

	$
Asset carrying amount ($16,000 × 5/8)	10,000
Recoverable amount	40,000
Impairment loss	nil

There has been no impairment loss. In fact, there has been a complete reversal of the first impairment loss. The asset can be reinstated to its depreciated historical cost i.e. to the carrying value at 31 December 20X5 if there never had been an earlier impairment loss.

Year 5 depreciated historical cost (30,000 × 5/10) = $15,000

Carrying amount: $10,000

Reversal of the loss: $5,000

The reversal of the loss is now recognised. The asset will be increased by $5,000 ($15,000 – $10,000) and a gain of $5,000 will be recognised in profit or loss.

It should be noted that the whole $8,000 original impairment cannot be reversed. The impairment can only be reversed to a maximum amount of depreciated historical cost, based upon the original cost and estimated useful life of the asset.

Test your understanding 8 – CGUs and impairment reversals

The goodwill impairment cannot be reversed.

The impairment of the PPE can be reversed. However, this is limited to the carrying value of the asset had no impairment loss been previously recognised.

The carrying amount of the PPE as at 31 December 20X3 is $150,000 ($180,000 × 5/6).

If the PPE had not been impaired, then its value at 31 December 20X3 would have been $250,000 ($400,000 × 5/8).

Therefore, the carrying amount of the PPE can be increased from $150,000 to $250,000. This will give rise to a gain of $100,000 in profit or loss.

Test your understanding 9 – Hyssop

(a) IFRS 5 states that in order to be classified as 'held for sale' the property should be available for immediate sale in its present condition. The property will not be sold until the work has been carried out, demonstrating that the facility is not available for immediate sale. Therefore the property cannot be classified as 'held for sale'.

(b) The subsidiary B does not meet the criteria for classification as 'held for sale'. Although actions to locate a buyer are in place, the subsidiary is not for sale at a price that is reasonable compared with its fair value. The fair value of the subsidiary is $2.5 million, but it is advertised for sale at $3 million. It cannot be classified as held for sale' until the sales price is reduced.

Test your understanding 10 – AB

Until 31 December 20X4 the building is a normal non-current asset and its accounting treatment is prescribed by IAS 16. The annual depreciation charge was $4,000 ($200,000/50). As such, the carrying amount at 31 December 20X4, prior to reclassification, was $184,000 ($200,000 – (4 × $4,000)).

(a) On 31 December 20X4 the building is reclassified as a non-current asset held for sale. It is measured at the lower of carrying amount ($184,000) and fair value less costs to sell ($220,000 – $10,000 = $210,000). This means that the building will continue to be measured at $184,000.

(b) On 31 December 20X4 the building is reclassified as a non-current asset held for sale. It is measured at the lower of carrying amount ($184,000) and fair value less costs to sell ($110,000 – $10,000 = $100,000). The building will therefore be measured at $100,000 as at 31 December 20X4. An impairment loss of $84,000 ($184,000 – $100,000) will be charged to the statement of profit or loss.

Test your understanding 11 – Nash

The building would have been recognised on 1 January 20X1 at its cost of $1m and depreciated over its 50 year life.

By 31 December 20X2, the carrying amount of the building would have been $960,000 ($1m – (($1m/50) × 2 years)).

The building was revalued on 31 December 20X2 to $1.2m, giving a gain on revaluation of $240,000 ($1.2m – $960,000). This gain will have been recorded in other comprehensive income and held within a revaluation surplus (normally as a part of other components of equity).

The building would then have been depreciated over its remaining useful life of 48 years. Depreciation in the year ended 20X3 was therefore $25,000 ($1.2m/48). The building had a carrying amount at 31 December 20X3 of $1,175,000 ($1.2m – $25,000).

At 31 December 20X3, the building is held for sale. Because it is held under the revaluation model, it must initially be revalued downwards to its fair value of $1,100,000. This loss of $75,000 ($1,175,000 – $1,100,000) is recorded in other comprehensive income because there are previous revaluation gains relating to this asset within equity.

The building will then be revalued to fair value less costs to sell. Therefore, the asset must be reduced in value by a further $50,000. This loss is charged to the statement of profit or loss.

Test your understanding 12 – Cows

Cows are biological assets and should be initially recognised at fair value less costs to sell.

The cows purchased in the year should be initially recognised at $1,176 ((20 × $60) × 98%). This will give rise to an immediate loss of $24 ((20 × $60) – $1,176) in the statement of profit or loss.

At year end, the whole herd should be revalued to fair value less costs to sell. Any gain or loss will be recorded in the statement of profit or loss.

The herd of cows will be held at $10,584 ((120 × $90) × 98%) on the statement of financial position.

This will give rise to a further loss of $592 (W1) in the statement of profit or loss.

(W1) **Loss on revaluation**

	$
Value at 1 January 20X1	10,000
New purchase	1,176
Loss (bal. fig)	(592)
Value at 31 December 20X1	10,584

Test your understanding 13 – GoodWine

Land is accounted for in accordance with IAS 16 Property, Plant and Equipment. If the revaluation model is chosen, then gains in the fair value of the land should be reported in other comprehensive income.

At 30 June 20X2, the land should be revalued to $2.1m and a gain of $100,000 ($2.1m – $2.0m) should be reported in other comprehensive income and held within a revaluation reserve in equity.

The grape vines are used to produce agricultural produce over many periods. This means that they are bearer plants and are therefore also accounted for under IAS 16. Except for land, GoodWine uses the cost model for property, plant and equipment. Therefore, depreciation of $15,000 ($300,000/20 years) will be charged to profit or loss in the year and the grape vines will have a carrying amount of $285,000 ($300,000 – $15,000) at 30 June 20X2.

The grapes growing on the vines are biological assets. They should be revalued at the year end to fair value less costs to sell with any gain or loss reported in profit or loss. GoodWine's biological assets should therefore be revalued to $520,000. A gain of $20,000 ($520,000 – $500,000) should be reported in profit or loss.

The grapes are agricultural produce and should initially be recognised at fair value less costs to sell. Any gain or loss on initial recognition is reported in profit or loss. The harvested grapes should be initially recognised at $100,000 with a gain of $100,000 reported in profit or loss. The harvested grapes are now accounted for under IAS 2 Inventories and will have a deemed cost of $100,000.

chapter

6

Foreign currency in individual financial statements

Chapter learning objectives

Upon completion of this chapter you will be able to:

- outline the principles for translating foreign currency amounts, including translations into the functional currency and presentation currency
- apply these principles.

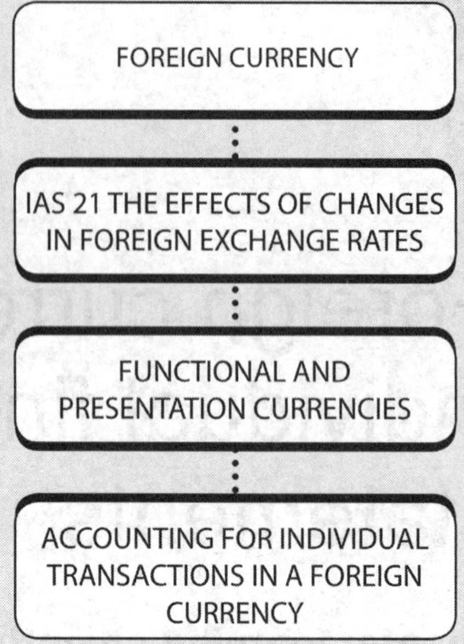

1 IAS 21 The effects of changes in foreign exchange rates

IAS 21 deals with:

- the definition of functional and presentation currencies
- accounting for individual transactions in a foreign currency
- translating the financial statements of a foreign operation.

Translating the financial statements of a foreign operation is covered in a later chapter.

Functional and presentation currencies

An entity maintains its day-to-day financial records in its functional currency.

Functional currency is the **'currency of the primary economic environment where the entity operates'** (IAS 21, para 8).

IAS 21 (para 9) says that an entity should consider the following primary factors when determining its functional currency:

- **'the currency that mainly influences sales prices for goods and services**
- **the currency of the country whose competitive forces and regulations mainly determine the sales price of goods and services**
- **the currency that mainly influences labour, materials and other costs of providing goods and services'.**

If the primary factors are inconclusive then the following secondary factors should also be considered:

- the currency in which funds from financing activities are generated
- the currency in which receipts from operating activities are retained.

There are times when a foreign subsidiary, rather than applying the above rules, should simply use the same functional currency as its parent. In determining this, IAS 21 says that the following factors should be considered:

- whether the foreign operation operates as an extension of the parent, rather than having significant autonomy
- the level of transactions with the parent
- whether cash flows are readily available for remittance to its parent
- whether the foreign operation has sufficient cash flows to service its debts without needing funds from its parent.

The **presentation currency** is defined by IAS 21 as the currency in which the entity presents its financial statements. This can be different from the functional currency.

Test your understanding 1 – Chive

Chive is an entity located in a country whose currency is dollars ($).

Seventy per cent of Chive's sales are denominated in dollars and 30% of them are denominated in sterling (£). Chive does not convert receipts from customers into other currencies. Chive buys most of its inventories, and pays for a large proportion of operating costs, in sterling.

Chive has two bank loans outstanding. Both of these loans are denominated in dollars.

Required:

What is the functional currency of Chive?

2 Accounting for individual transactions designated in a foreign currency

Where an entity enters into a transaction denominated in a currency other than its functional currency, that transaction must be translated into the functional currency before it is recorded.

The exchange rate used to initially record transactions should be either:

- the spot exchange rate on the date the transaction occurred, or
- an average rate over a period of time, providing the exchange rate has not fluctuated significantly.

Cash settlement

When cash settlement occurs, such as when cash is received from an overseas credit customer, the settled amount should be translated into the functional currency using the spot exchange rate on the settlement date. If this amount differs from that used when the transaction occurred, there will be an exchange difference.

Exchange differences on settlement

IAS 21 requires that exchange gains or losses on settlement of individual transactions are recognised in profit or loss in the period in which they arise.

IAS 21 is not definitive in stating where in profit or loss any such gains or losses are classified. It would seem reasonable to regard them as items of operating expense or income. However, other profit or loss headings may also be appropriate.

Illustration – Exchange differences on settlement

On 7 May 20X6 an entity with a functional currency of dollars ($) sold goods to a German entity for €48,000. On this date, the rate of exchange was $1 = € 3.2.

The sale is translated into the functional currency using the exchange rate in place on the transaction date.

	$
Dr Receivables (€48,000/3.2)	15,000
Cr Revenue	15,000

On 20 July 20X6 the customer paid the outstanding balance. On this date, the rate of exchange was $1 = €3.17.

The settlement is translated into the functional currency using the exchange rate in place on the settlement date.

	$
Dr Cash (€48,000/3.17)	15,142
Cr Receivables	15,000
Cr Profit or loss (exchange gain)	142

The $142 exchange gain forms part of the profit for the year.

Treatment of year-end balances

The treatment of any overseas items remaining in the statement of financial position at the year-end will depend on whether they are monetary or non-monetary. The rules in IAS 21 (para 8) stipulate the following:

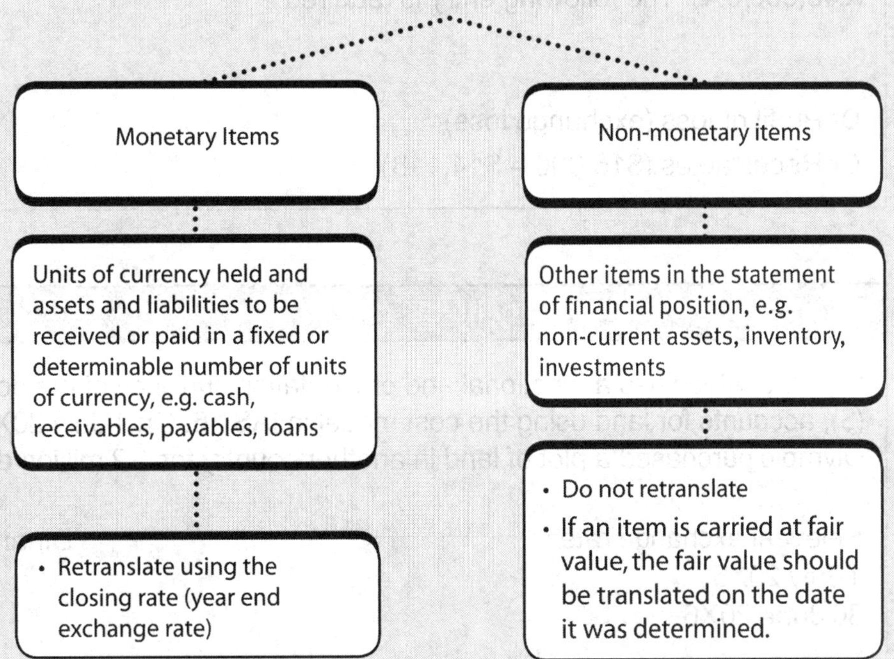

Monetary Items
Non-monetary items
Units of currency held and assets and liabilities to be received or paid in a fixed or determinable number of units of currency, e.g. cash, receivables, payables, loans
Other items in the statement of financial position, e.g. non-current assets, inventory, investments
• Retranslate using the closing rate (year end exchange rate)
• Do not retranslate
• If an item is carried at fair value, the fair value should be translated on the date it was determined.

Exchange differences on retranslation of monetary items

As with exchange differences arising on settlement, IAS 21 requires that exchange differences arising on retranslation of monetary assets and liabilities must be recognised in profit or loss.

IAS 21 does not specify the heading(s) under which such exchange gains or losses should be classified. It would seem reasonable to regard them as items of operating income or operating expense as appropriate.

Illustration – Monetary items

On 7 May 20X6 an entity with a functional currency of dollars ($) sold goods to a German entity for €48,000. On this date, the rate of exchange was $1 = € 3.2.

The sale is translated into the functional currency using the exchange rate in place on the transaction date.

	$
Dr Receivables (€48,000/3.2)	15,000
Cr Revenue	15,000

By the reporting date of 31 July 20X6, the invoice had not been settled. On this date, the rate of exchange was $1 = €3.4.

Receivables are a monetary item so must be retranslated into the entity's functional currency at the year end using the closing exchange rate.

The receivable at year end should therefore be held at $14,118 (€48,000/3.4). The following entry is required:

	$
Dr Profit or loss (exchange loss)	882
Cr Receivables ($15,000 – $14,118)	882

Illustration – Non-monetary items

Olympic, which has a functional and presentation currency of the dollar ($), accounts for land using the cost model in IAS 16. On 1 July 20X5, Olympic purchased a plot of land in another country for 1.2 million dinars.

Relevant exchange rates:	Dinars to $1
1 July 20X5	4.0
30 June 20X6	3.0

The land is initially recognised at cost. This should be translated into the functional currency using the exchange rate on the purchase date. The land is therefore initially recorded at $300,000 (1.2m dinars/4.0).

Land is not a monetary item so is therefore not retranslated. In accordance with IAS 16, no depreciation is charged. This means that the land remains at $300,000.

Illustration – Non-monetary items at fair value

Pallot, which has a functional and presentation currency of the dollar ($), accounts for land using the revaluation model in IAS 16. On 1 July 20X5, Pallot purchased a plot of land in another country for 1.2 million dinars. At 30 June 20X6, the fair value of the plot of land was 1.5 million dinars.

Relevant exchange rates:	Dinars to $1
1 July 20X5	4.0
30 June 20X6	3.0

The land is initially recognised at cost. This should be translated into the functional currency using the exchange rate on the purchase date. The land is therefore initially recorded at $300,000 (1.2m dinars/4.0).

Land is not a monetary item so its cost is not retranslated. However, in accordance with the revaluation model in IAS 16, a fair value has been determined. This valuation is in dinars and so must be translated into the functional currency using the exchange rate in place when the fair value was determined. This means that the land will must be revalued to $500,000 (1.5m dinars/3.0).

The increase in the carrying value of the land of $200,000 ($500,000 – $300,000) will be reported as a revaluation gain in other comprehensive income for the year and a revaluation reserve will be included within other components of equity on the statement of financial position at the reporting date.

Test your understanding 2 – Butler, Waiter and Attendant

(a) An entity, Butler, has a reporting date of 31 December and a functional currency of dollars ($). On 27 November 20X6 Butler plc buys goods from a Swedish supplier for SwK 324,000.

On 19 December 20X6 Butler plc pays the Swedish supplier in full.

Exchange rates were as follows:

27 November 20X6 – SwK 11.15: $1
19 December 20X6 – SwK 10.93: $1

Required:

Describe how the above transaction should be accounted for in the financial statements of Butler for the year ended 31 December 20X6.

(b) An entity, Waiter, has a reporting date of 31 December and the dollar ($) as its functional currency. Waiter borrows in the foreign currency of the Kram (K). The loan of K120,000 was taken out on 1 January 20X7. A repayment of K40,000 was made on 1 March 20X7.

Exchange rates were as follows

1 January 20X7 – K1: $2
1 March 20X7 – K1: $3
31 December 20X7 – K1: $3.5

Required:

Describe how the above should be accounted for in the financial statements of Waiter for the year ended 31 December 20X7.

(c) An entity, Attendant, has a reporting date of 31 December and has the dollar ($) as its functional currency. Attendant purchased a plot of land overseas on 1 March 20X0. The entity paid for the land in the currency of the Rylands (R). The purchase cost of the land at 1 March 20X0 was R60,000. The value of the land at the reporting date was R80,000.

Exchange rates were as follows:

1 March 20X0 – R8 : $1
31 December 20X0 – R10 :$1

Required:

Describe how the above transaction should be accounted for in the financial statements of Attendant for the year ended 31 December 20X0 if the land is measured at:

- **cost**
- **fair value.**

Test your understanding 3 – Highlight

(a) Highlight is an entity whose functional currency is the dollar ($) and has an annual reporting date of 31 December.

On 1 July 20X3, Highlight purchased an item of plant and equipment on credit for Dn400,000. On 1 November 20X3, Highlight made a payment of Dn180,000 to the supplier. The balance of the invoice remains outstanding.

Highlight has a policy of applying historical cost accounting and depreciating plant and equipment at the rate of 20% per annum. The item of plant and equipment is not expected to have any residual value at the end of its useful life.

Relevant exchange rates to $1 are as follows:

	Dn
1 July 20X3	10.0
1 November 20X3	7.2
1 December 20X3	9.0
31 December 20X3	8.0

Required:

Prepare relevant extracts from Highlight's financial statements for the year ended 31 December 20X3 to illustrate the impact of the above transactions.

(b) During 20X3, Highlight entered into a number of transactions with Eraser, an overseas customer.

On 1 November 20X3, Highlight made credit sales to Eraser on 3 months credit for Dn360,000. On 1 December 20X3, Highlight made further credit sales to Eraser on 3 months credit for Dn540,000.

By 31 December 20X3, Highlight had received no payment from Eraser. As the receivables were still within their credit period, they were not regarded as being impaired.

Relevant exchange rates to $1 are as follows:

	Dn
1 July 20X3	10.0
1 November 20X3	7.2
1 December 20X3	9.0
31 December 20X3	8.0

Required:

Prepare relevant extracts from Highlight's financial statements for the year ended 31 December 20X3 to illustrate the impact of the above transactions.

3 Chapter summary

FOREIGN CURRENCY

IAS 21 THE EFFECTS OF CHANGES IN FOREIGN EXCHANGE RATES

Functional currency:
The currency of the primary economic environment where the entity operates

Presentation currency:
The currency in which the entity presents its financial statements

Accounting for individual transactions in a foreign currency

- At transaction date
- On settlement
- At reporting date

Test your understanding answers

Test your understanding 1 – Chive

Firstly, the primary indicators of functional currency should be applied. Most of Chive's sales are denominated in dollars and so this would suggest that the dollar is its functional currency. However, since a lot of the costs of the business are denominated in sterling, it could be argued that its functional currency is sterling.

Since the primary indicators of functional currency are not clear cut, it is important to look at the secondary indicators. Receipts are retained in both dollars and sterling. However, funding is generated in the form of dollar loans, which further suggests that the dollar might be Chive's functional currency.

All things considered, it would seem that the functional currency of Chive is dollars. This means that any business transactions that are denominated in sterling must be translated into dollars in order to record them.

Test your understanding 2 – Butler, Waiter and Attendant

(a) The transaction on 27 November 20X6 must be translated using the exchange rate on the transaction date.

The transaction is recorded at $29,058 (SwK324,000/11.15).

Dr Purchases	$29,058
Cr Payables	$29,058

The cash settlement on 19 December 20X6 must be translated using the exchange rate on the settlement date.

The cash settlement is recorded at $29,643 (SwK324,000/10.93).

Dr Payables	$29,058
Dr Profit or loss	$585
Cr Cash	$29,643

An exchange loss of $585 has arisen and this is recorded in the statement of profit or loss.

(b) On 1 January 20X7, money was borrowed in Krams. This must be translated into the functional currency using the exchange rate on the transaction date.

The transaction is recorded at $240,000 (K120,000 × 2).

Dr Cash	$240,000
Cr Loans	$240,000

The cash settlement on 1 March 20X7 must be translated into the functional currency using the exchange rate on the settlement date.

The cash settlement is recorded at $120,000 (K40,000 × 3).

Dr Loans	$120,000
Cr Cash	$120,000

Loans are a monetary liability. At the reporting date, the remaining loan of K80,000 (K120,000 – K40,000) must be translated at the year end exchange rate. This gives a closing liability of $280,000 (K80,000 × 3.5).

The exchange loss on retranslation is calculated as follows:

	K	Rate	$
1 January 20X7	120,000	2.0	240,000
1 March 20X7	(40,000)	3.0	(120,000)
Exchange loss (bal. fig)			160,000
31 December 20X7	80,000	3.5	280,000

The double entry to record this loss:

Dr Profit or loss $160,000
Cr Loans $160,000

(c) The asset is initially recognised at cost. This should be translated into the functional currency using the exchange rate on the purchase date. The land is therefore initially recorded at $7,500 ($60,000/8).

Land is not a monetary item so is therefore not retranslated. If held under the cost model, it will remain at $7,500

If the land is held at fair value, then the valuation must be translated into dollars using the exchange rate in place when determined. Therefore, the land will be revalued to $8,000 (R80,000/10).

The carrying value of the land must be increased by $500 ($8,000 – $7,500).

If the land is held under IAS 40 Investment Property, then the gain will be recorded in profit or loss.

If the land is held under IAS 16 Property, Plant and Equipment, then the gain will be recorded in other comprehensive income.

Test your understanding 3 – Highlight

(a) Both the purchase of plant and equipment and the associated payable are recorded using the rate ruling at the date of the transaction (Dn10 = $1), giving a value of $40,000. The part-payment made on 1 November is recorded using the rate applicable on that date, with the remaining dinar liability being restated in dollars at the closing rate at the reporting date. The exchange difference, in this case a loss of $12,500 (see calculation below), is taken to profit or loss as an operating expense.

		Dn	Rate	$
1/7/X3	Payable recorded	400,000	10.0	40,000
1/11/X3	Part-payment made	(180,000)	7.2	(25,000)
	Exchange loss (bal. fig.)			12,500
31/12/X3	Payable outstanding	220,000	8.0	27,500

Plant and equipment, as a non-monetary item, is accounted for at historic cost and is therefore not retranslated. The depreciation charge is $4,000 ($40,000 × 1/5 × 6/12).

Extracts of the financial statements for the year ended 31 December 20X3 are as follows:

Statement of profit or loss:	$
Cost of sales (depreciation)	(4,000)
Operating expenses (exchange loss)	(12,500)
Statement of financial position:	
Property, plant and equipment ($40,000 – $4,000)	36,000
Current liabilities	27,500

(b) Each of the sales invoices denominated in Dn must be translated into $ using the spot rate on the date of each transaction. Each transaction will result in recognition of revenue and a trade receivable at the following amounts:

1 November 20X3: Dn360,000/7.2 = $50,000
1 December 20X3: Dn540,000/9.0 = $60,000

Both amounts remain outstanding at the reporting date and must be restated into dollars using the closing rate of Dn8 = $1. The exchange difference, in this case a gain of $2,500 (see calculation below), is taken to profit or loss as an item of other operating income.

		Dn	Rate	$
1/11/X3	Receivable recorded	360,000	7.2	50,000
1/12/X3	Receivable recorded	540,000	9.0	60,000
	Exchange gain (bal. fig.)			2,500
31/12/X3	Receivable outstanding	900,000	8.0	112,500

Extracts of the financial statements for the year ended 31 December 20X3 are as follows:

Statement of profit or loss:	$
Revenue ($50,000 + $60,000)	110,000
Other operating income (exchange gain)	2,500
Statement of financial position:	
Receivables	112,500

chapter

7

Leases

Chapter learning objectives

Upon completion of this chapter you will be able to:

- Apply and discuss the accounting for leases by lessees including the measurement of the right of use asset and liability
- Apply and discuss the accounting for leases by lessors
- Apply and discuss the circumstances where there may be re-measurement of the lease liability
- Apply and discuss the reasons behind the separation of the components of a lease contract into lease and non–lease elements
- Discuss the recognition exemptions under the current leasing standard
- Account for and discuss sale and leaseback transactions.

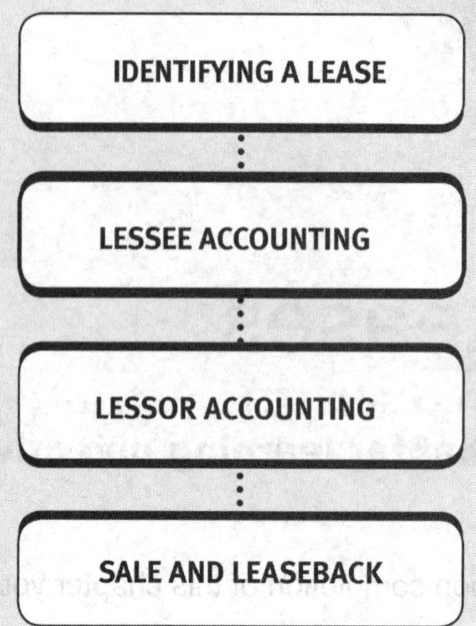

1 Leases: definitions

IFRS 16 Leases provides the following definitions:

A **lease** is a contract, or part of a contract, that conveys the right to use an underlying asset for a period of time in exchange for consideration.

The **lessor** is the entity that provides the right-of-use asset and, in exchange, receives consideration.

The **lessee** is the entity that obtains use of the right-of-use asset and, in exchange, transfers consideration.

A **right-of-use asset** is the lessee's right to use an underlying asset over the lease term.

2 Identifying a lease

IFRS 16 Leases requires lessees to recognise an asset and a liability for all leases, unless they are short-term or of a minimal value. As such, it is vital to assess whether a contract contains a lease, or whether it is simply a contract for a service.

A contract contains a lease if it conveys **'the right to control the use of an identified asset for a period of time in exchange for consideration'** (IFRS 16, para 9).

For this to be the case, IFRS 16 says that the contract must give the customer:

- the right to substantially all of the identified asset's economic benefits, and

- the right to direct the identified asset's use.

The right to direct the use of the asset can still exist if the lessor puts restrictions on its use within a contract (such as by capping the maximum mileage of a vehicle, or limiting which countries an asset can be used in). These restrictions define the scope of a lessee's right of use, rather than preventing them from directing use.

IFRS 16 says that a customer does not have the right to use an identified asset if the supplier has the practical ability to substitute the asset for an alternative and if it would be economically beneficial for them to do so.

Test your understanding 1 – Coffee Bean

Coffee Bean enters into a contract with an airport operator to use some space in the airport to sell its goods from portable kiosks for a three-year period. Coffee Bean owns the portable kiosks. The contract stipulates the amount of space and states that the space may be located at any one of several departure areas within the airport. The airport operator can change the location of the space allocated to Coffee Bean at any time during the period of use, and the costs that the airport operator would incur to do this would be minimal. There are many areas in the airport that are suitable for the portable kiosks.

Required:

Does the contract contain a lease?

Test your understanding 2 – AFG

AFG enters into a contract with Splash, the supplier, to use a specified ship for a five-year period. Splash has no substitution rights. During the contract period, AFG decides what cargo will be transported, when the ship will sail, and to which ports it will sail. However, there are some restrictions specified in the contract. Those restrictions prevent AFG from carrying hazardous materials as cargo or from sailing the ship into waters where piracy is a risk.

Splash operates and maintains the ship and is responsible for the safe passage of the cargo on board the ship. AFG is prohibited from hiring another operator for the ship, and from operating the ship itself during the term of the contract.

Required:

Does the contract contain a lease?

3 Lessee accounting

Basic principle

At the commencement of the lease, IFRS 16 requires that the lessee recognises a lease liability and a right-of-use asset.

Initial measurement

The liability

The lease liability is initially measured at the present value of the lease payments that have not yet been paid.

IFRS 16 states that lease payments include the following:

- Fixed payments
- Variable payments that depend on an index or rate, initially valued using the index or rate at the lease commencement date
- Amounts expected to be payable under residual value guarantees
- Options to purchase the asset that are reasonably certain to be exercised
- Termination penalties, if the lease term reflects the expectation that these will be incurred.

A residual value guarantee is when the lessor is promised that the underlying asset at the end of the lease term will not be worth less than a specified amount.

The discount rate should be the rate implicit in the lease. If this cannot be determined, then the entity should use its incremental borrowing rate (the rate at which it could borrow funds to purchase a similar asset).

The right-of-use asset

The right-of-use asset is initially recognised at cost.

IFRS 16 says that the initial cost of the right-of-use asset comprises:

- The amount of the initial measurement of the lease liability (see above)
- Lease payments made at or before the commencement date
- Initial direct costs
- The estimated costs of removing or dismantling the underlying asset as per the conditions of the lease.

The lease term

To calculate the initial value of the liability and right-of-use asset, the lessee must consider the length of the lease term. IFRS 16 says that the lease term comprises:

- Non-cancellable periods
- Periods covered by an option to extend the lease if reasonably certain to be exercised
- Periods covered by an option to terminate the lease if reasonably certain not to be exercised.

Test your understanding 3 – Dynamic

On 1 January 20X1, Dynamic entered into a two year lease for a lorry. The contract contains an option to extend the lease term for a further year. Dynamic believes that it is reasonably certain to exercise this option. Lorries have a useful economic life of ten years.

Lease payments are $10,000 per year for the initial term and $15,000 per year for the option period. All payments are due at the end of the year. To obtain the lease, Dynamic incurs initial direct costs of $3,000. The lessor reimburses $1,000 of these costs.

The interest rate within the lease is not readily determinable. Dynamic's incremental rate of borrowing is 5%.

Required:

Calculate the initial carrying amount of the lease liability and the right-of-use asset and provide the double entries needed to record these amounts in Dynamic's financial records.

Subsequent measurement

The liability

The carrying amount of the lease liability is increased by the interest charge. This interest is also recorded in the statement of profit or loss:

Dr Finance costs (P/L)	X
Cr Lease liability	X

The carrying amount of the lease liability is reduced by cash repayments:

Dr Lease liability	X
Cr Cash	X

The right-of-use asset

The right-of-use asset is measured using the cost model (unless another measurement model is chosen). This means that it is measured at its initial cost less accumulated depreciation and impairment losses.

Depreciation is calculated as follows:

- If ownership of the asset transfers to the lessee at the end of the lease term then depreciation should be charged over the asset's remaining useful economic life,
- Otherwise, depreciation is charged over the shorter of the useful life and the lease term (as defined previously).

Other measurement models

If the lessee measures investment properties at fair value then IFRS 16 requires that right-of-use assets that meet the definition of investment property should also be measued using the fair value model (e.g. right-of-use assets that are sub-leased under operating leases in order to earn rental income).

If the right-of-use asset belongs to a class of property, plant and equipment that is measured using the revaluation model, an entity **may** apply the IAS 16 Property, Plant and Equipment revaluation model to all right-of-use assets within that class.

Test your understanding 4 – Dynamic (cont.)

This question follows on from the previous 'test your understanding'.

Required:

Explain the subsequent treatment of Dynamic's lease in the year ended 31 December 20X1

Separating components

A contract may contain a lease component and a non-lease component.

Unless an entity chooses otherwise, the consideration in the contract should be allocated to each component based on the stand-alone selling price of each component.

Entities can, if they prefer, choose to account for the lease and non-lease component as a single lease. This decision must be made for each class of right-of-use asset. However this choice would increase the lease liability recorded at the inception of the lease, which may negatively impact perception of the entity's financial position.

Illustration – Separating components

On 1 January 20X1 Swish entered into a contract to lease a crane for three years. The lessor agrees to maintain the crane during the three year period. The total contract cost is $180,000. Swish must pay $60,000 each year with the payments commencing on 31 December 20X1. Swish accounts for non-lease components separately from leases.

If contracted separately it has been determined that the standalone price for the lease of the crane is $160,000 and the standalone price for the maintenance services is $40,000.

Swish can borrow at a rate of 5% a year.

Required:

Explain how the above will be accounted for by Swish in the year ended 31 December 20X1.

Solution

Allocation of payments

The annual payments of $60,000 should be allocated between the lease and non-lease components of the contract based on their standalone selling prices:

Lease of Crane: ($160/$160 + $40) × $60,000 = $48,000

Maintenance ($40/$160 + $40) × $60,000 = $12,000

Lease of Crane

The lease liability is calculated as the present value of the lease payments, as follows:

Date	Cash flow ($)	Discount rate	Present value ($)
31/12/X1	48,000	1/1.05	45,714
31/12/X2	48,000	$1/1.05^2$	43,537
31/12/X3	48,000	$1/1.05^3$	41,464
			130,715

There are no direct costs so the right-of-use asset is recognised at the same amount:

Dr Right-of-use asset	$130,715
Cr Lease liability	$130,715

Interest of $6,536 (W1) is charged on the lease liability.

Dr Finance costs (P/L)	$6,536
Cr Lease liability	$6,536

The cash payment reduces the liability.

Dr Lease liability	$48,000
Cr Cash	$48,000

The liability has a carrying amount of $89,251 at the reporting date.

The right-of-use asset is depreciated over the three year lease term. This gives a charge of $43,572 ($130,715/3 years).

Dr Depreciation (P/L)	$43,572
Cr Right-of-use asset	$43,572

The carrying amount of the right-of-use asset will be reduced to $87,143 ($130,715 – $43,572).

(W1) **Lease liability table**

Year-ended	Opening	Interest (5%)	Payments	Closing
	$	$	$	$
31/12/X1	130,715	6,536	(48,000)	89,251

Maintenance

The cost of one year's maintenance will be expensed to profit or loss:

Dr P/L	$12,000
Cr Cash	$12,000

Reassessing the lease liability

If changes to lease payments occur then the lease liability must be re-calculated and its carrying amount adjusted. A corresponding adjustment is posted against the carrying amount of the right-of-use asset.

Recalculating the discount rate

IFRS 16 says that the lease liability should be re-calculated using a revised discount rate if:

- the lease term changes
- the entity's assessment of an option to purchase the underlying asset changes.

The revised discount rate should be the interest rate implicit in the lease for the remainder of the lease term. If this cannot be readily determined, the lessee's incremental borrowing rate at the date of reassessment should be used.

Test your understanding 5 – Kingfisher

On 1 January 20X1, Kingfisher enters into a four year lease of property with annual lease payments of $1 million, payable at the beginning of each year. According to the contract, lease payments will increase every year on the basis of the increase in the Consumer Price Index for the preceding 12 months. The Consumer Price Index at the commencement date is 125. The interest rate implicit in the lease is not readily determinable. Kingfisher's incremental borrowing rate is 5 per cent per year.

At the beginning of the second year of the lease the Consumer Price Index is 140.

Required:

Discuss how the lease will be accounted for:

- **during the first year of the contract**
- **on the first day of the second year of the contract.**

Short-life and low value assets

If the lease is short-term (less than 12 months at the inception date) or of a low value then a simplified treatment is allowed.

In these cases, the lessee can choose to recognise the lease payments in profit or loss on a straight line basis. No lease liability or right-of-use asset would therefore be recognised.

Low value assets

IFRS 16 does not specify a particular monetary amount below which an asset would be considered 'low value'.

The standard gives the following examples of low value assets:

- tablets
- small personal computers
- telephones
- small items of furniture.

The assessment of whether an asset qualifies as having a 'low value' must be made based on its value when new. Therefore, a car would not qualify as a low value asset, even if it was very old at the commencement of the lease.

Lessees: presentation and disclosure

If right-of-use assets are not presented separately on the face of the statement of financial position then they should be included within the line item that would have been used if the assets were owned. The entity must disclose which line item includes right-of-use assets.

IFRS 16 requires lessees to disclose the following amounts:

- The depreciation charged on right-of-use assets
- Interest expenses on lease liabilities
- The expense relating to short-term leases and leases of low value assets
- Cash outflows for leased assets
- Right-of-use asset additions
- The carrying amount of right-of-use assets
- A maturity analysis of lease liabilities.

4 Lessor accounting

A lessor must classify its leases as finance leases or operating leases.

IFRS 16 provides the following definitions:

A **finance lease** is a lease where the risks and rewards of the underlying asset substantially transfer to the lessee.

An **operating lease** is a lease that does not meet the definition of a finance lease.

How to classify a lease

IFRS 16 Leases states that a lease is probably a finance lease if one or more of the following apply:

- Ownership is transferred to the lessee at the end of the lease
- The lessee has the option to purchase the asset for less than its expected fair value at the date the option becomes exercisable and it is reasonably certain that the option will be exercised
- The lease term (including any secondary periods) is for the major part of the asset's economic life
- At the inception of the lease, the present value of the lease payments amounts to at least substantially all of the fair value of the leased asset

- The leased assets are of a specialised nature so that only the lessee can use them without major modifications being made
- The lessee will compensate the lessor for their losses if the lease is cancelled
- Gains or losses from fluctuations in the fair value of the residual fall to the lessee (for example, by means of a rebate of lease payments)
- The lessee can continue the lease for a secondary period in exchange for substantially lower than market rent payments.

Test your understanding 6 – DanBob

DanBob is a lessor and is drawing up a lease agreement for a building.

The building has a remaining useful economic life of 50 years. The lease term, which would commence on 1 January 20X0, is for 30 years.

DanBob would receive 40% of the asset's value upfront from the lessee. At the end of each of the 30 years, DanBob will receive 6% of the asset's fair value as at 1 January 20X0.

Legal title at the end of the lease remains with DanBob, but the lessee can continue to lease the asset indefinitely at a rental that is substantially below its market value. If the lessee cancels the lease, it must make a payment to DanBob to recover its remaining investment.

Required:

Per IFRS 16 Leases, should the lease be classified as an operating lease or a finance lease?

Finance leases

Initial treatment

At the inception of a lease, lessors present assets held under a finance lease as a receivable. The value of the receivable should be equal to the **net investment in the lease**.

IFRS 16 requires that the net investment is calculated as the present value of:

- Fixed payments
- Variable payments that depend on an index or rate, valued using the index or rate at the lease commencement date
- Residual value guarantees

- Unguaranteed residual values
- Purchase options that are reasonably certain to be exercised
- Termination penalties, if the lease term reflects the expectation that these will be incurred.

Discount rate

The discount rate used to calculate the net investment in the lease is the rate of interest implicit in the lease.

IFRS 16 requires that the discount rate incorporates any initial direct costs of the lease (this means higher initial direct costs will lead to lower income being recognised over the lease term). There is therefore no need to add any direct costs onto the net investment separately.

Illustration – Calculating the net investment

On 31 December 20X1, Rain leases a machine to Snow on a three year finance lease and will receive $10,000 per year in arrears. Snow has guaranteed that the machine will have a market value at the end of the lease term of $2,000.

The interest rate implicit in the lease is 10%.

Required:

Calculate Rain's net investment in the lease at 31 December 20X1.

Solution

The net investment in the lease must include the present value of:

- fixed lease payments
- residual value guarantees that are expected to be paid.

Date	Description	Amount	Discount rate	Present value
		$		$
31/12/X2	Receipt	10,000	1/1.1	9,091
31/12/X3	Receipt	10,000	$1/1.1^2$	8,264
31/12/X4	Receipt	10,000	$1/1.1^3$	7,513
31/12/X4	Guaranteed residual value	2,000	$1/1.1^3$	1,503
				–––––––
	Net investment in lease			26,371
				–––––––

The net investment in the lease is $26,371. This is the value of the lease receivable that will be recognised by Rain.

Subsequent treatment

The subsequent treatment of the finance lease is as follows:

- The carrying amount of the lease receivable is increased by finance income earned, which is also credited to the statement of profit or loss.
- The carrying amount of the lease receivable is reduced by cash receipts.

Test your understanding 7 – Vache

Vache leases machinery to Toro. The lease is for four years at an annual cost of $2,000 payable annually in arrears. The present value of the lease payments is $5,710. The implicit rate of interest is 15%.

Required:

How should Vache account for their net investment in the lease?

Operating leases

A lessor recognises income from an operating lease on a straight line basis over the lease term.

Any direct costs of negotiating the lease are added to the cost of the underlying asset. The underlying asset should be depreciated in accordance with IAS 16 Property, Plant and Equipment or IAS 38 Intangible Assets.

Test your understanding 8 – Oroc

Oroc hires out industrial plant on long-term operating leases. On 1 January 20X1, it entered into a seven-year lease on a mobile crane. The terms of the lease are $175,000 payable on 1 January 20X1, followed by six rentals of $70,000 payable on 1 January 20X2 – 20X7. The crane will be returned to Oroc on 31 December 20X7. The crane originally cost $880,000 and has a 25-year useful life with no residual value.

Required:

Discuss the accounting treatment of the above in the year ended 31 December 20X1.

Lessors: presentation and disclosure

The underlying asset should be presented in the statement of financial position according to its nature.

For finance leases, IFRS 16 requires lessors to disclose:

- Profit or loss arising on the sale
- Finance income
- Data about changes in the carrying amount of the net investment in finance leases
- A maturity analysis of lease payments receivable

For operating leases, lessors should disclose a maturity analysis of undiscounted lease payments receivable.

5 Sale and leaseback

If an entity (the seller-lessee) transfers an asset to another entity (the buyer-lessor) and then leases it back, IFRS 16 requires that both entities assess whether the transfer should be accounted for as a sale.

For this purpose, entities must apply IFRS 15 Revenue from Contracts with Customers to decide whether a performance obligation has been satisfied. This normally occurs when the customer obtains control of a promised asset. Control of an asset refers to the ability to obtain substantially all of the remaining benefits.

Transfer is not a sale

If the transfer is not a sale then IFRS 16 states that:

- The seller-lessee continues to recognise the transferred asset and will recognise a financial liability equal to the transfer proceeds.
- The buyer-lessor will not recognise the transferred asset and will recognise a financial asset equal to the transfer proceeds.

In simple terms, the transfer proceeds are treated as a loan. The detailed accounting treatment of financial assets and financial liabilities is covered in Chapter 11.

Transfer is a sale

If the transfer does qualify as a sale then IFRS 16 states that:

- The seller-lessee must measure the right-of-use asset as the proportion of the previous carrying amount that relates to the rights retained.
  - This means that the seller-lessee will recognise a profit or loss based only on the rights transferred to the buyer-lessor.
- The buyer-lessor accounts for the asset purchase using the most applicable accounting standard (such as IAS 16 Property, Plant and Equipment). The lease is accounted for by applying lessor accounting requirements.

Test your understanding 9 – Painting

On 1 January 20X1, Painting sells an item of machinery to Collage for its fair value of $3 million. The asset had a carrying amount of $1.2 million prior to the sale. This sale represents the satisfaction of a performance obligation, in accordance with IFRS 15 Revenue from Contracts with Customers. Painting enters into a contract with Collage for the right to use the asset for the next five years. Annual payments of $500,000 are due at the end of each year. The interest rate implicit in the lease is 10%.

The present value of the annual lease payments is £1.9 million. The remaining useful economic life of the machine is much greater than the lease term.

Required:

Explain how the transaction will be accounted for on 1 January 20X1 by both Painting and Collage.

Sale and leaseback transactions not at fair value

If the sales proceeds or lease payments are not at fair value, IFRS 16 requires that:

- below market terms (e.g. when the sales proceeds are less than the asset's fair value) are treated as a prepayment of lease payments
- above market terms (e.g. when the sales proceeds exceed the asset's fair value) are treated as additional financing.

Illustration – Mosaic

On 1 January 20X1, Mosaic sells an item of machinery to Ceramic for $3 million. Its fair value was $2.8 million. The asset had a carrying amount of $1.2 million prior to the sale. This sale represents the satisfaction of performance obligation, in accordance with IFRS 15 Revenue from Contracts with Customers.

Mosaic enters into a contract with Ceramic for the right to use the asset for the next five years. Annual payments of $500,000 are due at the end of each year. The interest rate implicit in the lease is 10%. The present value of the annual lease payments is £1.9 million.

Required:

Explain how the transaction will be accounted for on 1 January 20X1 by both Mosaic and Ceramic.

Solution

The excess sales proceeds are $0.2 million ($3m – $2.8m). These are treated as additional financing.

The present value of the lease payments was $1.9 million. It is assumed that $0.2 million relates to the additional financing that Mosaic has been given. The remaining $1.7 million relates to the lease.

Mosaic

Mosaic must remove the carrying amount of the machine from its statement of financial position. It should instead recognise a right-of-use asset. This right-of-use asset will be measured as the proportion of the previous carrying amount that relates to the rights retained by Mosaic:

(1.7m/2.8m) × $1.2 million = $0.73 million.

The entry required is as follows:

Dr Cash	$3.00m
Dr Right-of-use asset	$0.73m
Cr Machine	$1.20m
Cr Lease liability	$1.70m
Cr Financial liability	$0.20m
Cr Profit or loss (bal. fig.)	$0.63m

Note: The gain in profit or loss is the proportion of the overall $1.6 million gain on disposal ($2.8m – $1.2m) that relates to the rights transferred to Ceramic. This can be calculated as follows:

((2.8m – 1.7m)/2.8m) × $1.6 million = $0.63 million.

The right of use asset and the lease liability will then be accounted for using normal lessee accounting rules. The financial liability is accounted for in accordance with IFRS 9 Financial Instruments.

Ceramic

Ceramic will post the following:

Dr Machine	$2.80m
Dr Financial asset	$0.20m
Cr Cash	$3.00m

It will then account for the lease using normal lessor accounting rules.

Note

The payments/receipts will be allocated between the lease and the additional finance. This is based on the proportion of the total present value of the payments that they represent:

- The payment/receipt allocated to the lease will be $447,368 ((1.7/1.9) × $500,000).
- The payment/receipt allocated to the additional finance will be $52,632 ((0.2/1.9) × $500,000).

6 Other issues

Current issue: IFRS 16 Leases vs IAS 17 Leases

IFRS 16 Leases replaced IAS 17 Leases. The most important difference between the two standards relates to lessee accounting.

When entering into leasing arrangements, IAS 17 required lessees to decide if the lease was a finance lease or an operating lease.

If the lease was a finance lease then the lessee recognised the asset and a lease liability on its statement of financial position because, in substance, the lessee controlled the asset. If the lease was an operating lease then no asset or liability was recognised because, in substance, the lessee did not control the asset.

This approach was heavily criticised, most notably for its treatment of lease liabilities. Signing an operating lease agreement gave rise to a contractual obligation to make lease payments, yet no liability was recognised in the statement of financial position. This 'off balance sheet' financing was seen to lack transparency as it caused users of an entity's financial statements to underestimate its gearing levels. Although operating lease commitments were disclosed in the notes to the financial statements, these disclosures lacked prominence.

The treatment of operating leases in the financial statements of lessees also caused comparability issues. Users could not easily compare entities that leased assets under operating leases with those that purchased them, thus hindering investment decisions. Moreover, the same leasing arrangement might be accounted for very differently by two entities depending upon their perception and interpretation of the relevant risks and rewards criteria.

As you have learned in this chapter, IFRS 16 addressed criticisms of lessee accounting by requiring entities to recognise an asset and a liability for all leases (unless they are short-term or of minimal value). IFRS 16 did not change lessor accounting requirements, because the cost involved was deemed to outweigh the benefits.

7 Chapter summary

IDENTIFYING A LEASE
A contract that conveys the right to control the use of an identified asset for a period of time in exchange for consideration.

LESSEE ACCOUNTING
Recognise a lease liability and a right-of-use asset (unless the lease is short-term or of low value)

LESSOR ACCOUNTING
Classify the lease as a finance lease or an operating lease

SALE AND LEASEBACK
Determine whether the transfer qualifies as a 'sale'

Test your understanding answers

Test your understanding 1 – Coffee Bean

The contract does not contain a lease because there is no identified asset.

The contract is for space in the airport, and the airport operator has the practical right to substitute this during the period of use because:

- There are many areas available in the airport that would meet the contract terms, providing the operator with a practical ability to substitute
- The airport operator would benefit economically from substituting the space because there would be minimal cost associated with it. This would allow the operator to make the most effective use of its available space, thus maximising profits.

Test your understanding 2 – AFG

AFG has the right to use an identified asset (a specific ship) for a period of time (five years). Splash cannot substitute the specified ship for an alternative.

AFG has the right to control the use of the ship throughout the five-year period of use because:

- it has the right to obtain substantially all of the economic benefits from use of the ship over the five-year period due to its exclusive use of the ship throughout the period of use.
- it has the right to direct the use of the ship. Although contractual terms exist that limit where the ship can sail and what cargo can be transported, this acts to define the scope of AFG's right to use the ship rather than restricting AFG's ability to direct the use of the ship. Within the scope of its right of use, AFG makes the relevant decisions about how and for what purpose the ship is used throughout the five-year period of use because it decides whether, where and when the ship sails, as well as the cargo it will transport.

Splash's operation and maintenance of the ship does not prevent AFG from directing how, and for what purpose, the ship is used.

Therefore, based on the above, the contract contains a lease.

Test your understanding 3 – Dynamic

The lease term is three years. This is because the option to extend the lease is reasonably certain to be exercised.

The lease liability calculated as follows:

Date	Cash flow ($)	Discount rate	Present value ($)
31/12/X1	10,000	1/1.05	9,524
31/12/X2	10,000	$1/1.05^2$	9,070
31/12/X3	15,000	$1/1.05^3$	12,958
			31,552

The initial cost of the right-of-use asset is calculated as follows:

	$
Initial liability value	31,552
Direct costs	3,000
Reimbursement	(1,000)
	33,552

The double entries to record this are as follows:

Dr Right-of-use asset	$31,552
Cr Lease liability	$31,552

Dr Right-of-use asset	$3,000
Cr Cash	$3,000

Dr Cash	$1,000
Cr Right-of-use asset	$1,000

Test your understanding 4 – Dynamic (cont.)

Interest of $1,578 (W1) is charged on the lease liability.

Dr Finance costs (P/L)	$1,578
Cr Lease liability	$1,578

The cash payment reduces the liability.

Dr Liability	$10,000
Cr Cash	$10,000

The liability has a carrying amount of $23,130 at the reporting date. Of this, $14,287 (W1) is non-current and $8,843 ($23,130 – $14,287) is current.

The right-of-use asset is depreciated over the three year lease term, because it is shorter than the useful economic life. This gives a charge of $11,184 ($33,552/3 years).

Dr Depreciation (P/L)	$11,184
Cr Right-of-use asset	$11,184

The carrying amount of the right-of-use asset will be reduced to $22,368 ($33,552 – $11,184).

(W1) **Lease liability table**

Year-ended	Opening	Interest (5%)	Payments	Closing
	$	$	$	$
31/12/X1	31,552	1,578	(10,000)	23,130
31/12/X2	23,130	1,157	(10,000)	14,287

Test your understanding 5 – Kingfisher

The first year

The first payment occurs on the commencement date so is included in the initial cost of the right-of-use asset:

Dr Right-of-use asset	$1m
Cr Cash	$1m

The liability should be measured at the present value of the lease payments not yet made. The payments are variable as they depend on an index. They should be valued using the index at the commencement date (i.e. it is assumed that the index will remain at 125 and so the payments will remain at $1 million a year).

Date	Cash flow ($m)	Discount rate	Present value ($m)
1/1/X2	1.0	1/1.05	0.95
1/1/X3	1.0	$1/1.05^2$	0.91
1/1/X4	1.0	$1/1.05^3$	0.86
			2.72

Dr Right-of-use asset	$2.72m
Cr Lease liability	$2.72m

The asset is depreciated over the lease term of four years, giving a charge of $0.93 million (($1m + $2.72m)/4).

Dr Depreciation (P/L)	$0.93m
Cr Right-of-use asset	$0.93m

The asset has a carrying amount at the reporting date of $2.79 million ($1m + $2.72m – $0.93m).

The interest charge on the liability is $0.14 million (W1).

Dr Finance costs (P/L)	$0.14m
Cr Lease liability	$0.14m

The liability has a carrying amount at the reporting date of $2.86m (W1).

(W1) **Lease liability table**

Year-ended	**Opening**	**Interest (5%)**	**Closing**
	$m	$m	$m
31/12/X1	2.72	0.14	2.86

The first day of the second year

There are three remaining payments to make. The payment for the second year that is now due is \$1.12 million (\$1m × 140/125). The lease liability is remeasured to reflect the revised lease payments (three payments of \$1.12 million).

Date	Cash flow (\$m)	Discount rate	Present value (\$m)
1/1/X2	1.12	1	1.12
1/1/X3	1.12	1/1.05	1.07
1/1/X4	1.12	$1/1.05^2$	1.02
			3.21

The lease liability must be increased by \$0.35 million (\$3.21 – \$2.86m). A corresponding adjustment is made to the right-of-use asset:

Dr Right-of-use asset	\$0.35m
Cr Lease liability	\$0.35m

The payment of \$1.12 million will then reduce the lease liability:

Dr Lease liability	\$1.12m
Cr Cash	\$1.12m

The right-of-use asset's carrying amount of \$3.14 million (\$2.79 + \$0.35m) will be depreciated over the remaining lease term of three years.

Test your understanding 6 – DanBob

A finance lease is defined by IFRS 16 as a lease where the risks and rewards of ownership transfer from the lessor to the lessee.

Key indications, according to IFRS 16, that a lease is a finance lease are as follows:

- The lease transfers ownership of the asset to the lessee by the end of the lease term.
- The lease term is for the major part of the asset's economic life.
- At the inception of the lease, the present value of the lease payments amounts to at least substantially all of the fair value of the leased asset.
- If the lessee can cancel the lease, the lessor's losses are borne by the lessee.
- The lessee can continue the lease for a secondary period in exchange for substantially lower than market rent payments.

The lease term is only for 60% (30 years/50 years) of the asset's useful life. Legal title also does not pass at the end of the lease. These factors suggest that the lease is an operating lease.

However, the lessee can continue to lease the asset at the end of the lease term for a value that is substantially below market value. This suggests that the lessee will benefit from the building over its useful life and is therefore an indication of a finance lease.

The lessee is also unable to cancel the lease without paying DanBob. This is an indication that DanBob is guaranteed to recoup its investment and therefore that they have relinquished the risks of ownership.

It also seems likely that the present value of the minimum lease payments will be substantially all of the asset's fair value. The minimum lease payments (ignoring discounting) equate to 40% of the fair value, payable upfront, and then another 180% (30 years × 6%) of the fair value over the lease term. Therefore this again suggests that the lease is a finance lease.

All things considered, it would appear that the lease is a finance lease.

Test your understanding 7 – Vache

Vache recognises the net investment in the lease as a receivable. This is the present value of the lease payments of $5,710.

The receivable is increased by finance income. The receivable is reduced by the cash receipts.

Year	Opening balance	Finance income (15%)	Cash received	Closing balance
	$	$	$	$
1	5,710	856	(2,000)	4,566
2	4,566	685	(2,000)	3,251
3	3,251	488	(2,000)	1,739
4	1,739	261	(2,000)	–

Extract from the statement of financial position at the end of Year 1

	$
Non-current assets:	
Net investment in finance leases (see note)	3,251
Current assets:	
Net investment in finance leases	1,315

Note: the current asset is the next instalment less next year's interest ($2,000 – $685). The non-current asset is the remainder ($4,566 – $1,315).

Test your understanding 8 – Oroc

Oroc holds the crane in its statement of financial position and depreciates it over its useful life. The annual depreciation charge is $35,200 ($880,000/25 years).

Rental income must be recognised in profit or loss on a straight line basis. Total lease receipts are $595,000 ($175,000 + ($70,000 × 6 years)). Annual rental income is therefore $85,000 ($595,000/7 years). The statement of financial position includes a liability for deferred income of $90,000 ($175,000 – $85,000).

Test your understanding 9 – Painting

Painting

Painting must remove the carrying amount of the machine from its statement of financial position. It should instead recognise a right-of-use asset. This right-of-use asset will be measured as the proportion of the previous carrying amount that relates to the rights retained by Painting:

(1.9m/3m) × $1.2 million = $0.76 million.

The entry required is as follows:

Dr Cash	$3.00m
Dr Right-of-use asset	$0.76m
Cr Machine	$1.20m
Cr Lease liability	$1.90m
Cr Profit or loss (bal. fig.)	$0.66m

Note: The gain in profit or loss is the proportion of the overall $1.8 million gain on disposal ($3m – $1.2m) that relates to the rights transferred to Collage. This can be calculated as follows:

((3m – 1.9m)/3m) × $1.8m = $0.66 million.

The right of use asset and the lease liability will then be accounted for using normal lessee accounting rules.

Collage

Collage will post the following:

Dr Machine	$3.00m
Cr Cash	$3.00m

Normal lessor accounting rules apply. The lease is an operating lease because the present value of the lease payments is not substantially the same as the asset's fair value, and the lease term is not for the majority of the asset's useful life. Collage will record rental income in profit or loss on a straight line basis.

chapter

8

Employee benefits

Chapter learning objectives

Upon completion of this chapter you will be able to:

- apply and discuss the accounting treatment of short term and long term employee benefits and defined contribution and defined benefit plans
- account for gains and losses on settlements and curtailments
- account for the 'asset ceiling' test and the reporting of remeasurement gains and losses.

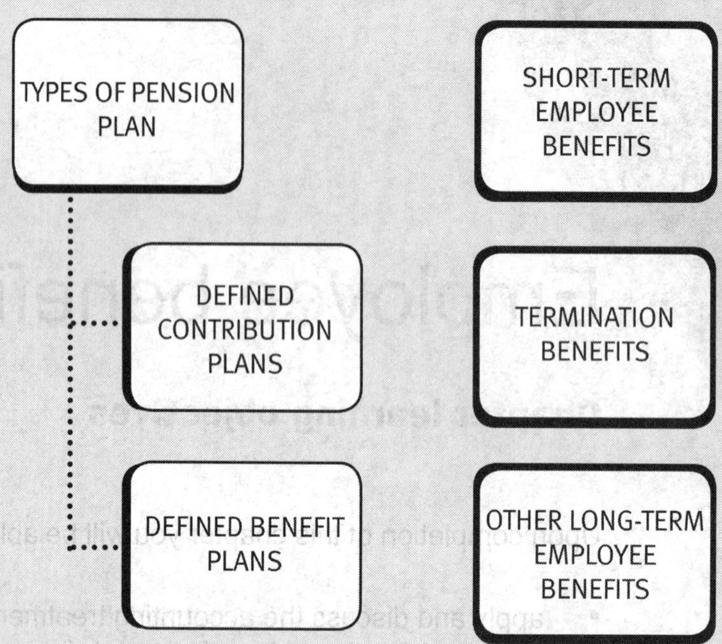

1 Introduction

Types of employee benefit

IAS 19 identifies four types of employee benefit as follows:

- **Post-employment benefits**. This normally relates to retirement benefits.
- **Short-term employee benefits**. This includes wages and salaries, bonuses and other benefits.
- **Termination benefits**. Termination benefits arise when benefits become payable upon employment being terminated, either by the employer or by the employee accepting terms to have employment terminated.
- **Other long-term employee benefits**. This comprises other items not within the above classifications and will include long-service leave or awards, long-term disability benefits and other long-service benefits.

Each will be considered within this chapter, with particular emphasis upon post-employment defined benefit plans.

2 Post-employment benefit plans

A pension plan (sometimes called a post-employment benefit plan or scheme) consists of a pool of assets, together with a liability for pensions owed. Pension plan assets normally consist of investments, cash and (sometimes) properties. The return earned on the assets is used to pay pensions.

There are two main types of pension plan:

- defined contribution plans
- defined benefit plans.

This distinction is important because the accounting treatment of the two types of pension plan is very different.

Defined contribution plans are benefit plans where the entity **'pays fixed contributions into a separate entity and will have no legal or constructive obligation to pay further contributions if the fund does not hold sufficient assets to pay all employee benefits relating to their service'** (IAS 19, para 8).

Defined benefit plans are post-employment plans that are not defined contribution plans.

A defined contribution plan

An entity pays fixed contributions of 5% of employee salaries into a pension plan each month. The entity has no obligation outside of its fixed contributions.

The lack of any obligation to contribute further assets into the fund means that this is a defined contribution plan.

A defined benefit plan

An entity guarantees a particular level of pension benefit to its employees upon retirement. The annual pension income that employees will receive is based on the following formula:

Salary at retirement × (no. of years worked/60 years)

The entity has an obligation to pay extra funds into the pension plan to meet this promised level of pension benefits. This is therefore a defined benefit plan.

Test you understanding 1 – Deller

Deller has a defined contribution pension scheme. However, during the year, it introduced a new post-employment plan (the Fund) for its employees as a way of enhancing the benefits they will receive when they retire. Deller makes monthly contributions into the Fund that are equal to a set percentage of the salary cost.

Upon retirement, employees will receive annual payments from the Fund based on their number of years of service and their final salary.

The Fund is voluntary and Deller can cancel it at any point.

Deller has a history of paying employees benefits that are substantially above the national average, with annual increases in excess of inflation. Deller has won many accolades as a 'top employer' and received positive coverage from the national press when the Fund was announced. The leadership team are well trusted by the employees.

Required:

Advise Deller on whether the Fund is a defined benefit plan or a defined contribution plan.

3 Accounting for defined contribution plans

The entity should charge the agreed pension contribution to profit or loss as an employment expense in each period.

The expense of providing pensions in the period is often the same as the amount of contributions paid. However, an accrual or prepayment arises if the cash paid does not equal the value of contributions due for the period.

Test your understanding 2 – Defined contribution scheme

An entity makes contributions to the pension fund of employees at a rate of 5% of gross salaries. For convenience, the entity pays $10,000 per month into the pension scheme with any balance being paid in the first month of the following accounting year. The wages and salaries for 20X6 are $2.7 million.

Required:

Calculate the pension expense for 20X6, and the accrual/ prepayment at the end of the year.

4 Accounting for defined benefit plans

The statement of financial position

Under a defined benefit plan, an entity has an obligation to its employees. The entity therefore has a long-term liability that must be measured at present value.

The entity will also be making regular contributions into the pension plan. These contributions will be invested and the investments will generate returns. This means that the entity has assets held within the pension plan, which IAS 19 states must be measured at fair value.

On the statement of financial position, an entity offsets its pension obligation and its plan assets and reports the net position:

- If the obligation exceeds the assets, there is a plan deficit (the usual situation) and a liability is reported in the statement of financial position.
- If the assets exceed the obligation, there is a surplus and an asset is reported in the statement of financial position.

It is difficult to calculate the size of the defined benefit pension obligation and plan assets. It is therefore recommended that entities use an expert known as an actuary.

Measuring the plan assets and liabilities

In practice, an actuary measures the plan assets and liabilities by applying carefully developed estimates and assumptions relevant to the defined benefit pension plan.

- The plan liability is measured at the present value of the defined benefit obligation, using the Projected Unit Credit Method. This is an actuarial valuation method.
- Discounting is necessary because the liability will be settled many years in the future and, therefore, the effect of the time value of money is material. The discount rate used should be determined by market yields on high quality corporate bonds at the start of the reporting period, and applied to the net liability or asset at the start of the reporting period.
- Plan assets are measured at fair value. IFRS 13 Fair Value Measurement provides a framework for determining how fair value should be established.

- IAS 19 does not prescribe a maximum time interval between valuations. However, valuations should be carried out with sufficient regularity to ensure that the amounts recognised in the financial statements do not differ materially from actual fair values at the reporting date.
- Where there are unpaid contributions at the reporting date, these are not included in the plan assets. Unpaid contributions are treated as a liability owed by the entity/employer to the plan.

The year-on-year movement

An entity must account for the year-on-year movement in its defined benefit pension scheme deficit (or surplus).

The following proforma shows the movement on the defined benefit deficit (surplus) over a reporting period:

	$000
Net deficit/(asset) brought forward (Obligation bfd – assets bfd)	X/(X)
Net interest component	X/(X)
Service cost component	X
Contributions into plan	(X)
Benefits paid	–
	X/(X)
Remeasurement component (bal. fig)	X/(X)
Net deficit/(asset) carried forward (Obligation cfd – assets cfd)	X/(X)

The net interest component: this is charged (or credited) to profit or loss and represents the change in the net pension liability (or asset) due to the passage in time. It is computed by applying the discount rate at the start of the year to the net defined benefit liability (or asset).

The service cost component: this is charged to profit or loss and is comprised of three elements:

- **'Current service cost, which is the increase in the present value of the obligation arising from employee service in the current period. period.**
- **Past service cost, which is the change in the present value of the obligation for employee service in prior periods, resulting from a plan amendment or curtailment**

- **Any gain or loss on settlement'** (IAS 19, para 8).

Contributions into the plan: these are the cash payments paid into the plan during the reporting period by the employer. This has no impact on the statement of profit or loss and other comprehensive income.

Benefits paid: these are the amounts paid out of the plan assets to retired employees during the period. These payments reduce both the plan obligation and the plan assets. Therefore, this has no overall impact on the net pension deficit (or asset).

After accounting for the above, the net pension deficit will differ from the amount calculated by the actuary as at the current year end. This is for a number of reasons, that include the following:

- The actuary's calculation of the value of the plan obligation and assets is based on assumptions, such as life expectancy and final salaries, and these will have changed year-on-year.
- The actual return on plan assets is different from the amount taken to profit or loss as part of the net interest component.

An adjustment, known as the **remeasurement component**, must therefore be posted. This is charged or credited to other comprehensive income for the year and identified as an item that will not be reclassified to profit or loss in future periods.

Explanation of terms

A **past service cost** is the **'change in the present value of the defined benefit obligation for employee service in prior periods, resulting from a plan amendment or a curtailment'** (IAS 19, para 8).

- Past service costs could arise when there has been an improvement in the benefits to be provided under the plan. This will apply whether or not the benefits have vested (i.e. whether or not employees are immediately entitled to those enhanced benefits), or whether they are obliged to provide additional work and service to become eligible for those enhanced benefits.
- Past service costs are included within the service cost component for the year.
- Past service costs are recognised at the earlier of:
  - **'when the plan amendment or curtailment occurs**
  - **when the entity recognises related restructuring costs or termination benefit'** (IAS 19, para 103).

A curtailment is a significant reduction in the number of employees covered by a pension plan. This may be a consequence of an individual event such as plant closure or discontinuance of an operation, which will typically result in employees being made redundant.

A settlement occurs when an entity enters into a transaction to eliminate the obligation for part or all of the benefits under a plan. For example, an employee may leave the entity for a new job elsewhere, and a payment is made from that pension plan to the pension plan operated by the new employer.

- The gain or loss on settlement comprises the difference between the fair value of the plan assets paid out and the reduction in the present value of the defined benefit obligation and is included as part of the service cost component.
- The gain or loss on settlement is recognised on the date when the entity eliminates the obligation for all or part of the benefits provided under the defined benefit plan.

Separate disclosure of the plan assets and obligation

For the purposes of the P2 exam it will be quicker to account for the net pension obligation, as outlined in the section above.

However, in a set of published financial statements that are prepared in accordance with IFRS Standards, an entity should disclose separate reconciliations for the defined benefit obligation and the plan assets, showing the movement between the opening and closing balances. These would appear as follows:

	Obligation	**Assets**
	$000	$000
Brought forward	X	X
Interest on obligation	X	
Interest on plan assets		X
Service cost component	X	
Contributions into plan		X
Benefits paid	(X)	(X)
	X	X
Remeasurement component (bal. fig)	X/(X)	X/(X)
Carried forward	X	X

Summary of the amounts recognised in the financial statements

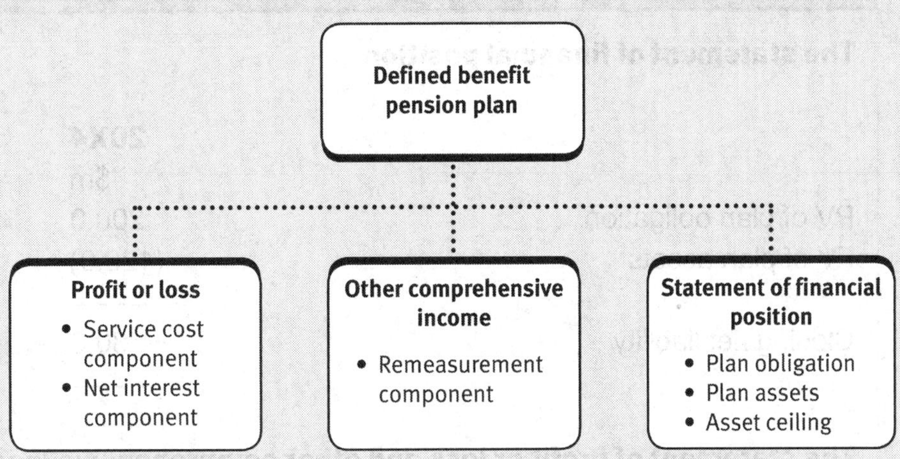

Illustration 1 – Defined benefit plan – Celine

The following information is provided in relation to a defined benefit plan operated by Celine. At 1 January 20X4, the present value of the obligation was $140 million and the fair value of the plan assets amounted to $80 million.

	20X4	20X5
Discount rate at start of year	4%	3%
Current and past service cost ($m)	30	32
Benefits paid ($m)	20	22
Contributions into plan ($m)	25	30
Present value of obligation at 31 December ($m)	200	230
Fair value of plan assets at 31 December ($m)	120	140

Required:

Determine the net plan obligation or asset at 31 December 20X4 and 20X5 and the amounts to be taken to profit or loss and other comprehensive income for both financial years.

Solution

The statement of financial position

	20X4	20X5
	$m	$m
PV of plan obligation	200.0	230.0
FV of plan assets	(120.0)	(140.0)
Closing net liability	80.0	90.0

The statement of profit or loss and other comprehensive income

Both the service cost component and the net interest component are charged to profit or loss for the year. The remeasurement component, which comprises actuarial gains and losses, together with returns on plan assets to the extent that they are not included within the net interest component, is taken to other comprehensive income.

	20X4	20X5
Profit or loss	$m	$m
Service cost component	30.0	32.0
Net interest component	2.4	2.4
	32.4	34.4
Other comprehensive income		
Remeasurement component	12.6	5.6
Total comprehensive income charge for year	45.0	40.0

Reconciliation of the net obligation for 20X4 and 20X5

	20X4	20X5
	$m	$m
Obligation bal b/fwd 1 January	140.0	200.0
Asset bal b/fwd at 1 January	(80.0)	(120.0)
Net obligation b/fwd at 1 January	60.0	80.0
Service cost component	30.0	32.0
Net interest component		
4% × $60m	2.4	
3% × $80m		2.4
Contributions into plan	(25.0)	(30.0)
Benefits paid	–	–
Remeasurement component (bal. fig.)	12.6	5.6
Net obligation c/fwd at 31 December	80.0	90.0

Illustration – Accounting for past service costs

An entity operates a pension plan that provides a pension of 2% of final salary for each year of service. On 1 January 20X5, the entity improves the pension to 2.5% of final salary for each year of service, including service before this date. Employees must have worked for the entity for at least five years in order to obtain this increased benefit. At the date of the improvement, the present value of the additional benefits for service from 1 January 20X1 to 1 January 20X5, is as follows:

	$000
Employees with more than five years' service at 1.1.X5	150
Employees with less than five years' service at 1.1.X5 (average length of service: two years)	120
	270

Required:

Explain how the additional benefits are accounted for in the financial statements of the entity.

Solution

The entity recognises all $270,000 immediately as an increase in the defined benefit obligation following the amendment to the plan on 1 January 20X5. This will form part of the service cost component. Whether or not the benefits have vested by the reporting date is not relevant to their recognition as an expense in the financial statements.

Illustration – Curtailments

AB decides to close a business segment. The segment's employees will be made redundant and will earn no further pension benefits after being made redundant. Their plan assets will remain in the scheme so that the employees will be paid a pension when they reach retirement age (i.e. this is a curtailment without settlement).

Before the curtailment, the scheme assets had a fair value of $500,000, and the defined benefit obligation had a present value of $600,000. It is estimated that the curtailment will reduce the present value of the future obligation by 10%, which reflects the fact that employees will not benefit from future salary increases and therefore will be entitled to a smaller pension than previously estimated.

Required:

What is net gain or loss on curtailment and how will this be treated in the financial statements?

Solution

The obligation is to be reduced by 10% × $600,000 = $60,000, with no change in the fair value of the assets as they remain in the plan. The reduction in the obligation represents a gain on curtailment which should be included as part of the service cost component and taken to profit or loss for the year. The net position of the plan following curtailment will be:

	Before	**On curtailment**	**After**
	$000	$000	$000
Present value of obligation	600	(60)	540
Fair value of plan assets	(500)	–	(500)
Net obligation in SOFP	100	(60)	40

The gain on curtailment is $60,000 and this will be included as part of the service cost component in profit or loss for the year.

Test your understanding 3 – Fraser

The following information relates to a defined benefit plan operated by Fraser. At 1 January 20X1, the present value of the obligation was $1,000,000 and the fair value of the plan assets amounted to $900,000.

	20X1	**20X2**	**20X3**
Discount rate at start of year	10%	9%	8%
Current and past service cost ($000)	125	130	138
Benefits paid ($000)	150	155	165
Contributions paid into plan ($000)	90	95	105
PV of obligation at 31 December ($000)	1,350	1,340	1,450
FV of plan assets at 31 December ($000)	1,200	1,150	1,300

Required:

Show how the defined benefit plan would be shown in the financial statements for each of the years ended 31 December 20X1, 20X2 and 20X3 respectively.

Test your understanding 4 – TC

TC has a defined benefit pension plan and prepares financial statements to 31 March each year. The following information is relevant for the year ended 31 March 20X3:

- The net pension obligation at 31 March 20X3 was $55 million. At 31 March 20X2, the net obligation was $48 million, comprising the present value of the plan obligation stated at $100 million, together with plan assets stated at fair value of $52 million.
- The discount rate relevant to the net obligation was 6.25% and the actual return on plan assets for the year was $4 million.
- The current service cost was $12 million.
- At 31 March 20X3, TC granted additional benefits to those currently receiving benefits that are due to vest over the next four years and which have a present value of $4 million at that date. They were not allowed for in the original actuarial assumptions.
- During the year, TC made pension contributions of $8 million into the scheme and the scheme paid pension benefits in the year amounting to $3 million.

Required:

Explain the accounting treatment of the TC pension scheme for the year to 31 March 20X3, together with supporting calculations.

Test your understanding 5 – Mickleover

On 1 July 20X3 Mickleover started a defined benefit pension scheme for its employees and immediately contributed $4m cash into the scheme. The actuary has stated that the net obligation was $0.4m as at 30 June 20X4. The interest rate for good quality corporate bonds was 10% at 1 July 20X3 but 12% by 30 June 20X4. The actual return on the plan assets was 11%. The increased cost from the employee's service in the year was $4.2m which can be assumed to accrue at the year end.

On 30 June 20X4 Mickleover paid $0.3m in settlement of a defined benefit obligation with a present value of $0.2m. This related to staff that were to be made redundant although, as at 30 June 20X4, they still had an average remaining employment term of one month. The redundancies were not foreseen at the start of the year.

Required:

Discuss the correct accounting treatment of the above transaction in the financial statements of Mickleover for the year ended 30 June 20X4.

5 The asset ceiling

Most defined benefit pension plans are in deficit (i.e. the obligation exceeds the plan assets). However, some defined benefit pension plans do show a surplus.

If a defined benefit plan is in surplus, IAS 19 states that the surplus must be measured at the lower of:

- the amount calculated as normal (per earlier examples and illustrations)
- the total of the present value of any economic benefits available in the form of refunds from the plan or reductions in future contributions to the plan.

This is known as applying the 'asset ceiling'. It means that a surplus can only be recognised to the extent that it will be recoverable in the form of refunds or reduced contributions in the future. In other words, it ensures that the surplus recognised in the financial statements meets the definition of an 'asset' (a resource controlled by the entity that will lead to a probable inflow of economic benefits).

Illustration 2 – The asset ceiling

The following information relates to a defined benefit plan:	$000
Fair value of plan assets	950
Present value of pension liability	800
Present value of future refunds and reductions in future contributions	70

Required:

What is the value of the asset that recognised in the financial statements?

Solution

The amount that can be recognised is the lower of:

	$000
Present value of plan obligation	800
Fair value of plan assets	(950)
	(150)

	$000
PV of future refunds and/or reductions in future contributions	(70)

Therefore the asset that can be recognised is restricted to $70,000.

Test your understanding 6 – Arc

The following information relates to the defined benefit plan operated by Arc for the year ended 30 June 20X4:

	$m
FV of plan assets b/fwd at 30 June 20X3	2,600
PV of obligation b/fwd at 30 June 20X3	2,000
Current service cost for the year	100
Benefits paid in the year	80
Contributions into plan	90
FV of plan assets at 30 June 20X4	3,100
PV of plan obligation at 30 June 20X4	2,400

Discount rate for the defined benefit obligation – 10%

Arc has identified that the asset ceiling at 30 June 20X3 and 30 June 20X4, based upon the present value of future refunds from the plan and/or reductions in future contributions amounts to $200m at 30 June 20X3 and 30 June 20X4.

Required:

Explain, with supporting calculations, the accounting treatment of the pension scheme for the year ended 30 June 20X4.

6 Other issues

Disclosure requirements

IAS 19 has extensive disclosure requirements. An entity should disclose the following information about defined benefit plans:

- explanation of the regulatory framework within which the plan operates, together with explanation of the nature of benefits provided by the plan
- explanation of the nature of the risks the entity is exposed to as a consequence of operating the plan, together with explanation of any plan amendments, settlements or curtailments in the year
- the entity's accounting policy for recognising actuarial gains and losses, together with disclosure of the significant actuarial assumptions used to determine the net defined benefit obligation or assets. Although there is no longer a choice of accounting policy for actuarial gains and losses, it may still be helpful to users to explain how they have been accounted for within the financial statements.

- a general description of the type of plan operated
- a reconciliation of the assets and liabilities recognised in the statement of financial position
- a reconciliation showing the movements during the period in the net liability (or asset) recognised in the statement of financial position
- the charge to total comprehensive income for the year, separated into the appropriate components
- analysis of the remeasurement component to identify returns on plan assets, together with actuarial gains and losses arising on the net plan obligation
- sensitivity analysis and narrative description of how the defined benefit plan may affect the nature, timing and uncertainty of the entity's future cash flows.

Other employee benefits

IAS 19 covers a number of other issues in addition to post-employment benefits as follows:

Short-term employee benefits – This includes a number of issues including:

- **Wages and salaries and bonuses and other benefits.** The general principle is that wages and salaries costs are expenses as they are incurred on a normal accruals basis, unless capitalisation is permitted in accordance with another reporting standard, such as IAS 16 or IAS 38. Bonuses and other short-term payments are recognised using normal criteria of establishing an obligation based upon past events which can be reliably measured.
- **Compensated absences.** This covers issues such as holiday pay, sick leave, maternity leave, jury service, study leave and military service. The key issue is whether the absences are regarded as being accumulating or non-accumulating:
  - accumulating benefits are earned over time and are capable of being carried forward. In this situation, the expense for future compensated absences is recognised over the period services are provided by the employee. This will typically result in the recognition of a liability at the reporting date for the expected cost of the accumulated benefit earned but not yet claimed by an employee. An example of this would be a holiday pay accrual at the reporting date where unused holiday entitlement can be carried forward and claimed in a future period.

- for non-accumulating benefits, an expense should only be recognised when the absence occurs. This may arise, for example, where an employee continues to receive their normal remuneration whilst being absent due to illness or other permitted reason. A charge to profit or loss would be made only when the authorised absence occurs; if there is no such absence, there will be no charge to profit or loss.

- **Benefits in kind.** Recognition of cost should be based on the same principles as benefits payable in cash; it should be measured based upon the cost to the employer of providing the benefit and recognised as it is earned.

Termination benefits

Termination benefits may be defined as benefits payable as a result of employment being terminated, either by the employer, or by the employee accepting voluntary redundancy. Such payments are normally in the form of a lump sum; entitlement to such payments is not accrued over time, and only become available in a relatively short period prior to any such payment being agreed and paid to the employee.

The obligation to pay such benefits is recognised either when the employer can no longer withdraw the offer of such benefits (i.e. they are committed to paying them), or when it recognises related restructuring costs (normally in accordance with IAS 37). Payments which are due to be paid more than twelve months after the reporting date should be discounted to their present value.

Other long-term employee benefits

This comprises other items not within the above classifications and will include long-service leave, long-term disability benefits and other long-service benefits. These employee benefits are accounted for in a similar manner to accounting for post-employment benefits, typically using the projected unit credit method, as benefits are payable more than twelve months after the period in which services are provided by an employee.

Criticisms of IAS 19

Retirement benefit accounting continues to be a controversial area. Commentators have perceived the following problems with the IAS 19 approach:

- The fair values of plan assets may be volatile or difficult to measure reliably. This could lead to significant fluctuations in the statement of financial position.
- IAS 19 requires plan assets to be valued at fair value. Fair values of plan assets are not relevant to the economic reality of most pension schemes. Under the requirements of IAS 19, assets are valued at short-term amounts, but most pension scheme assets and liabilities are held for the long term. The actuarial basis of valuing plan assets would better reflect the long-term costs of funding a pension scheme. However, such a move would be a departure from IFRS 13 Fair Value Measurement which seeks to standardise the application of fair value measurement when it is required by a particular reporting standard.
- The treatment of pension costs in the statement of profit or loss and other comprehensive income is complex and may not be easily understood by users of the financial statements. It has been argued that all the components of the pension cost are so interrelated that it does not make sense to present them separately.

7 Chapter summary

Post-employment benefit plans

Defined contribution plans
- Normal accruals accounting

Defined benefit plans
- SOFP
  - Plan obligation at PV
  - Plan assets at FV
  - Asset ceiling
- Profit or loss
  - Service cost component
  - Current and past service cost
  - Curtailments and settlements
  - Net interest component
- Other comprehensive income
  - Remeasurement component

Other long-term employee benefits
- Account for in similar way to defined benefit pension plans – spread cost over service period

Short-term employee benefits
- Normal accruals accounting
- Cumulating or non-cumulating

Termination benefits
- Recognise when an obligation or when related restructuring costs recognised

Test your understanding answers

Test you understanding 1 – Deller

It is possible that there will be insufficient assets in the Fund to pay the benefits due to retired employees, particularly if final salaries or life expectancy rise substantially. Deller therefore bears actuarial and investment risk because, if it continues with the Fund, it would need to make up for any shortfall.

Although the Fund is voluntary and can be cancelled, Deller has a history of remunerating its employees above the national average as well as a strong reputation as a good and honest employer. Deller therefore has a constructive obligation to continue with the Fund and to ensure that its level of assets is sufficient.

As a result of the above, the Fund should be accounted for as a defined benefit plan.

Test your understanding 2 – Defined contribution scheme

This appears to be a defined contribution scheme.

The charge to profit or loss should be:

$2.7m × 5% = $135,000

The statement of financial position will therefore show an accrual of $15,000, being the difference between the $135,000 expense and the $120,000 ($10,000 × 12 months) cash paid in the year.

Test your understanding 3 – Fraser

Statement of financial position

	20X1	20X2	20X3
	$000	$000	$000
Net pension (asset)/liability	150	190	150

Profit or loss and other comprehensive income for the year

	20X1	20X2	20X3
	$000	$000	$000
Profit or loss			
Service cost component	125	130	138
Net interest component	10	14	15
Charge to profit or loss	135	144	153
Other comprehensive income:			
Remeasurement component	5	(9)	(88)
Total charge to comprehensive income	140	135	65

The remeasurement component on the net obligation

	20X1	20X2	20X3
	$000	$000	$000
Net obligation at start of the year	100	150	190
Net interest component (10% X1/9% X2/8% X3)	10	14	15
Service cost component	125	130	138
Contributions into plan	(90)	(95)	(105)
Remeasurement (gain)/loss (bal. fig)	5	(9)	(88)
Net obligation at end of the year	150	190	150

Test your understanding 4 – TC

		$m
Net obligation brought forward		48
Net interest component (6.25% × 48)		3
Service cost component:		
Current service cost	12	
Past service cost	4	
		16
Contributions into the plan		(8)
Benefits paid		–
Remeasurement component (bal fig)		(4)
Net obligation carried forward		55

Explanation:

- The discount rate is applied to the net obligation brought forward. The net interest component is $3m and this is charged to profit or loss.
- The current year service cost, together with the past service cost forms the service cost component. Past service cost is charged in full, usually when the scheme is amended, rather than when the additional benefits vest. The total service cost component is $16m and this is charged to profit or loss.
- To the extent that there has been a return on assets in excess of the amount identified by application of the discount rate to the fair value of plan assets, this is part of the remeasurement component (i.e. $4m – $3.25m ($52m × 6.25%) = $0.75m).
- Contributions paid into the plan during the year of $8m reduce the net obligation.
- Benefits paid of $3 million will reduce both the scheme assets and the scheme obligation, so have no impact on the net obligation.
- The statement of financial position as at 31 March 20X3 will show a net deficit (a liability) of $55m.

Test your understanding 5 – Mickleover

The accounting treatment of a defined benefit plan is as follows:

- the amount recognised in the statement of financial position is the present value of the defined benefit obligation less the fair value of the plan assets as at the reporting date.
- The opening net position should be unwound using a discount rate that applies to good quality corporate bonds. This should be charged/credited to profit or loss.
- The increased cost from the employees' service during the past year is known as a current service cost. This should be expensed against profits as part of the service cost component and credited to the pension scheme obligation.
- Curtailments should be recognised at the earlier of when the curtailment occurs or when the related termination benefits are recognised.
- The remeasurement component should be included in other comprehensive income and identified as an item which will not be reclassified to profit and loss in future periods.

In relation to Mickleover:

- The net liability on the statement of financial position as at 30 June 20X4 is $0.4m.
- Although this is the first year of the scheme cash of $4m was introduced at the start of the year and so this should be unwound at 10%.
- The net interest component credited to profit and loss will therefore be $0.4m (10% × $4m). The service cost arises at the year end and so is not unwound.
- Although the employees have not yet been made redundant, the costs related to the redundancy will have been recognised during the current reporting period. Therefore, a loss on curtailment of $0.1m ($0.3m – $0.2m) should also be recognised in the current year. As the curtailment was not foreseen and would not have been included within the actuarial assumptions, the $0.1m should be charged against profits within the service cost component.
- The remeasurement loss, which includes the difference between the actual returns on plan assets and the amount taken to profit or loss as part of the net interest component, is $0.5m (W1).

(W1) **Remeasurement component**

		$m
Net obligation brought forward		0
Contributions		(4)
Net interest component (10% × $4m)		(0.4)
Service cost component:		
Current service cost	4.2	
Loss on curtailment	0.1	
		4.3
Benefits paid		–
Remeasurement component (bal fig)		**0.5**
Net obligation carried forward		0.4

Test your understanding 6 – Arc

	Net plan asset before ceiling adj	Ceiling adj*	Net plan asset after ceiling adj	Note
	$m	$m	$m	
Balance b/fwd	(600)	400	(200)	1
Net interest component (10%)	(60)	40	(20)	2
Service cost component	100	–	100	3
Benefits paid	–	–	–	4
Contributions in	(90)	–	(90)	5
Sub-total:	(650)	440	(210)	
Remeasurement component:	(50)	60	10	6
Balance c/fwd	(700)	500	(200)	

* note that this is effectively a balancing figure.

Explanation:

(1) The asset ceiling adjustment at the previous reporting date of 30 June 20X3 measures the net defined benefit asset at the amount recoverable by refunds and/or reduced future contributions, stated at $200m. In effect, the value of the asset was reduced for reporting purposes at 30 June 20X3.

(2) Interest charged on the obligation or earned on the plan assets is based upon the discount rate for the obligation, stated at 10%. This will then require adjustment to agree with the net return on the net plan asset at the beginning of the year. Net interest earned is taken to profit or loss for the year.

(3) The current year service cost increases the plan obligation, which therefore reduces the net plan asset. The current year service cost is taken to profit or loss for the year.

(4) Benefits paid in the year reduce both the plan obligation and the plan assets by the same amount.

(5) Contributions into the plan increase the fair value of plan assets, and also the net plan asset during the year.

(6) The remeasurement component, including actuarial gains and losses for the year, is identified to arrive at the present value of the plan obligation and the fair value of the plan assets at 30 June 20X4. As there is a net asset of $700m ($3,100m – $2,400m) for the defined benefit pension plan, the asset ceiling test is applied to restrict the reported asset to the expected future benefits in the form of refunds and/or reduced future contributions. This is stated in the question to be $200m. To the extent that an adjustment is required to the net asset at the reporting date, this is part of the net remeasurement component.

Statement of financial position

	$000
Net pension asset	200

Profit or loss and other comprehensive income for the year

	$000
Profit or loss	
Service cost component	100
Net interest component	(20)
Charge to profit or loss	80
Other comprehensive income:	
Remeasurement component	10
Total charge to comprehensive income	90

chapter

9

Share-based payment

Chapter learning objectives

Upon completion of this chapter you will be able to:

- apply and discuss the recognition and measurement criteria for share-based payment transactions
- account for modifications, cancellations and settlements of share-based payment transactions.

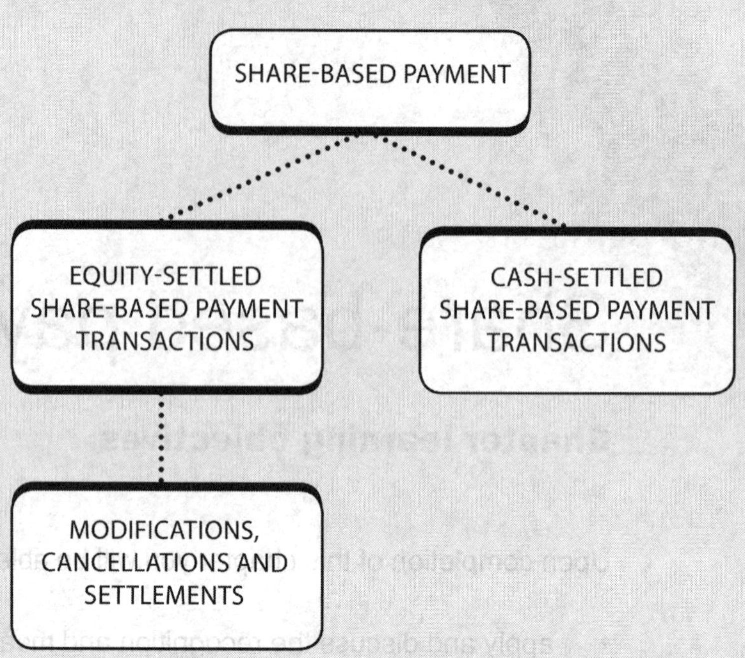

1 Share-based payment

Introduction

Share-based payment has become increasingly common. Share-based payment occurs when an entity buys goods or services from other parties (such as employees or suppliers) and:

- settles the amounts payable by issuing shares or share options, or
- incurs liabilities for cash payments based on its share price.

The problem

If a company pays for goods or services in cash, an expense is recognised in profit or loss. If a company 'pays' for goods or services in share options, there is no cash outflow and therefore, under traditional accounting, no expense would be recognised.

If a company issues shares to employees, a transaction has occurred. The employees have provided a valuable service to the entity, in exchange for the shares/options. It is inconsistent not to recognise this transaction in the financial statements.

IFRS 2 Share-based Payment was issued to deal with this accounting anomaly. IFRS 2 requires that all share-based payment transactions must be recognised in the financial statements when the transaction takes place.

Arguments against recognising share-based payments

There are a number of arguments against recognising share-based payments. IFRS 2 rejects them all.

No cost therefore no charge

A charge for shares or options should not be recognised because the entity does not have to sacrifice cash or other assets. There is no cost to the entity.

This argument ignores the fact that a transaction has occurred. The employees have provided valuable services to the entity in return for valuable shares or options. If this argument were accepted, the financial statements would fail to reflect the economic transactions that had occurred.

Earnings per share would be hit twice

The charge to profit for the employee services consumed reduces the entity's earnings. At the same time there is an increase in the number of shares issued.

However, the double impact on earnings per share simply reflects the two economic events that have occurred: the entity has issued shares, thus increasing the denominator of the EPS calculation, and it has also consumed the resources it received for those shares, thus reducing the numerator. Issuing shares to employees, instead of paying them in cash, requires a greater increase in the entity's earnings in order to maintain its earnings per share. Recognising the transaction ensures that its economic consequences are reported.

Adverse economic consequences

Recognition of employee share-based payment might discourage entities from introducing or continuing employee share plans.

However, accounting for share-based payments avoids the economic distortion created when entities consume resources without having to account for such transactions.

Types of transaction

IFRS 2 applies to all share-based payment transactions. There are two main types.

- **Equity-settled share-based payments:** the entity acquires goods or services in exchange for equity instruments of the entity (e.g. shares or share options)
- **Cash-settled share-based payments:** the entity acquires goods or services in exchange for amounts of cash measured by reference to the entity's share price.

The most common type of share-based payment transaction is where share options are granted to employees or directors as part of their remuneration.

2 Equity-settled share-based payment transactions

Accounting treatment

When an entity receives goods or services as a result of an equity-settled share-based payment transaction, it posts the following double entry:

Dr Expense/asset
Cr Equity

The entry to equity is normally reported in 'other components of equity'. Share capital is not affected until the share-based payment has 'vested' (covered later in the chapter).

Measurement

The basic principle is that all transactions are measured at fair value.

How fair value is determined:

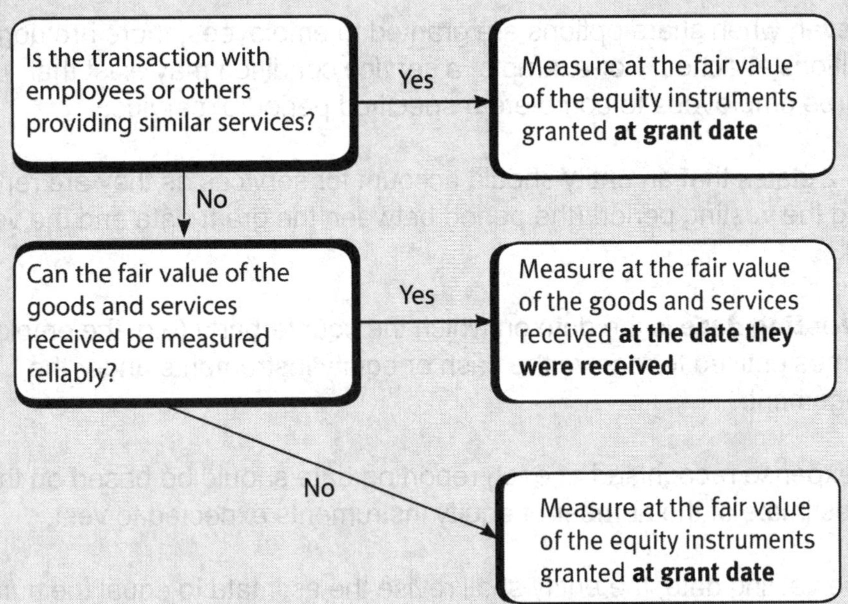

The **grant date** is the date at which the entity and another party agree to the arrangement.

Determining fair value

Where a share-based payment transaction is with parties other than employees, it is assumed that the fair value of the goods and services received can be measured reliably, at their cash price for example.

Where shares or share options are granted to employees as part of their remuneration, it is not usually possible to arrive at a reliable value for the services received in return. For this reason, the entity measures the transaction by reference to the fair value of the equity instruments granted.

The fair value of equity instruments is market value, if this is available. Where no market price is available (for example, if the instruments are unquoted), a valuation technique or model is used.

The fair value of share options is harder to determine. In rare cases there may be publicly quoted traded options with similar terms, whose market value can be used as the fair value of the options we are considering. Otherwise, the fair value of options must be estimated using a recognised option-pricing model. IFRS 2 does not require any specific model to be used. The most commonly used is the Black-Scholes model.

Allocating the expense to reporting periods

Some equity instruments vest immediately. In other words, the holder is unconditionally entitled to the instruments. In this case, the transaction should be accounted for in full on the grant date.

However, when share options are granted to employees, there are normally conditions attached. For example, a service condition may exist that requires employees to complete a specified period of service.

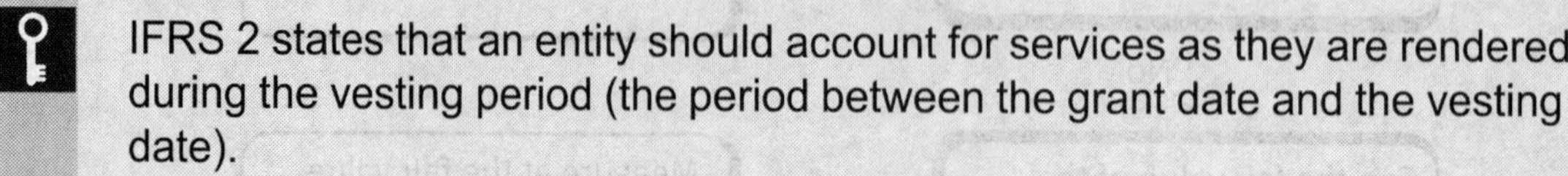

IFRS 2 states that an entity should account for services as they are rendered during the vesting period (the period between the grant date and the vesting date).

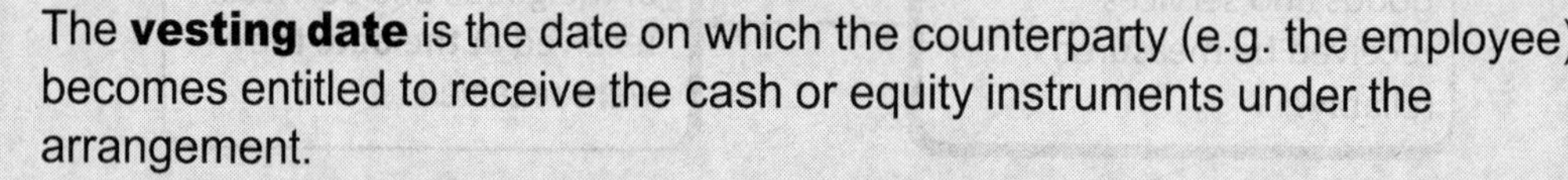

The **vesting date** is the date on which the counterparty (e.g. the employee) becomes entitled to receive the cash or equity instruments under the arrangement.

The expense recognised at each reporting date should be based on the best estimate of the number of equity instruments expected to vest.

On the vesting date, the entity shall revise the estimate to equal the number of equity instruments that ultimately vest.

Illustration 1 – When to recognise the transaction

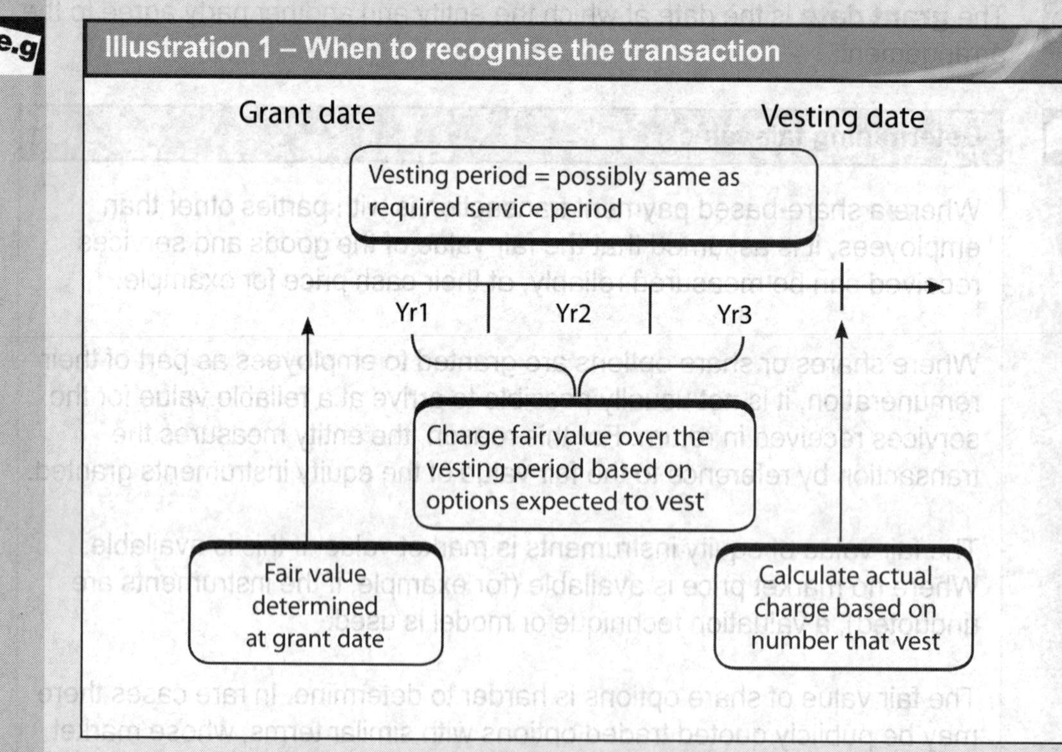

Test your understanding 1 – Equity-settled share-based

An entity has a reporting date of 31 December.

On 1 January 20X1 it grants 100 share options to each of its 500 employees. Each grant is conditional upon the employee working for the entity until 31 December 20X3. At the grant date the fair value of each share option is $15.

During 20X1, 20 employees leave and the entity estimates that a total of 20% of the 500 employees will leave during the three-year period.

During 20X2, a further 20 employees leave and the entity now estimates that only 15% of the original 500 employees will leave during the three-year period.

During 20X3, a further 10 employees leave.

Required:

Calculate the remuneration expense that will be recognised in each of the three years of the share-based payment scheme.

Performance conditions

In addition to service conditions, some share based payment schemes have **performance conditions** that must be satisfied before they vest, such as:

- achieving a specified increase in the entity's profit
- the completion of a research project
- achieving a specified increase in the entity's share price.

Performance conditions can be classified as either market conditions or non-market conditions.

- A **market condition** is defined by IFRS 2 as one that is related to the market price of the entity's equity instruments. An example of a market condition is that the entity must attain a minimum share price by the vesting date for scheme members to be eligible to participate in the share-based payment scheme.
- **Non-market performance conditions** are not related to the market price of the entity's equity instruments. Examples of non-market performance conditions include EPS or profit targets.

Conditions attaching to share-based payment transactions: a summary

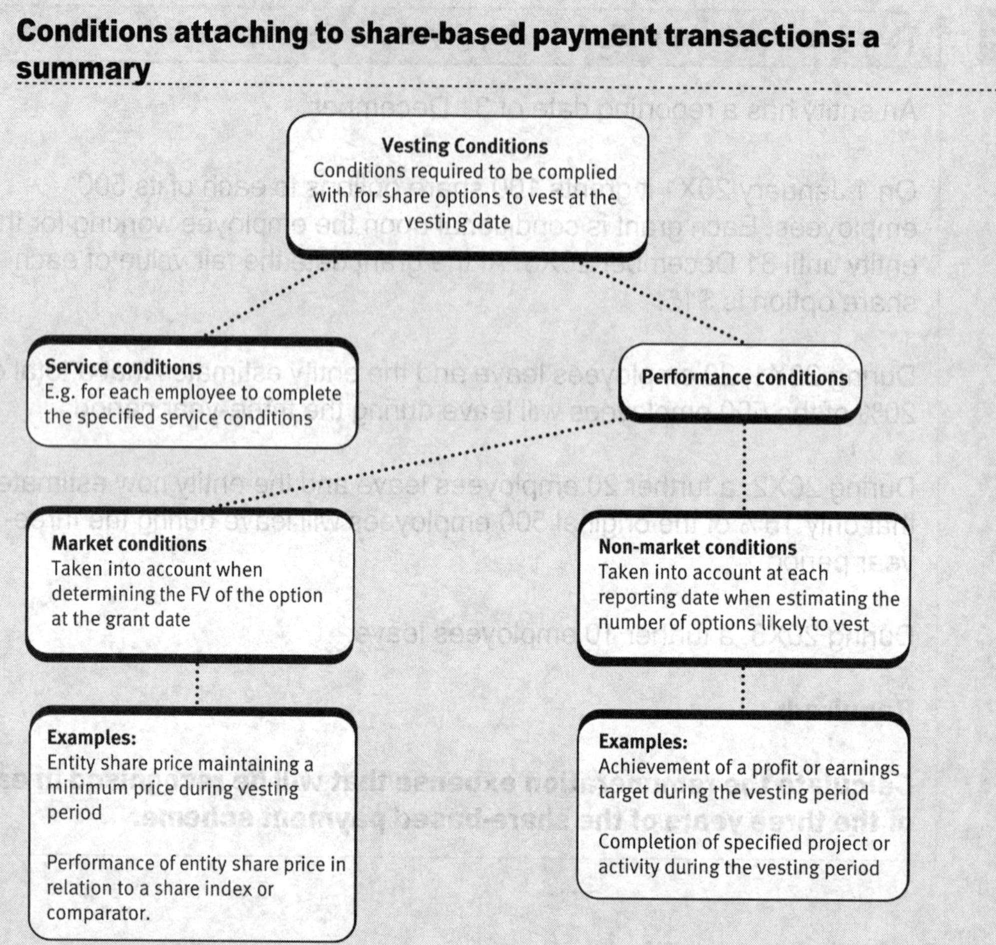
Vesting Conditions
Conditions required to be complied with for share options to vest at the vesting date
Service conditions
E.g. for each employee to complete the specified service conditions
Performance conditions
Market conditions
Taken into account when determining the FV of the option at the grant date
Non-market conditions
Taken into account at each reporting date when estimating the number of options likely to vest
Examples:
Entity share price maintaining a minimum price during vesting period
Performance of entity share price in relation to a share index or comparator.
Examples:
Achievement of a profit or earnings target during the vesting period
Completion of specified project or activity during the vesting period

The impact of performance conditions

- **Market based conditions** have already been factored into the fair value of the equity instrument at the grant date. Therefore, an expense is recognised irrespective of whether market conditions are satisfied.
- **Non-market based conditions** must be taken into account in determining whether an expense should be recognised in a reporting period.

Test your understanding 2 – Market based conditions

On 1 January 20X1, one hundred employees were given 50 share options each. These will vest if the employees still work for the entity on 31 December 20X2 and if the share price on that date is more than $5.

On 1 January 20X1, the fair value of the options was $1. The share price on 31 December 20X1 was $3 and it was considered unlikely that the share price would rise to $5 by 31 December 20X2. Ten employees left during the year ended 31 December 20X1 and a further ten are expected to leave in the following year.

Required:

How should the above transaction be accounted for in the year ended 31 December 20X1?

Test your understanding 3 – Blueberry

On 1 January 20X4 an entity, Blueberry, granted share options to each of its 200 employees, subject to a three-year vesting period, provided that the volume of sales increases by a minimum of 5% per annum throughout the vesting period. A maximum of 300 share options per employee will vest, dependent upon the increase in the volume of sales throughout each year of the vesting period as follows:

- If the volume of sales increases by an average of between 5% and 10% per year, each eligible employee will receive 100 share options.
- If the volume of sales increases by an average of between 10% and 15% per year, each eligible employee will receive 200 share options.
- If the volume of sales increases by an average of over 15% per year, each eligible employee will receive 300 share options.

At the grant date, Blueberry estimated that the fair value of each option was $10 and that the increase in the volume of sales each year would be between 10% and 15%. It was also estimated that a total of 22% of employees would leave prior to the end of the vesting period. At each reporting date within the vesting period, the situation was as follows:

Reporting date	Employees leaving in year	Further leavers expected prior to vesting date	Annual increase in sales volume	Expected sales volume increase over remaining vesting period	Average annual increase in sales volume to date
31 Dec X4	8	18	14%	14%	14%
31 Dec X5	6	4	18%	16%	16%
31 Dec X6	2		16%		16%

Required:

Calculate the impact of the above share-based payment scheme on Blueberry's financial statements in each reporting period.

Accounting after the vesting date

IFRS 2 states that no further adjustments to **total equity** should be made after the vesting date. This applies even if some of the equity instruments do not vest (for example, because a market based condition was not met).

Entities may, however, transfer any balance from 'other components of equity' to retained earnings.

Test your understanding 4 – Beginner

Beginner offered directors an option scheme conditional on a three-year period of service. The number of options granted to each of the ten directors at the inception of the scheme was 1 million. The options were exercisable shortly after the end of the third year. Upon exercise of the share options, those directors eligible would be required to pay $2 for each share of $1 nominal value.

The fair value of the options and the estimates of the number of options expected to vest at various points in time were as follows:

Year	Rights expected to vest	Fair value of the option $
Start of Year One	8m	0.30
End of Year One	7m	0.33
End of Year Two	8m	0.37

At the end of year three, 9 million rights actually vested.

Required:

(a) **Show how the option scheme will affect the financial statements for each of the three years of the vesting period.**

(b) **Show the accounting treatment at the vesting date for each of the following situations:**

(i) **The fair value of a share was $5 and all eligible directors exercised their share options immediately.**

(ii) **The fair value of a share was $1.50 and all eligible directors allowed their share options to lapse.**

Modifications to the terms on which equity instruments are granted

An entity may alter the terms and conditions of share option schemes during the vesting period. For example:

- it might increase or reduce the exercise price of the options (the price that the holder of the options has to pay for shares when the options are exercised). This makes the scheme less favourable or more favourable to employees.
- it might change the vesting conditions, to make it more likely or less likely that the options will vest.

If a modification to an equity-settled share-based payment scheme occurs, the entity must continue to recognise the grant date fair value of the equity instruments in profit or loss, unless the instruments do not vest because of a failure to meet a non-market based vesting condition.

If the modification increases the fair value of the equity instruments, then an extra expense must be recognised:

- The difference between the fair value of the new arrangement and the fair value of the original arrangement (the incremental fair value) at the date of the modification must be recognised as a charge to profit or loss. The extra expense is spread over the period from the date of the change to the vesting date.

Test your understanding 5 – Modifications

An entity grants 100 share options to each of its 500 employees, provided that they remain in service over the next three years. The fair value of each option is $20.

During year one, 50 employees leave. The entity estimates that a further 60 employees will leave during years two and three.

At the end of year one the entity reprices its share options because the share price has fallen. The other vesting conditions remain unchanged. At the date of repricing, the fair value of each of the original share options granted (before taking the repricing into account) was $10. The fair value of each repriced share option is $15.

During year two, a further 30 employees leave. The entity estimates that a further 30 employees will leave during year three.

During year three, a further 30 employees leave.

Required:

Calculate the amounts to be recognised in the financial statements for each of the three years of the scheme.

Further illustration on modifications

An entity grants 100 share options to each of the 15 employees in its sales team, on condition that they remain in service over the next three years. There is also a performance condition: the team must sell more than 40,000 units of a particular product over the three-year period. At the grant date the fair value of each option is $20.

During Year 2, the entity increases the sales target to 70,000 units. By the end of Year 3, only 60,000 units have been sold and the share options do not vest.

All 15 employees remain with the entity for the full three years.

Required:

Calculate the amounts to be recognised in the financial statements for each of the three years of the scheme.

Solution

IFRS 2 states that when a share option scheme is modified, the entity must recognise, as a minimum, the services received measured at the fair value at the grant date. The employees have not met the modified sales target, but **did** meet the original target set on grant date.

This means that the entity must recognise the expense that it would have incurred had the original scheme continued in force.

The total amount recognised in equity is $30,000 (15 × 100 × 20). The entity recognises an expense of $10,000 for each of the three years.

Cancellations and settlements

An entity may cancel or settle a share option scheme before the vesting date.

- If the cancellation or settlement occurs during the vesting period, the entity immediately recognises the amount that would otherwise have been recognised for services received over the vesting period (**'an acceleration of vesting'** (IFRS 2, para 28a)).

- Any payment made to employees up to the fair value of the equity instruments granted at cancellation or settlement date is accounted for as a deduction from equity.
- Any payment made to employees in excess of the fair value of the equity instruments granted at the cancellation or settlement date is accounted for as an expense in profit or loss.

Test your understanding 6 – Cancellations and settlements

An entity introduced an equity-settled share-based payment scheme on 1 January 20X0 for its 5 directors. Under the terms of the scheme, the entity will grant 1,000 options to each director if they remain in employment for the next three years. All five directors are expected to stay for the full three years. The fair value of each option at the grant date was $8.

On 30 June 20X1, the entity decided to base its share-based payment schemes on profit targets instead. It therefore cancelled the existing scheme. On 30 June 20X1, it paid compensation of $10 per option to each of the 5 directors. The fair value of the options at 30 June 20X1 was $9.

Required:

Explain, with calculations, how the cancellation and settlement of the share-based payment scheme should be accounted for in the year ended 31 December 20X1.

3 Cash-settled share-based payment transactions

Examples of cash-settled share-based payment transactions include:

- share appreciation rights (SARs), where employees become entitled to a future cash payment based on the increase in the entity's share price from a specified level over a specified period of time
- the right to shares that are redeemable, thus entitling the holder to a future payment of cash.

Accounting treatment

The double entry for a cash-settled share-based payment transaction is:

Dr Profit or loss/Asset
Cr Liabilities

Measurement

The entity remeasures the fair value of the liability arising under a cash-settled scheme at each reporting date.

This is different from accounting for equity-settled share-based payments, where the fair value is fixed at the grant date.

Allocating the expense to reporting periods

Where services are received in exchange for cash-settled share-based payments, the expense is recognised over the period that the services are rendered (the vesting period).

This is the same principle as for equity-settled transactions.

Illustration 2 – Cash-settled share-based payment transactions

An entity has a reporting date of 31 December.

On 1 January 20X1 the entity grants 100 share appreciation rights (SARs) to each of its 300 employees, on the condition that they continue to work for the entity until 31 December 20X3.

During 20X1, 20 employees leave. The entity estimates that a further 40 will leave during 20X2 and 20X3.

During 20X2, 10 employees leave. The entity estimates that a further 20 will leave during 20X3.

During 20X3, 10 employees leave.

The fair value of a SAR at each reporting date is shown below:

	$
20X1	10.00
20X2	12.00
20X3	15.00

Required:

Calculate the expense for each of the three years of the scheme, and the liability to be recognised in the statement of financial position as at 31 December for each of the three years.

Solution

Year	**Liability at year-end**	**Expense for year**
	$000	$000
20X1 ((300 – 20 – 40) × 100 × $10 × 1/3)	80	80
20X2 ((300 – 20 – 10 – 20) × 100 × $12 × 2/3)	200	120
20X3 ((300 – 20 – 10 – 10) × 100 × $15)	390	190

Note that the fair value of the liability is remeasured at each reporting date. This is then spread over the vesting period.

The value of share appreciation rights (SARs)

SARs may be exercisable over a period of time. The fair value of each SAR comprises the intrinsic value (the cash amount payable based upon the share price at that date) together with its time value (based upon the fact that the share price will vary over time).

When SARs are exercised, they are accounted for at their intrinsic value at the exercise date. The fair value of a SAR could exceed its intrinsic value at this date. This is because SAR holders who do not exercise their rights at that time have the ability to benefit from future share price rises.

At the end of the exercise period, the intrinsic value of a SAR will equal its fair value. The liability will be cleared and any remaining balance taken to profit or loss.

Test your understanding 7 – Growler

On 1 January 20X4 Growler granted 200 share appreciation rights (SARs) to each of its 500 employees on the condition that they continue to work for the entity for two years. At 1 January 20X4, the entity expects that 25 of those employees will leave each year.

During 20X4, 20 employees leave Growler. The entity expects that the same number will leave in the second year.

During 20X5, 24 employees leave.

The SARs vest on 31 December 20X5 and can be exercised during 20X6 and 20X7. On 31 December 20X6, 257 of the eligible employees exercised their SARs in full. The remaining eligible employees exercised their SARs in full on 31 December 20X7.

The fair value and intrinsic value of each SAR was as follows:

Reporting date	FV per SAR	Intrinsic value per SAR
31 December 20X4	$5	
31 December 20X5	$7	
31 December 20X6	$8	$7
31 December 20X7	$10	$10

Required:

(a) **Calculate the amount to be recognised as a remuneration expense in the statement of profit or loss, together with the liability to be recognised in the statement of financial position, for each of the two years to the vesting date.**

(b) **Calculate the amount to be recognised as a remuneration expense and reported as a liability in the financial statements for each of the two years ended 31 December 20X6 and 20X7.**

Replacing an equity scheme with a cash scheme

An entity may modify the terms of an equity-settled share-based payment scheme so that it becomes classified as a cash-settled scheme. If this is the case, IFRS 2 requires the entity to:

- Measure the transaction by reference to the modification fair value of the equity instruments granted
- Derecognise the liability and recognise equity to the extent of the services rendered by the modification date
- Recognise a profit or loss for the difference between the liability derecognised and the equity recognised.

4 Other issues

Hybrid transactions

If a share-based payment transaction gives the entity a choice over whether to settle in cash or by issuing equity instruments, IFRS 2 states that:

- The scheme should be accounted for as a cash-settled share-based payment transaction if the entity has an obligation to settle in cash.
- If no obligation exists to settle in cash, then the entity accounts for the transaction as an equity-settled share-based payment scheme.

Some entities enter into share-based payment transactions that give the counterparty the choice of settling in cash or in equity instruments. In this case, the entity has granted a compound financial instrument that must be split accounted (part is recorded as debt and part is recorded as equity).

Group share-based payment transactions

A subsidiary might receive goods or services from employees or suppliers but the parent (or another entity in the group) might issue equity or cash settled share-based payments as consideration.

In accordance with IFRS 2, the entity that receives goods or services in a share-based payment arrangement must account for those goods or services irrespective of which entity in the group settles the transaction, or whether the transaction is settled in shares or cash.

Disclosures

The main disclosures required by IFRS 2 are as follows:

- a description of share-based payment arrangements
- the number of share options granted or exercised during the year, and outstanding at the end of the year.

Entities should also disclose information that enables users of the financial statements to understand the effect of share-based payment transactions on the entity's profit or loss for the period and on its financial position, that is:

- the total share-based payment expense
- the total carrying amount of liabilities arising from share-based payment transactions.

IFRS 2 requires disclosures that enable users to understand how fair values have been determined.

5 Chapter summary

Share-based payment
- What it is
- Types of transaction
- Basic principles

Equity-settled share-based payment transactions
- Measurement
- Allocating the expense to reporting periods

Cash-settled share-based payment transactions
- Measurement
- Accounting treatment

Modifications, cancellations and settlements
- Accounting treatment of modifications
- Accounting treatment of cancellations and settlements

Test your understanding answers

Test your understanding 1 – Equity-settled share-based

The total expense recognised is based on the fair value of the share options granted at the grant date (1 January 20X1). The entity recognises the remuneration expense as the employees' services are received during the three-year vesting period.

Year ended 31 December 20X1

At 31 December 20X1, the entity must estimate the number of options expected to vest by predicting how many employees will remain in employment until the vesting date. It believes that 80% of the employees will stay for the full three years and therefore calculates an expense based on this assumption:

(500 employees × 80%) × 100 options × \$15 FV × 1/3 = \$200,000

Therefore, an expense is recognised for \$200,000 together with a corresponding increase in equity.

Year ended 31 December 20X2

The estimate of the number of employees staying for the full three years is revised at each year end. At 31 December 20X2, it is estimated that 85% of the 500 employees will stay for the full three years. The calculation of the share based payment expense is therefore as follows:

	$
(500 employees × 85%) × 100 options × \$15 FV × 2/3	425,000
Less previously recognised expense	(200,000)
Expense in year ended 31 December 20X2	225,000

Equity will be increased by \$225,000 to \$425,000 (\$200,000 + \$225,000).

Year ended 31 December 20X3

A total of 50 (20 + 20 + 10) employees left during the vesting period. The expense recognised in the final year of the scheme is as follows:

	$
(500 – 50 employees) × 100 options × $15 FV × 3/3	675,000
Less previously recognised expense	(425,000)
Expense in year ended 31 December 20X3	250,000

The financial statements will include the following amounts:

Statement of profit or loss	20X1	20X2	20X3
	$	$	$
Staff costs	200,000	225,000	250,000

Statement of financial position	20X1	20X2	20X3
	$	$	$
Other components of equity	200,000	425,000	675,000

Test your understanding 2 – Market based conditions

The expense recognised is based on the fair value of the options at the grant date. This should be spread over the vesting period.

There are two types of conditions attached to the share based payment scheme:

- A service condition (employees must complete a minimum service period)
- A market based performance condition (the share price must be $5 at 31 December 20X2).

Although it looks unlikely that the share price target will be hit, this condition has already been factored into the fair value of the options at the grant date. Therefore, this condition can be ignored when determining the charge to the statement of profit or loss.

The expense to be recognised should therefore be based on how many employees are expected to satisfy the service condition only. The calculation is as follows:

(100 employees – 10 – 10) × 50 options × $1 FV × 1/2 = $2,000.

The entry to recognise this is:

Dr Profit or loss	$2,000
Cr Equity	$2,000

Test your understanding 3 – Blueberry

Rep. date	Calculation of equity	Equity	Expense	Note
		$000	$000	
31/12/X4	(174 × 200 × $10) × 1/3	116	116	1
31/12/X5	(182 × 300 × $10) × 2/3	364	248	2
31/12/X6	(184 × 300 × $10) × 3/3	552	188	3

Notes:

(1) At 31/12/X4 a total of 26 employees (8 + 18) are expected to leave by the vesting date meaning that 174 are expected to remain. Blueberry estimates that average annual growth in sales volume will be 14%. Consequently, it is estimated that eligible employees would each receive 200 share options at the vesting date.

(2) At 31/12/X5, a total of 18 employees (8 + 6 + 4) are expected to leave by the vesting date meaning that 182 are expected to remain. Blueberry estimates that the average growth in sales volume will be 16%. Consequently, it is estimated that eligible employees will each receive 300 share options at the vesting date.

(3) A t 31/12/X6, it is known that total of 16 employees (8 + 6 + 2) have left at some point during the vesting period, leaving 184 eligible employees. As average annual growth in sales volume over the vesting period was 16%, eligible employees are entitled to 300 share options each.

Test your understanding 4 – Beginner

Year		**Equity**	**Expense**
		$000	$000
Year 1	(7m × $0.3 × 1/3)	700	700
Year 2	(8m × $0.3 × 2/3)	1,600	900
Year 3	(9m × $0.3)	2,700	1,100

Note: Equity-settled share-based payments are measured using the fair value of the instrument at the grant date (the start of year one).

(i) All eligible directors exercised their options:

The entity will post the following entry:

Dr Cash (9m × $2)	$18.0m
Dr Equity reserve	$2.7m
Cr Share capital (9m × $1)	$9.0m
Cr Share premium (bal. fig.)	$11.7m

(ii) No options are exercised

The amount recognised in equity ($2.7m) remains. The entity can choose to transfer this to retained earnings.

Test your understanding 5 – Modifications

The repricing means that the total fair value of the arrangement has increased and this will benefit the employees. This in turn means that the entity must account for an increased remuneration expense. The increased cost is based upon the difference in the fair value of the option, immediately before and after the repricing. Under the original arrangement, the fair value of the option at the date of repricing was $10, which increased to $15 following the repricing of the options, for each share estimated to vest. The additional cost is recognised over the remainder of the vesting period (years two and three).

The amounts recognised in the financial statements for each of the three years are as follows:

	Equity	**Expense**
	$	$
Year one original		
(500 – 50 – 60) × 100 × $20 × 1/3	260,000	260,000
Year two original		
(500 – 50 – 30 – 30) × 100 × $20 × 2/3	520,000	260,000
Incremental		
(500 – 50 – 30 – 30) × 100 × $5 × 1/2	97,500	97,500
	617,500	357,500
Year three original		
(500 – 50 – 30 – 30) × 100 × $20	780,000	260,000
Incremental		
(500 – 50 – 30 – 30) × 100 × $5	195,000	97,500
	975,000	357,500

Test your understanding 6 – Cancellations and settlements

The share option scheme has been cancelled. This means that all the expense not yet charged through profit or loss must now be recognised in the year ended 31 December 20X1:

	$
Total expense (5 directors × 1,000 options × $8)	40,000
Less expense recognised in year ended 31 December 20X0 (5 directors × 1,000 options × $8 × 1/3)	(13,333)
Expense to be recognised	26,667

To recognise the remaining expense, the following entry must be posted:

Dr Profit or loss	$26,667
Cr Equity	$26,667

Any payment made in compensation for the cancellation that is up to the fair value of the options is recognised as a deduction to equity. Any payment in excess of the fair value is recognised as an expense.

The compensation paid to the director for each option exceeded the fair value by $1 ($10 – $9). Therefore, an expense of $1 per option should be recognised in profit or loss.

The following accounting entry is required:

Dr Equity (5 directors × 1,000 options × $9)	$45,000
Dr Profit or loss (5 directors × 1,000 options × $1)	$5,000
Cr Cash (5 directors × 1,000 options × $10)	$50,000

Test your understanding 7 – Growler

(a) The liability is remeasured at each reporting date, based upon the current information available relating to known and expected leavers, together with the fair value of the SAR at each date. The remuneration expense recognised is the movement in the liability from one reporting date to the next as summarised below:

Rep. date	**Workings**	**Liability (SFP)**	**Expense (P/L)**
		$	$
31/12/X4	(500 – 20 – 20) × 200 × $5 × 1/2	230,000	230,000
31/12/X5	(500 – 20 – 24) × 200 × $7 × 2/2	638,400	408,400

(b) The number of employees eligible for a cash payment is 456 (500 – 20 – 24). Of these, 257 exercise their SARs at 31/12/X6 and the remaining 199 exercise their SARs at 31/12/X7.

The liability is measured at each reporting date, based upon the current information available at that date, together with the fair value of each SAR at that date. Any SARs exercised are reflected at their intrinsic value at the date of exercise.

Year ended 31/12/X6

	$
Liability b/fwd	638,400
Cash payment (257 × 200 × $7)	(359,800)
Profit or loss (bal. fig)	39,800
Liability c/fwd (199 × 200 × $8)	318,400

Year ended 31/12/X7

	$
Liability b/fwd	318,400
Cash payment (199 × 200 × $10)	(398,000)
Profit or loss (bal. fig)	79,600
Liability c/fwd	nil

chapter

10

Events after the reporting period, provisions and contingencies

Chapter learning objectives

Upon completion of this chapter you will be able to:

- apply and discuss accounting for events after the reporting date
- determine and report going concern issues arising after the reporting date
- apply and discuss the recognition, derecognition and measurement of provisions, contingent liabilities and contingent assets including environmental provisions
- calculate and discuss restructuring provisions.

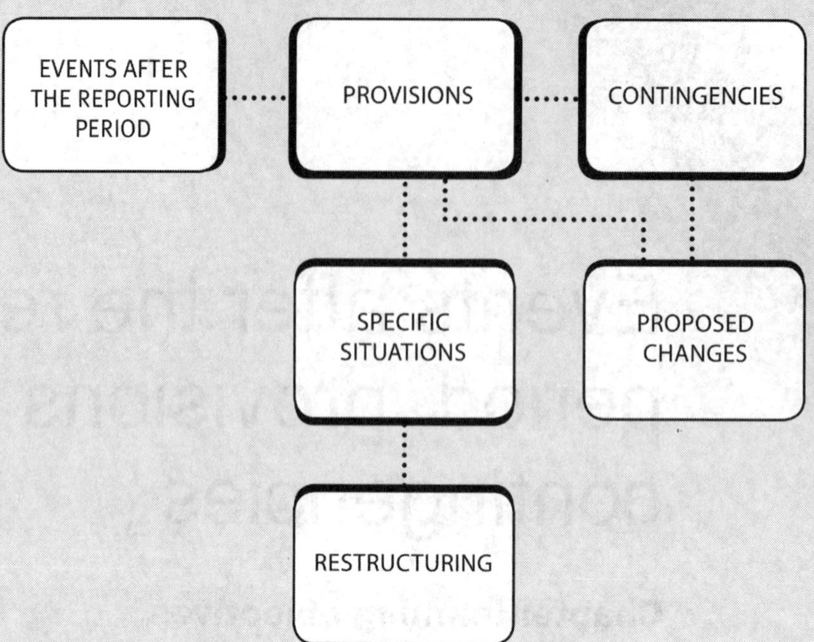

1 IAS 10 Events after the reporting period

Definition

Events after the reporting period **'are those events, both favourable and unfavourable, that occur between the reporting date and the date on which the financial statements are authorised for issue'** (IAS 10, para 3).

There are two types of event after the reporting period:

- adjusting events
- non-adjusting events.

Financial statements are prepared on the basis of conditions existing at the reporting date.

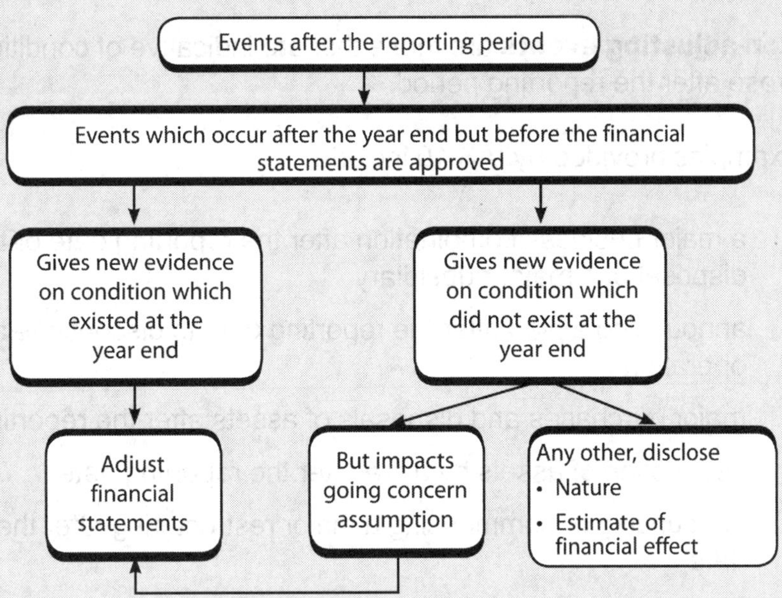

Adjusting and non-adjusting events

Adjusting events provide evidence of conditions that existed at the reporting date.

Examples provided by IAS 10 include:

- the sale of inventory after the reporting date – this gives evidence about the net realisable value of inventory at the reporting date
- the bankruptcy of a customer after the reporting date – this confirms that an allowance is required against a receivables balance at the reporting date
- the discovery of fraud or errors – this shows that the financial statements are incorrect
- the settlement after the reporting period of a court case – this confirms the existence and value of the entity's obligation at the reporting date.

Adjusting events result in changes to the figures recognised in the financial statements.

Non-adjusting events are those that are indicative of conditions that arose after the reporting period.

Examples provided by IAS 10 include:

- a major business combination after the reporting date or the disposal of a major subsidiary
- announcing a plan after the reporting date to discontinue an operation
- major purchases and disposals of assets after the reporting date
- destruction of assets by a fire after the reporting date
- announcing or commencing a major restructuring after the reporting date
- large changes after the reporting date in foreign exchange rates
- equity dividends declared or proposed after the reporting date.

Non-adjusting events do not affect any items in the statement of financial position or the statement of profit or loss and other comprehensive income. However, for material non-adjusting events, IAS 10 requires the following disclosures:

- a description of the event
- its estimated financial effect.

Problems with events after the reporting period

Judgement is involved when deciding if an event is adjusting or non-adjusting.

Suppose that an item of property, plant and equipment is valued shortly after the year-end and that this valuation reveals a significant fall in value. It may be that the fall in value occurred over a period of several months before the year-end, in which case the loss would be an adjusting event. However, it may be that the fall in value occurred after the year-end as a result of a particular event, such as an interest rate rise.

Test your understanding 1 – Adjusting events

The following material events have occurred after the reporting period and prior to the date of approval of the financial statements by the directors.

(i) The insolvency of a major credit customer

(ii) The uninsured loss of inventory in a fire

(iii) The proposal of a final equity dividend

(iv) A change in foreign exchange rates.

Required:

State whether the above are adjusting or non-adjusting events.

Going concern issues arising after the reporting date

There is an exception to the rule that the financial statements reflect conditions at the reporting date. If, after the reporting date, management decides to liquidate the entity or cease trading (or decides that it has no realistic alternative to these actions), the financial statements cannot be prepared on a going concern basis.

- In accordance with IAS 1, management must disclose any material uncertainties relating to events or conditions that cast significant doubt upon an entity's ability to continue trading. This applies if the events have arisen since the reporting period.
- If the going concern assumption is no longer appropriate then IAS 10 states that a fundamental change in the basis of accounting is required. In this case, entities will prepare their financial statements using the 'break up' basis.
- If the financial statements are not prepared on a going concern basis, that fact must be disclosed.

Going concern considerations

IAS 1 states that management should assess whether the going concern assumption is appropriate. Management should take into account all available information about events within at least twelve months of the end of the reporting period.

The following are indicators of a going concern uncertainty:

- A lack of cash and cash equivalents
- Increased levels of overdrafts and other forms of short-term borrowings
- Major debt repayments due in the next 12 months
- A rise in payables days – this may suggest that payments to suppliers are being delayed
- Increased levels of gearing
- Negative cash flows, particularly in relation to operating activities
- Disclosures or provisions relating to material legal claims
- Large impairment losses – this might suggest a decline in demand or productivity.

Where there is uncertainty, management should consider all available information about the future, including current and expected profitability, debt repayment finance and potential sources of alternative finance. If there is greater doubt or uncertainty, then more work will be required to evaluate whether or not the entity can be regarded as a going concern. Here, 'the future' means at least twelve months from the reporting date.

2 Provisions

Introduction

Liabilities are obligations arising from a past event that will lead to an outflow of economic resources.

Most liabilities can be measured accurately. For example, if you take out a bank loan then you know exactly how much you have to repay, and when the repayments are due. Provisions, however, involve more uncertainty.

According to IAS 37 Provisions, Contingent Liabilities and Contingent Assets (para 10), **'a provision is a liability of uncertain timing or amount'**.

Recognition

IAS 37 (para 14) requires that a provision should be recognised when and only when:

- **'an entity has a present obligation (legal or constructive) as a result of a past event**
- **it is probable that an outflow of resources embodying economic benefits will be required to settle the obligation**
- **a reliable estimate can be made of the amount of the obligation'.**

An obligation is something that cannot be avoided:

- **A constructive obligation** arises when an entity's past practice or published policies creates a valid expectation amongst other parties that it will discharge certain responsibilities.
- **A legal obligation** arises from a contract or from laws and legislation.

An outflow of economic benefits is regarded as probable if it is more likely than not to occur. Only in extremely rare cases is it impossible to make a reliable estimate of the amount of the obligation.

Measurement

IAS 37 requires that provisions are measured at the best estimate of the expenditure required to settle the obligation as at the reporting date.

The best estimate of a provision will be:

- the most likely amount payable for a single obligation (such as a court case)
- an expected value for a large population of items (such as a warranty provision).

An entity should use its own judgement in deriving the best estimate, supplemented by past experience and the advice of experts (such as lawyers).

If the effect of the time value of money is material, then the provision should be discounted to present value. The discount rate should be pre-tax and risk-specific.

Test your understanding 2 – Warranty

Clean sells domestic appliances such as washing machines.

On 31 December 20X1, Clean decides to start selling washing machines with a warranty. Under the terms of the warranty, Clean will repair washing machines at no charge to the customer if they break within the warranty period. The entity estimates, based on past-correspondence with customers, that 20% of the washing machines sold will require repair within the warranty period at an average cost to Clean of $50 per machine.

Clean sold 200 washing machines on 31 December 20X1.

The time value of money should be ignored.

Required:

Calculate the warranty provision required.

Subsequent measurement

If a provision has been discounted to present value, then the discount must be unwound and presented in finance costs in the statement of profit or loss:

Dr Finance costs (P/L)
Cr Provisions (SFP)

Provisions should be remeasured to reflect the best estimate of the expenditure required to settle the liability as at each reporting date.

Derecognition

IAS 37 states that provisions should be used only for expenditure that relates to the matter for which the provision was originally recognised.

At the reporting date, a provision should be reversed if it is no longer probable that an outflow of economic benefits will be required to settle the obligation.

3 Contingent liabilities

A contingent liability is defined by IAS 37 as:

- a possible obligation that arises from past events and whose existence will be confirmed by the outcome of uncertain future events which are outside of the control of the entity, or
- a present obligation that arises from past events, but does not meet the criteria for recognition as a provision. This is either because an outflow of economic benefits is not probable or (more rarely) because it is not possible to make a reliable estimate of the obligation.

A contingent liability is disclosed, unless the possibility of a future outflow of economic benefits is remote.

If an outflow of economic benefits becomes probable then contingent liabilities must be reclassified as provisions.

4 Contingent assets

IAS 37 defines a contingent asset as a possible asset that arises from past events and whose existence will be confirmed by uncertain future events that are outside of the entity's control.

A contingent asset should not be recognised:

- A contingent asset should be disclosed if the an inflow of future economic benefits is at least probable
- If the future inflow of benefits is virtually certain, then it ceases to be a contingent asset and should be recognised as a normal asset.

Summary

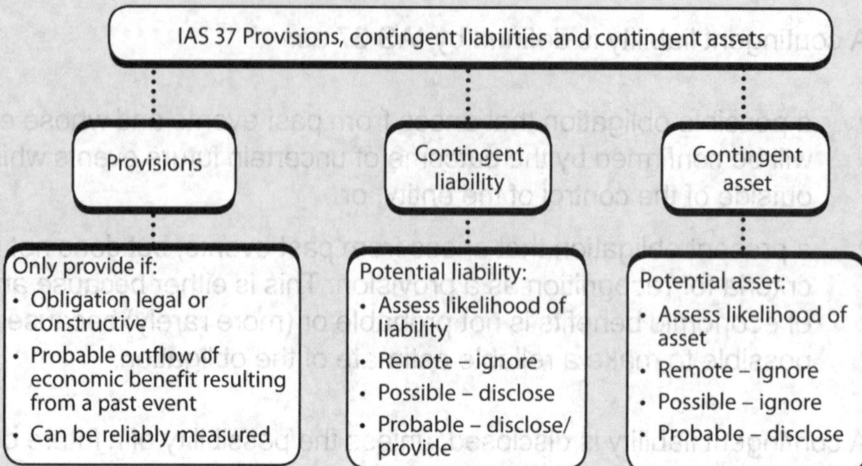
IAS 37 Provisions, contingent liabilities and contingent assets
Provisions
Contingent liability
Contingent asset
Only provide if:
• Obligation legal or constructive
• Probable outflow of economic benefit resulting from a past event
• Can be reliably measured
Potential liability:
• Assess likelihood of liability
• Remote – ignore
• Possible – disclose
• Probable – disclose/ provide
Potential asset:
• Assess likelihood of asset
• Remote – ignore
• Possible – ignore
• Probable – disclose

5 Provisions and contingencies: specific situations

Losses, contracts and repairs

Future operating losses

IAS 37 says that provisions should not be recognised for future operating losses because:

- They relate to future, rather than past, events
- The loss-making business could be closed and the losses avoided, meaning that there is no obligation to make the losses.

An expectation of future operating losses is an indication that assets may be impaired. An impairment review should be conducted in accordance with IAS 36 Impairment of Assets.

Onerous contracts

IAS 37 defines an onerous contract as one **'in which the unavoidable costs of meeting the contract exceed the economic benefits expected to be received under it'** (IAS 37, para 10).

If an entity has an onerous contract, a provision should be recognised for the present obligation under the contract. The provision is measured at the lower of:

- the cost of fulfilling the contract, or
- the cost of terminating it and suffering any penalties.

Some assets may have been bought specifically for use in fulfilling the onerous contract. These should be reviewed for impairment before any separate provision is made for the contract itself.

Future repairs to assets

Some assets need to be repaired or to have parts replaced every few years. For example, an airline may be required by law to overhaul all its aircraft every three years.

Provisions cannot normally be recognised for the cost of future repairs or replacement parts. This is because there is no current obligation to incur the expense – even if the future expenditure is required by law, the entity could avoid it by selling the asset.

Test your understanding 3 – Danboy

Danboy is a company that owns several shops and which has a year end of 31 December 20X1.

One of the shops is loss-making. At 31 December 20X1, Danboy forecasts that this shop will make a loss of $50,000 in the year ended 31 December 20X2.

As at 31 December 20X1, one of the shop buildings requires repair. The cost has been reliably estimated at the reporting date at $10,000. The repair is made in the following accounting period at a cost $12,000.

Required:

Discuss the accounting treatment of the above in the financial statements for the year ended 31 December 20X1.

Test your understanding 4 – Smoke filters

Under new legislation, an entity is required to fit smoke filters to its factories by 31 December 20X7. At the reporting date of 30 June 20X7, the entity has not fitted the smoke filters.

Required:

Should a provision be made at the reporting date for the estimated cost of fitting the filters?

Environmental provisions

Environmental provisions are often referred to as clean-up costs because they usually relate to the cost of decontaminating and restoring an industrial site after production has ceased.

A provision is recognised if a past event has created an obligation to repair environmental damage:

- A provision can only be set up to rectify environmental damage that has already happened. There is no obligation to restore future environmental damage because the entity could cease its operations.
- Merely causing damage or intending to clean-up a site does not create an obligation.
  - An entity may have a constructive obligation to repair environmental damage if it publicises policies that include environmental awareness or explicitly undertakes to clean up the damage caused by its operations

The full cost of an environmental provision should be recognised as soon as the obligation arises.

- The effect of the time value of money is usually material. Therefore, an environmental provision is normally discounted to its present value.
- If the expenditure results in future economic benefits then an equivalent asset can be recognised. This is depreciated over its useful life, which is the same as the 'life' of the provision.

Test your understanding 5 – Environmental provisions

(a) An entity has a policy of only carrying out work to rectify damage caused to the environment when it is required to do so by local law. For several years the entity has been operating an overseas oil rig which causes environmental damage. The country in which the oil rig is located has not had legislation in place that required this damage to be rectified.

A new government has recently been elected in the country. At the reporting date, it is virtually certain that legislation will be enacted that will require damage rectification. This legislation will have retrospective effect.

(b) Under a licence granted by a local government, an entity has constructed a rock-crushing plant to process material mined from the surrounding area. Mining activities have already started. Under the terms of the licence, the entity must remove the rock-crushing plant when mining activities have been completed and must landscape the mined area, so as to create a national park.

Required:

For each of the situations, explain whether a provision should be recognised.

Test your understanding 6 – Scrubber

On 1 January 20X6, Scrubber spent $5m on erecting infrastructure and machinery near to an area of natural beauty. These assets will be used over the next three years. Scrubber is well-known for its environmentally friendly behaviour and is therefore expected to restore the site after its use.

The estimated cost of removing these assets and cleaning up the area on 1 January 20X9 is $3m.

The pre-tax, risk-specific discount rate is 10%. Scrubber has a reporting date of 31 December.

Required:

Explain how the above should be treated in the financial statements of Scrubber.

6 Restructuring

Restructuring provisions

Definition

A **restructuring** is a programme that is planned and controlled by management and has a material effect on:

- the scope of a business undertaken by the reporting entity in terms of the products or services it provides
- the manner in which a business undertaken by the reporting entity is conducted.

IAS 37 says that a restructuring could include:

- the closure or sale of a line of business
- the closure of business locations in a country
- the relocation of business activities from one country to another.

When can a provision be recognised?

A restructuring provision can only be recognised where an entity has a **constructive obligation** to carry out the restructuring.

A board decision alone does not create a constructive obligation. IAS 37 states that a constructive obligation exists only if:

- there is a detailed formal plan for restructuring, that identifies the businesses, locations and employees affected as well as an estimate of the cost and timings involved
- the employees affected have a valid expectation that the restructuring will be carried out, either because the plan has been formally announced or because the plan has started to be implemented.

The constructive obligation must exist at the reporting date. An obligation arising after the reporting date requires disclosure as a non-adjusting event under IAS 10 Events after the Reporting Period.

Measuring a restructuring provision

A restructuring provision should only include the direct costs of restructuring. These must be both:

- **'necessarily entailed by the restructuring**
- **not associated with the ongoing activities of the entity'** (IAS 37, para 80).

IAS 37 prohibits the following costs from being included in a restructuring provision:

- retraining staff
- relocating staff
- marketing products
- expenditure on new systems
- future operating losses (unless these arise from an onerous contract)
- profits on disposal of assets

The amount recognised should be the best estimate of the expenditure required and it should take into account expected future events. This means that expenses should be measured at their actual cost, where this is known, even if this was only discovered after the reporting date (this is an adjusting event after the reporting period per IAS 10).

Test your understanding 7 – Restructuring provisions

On 15 January 20X5, the Board of Directors of Shane voted to proceed with two reorganisation schemes involving the closure of two factories. Shane's reporting date is 31 March, and the financial statements will be authorised for issue on 30 June.

Scheme 1

The closure costs will amount to $125,000. The closure will be announced in June, and will commence in August.

Scheme 2

The costs will amount to $45,000 (after crediting $105,000 profit on disposal of certain machines). The closure will take place in July, but redundancy negotiations began with the staff in March.

Required:

For each of the two schemes discuss whether a provision should be recognised and, if so, at what amount.

Test your understanding 8 – Delta

On 30 June 20X2, the directors of Delta decided to close down a division. This decision was announced to the employees affected on 15 July 20X2 and the actual closure occurred on 31 August 20X2, prior to the 20X2 financial statements being authorised for issue on 15 September.

Expenses and other items connected with the closure were as follows:

	$m
Redundancy costs (estimated)	22
Staff retraining (actual)	10
Operating loss for the 2 months to 31 August 20X2 (estimated at 30 June)	12
Profit on sale of property	5

The actual redundancy costs were $20 million and the actual operating loss for the two months to 31 August 20X2, was $15 million.

Required:

What is the amount of the restructuring provision to be recognised in the financial statements of Delta plc for the year ended 31 July 20X2?

7 Current issues

Criticisms of IAS 37

In 2012, the Board decided to make IAS 37 a research project. The project will focus on identifying aspects of IAS 37 that cause difficulties in application. These will be used as test cases for developing the Conceptual Framework.

The following criticisms have been made of IAS 37:

- IAS 37 requires entities to exercise a lot of judgement, which may increase the risk of bias and reduce comparability between entities.
- IAS 37 was issued many years ago and does not reflect the current thinking of the International Accounting Standards Board.
- The notion of a 'present obligation' is vague. It is unclear how unavoidable an obligation needs to be in order to not recognise a provision.
- There are differences between IAS 37 and US GAAP, which limit comparability.
- Provisions for single obligations are recognised at the 'best estimate' of the expenditure that will be incurred. Guidance in this area is lacking.
- IAS 37 does not specify what types of costs should be included when measuring a provision. For example, some entities include legal costs within provisions, but others do not.
- IAS 37 states that entities may need to make a risk adjustment to provisions, but it does not explain when to do this or how to calculate the adjustment.
- Contingent assets are not recognised unless the inflow of benefits is 'virtually certain'. There is a lack of guidance about the meaning of 'virtually certain'.
- With regards to contingencies, there can be timing differences between when one entity recognises a contingent liability and when the other entity recognises a contingent asset.

8 Chapter summary

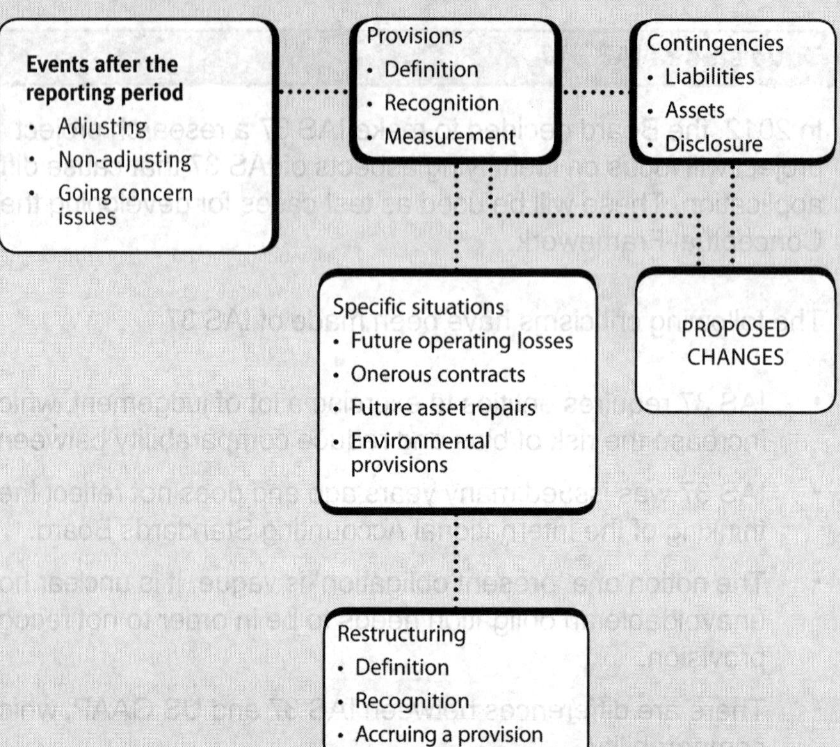

Test your understanding answers

Test your understanding 1 – Adjusting events

(i) Adjusting.

(ii) Non-adjusting.

(iii) Non-adjusting.

(iv) Non-adjusting.

Test your understanding 2 – Warranty

A provision is required.

A past event (the sale) has created a legal obligation to spend money on repairing machines in the future.

The best estimate can be determined using an expected value:

200 machines × 20% × $50 = $2,000.

Test your understanding 3 – Danboy

IAS 37 states that no provision should be made for future operating losses. Therefore, no provision should be made for the $50,000 forecast losses.

No provision should be made for future repairs despite it being probable and capable of being reliably measured. This is because there is no obligation at the year end. The repairs expenditure of $12,000 is expensed to profit or loss as it is incurred.

Test your understanding 4 – Smoke filters

No provision should be made for this future expenditure despite it being probable and capable of being reliably measured. There has been no obligating past event (the fitting of the filters).

Test your understanding 5 – Environmental provisions

For each situation, ask two questions.

(a) Is there a present obligation as the result of a past event?

(b) Is an outflow of economic benefits probable as a result?

A provision should be recognised if the answer to both questions is yes. In the absence of information to the contrary, it is assumed that any future costs can be estimated reliably.

(a) Present obligation? Yes. Because the new legislation with retrospective effect is virtually certain to be enacted, the damage caused by the oil rig is the past event that gives rise to a present obligation.

Outflow of economic benefits probable? Yes.

Conclusion – Recognise a provision.

(b) Present obligation? Yes. There is a legal obligation under the licence to remove the rock-crushing plant and to make good damage caused by the mining activities to date (but not any that may be caused by these activities in the future, because mining activities could be stopped and no such damage caused).

Outflow of economic benefits probable? Yes.

Conclusion – Recognise a provision for the best estimate of the eventual costs of rectifying the damage caused up to the reporting date.

Test your understanding 6 – Scrubber

Scrubber has a constructive obligation to restore the area to its original condition as a result of a past event (erecting the infrastructure). Therefore, it should recognise a provision at 1 January 20X6. The best estimate of the expenditure is $3m, but this must be discounted to its present value of $2,253,000 ($3m × 0.751).

Scrubber could not carry out its operations without incurring the clean-up costs. This means that incurring the costs gives it access to future economic benefits. The estimated clean-up costs are therefore included in the cost of the property, plant and equipment (PPE):

Dr PPE	$2,253,000
Cr Provisions	$2,253,000

Each year, the discount unwinds and the provision increases. The unwinding of the discount is charged to the statement of profit or loss as a finance cost.

Movement on provision	20X6	20X7	20X8	20X9
	$000	$000	$000	$000
Opening balance	2,253	2,478	2,727	3,000
Finance cost at 10%	225	249	273	–
Utilisation	–	–	–	(3,000)
Closing balance	2,478	2,727	3,000	–

Initial cost of PPE	$000
Cash paid 1 January 20X6	5,000
PV of clean-up costs	2,253
Total	7,253

The effect on the financial statements is shown below:

Statements of profit or loss	**20X6**	**20X7**	**20X8**	**20X9**
	$000	$000	$000	$000
Operating costs				
Depreciation ($7,253/3 years)	2,418	2,418	2,417	–
Finance costs				
Unwinding of discount	225	249	273	–

Statement of financial position	$000	$000	$000	$000
PPE				
Cost	7,253	7,253	7,253	–
Depreciation	(2,418)	(4,836)	(7,253)	–
Carrying value	4,835	2,417	–	–
Liabilities				
Clean-up provision	2,478	2,727	3,000	–

Test your understanding 7 – Restructuring provisions

Scheme 1

The obligating event is the announcement of the plan, which occurs in June. This is after the year-end, so there can be no provision. However, the announcement in June should be disclosed as a non-adjusting event after the reporting date.

Scheme 2

Although the closure will not begin until July, the employees will have had a valid expectation that it would happen when the redundancy negotiations began in March. Therefore, a provision should be recognised. The provision will be for $150,000 because the expected profit on disposal cannot be netted off against the expected costs.

Test your understanding 8 – Delta

The only item which can be included in the provision is the redundancy costs, measured at their actual amount of $20 million.

IAS 37 prohibits the recognition of future operating losses, staff retraining and profits on disposals of assets.

chapter

11

Financial instruments

Chapter learning objectives

Upon completion of this chapter you will be able to:

- apply and discuss the recognition and derecognition of financial assets or financial liabilities
- apply and discuss the classification of financial assets or financial liabilities and their measurement
- apply and discuss the treatment of gains and losses arising on financial assets and financial liabilities
- apply and discuss the treatment of the expected loss impairment model
- account for derivative financial instruments, and simple embedded derivatives
- outline the principle of hedge accounting, and account for fair value hedges and cash flow hedges including hedge effectiveness.

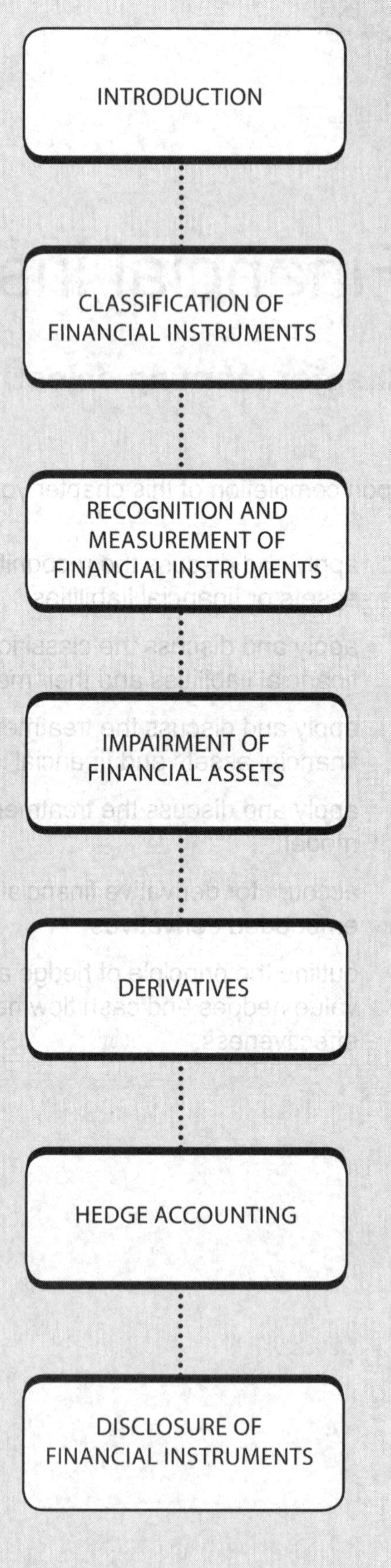
INTRODUCTION
CLASSIFICATION OF FINANCIAL INSTRUMENTS
RECOGNITION AND MEASUREMENT OF FINANCIAL INSTRUMENTS
IMPAIRMENT OF FINANCIAL ASSETS
DERIVATIVES
HEDGE ACCOUNTING
DISCLOSURE OF FINANCIAL INSTRUMENTS

1 Introduction

Definitions

A financial instrument is **'any contract that gives rise to a financial asset of one entity and a financial liability or equity instrument of another entity'** (IAS 32, para 11).

A **financial asset** is any asset that is:

- **'cash**
- **an equity instrument of another entity**
- **a contractual right to receive cash or another financial asset from another entity**
- **a contractual right to exchange financial instruments with another entity under conditions that are potentially favourable to the entity**
- **a non-derivative contract for which the entity is or may be obliged to receive a variable number of the entity's own equity instruments'** (IAS 32, para 11).

A **financial liability** is any liability that is a:

- **'contractual obligation to deliver cash or another financial asset to another entity**
- **contractual obligation to exchange financial instruments with another entity under conditions that are potentially unfavourable**
- **a non-derivative contract for which the entity is or may be obliged to deliver a variable number of the entity's own equity instruments.'** (IAS 32, para 11).

An equity instrument is **'any contract that evidences a residual interest in the assets of an entity after deducting all of its liabilities'** (IAS 32, para 11).

Reporting standards

There are three reporting standards within the P2 syllabus that deal with financial instruments:

- IAS 32 Financial Instruments: Presentation
- IFRS 7 Financial Instruments: Disclosures
- IFRS 9 Financial Instruments

IAS 32 deals with the classification of financial instruments and their financial statement presentation.

IFRS 7 deals with the disclosure of financial instruments in financial statements.

IFRS 9 is concerned with the initial and subsequent measurement of financial instruments.

2 Classification of financial liabilities and equity

IAS 32 provides rules on classifying financial instruments.

The issuer of a financial instrument must classify it as a financial liability or equity instrument on initial recognition according to its substance and the definitions provided at the start of this chapter.

Test your understanding 1 – Liabilities or equity?

Coasters wishes to purchase a new ride for its 'Animation Galaxy' theme park but requires extra funding. On 30 September 20X3, Coasters issued the following preference shares:

- 1 million preference shares for $3 each. No dividends are payable. Coasters will redeem the preference shares in three years' time by issuing ordinary shares worth $3 million. The exact number of ordinary shares issuable will be based on their fair value on 30 September 20X6.
- 2 million preference shares for $2.80 each. No dividends are payable. The preference shares will be redeemed in two years' time by issuing 3 million ordinary shares.
- 4 million preference shares for $2.50 each. They are not mandatorily redeemable. A dividend is payable if, and only if, dividends are paid on ordinary shares.

Required:

Discuss whether these financial instruments should be classified as financial liabilities or equity in the financial statements of Coasters for the year ended 30 September 20X3.

Interest, dividends, losses and gains

The accounting treatment of interest, dividends, losses and gains relating to a financial instrument follows the treatment of the instrument itself.

- Dividends paid in respect of preference shares classified as a liability will be charged as a finance expense through profit or loss
- Dividends paid on shares classified as equity will be reported in the statement of changes in equity.

The impact of classification

The classification of a financial instrument as either a liability or as equity will have a major impact on the financial statements.

- If an entity issues an instrument and classifies it as a liability, then gearing will rise and the entity will appear more risky to potential investors. The servicing of the finance will be charged to profit or loss reducing profits.
- If an entity issues an instrument and classifies it as equity then gearing will fall. The servicing of the finance will be charged directly to retained earnings and so will not impact profit.

Offsetting financial assets and liabilities

IAS 32 states that a financial asset and a financial liability may only be offset in very limited circumstances. The net amount may only be reported when the entity:

- **'has a legally enforceable right to set off the amounts**
- **intends either to settle on a net basis, or to realise the asset and settle the liability simultaneously'** (IAS 32, para 42).

3 Recognition and measurement of financial liabilities

Initial recognition of financial liabilities

At initial recognition, financial liabilities are measured at fair value.

- If the financial liability will be held at fair value through profit or loss, transaction costs should be expensed to the statement of profit or loss
- If the financial liability will not be held at fair value through profit or loss, transaction costs should be deducted from its carrying amount.

Subsequent measurement of financial liabilities

The subsequent treatment of a financial liability is that they can be measured at either:

- amortised cost
- fair value through profit or loss.

Amortised cost

Most financial liabilities, such as borrowings, are subsequently measured at amortised cost using the effective interest method. This is considered in more detail below:

Effective rate of interest

Assume that a company takes out a $10m bank loan for 5 years. Interest of 10% is payable annually in arrears:

- The interest payable each year is $1m ($10m × 10%)
- The total cost of the loan is $5m ($1m × 5 years).

Now assume that a company issues a bond. This has a nominal value of $10m and interest of 10% is payable annually in arrears. However, the company issues the bond for only $9m and has agreed to repay $12m to the bond holders in five years' time.

- Interest of $1m ($10m × 10%) will be paid per year
- Total interest payments over the life of the bond are $5m ($1m × 5 years).
- On top of this interest, the entity must pay back $3m more ($12m – $9m) than it received.

The total cost of the loan is actually $8m ($5m + $3m) and, in accordance with the accruals concept, this should be spread over the 5 year period. This is achieved by charging interest on the liability using the **effective rate of interest**. The effective rate is the internal rate of return of the investment.

Calculating amortised cost

The initial carrying amount of a financial liability measured at amortised cost is its fair value less any transaction costs (the 'net proceeds' from issue).

A finance cost is charged on the liability using the effective rate of interest. This will increase the carrying amount of the liability:

Dr Finance cost (P/L)
Cr Liability

The liability is reduced by any cash payments made during the year:

Dr Liability
Cr Cash

Amortised cost table

In the exam, assuming interest is paid in arrears, you might find the following working useful:

Opening liability	**Finance cost** (op. liability × effective %)	**Cash payments** (nom. value × coupon %)	**Closing liability**
X	X	(X)	X

The finance cost is charged to the statement of profit or loss.

The cash payment will be part of 'interest paid' in the statement of cash flows.

The closing liability will appear on the statement of financial position.

Illustration 1 – Loan issues at a discount

On 1 January 20X1 James issued a loan note with a $50,000 nominal value. It was issued at a discount of 16% of nominal value. The costs of issue were $2,000. Interest of 5% of the nominal value is payable annually in arrears. The bond must be redeemed on 1 January 20X6 (after 5 years) at a premium of $4,611.

The effective rate of interest is 12% per year.

Required:

How will this be reported in the financial statements of James over the period to redemption?

Solution

The liability will be initially recognised at the net proceeds received:

	$
Face value	50,000
Less: 16% discount	(8,000)
Less: Issue costs	(2,000)
Initial recognition of liability	40,000

The liability is then measured at amortised cost:

Year	Opening balance	Finance cost (Liability × 12%)	Cash payments ($50,000 × 5%)	Closing balance
	$	$	$	$
1	40,000	4,800	(2,500)	42,300
2	42,300	5,076	(2,500)	44,876
3	44,876	5,385	(2,500)	47,761
4	47,761	5,731	(2,500)	50,992
5	50,992	6,119	(2,500)	54,611
		27,111	(12,500)	
		To: Profit or loss	To: Statement of cash flows	To: SOFP

According to the above working, the total cost of the loan over the five year period is $27,111.

This is made up as follows:

	$	$
Repayments:		
Capital	50,000	
Premium	4,611	
		54,611
Interest ($50,000 × 5% × 5 years)		12,500
		67,111
Cash received		(40,000)
Total finance cost		27,111

The finance charge taken to profit or loss in each year is greater than the actual interest paid. This means that the value of the liability increases over the life of the instrument until it equals the redemption value at the end of its term.

In Years 1 to 4 the balance shown as a liability is less than the amount that will be payable on redemption. Therefore the full amount payable must be disclosed in the notes to the accounts.

Test your understanding 2 – Hoy

Hoy raised finance on 1 January 20X1 by the issue of a two-year 2% bond with a nominal value of $10,000. It was issued at a discount of 5% and is redeemable at a premium of $1,075. Issue costs can be ignored. The bond has an effective rate of interest of 10%.

Wiggins raised finance by issuing $20,000 6% four-year loan notes on 1 January 20X4. The loan notes were issued at a discount of 10%, and will be redeemed after four years at a premium of $1,015. The effective rate of interest is 12%. The issue costs were $1,000.

Cavendish raised finance by issuing zero coupon bonds at par on 1 January 20X5 with a nominal value of $10,000. The bonds will be redeemed after two years at a premium of $1,449. Issue costs can be ignored. The effective rate of interest is 7%.

The reporting date for each entity is 31 December.

Required:

Illustrate and explain how these financial instruments should be accounted for by each company.

Fair value through profit or loss

Out of the money derivatives and liabilities held for trading are measured at fair value through profit or loss.

It is also possible to measure a liability at fair value when it would normally be measured at amortised cost if it would eliminate or reduce an accounting mismatch. In this case, IFRS 9 says that any movement in fair value is split into two components:

- the fair value change due to own credit risk (the risk that the entity which has issued the financial liability will be unable to repay or discharge it), which is presented in other comprehensive income
- the remaining fair value change, which is presented in profit or loss.

Illustration – Fair value through profit or loss

On 1 January 20X1, McGrath issued a financial liability for its nominal value of $10 million. Interest is payable at a rate of 5% in arrears. The liability is repayable on 31 December 20X3. McGrath trades financial liabilities in the short-term.

At 31 December 20X1, market rates of interest have risen to 10%.

Required:

Discuss the accounting treatment of the liability at 31 December 20X1.

Solution

The financial liability is traded in the short-term and so is measured at fair value through profit or loss.

The liability must be remeasured to fair value at the reporting date. Assuming that the fair value of the liability cannot be observed from an active market, it can be calculated by discounting the future cash flows at a market rate of interest.

Date	Cash flow ($m)	Discount rate	Present value ($m)
31/12/X2	0.5*	1/1.1	0.45
31/12/X3	10.5	$1/1.1^2$	8.68
			9.13

* The interest payments are $10m × 5% = $0.5m

The fair value of the liability at the year-end is $9.13 million.

The following adjustment is required:

Dr Liability ($10m – $9.13m)	$0.87m
Cr Profit or loss	$0.87m

Test your understanding 3 – Bean

Bean regularly invests in assets that are measured at fair value through profit or loss. These asset purchases are funded by issuing bonds. If the bonds were not remeasured to fair value, an accounting mismatch would arise. Therefore, Bean designates the bonds to be measured at fair value through profit or loss.

The fair value of the bonds fell by $30m during the reporting period, of which $10m related to Bean's credit worthiness.

Required:

How should the bonds be accounted for?

4 Compound instruments

A **compound instrument** is a financial instrument that has characteristics of both equity and liabilities. An example would be debt that can be redeemed either in cash or in a fixed number of equity shares.

Presentation of compound instruments

IAS 32 requires compound financial instruments be split into two components:

- a financial liability (the liability to repay the debt holder in cash)
- an equity instrument (the option to convert into shares).

These two elements must be shown separately in the financial statements.

The initial recognition of compound instruments

On initial recognition, a compound instrument must be split into a liability component and an equity component:

- The liability component is calculated as the present value of the repayments, discounted at a market rate of interest for a similar instrument without conversion rights.
- The equity component is calculated as the difference between the cash proceeds from the issue of the instrument and the value of the liability component.

Illustration 2 – Compound instruments

On 1 January 20X1 Daniels issued a $50m three-year convertible bond at par.

- There were no issue costs.
- The coupon rate is 10%, payable annually in arrears on 31 December.
- The bond is redeemable at par on 1 January 20X4.
- Bondholders may opt for conversion in the form of shares. The terms of conversion are two 25-cent equity shares for every $1 owed to each bondholder on 1 January 20X4.
- Bonds issued by similar entities without any conversion rights currently bear interest at 15%.
- Assume that all bondholders opt for conversion in shares.

Required:

How will this be accounted for by Daniels?

Solution

On initial recognition, the proceeds received must be split between liabilities and equity.

- The liability component is calculated as the present value of the cash repayments at the market rate of interest for an instrument similar in all respects, except that it does not have conversion rights.
- The equity component is the difference between the proceeds of the issue and the liability component.

(1) **Splitting the proceeds**

The cash payments on the bond should be discounted to their present value using the interest rate for a bond without the conversion rights, i.e. 15%.

Date		**Cash flow**	**Discount factor (15%)**	**Present value**
		$000		$000
31-Dec-X1	Interest	5,000	1/1.15	4,347.8
31-Dec-X2	Interest	5,000	$1/1.15^2$	3,780.7
31-Dec-X3	Interest	5,000	$1/1.15^3$	3,287.6
1-Jan-X4	Principal	50,000	$1/1.15^3$	32,875.8
Liability component		A		44,291.9
Net proceeds of issue		B		50,000.0
Equity component		B – A		5,708.1

(2) Measuring the liability at amortised cost

The liability component is measured at amortised cost. The working below shows the finance costs recorded in the statement of profit or loss for each year as well as the carrying value of the liability in the statement of financial position at each reporting date.

	Opening bal.	Finance cost (15%)	Payments	Closing bal.
	$000	$000	$000	$000
20X1	44,291.9	6,643.8	(5,000)	45,935.7
20X2	45,935.7	6,890.4	(5,000)	47,826.1
20X3	47,826.1	7,173.9	(5,000)	50,000.0

(3) The conversion of the bond

The carrying amounts at 1 January 20X4 are:

	$000
Equity	5,708.1
Liability – bond	50,000.0
	55,708.1

The conversion terms are two 25-cent equity shares for every $1. Therefore 100m shares ($50m × 2), will be issued which have a nominal value of $25m. The remaining $30,708,100 should be classified as the share premium, also within equity. There is no remaining liability, because conversion has extinguished it.

The double entry is as follows:

	$000
Dr Other components of equity	5,708.1
Dr Liability	50,000.0
Cr Share capital	25,000.0
Cr Share premium	30,708.1

Test your understanding 4 – Craig

Craig issues a $100,000 4% three-year convertible loan on 1 January 20X6. The market rate of interest for a similar loan without conversion rights is 8%. The conversion terms are one equity share ($1 nominal value) for every $2 of debt. Conversion or redemption at par takes place on 31 December 20X8.

Required:

How should this be accounted for:

(a) **if all holders elect for the conversion?**

(b) **no holders elect for the conversion?**

5 Initial recognition of financial assets

IFRS 9 says that an entity should recognise a financial asset **'when, and only when, the entity becomes party to the contractual provisions of the instrument'** (IFRS 9, para 3.1.1).

Examples of this principle are as follows:

- A trading commitment to buy or sell goods is not recognised until one party has fulfilled its part of the contract. For example, a sales order will not be recognised as revenue and a receivable until the goods have been delivered.
- Forward contracts are accounted for as derivative financial assets and are recognised on the commitment date, not on the date when the item under contract is transferred from seller to buyer.
- Option contracts are accounted for as derivative financial assets and are recognised on the date the contract is entered into, not on the date when the item subject to the option is acquired.

6 Accounting for investments in equity instruments

Classification

Investments in equity instruments (such as an investment in the ordinary shares of another entity) are measured at either:

- fair value either through profit or loss, or
- fair value through other comprehensive income.

Fair value through profit or loss

The normal expectation is that equity instruments will have the designation of fair value through profit or loss.

Fair value through other comprehensive income

It is possible to designate an equity instrument as fair value through other comprehensive income, provided that the following conditions are complied with:

- the equity instrument must not be held for trading, and
- there must have been an irrevocable choice for this designation upon initial recognition of the asset.

Measurement

Fair value through profit or loss

Investments in equity instruments that are classified as fair value through profit or loss are initially recognised at fair value. Transaction costs are expensed to profit or loss.

At the reporting date, the asset is revalued to fair value with the gain or loss recorded in the statement of profit or loss.

Fair value through other comprehensive income

Investments in equity instruments that are classified as fair value through other comprehensive income are initially recognised at fair value plus transaction costs.

At the reporting date, the asset is revalued to fair value with the gain or loss recorded in other comprehensive income. This gain or loss will not be reclassified to profit or loss in future periods.

Test your understanding 5 – Ashes' financial assets

Ashes holds the following financial assets:

(1) Investments in ordinary shares that are held for short-term speculation.

(2) Investments in ordinary shares that, from the purchase date, are intended to be held for the long term.

Required:

How should Ashes classify and account for its financial assets?

Summary

Investments in equity
Fair value through other comprehensive income can be used if:
• not held for trade, and
• irrevocably designated.
Fair value through profit or loss

7 Accounting for investments in debt instruments

Classification

Financial assets that are debt instruments can be measured in one of three ways:

- Amortised cost
- Fair value through other comprehensive income
- Fair value through profit or loss.

Amortised cost

IFRS 9 says that an investment in a debt instrument is measured at amortised cost if:

- The entity's business model is to collect the asset's contractual cash flows
  - This means that the entity does not plan on selling the asset prior to maturity but rather intends to hold it until redemption.
- The contractual terms of the financial asset give rise to cash flows that are solely payments of principal, and interest on the principal amount outstanding
  - For example, the interest rate on convertible bonds is lower than market rate because the holder of the bond gets the benefit of choosing to take redemption in the form of cash or shares. The contractual cash flows are therefore not solely payments of principal and interest on the principal amount outstanding.

Fair value through other comprehensive income

An investment in a debt instrument is measured at fair value through other comprehensive income if:

- The entity's business model involves both collecting contractual cash flows and selling financial assets
  - This means that sales will be more frequent than for debt instruments held at amortised cost. For instance, an entity may sell investments if the possibility of buying another investment with a higher return arises.
- The contractual terms of the financial asset give rise to cash flows that are solely payments of principal and interest on the principal amount outstanding.

Fair value through profit or loss

An investment in a debt instrument that is not measured at amortised cost or fair value through other comprehensive income will be measured, according to IFRS 9, at fair value through profit or loss.

Test your understanding 6 – Paloma

Paloma purchased a new financial asset on 31 December 20X3. The asset is a bond that will mature in three years. Paloma buys debt investments with the intention of holding them to maturity although has, on occasion, sold some investments if cash flow deteriorated beyond acceptable levels. The bond pays a market rate of interest. The Finance Director is unsure as to whether this financial asset can be measured at amortised cost.

Required:

Advise the Finance Director on how the bond will be measured.

Re-classification of financial assets

Financial assets are classified in accordance with IFRS 9 when initially recognised.

If an entity changes its business model for managing financial assets, all affected financial assets are reclassified (e.g. from fair value through profit or loss to amortised cost). This will only apply to investments in debt.

Measurement

Amortised cost

For investments in debt that are measured at amortised cost:

- The asset is initially recognised at fair value plus transaction costs.
- Interest income is calculated using the effective rate of interest.

Fair value through other comprehensive income

For investments in debt that are measured at fair value through other comprehensive income:

- The asset is initially recognised at fair value plus transaction costs.
- Interest income is calculated using the effective rate of interest.
- At the reporting date, the asset will be revalued to fair value with the gain or loss recognised in other comprehensive income. This will be reclassified to profit or loss when the asset is disposed.

Fair value through profit or loss

For investments in debt that are measured at fair value through profit or loss:

- The asset is initially recognised at fair value, with any transaction costs expensed to the statement of profit or loss.
- At the reporting date, the asset will be revalued to fair value with the gain or loss recognised in the statement of profit or loss.

Note on loss allowances

For debt instruments measured at amortised cost or at fair value through other comprehensive income, a loss allowance must also be recognised. This detail is covered in the next section.

Test your understanding 7 – Tokyo

On 1 January 20X1, Tokyo bought a $100,000 5% bond for $95,000, incurring issue costs of $2,000. Interest is received in arrears. The bond will be redeemed at a premium of $5,960 over nominal value on 31 December 20X3. The effective rate of interest is 8%.

The fair value of the bond was as follows:

31/12/X1 $110,000
31/12/X2 $104,000

Required:

Explain, with calculations, how the bond will have been accounted for over all relevant years if:

(a) **Tokyo's business model is to hold bonds until the redemption date.**

(b) **Tokyo's business model is to hold bonds until redemption but also to sell them if investments with higher returns become available.**

(c) **Tokyo's business model is to trade bonds in the short-term. Assume that Tokyo sold this bond for its fair value on 1 January 20X2.**

The requirement to recognise a loss allowance on debt instruments held at amortised cost or fair value through other comprehensive income should be ignored.

Test your understanding 8 – Magpie

On 1 January 20X1, Magpie lends $2 million to an important supplier. The loan, which is interest-free, will be repaid in two years' time. The asset is classified to be measured at amortised cost. There are no transaction fees.

Market rates of interest are 8%. The loss allowance is highly immaterial and can be ignored.

Required:

Explain the accounting entries that Magpie needs to post in the year ended 31 December 20X1 to account for the above.

Summary

Investments in debt

- Amortised cost if:
  - Contractual cash flow characteristics test passed
  - Business model is to hold until maturity
- FVOCI if:
  - Contractual cash flow characteristics test passed
  - Business model involves holding to maturity and selling
- FVPL if not measured at either:
  - Amortised cost
  - FVOCI

8 Impairment of financial assets

From incurred losses to expected losses

Under previous accounting standards, a financial asset could only be impaired if there was objective evidence of impairment. Losses expected as a result of future events, no matter how likely, could not be recognised. This was known as an incurred loss model.

Following the credit crunch, it was argued that many banks had not written down assets, despite having little expectation of receiving any benefits. With the benefit of hindsight this resulted in profit and assets being overstated. No early warning system was in place.

In response, the Board has introduced an expected loss model for financial asset impairment accounting. Entities now determine and account for expected credit losses instead of waiting for an actual default.

The expected loss model makes it is less likely that assets will be over-stated. It also provides timely information to the users of the financial statements because they will be warned about potential losses relatively early.

However, the expected loss model requires a lot of judgement. This could be argued to reduce verifiability and also to increase the scope for the manipulation of profits. The expected loss model also differs from the US GAAP treatment of financial asset impairments, therefore reducing comparability between companies. Another criticism is that the cost of implementing the expected loss model will be high for businesses that hold large volumes of financial assets (such as banks).

Loss allowances

IFRS 9 says that loss allowances must be recognised for financial assets that are debt instruments and which are measured at amortised cost or at fair value through other comprehensive income.

- If the credit risk on the financial asset has not increased significantly since initial recognition, the loss allowance should be equal to 12-month expected credit losses.
- If the credit risk on the financial asset has increased significantly since initial recognition then the loss allowance should be equal to the lifetime expected credit losses.

Adjustments to the loss allowance are charged (or credited) to the statement of profit or loss.

Unless credit impaired, interest income is recognised on the asset's gross carrying amount (i.e. excluding the loss allowance).

Definitions

'Credit loss: The difference between all contractual cash flows that are due to an entity in accordance with the contract and all the cash flow that the entity expects to receive (i.e. all cash shortfalls), discounted at the original effective interest rate

Expected credit losses: The weighted average of credit losses with the respective risks of a default occurring as the weights.

Lifetime expected credit losses: The expected credit losses that result from all possible default events over the expected life of a financial instrument.

12-month expected credit losses: The portion of lifetime expected credit losses that represent the expected credit losses that result from default events on a financial instrument that are possible within the 12 months after the reporting date' (IFRS 9, Appendix A).

Significant increases in credit risk

To assess whether there has been a significant increase in credit risk, IFRS 9 requires entities to compare the asset's risk of default at the reporting date with its risk of default at the date of initial recognition.

Entities should not rely solely on past information when determining if credit risk has increased significantly.

An entity can assume that credit risk has not increased significantly if the instrument has a low credit risk at the reporting date.

Credit risk can be assumed to have increased significantly if contractual payments are more than 30 days overdue at the reporting date.

Test you understanding 9 – Tahoe

San Fran is a company that has issued a public bond. It reports to its shareholders on a bi-annual basis.

Tahoe, a company which holds financial assets until maturity, is one of many investors in San Fran's bond. On purchase, Tahoe deemed the bond to have a low credit risk due to San Fran's strong capacity to fulfil its short-term obligations. It was perceived, however, that adverse changes in the economic environment could have a detrimental impact on San Fran's liquidity.

At Tahoe's reporting date, it has access to the following information about San Fran:

- Sales have declined 15% over the past 6 months
- External agencies are reviewing its credit rating, but no changes have yet been made
- Although market bond prices have remained static, San Fran's bond price has fallen dramatically.

Required:

Discuss the accounting treatment of the bond in Tahoe's financial statements at the reporting date.

Measuring expected losses

An entity's estimate of expected credit losses should be:

- unbiased and probability-weighted
- reflective of the time value of money
- based on information about past events, current conditions and forecasts of future economic conditions.

If an asset is credit impaired at the reporting date, IFRS 9 says that the expected credit losses should be measured as the difference between the asset's gross carrying amount and the present value of the estimated future cash flows when discounted at the original effective rate of interest.

Indications of credit impairment

IFRS 9 says that the following events may suggest the asset is credit-impaired:

- significant financial difficulty of the issuer or the borrower
- a breach of contract, such as a default
- the borrower being granted concessions
- it becoming probable that the borrower will enter bankruptcy

If an asset is credit-impaired, interest income is calculated on the asset's net carrying amount (i.e. the gross carrying amount less the loss allowance).

Test your understanding 10 – Napa

On 1 January 20X1, Napa purchased a bond for $1m which is measured at amortised cost. Interest of 10% is payable in arrears. Repayment is due on 31 December 20X3. The effective rate of interest is 10%.

On 31 December 20X1, Napa received interest of $100,000. It estimated that the probability of default on the bond within the next 12 months would be 0.5%. If default occurs within the next 12 months then Napa estimated that no further interest will be received and that only 50% of the capital will be repaid on 31 December 20X3.

The asset's credit risk at 31 December 20X1 is low.

Required:

Discuss the accounting treatment of the financial asset at 31 December 20X1.

Test your understanding 11 – Eve

On 1 February 20X6, Eve made a four-year loan of $10,000 to Fern. The coupon rate on the loan is 6%, the same as the effective rate of interest. Interest is received at the end of each year.

On 1 February 20X9, Fern tells Eve that it is in significant financial difficulties. At this time the current market interest rate is 8%.

Eve estimates that it will receive no more interest from Fern. It also estimates that only $6,000 of the capital will be repaid on the redemption date.

Eve has already recognised a loss allowance of $1,000 in respect of its loan to Fern.

Required:

How should this be accounted for?

Purchased or originated credit impaired financial assets

A purchased or originated credit-impaired financial asset is one that is credit-impaired on initial recognition. Interest income is calculated on such assets using the **credit-adjusted effective interest rate**.

The credit adjusted effective interest rate incorporates all the contractual terms of the financial asset as well as expected credit losses. In other words, the higher the expected credit losses, the lower the credit adjusted effective interest rate.

Since credit losses anticipated at inception will be recognised through the credit-adjusted effective interest rate, the loss allowance on purchased or originated credit-impaired financial assets should be measured only as the **change in the lifetime expected credit losses** since initial recognition.

Debt instruments at fair value through other comprehensive income

These assets are held at fair value at the reporting date and therefore the loss allowance should not reduce the carrying amount of the asset in the statement of financial position. Instead, the allowance is recorded against other comprehensive income.

Test your understanding 12 – FVOCI and expected losses

An entity purchases a debt instrument for $1,000 on 1 January 20X1. The interest rate on the bond is the same as the effective rate. After accounting for interest for the year to 31 December 20X1, the carrying amount of the bond is still $1,000.

At the reporting date of 31 December 20X1, the fair value of the instrument has fallen to $950. There has not been a significant increase in credit risk since inception so expected credit losses should be measured at 12-month expected credit losses. This is deemed to amount to $30.

Required:

Explain how the revaluation and impairment of the financial asset should be accounted for.

Simplifications

IFRS 9 permits some simplifications:

- The loss allowance should always be measured at an amount equal to lifetime credit losses for trade receivables and contract assets (recognised in accordance with IFRS 15 Revenue from Contracts with Customers) if they do not have a significant financing component.
- For lease receivables, as well as trade receivables and contract assets with a significant financing component, the entity can choose as its accounting policy to measure the loss allowance at an amount equal to lifetime credit losses.

Impairment reversals

At each reporting date, the loss allowance is recalculated.

It may be that the allowance was previously equal to lifetime credit losses but now, due to reductions in credit risk, only needs to be equal to 12-month expected credit losses. As such, there may be a substantial reduction in the allowance required.

Gains or losses on remeasurement of the loss allowance are recorded in profit or loss.

9 Derecognition of financial instruments

A **financial asset** should be derecognised if one of the following has occurred:

- The contractual rights have expired.
  - For example, an option held by the entity may have lapsed and become worthless.
- The financial asset has been sold and substantially all the risks and rewards of ownership have been transferred from the seller to the buyer.

The analysis of where the risks and rewards of ownership lie after a transaction is critical. If an entity has retained substantially all of the risks and rewards of a financial asset then it should not be derecognised, even if it has been legally 'sold' to another entity.

A **financial liability** should be derecognised when the obligation is discharged, cancelled or expires.

The accounting treatment of derecognition is as follows:

- The difference between the carrying amount of the asset or liability and the amount received or paid for it should be recognised in profit or loss for the period.
- For investments in equity instruments held at fair value through other comprehensive income, the cumulative gains and losses recognised in other comprehensive income **are not** recycled to profit or loss on disposal.
- For investments in debt instruments held at fair value through other comprehensive income, the cumulative gains and losses recognised in other comprehensive income **are** recycled to profit or loss on disposal.

Test your understanding 13 – Ming

Ming has two receivables that it has factored to a bank in return for immediate cash proceeds. Both receivables are due from long standing customers who are expected to pay in full and on time. Ming had agreed a three-month credit period with both customers.

The first receivable is for $200,000. In return for assigning the receivable, Ming has received $180,000 from the factor. Under the terms of the factoring arrangement, Ming will not have to repay this money, even if the customer does not settle the debt (the factoring arrangement is said to be 'without recourse').

The second receivable is for $100,000. In return for assigning the receivable, Ming has received $70,000 from the factor. The terms of this factoring arrangement state that Ming will receive a further $5,000 if the customer settles the account on time.

If the customer does not settle the account in accordance with the agreed terms then the receivable will be reassigned back to Ming who will then be obliged to refund the factor with the original $70,000 (this factoring arrangement is said to be 'with recourse').

Required:

Discuss the accounting treatment of the two factoring arrangements.

Test your understanding 14 – Case

Case holds equity investments at fair value through profit or loss. Due to short-term cash flow shortages, Case sold some equity investments for $5 million when the carrying amount was $4 million. The terms of the disposal state that Case has the right to repurchase the shares at any point over the next two years at their fair value on the repurchase date. Case has not derecognised the investment because its directors believe that a repurchase is highly likely.

Required:

Advise the directors of Case as to the acceptability of the above accounting treatment.

Test your understanding 15 – Jones

Jones bought an investment in equity shares for $40 million plus associated transaction costs of $1 million. The asset was designated upon initial recognition as fair value through other comprehensive income. At the reporting date the fair value of the financial asset had risen to $60 million. Shortly after the reporting date the financial asset was sold for $70 million.

Required:

(a) **How should the investment be accounted for?**

(b) **How would the answer have been different if the investment had been classified to be measured at fair value through profit and loss?**

10 Derivatives

Definitions

IFRS 9 says that a derivative is a financial instrument with the following characteristics:

(a) Its value changes in response to the change in a specified interest rate, security price, commodity price, foreign exchange rate, index of prices or rates, a credit rating or credit index or similar variable (called the 'underlying').

(b) It requires little or no initial net investment relative to other types of contract that have a similar response to changes in market conditions.

(c) It is settled at a future date.

The problems of derivatives

Derivatives were originally designed to hedge against fluctuations in agricultural commodity prices on the Chicago Stock Exchange. A speculator would pay a small amount (say $100) now for the contractual obligation to buy a thousand units of wheat in three months' time for $10,000. If in three months' time one thousand units of wheat costs $11,000, then the speculator would make a profit of $900 (11,000 – 100 – 10,000). This would be a 900% return on the original investment over 3 months. But if the price had dropped to $9,000, then the trader would have made a loss of $1,100 (100 + 1,000) despite the initial investment only having been $100.

This shows that losses on derivatives can be far greater than their historical cost. Therefore, it is important that derivatives are recognised and disclosed in the financial statements as they have very little initial outlay yet expose the entity to significant gains and losses.

Typical derivatives

Derivatives include the following types of contracts:

Forward contracts

- The holder of a forward contract is obliged to buy or sell a defined amount of a specific underlying asset, at a specified price at a specified future date.
- For example, a forward contract for foreign currency might require £100,000 to be exchanged for $150,000 in three months' time. Both parties to the contract have both a financial asset and a financial liability. For example, one party has the right to receive $150,000 and the obligation to pay £100,000.
- Forward currency contracts may be used to minimise the risk on amounts receivable or payable in foreign currencies.

Forward rate agreements

- Forward rate agreements can be used to fix the interest charge on a floating rate loan.
- For example, an entity has a $1m floating rate loan, and the current rate of interest is 7%. The rates are reset to the market rate every six months, and the entity cannot afford to pay more than 9% interest. The entity enters into a six-month forward rate agreement (with, say, a bank) at 9% on $1m. If the market rates go up to 10%, then the bank will pay them $5,000 (1% of $1m for 6 months) which in effect reduces their finance cost to 9%. If the rates only go up to 8% then the entity pays the bank $5,000. The forward rate agreement effectively fixes the interest rate payable at 9% for the period.

Futures contracts

- Futures contracts oblige the holder to buy or sell a standard quantity of a specific underlying item at a specified future date.
- Futures contracts are very similar to forward contracts. The difference is that futures contracts have standard terms and are traded on a financial exchange, whereas forward contracts are tailor-made and are not traded on a financial exchange. Also, whilst forward contracts will always be settled, a futures contract will rarely be held to maturity.

Swaps

- Two parties agree to exchange periodic payments at specified intervals over a specified time period.
- For example, in an interest rate swap, the parties may agree to exchange fixed and floating rate interest payments calculated by reference to a notional principal amount.
- This enables companies to keep a balance between their fixed and floating rate interest payments without having to change the underlying loans.

Options

- These give the holder the right, but not the obligation, to buy or sell a specific underlying asset on or before a specified future date.

A contract to buy or sell a non-financial item (such as inventory or property, plant and equipment) is only a derivative if:

- it can be settled net in cash (or using another financial asset), and
- the contract was not entered into for the purpose of receipt or delivery of the item to meet the entity's operating requirements.

Derivatives and net settlement

IFRS 9 says that a contract to buy or sell a non-financial item is considered to be settled net in cash when:

- the terms of the contract permit either party to settle the contract net
- the entity has a practice of settling similar contracts net
- the entity, for similar contracts, has a practice of taking delivery of the item and then quickly selling it in order to benefit from fair value changes
- the non-financial item is readily convertible to cash.

If the contract is not a derivative then it is a simple executory contract (a contract where neither party has yet performed its obligations). Such contracts are not normally accounted for until the sale or purchase date.

Measurement of derivatives

On initial recognition, derivatives should be measured at fair value. Transaction costs are expensed to the statement of profit or loss.

At the reporting date, derivatives are remeasured to fair value. Movements in fair value are recognised in profit or loss.

Accounting for derivatives

Entity A has a reporting date of 30 September. It enters into an option on 1 June 20X5, to purchase 10,000 shares in another entity on 1 November 20X5 for $10 per share. The purchase price of each option is $1. This is recorded as follows:

Debit	Option (10,000 × $1)	$10,000
Credit	Cash	$10,000

By 30 September the fair value of each option has increased to $1.30.

This increase is recorded as follows:

Debit	Option (10,000 × ($1.30 – 1))	$3,000
Credit	Profit or loss	$3,000

On 1 November, the fair value per option increases to $1.50. The share price on the same date is $11.50. A exercises the option on 1 November and the shares are classified at fair value through profit or loss. Financial assets are recognised at their fair value so the shares are initially measured at $115,000 (10,000 × $11.50):

Debit	Investment in shares (at fair value)	$115,000
Credit	Cash (10,000 × $10)	$100,000
Credit	Option ($10,000 + $3,000)	$13,000
Credit	Profit or loss (gain on option)	$2,000

Test your understanding 16 – Hoggard

Hoggard buys 100 options on 1 January 20X6 for $5 per option. Each option gives Hoggard the right to buy a share in Rowling on 31 December 20X6 for $10 per share.

Required:

How should this be accounted for, given the following outcomes?

(a) **The options are sold on 1 July 20X6 for $15 each.**

(b) **On 31 December 20X6, Rowling's share price is $8 and Hoggard lets the option lapse unexercised.**

(c) **The option is exercised on 31 December when Rowling's share price is $25. The shares are classified as held for trading.**

Embedded derivatives

An embedded derivative is a **'component of a hybrid contract that also includes a non-derivative host, with the effect that some of the cash flows of the combined instrument vary in a way similar to a stand-alone derivative'** (IFRS 9, para 4.3.3).

With regards to the accounting treatment of an embedded derivative, if the host contract is within the scope of IFRS 9 then the entire contract must be classified and measured in accordance with that standard.

If the host contract is not within the scope of IFRS 9 (i.e. it is not a financial asset or liability), then the embedded derivative can be separated out and measured at fair value through profit or loss if:

(i) **'the economic risks and characteristics of the embedded derivative are not closely related to those of the host contract**

(ii) **a separate instrument with the same terms as the embedded derivative would meet the definition of a derivative, and**

(iii) **the entire instrument is not measured at fair value with changes in fair value recognised in profit or loss'** (IFRS 9, para 4.3.3).

Because of the complexity involved in splitting out and measuring an embedded derivative, IFRS 9 permits a hybrid contract where the host element is outside the scope of IFRS 9 to be measured at fair value through profit or loss in its entirety.

Therefore, for the vast majority of embedded derivatives, the whole contract will simply be measured at fair value through profit or loss.

Embedded derivatives: an example

An entity has an investment in a convertible bond, which can be converted into a fixed number of equity shares at a specified future date. The bond is a non-derivative host contract and the option to convert to shares is therefore a derivative element.

The host contract, the bond, is a financial liability and so is within the scope of IFRS 9. This means that the rules of IFRS 9 must be applied to the entire contract.

The bond would fail the contractual cash flow characteristics test and therefore the entire contract should be measured at fair value through profit or loss.

11 Hedge accounting

The need for hedge accounting

An entity has inventories of gold that cost $8m and whose value has increased to $10m. The entity is worried that the fair value of this inventory will fall, so it enters into a futures contract on 1 October 20X1 to sell the inventory for $10m in 6 months' time.

By the reporting date, the fair value of the inventory had fallen by $1m to $9m. There was a $1m increase in the fair value of the derivative.

In accordance with IFRS 9, the $1m gain on the derivative will be recognised through profit or loss:

Dr Derivative	$1m
Cr Profit or loss	$1m

In accordance with IAS 2, the $1m decline in the inventory's fair value will not be recognised because inventories are measured at the lower of cost ($8m) and NRV ($9m, assuming no selling costs).

The derivative has created volatility in profit or loss. However, if the entity had chosen to apply hedge accounting, this volatility would have been eliminated. This section of the text will outline the criteria for, and accounting treatment of, hedge accounting in more detail.

Definitions

Hedge accounting is a method of managing risk by designating one or more hedging instruments so that their change in fair value is offset, in whole or in part, by the change in fair value or cash flows of a hedged item.

A **hedged item** is an asset or liability that exposes the entity to risks of changes in fair value or future cash flows (and is designated as being hedged). There are 3 types of hedged item:

- A recognised asset or liability
- An unrecognised firm commitment – a binding agreement for the exchange of a specified quantity of resources at a specified price on a specified future date
- A highly probable forecast transaction – an uncommitted but anticipated future transaction.

A **hedging instrument** is a designated derivative, or a non-derivative financial asset or financial liability, whose fair value or cash flows are expected to offset changes in fair value or future cash flows of the hedged item.

Types of hedge accounting

IFRS 9 identifies three types of hedge. Two of these are within the P2 syllabus:

(1) **'Fair value hedge: a hedge of the exposure to changes in fair value of a recognised asset or liability or an unrecognised firm commitment that is attributable to a particular risk and could affect profit or loss (or other comprehensive income for equity investments measured at fair value through other comprehensive income).**

(2) **Cash flow hedge: a hedge of the exposure to variability in cash flows that is attributable to a particular risk associated with a recognised asset or liability or a highly probable forecast transaction and that could affect profit or loss'** (IFRS 9, para 6.5.2).

Criteria for hedge accounting

Under IFRS 9, hedge accounting rules can only be applied if the hedging relationship meets the following criteria:

(1) The hedging relationship consists only of eligible hedging instruments and hedged items.

(2) At the inception of the hedge there must be formal documentation identifying the hedged item and the hedging instrument.

(3) The hedging relationship meets all effectiveness requirements (see latter section for more details).

Accounting treatment of a fair value hedge

At the reporting date:

- The hedging instrument will be remeasured to fair value.
- The carrying amount of the hedged item will be adjusted for the change in fair value since the inception of the hedge.

The gain (or loss) on the hedging instrument and the loss (or gain) on the hedged item will be recorded:

- in profit or loss in most cases, but
- in other comprehensive income if the hedged item is an investment in equity that is measured at fair value through other comprehensive income.

Simple fair value hedge

An entity has inventories of gold that cost $8m but whose value has increased to $10m. The entity is worried that the fair value of this inventory will fall, so it enters into a futures contract on 1 October 20X1 to sell the inventory for $10m in 6 months' time. This was designated as a fair value hedge.

By the reporting date of 31 December 20X1, the fair value of the inventory had fallen from $10m to $9m. There was a $1m increase in the fair value of the derivative.

The entity believes that all effectiveness criteria have been met.

Under a fair value hedge, the movement in the fair value of the item and instrument since the inception of the hedge are accounted for. The gains and losses will be recorded in profit or loss.

The $1m gain on the future and the $1m loss on the inventory will be accounted for as follows:

Dr Derivative	$1m
Cr Profit or loss	$1m
Dr Profit or loss	$1m
Cr Inventory	$1m

By applying hedge accounting, the profit impact of remeasuring the derivative to fair value has been offset by the movement in the fair value of the inventory. Volatility has, in this example, been eliminated.

Note that the inventory will now be held at $7m (cost of $8m – $1m fair value decline). This is neither cost nor NRV. The normal accounting treatment of inventory has been changed by applying hedge accounting rules.

Test your understanding 17 – Fair value hedge

On 1 January 20X8 an entity purchased equity instruments for their fair value of $900,000. They were designated upon initial recognition to be classified as fair value through other comprehensive income.

At 30 September 20X8, the equity instrument was still worth $900,000 but the entity became worried about the risk of a decline in value. It therefore entered into a futures contract to sell the shares for $900,000 in six months' time. It identified the futures contract as a hedging instrument as part of a fair value hedging arrangement. The fair value hedge was correctly documented and designated upon initial recognition. All effectiveness criteria have been complied with.

By the reporting date of 31 December 20X8, the fair value of the equity instrument had fallen to $800,000, and the fair value of the futures contract had risen by $90,000.

Required:

Explain the accounting treatment of the fair value hedge arrangement based upon the available information.

Test your understanding 18 – Firm commitments

Chive has a firm commitment to buy an item of machinery for CU2m on 31 March 20X2. The Directors are worried about the risk of exchange rate fluctuations.

On 1 October 20X1, when the exchange rate is CU2:$1, Chive enters into a futures contract to buy CU2m for $1m on 31 March 20X2.

At 31 December 20X1, CU2m would cost $1,100,000. The fair value of the futures contract has risen to $95,000. All effectiveness criteria have been complied with.

Required:

Explain the accounting treatment of the above in the financial statements for the year ended 31 December 20X1 if:

(a) **Hedge accounting was not used.**

(b) **On 1 October 20X1, the futures contract was designated as a fair value hedge of the movements in the fair value of the firm commitment to purchase the machine.**

Accounting treatment of a cash flow hedge

For cash flow hedges, the hedging instrument will be remeasured to fair value at the reporting date. The gain or loss is recognised in other comprehensive income.

However, if the gain or loss on the hedging instrument since the inception of the hedge is greater than the loss or gain on the hedged item then the **excess** gain or loss on the instrument must be recognised in profit or loss.

Test your understanding 19 – Cash flow hedge

A company enters into a derivative contract in order to protect its future cash inflows relating to a recognised financial asset. At inception, when the fair value of the hedging instrument was nil, the relationship was documented as a cash flow hedge.

By the reporting date, the loss in respect of the future cash flows amounted to $9,100 in fair value terms. It has been determined that the hedging relationship meets all effectiveness criteria.

Required:

Explain the accounting treatment of the cash flow hedge if the fair value of the hedging instrument at the reporting date is:

(a) **$8,500**

(b) **$10,000.**

- If the hedged item eventually results in the recognition of a financial asset or a financial liability, the gains or losses that were recognised in equity shall be reclassified to profit or loss as a reclassification adjustment in the same period during which the hedged forecast cash flows affect profit or loss (e.g. in the period when the hedged forecast sale occurs).
- If the hedged item eventually results in the recognition of a non-financial asset or liability, the gain or loss held in equity must be adjusted against the carrying amount of the non-financial asset/liability. This is not a reclassification adjustment and therefore it does not affect other comprehensive income.

Test your understanding 20 – Bling

On 31 October 20X1, Bling had inventories of gold which cost $6.4m to buy and which could be sold for $7.7m. The management of Bling are concerned about the risk of fluctuations in future cash inflows from the sale of this gold.

To mitigate this risk, Bling entered into a futures contract on 31 October 20X1 to sell the gold for $7.7m. The contracts mature on 31 March 20X2. The hedging relationship was designated and documented at inception as a cash flow hedge. All effectiveness criteria are complied with.

On 31 December 20X1, the fair value of the gold was $8.6m. The fair value of the futures contract had fallen by $0.9m.

There is no change in fair value of the gold and the futures contract between 31 December 20X1 and 31 March 20X2. On 31 March 20X2, the inventory is sold for its fair value and the futures contract is settled net with the bank.

Required:

(a) **Discuss the accounting treatment of the hedge in the year ended 31 December 20X1.**

(b) **Outline the accounting treatment of the inventory sale and the futures contract settlement on 31 March 20X2.**

Test your understanding 21 – Grayton

In January, Grayton, whose functional currency is the dollar ($), decided that it was highly probable that it would buy an item of plant in one year's time for KR 200,000. As a result of being risk averse, it wished to hedge the risk that the cost of buying KRs would rise and so entered into a forward rate agreement to buy KR 200,000 in one year's time for the fixed sum of $100,000. The fair value of this contract at inception was zero and it was designated as a hedging instrument.

At Grayton's reporting date of 31 July, the KR had depreciated and the value of KR 200,000 was $90,000. The fair value of the derivative had declined by $10,000. These values remained unchanged until the plant was purchased.

Required:

How should this be accounted for?

Hedge effectiveness

Hedge accounting can only be used if the hedging relationship meets all effectiveness requirements. In the examples so far, it has been assumed that this is the case.

According to IFRS 9, an entity must assess at the inception of the hedging relationship, and at each reporting date, whether a hedging relationship meets the hedge effectiveness requirements. The assessment should be **forward-looking.**

The hedge effectiveness requirements are as follows

(1) **'There must be an economic relationship between the hedged item and the hedging instrument'** (IFRS 9, para 6.4.1).

- For example, if the price of a share falls below $10, the fair value of a futures contract to sell the share for $10 rises.

(2) **'The effect of credit risk does not dominate the value changes that result from that economic relationship'** (IFRS 9, para 6.4.1).

- Credit risk may lead to erratic fair value movements in either the hedged item or the hedging instrument. For example, if the counterparty of a derivative experiences a decline in credit worthiness, the fair value of the derivative (the hedging instrument) may fall substantially. This movement is unrelated to changes in the fair value of the item and would lead to hedge ineffectiveness.

(3) **'The hedge ratio of the hedging relationship is the same as that resulting from the quantity of the hedged item that the entity actually hedges and the quantity of the hedging instrument that the entity actually uses to hedge that quantity of hedged item'** (IFRS 9, para 6.4.1).

Hedge ratios – example 1

An entity owns 120,000 gallons of oil. It enters into 1 futures contract to sell 40,000 gallons of oil at a fixed price.

It wishes to designate this as a fair value hedge, with 120,000 gallons of oil as the hedged item and the futures contract as the hedging instrument. If deemed effective, this would mean that the fair value gain or loss on the hedged item (the oil) and the fair value loss or gain on the hedging instrument (the futures contract) would be recorded and recognised in profit or loss.

However, the hedge ratio means that the gain or loss on the item would probably be much bigger than the loss or gain on the instrument. This would create volatility in profit or loss that is at odds with the purpose of hedge accounting. Therefore, the hedge ratio must be adjusted to avoid the imbalance.

It may be that the hedged item should be designated as 40,000 gallons of oil, with the hedging instrument as 1 futures contract. The other 80,000 gallons of oil would be accounted for in accordance with normal accounting rules (IAS 2 Inventories).

Hedge ratios – example 2

In deciding whether the hedge ratio is appropriate, an entity should consider if there is a commercial reason for any imbalance between the quantity of the designated item and the quantity of the designated instrument.

Example

An entity wishes to fix the purchase price of 100 tonnes of coffee. Coffee futures contracts are denominated in Llbs (pounds).These contracts are traded in standard amounts, and therefore it is not possible to hedge 100 tonnes exactly. Five contracts would hedge the equivalent of 85 tonnes of coffee whilst six contracts would hedge the equivalent of 102.1 tonnes of coffee.

Although this is an imbalance that will lead to ineffectiveness (the movements on the item and instrument will most likely not offset), there is a commercial reason for this that is not at odds with the aim of hedge accounting. Therefore, the hedging ratio should not be adjusted.

Assuming that the entity enters into five futures contracts, then the hedged ratio is 20 tonnes of coffee to 1 contract:

- If the item is designated as the purchase of 100 tonnes of coffee, then the hedging instrument should be designated as five futures contracts.
- If the item is designated as the purchase of 60 tonnes of coffee, then the hedging instrument should be designated as three futures contracts. The other two futures contracts will be accounted for as derivatives in the usual way (fair value through profit or loss).

12 Discontinuing hedge accounting

Discontinuance

An entity must cease hedge accounting if any of the following occur:

- The hedging instrument expires or is exercised, sold or terminated.
- The hedge no longer meets the hedging criteria.
- A forecast future transaction that qualified as a hedged item is no longer highly probable.

The discontinuance should be accounted for prospectively (entries posted to date are not reversed).

Upon discontinuing a cash flow hedge, the treatment of the accumulated gains or losses on the hedging instrument within reserves depends on the reason for the discontinuation. IFRS 9 says:

- If the forecast transaction is no longer expected to occur, gains and losses recognised in other comprehensive income must be taken to profit or loss immediately.
- If the transaction is still expected to occur, the gains and losses will be retained in equity until the former hedged transaction occurs.

13 Disclosure of financial instruments

IFRS 7 provides the disclosure requirements for financial instruments.

The main disclosures required are:

(1) Information about the significance of financial instruments for an entity's financial position and performance.

(2) Information about the nature and extent of risks arising from financial instruments.

IFRS 7 Disclosures

Significance of financial instruments

- An entity must disclose the **significance** of financial instruments for their financial position and performance. The disclosures must be made for each class of financial instruments.
- An entity must disclose items of income, expense, gains, and losses, with separate disclosure of gains and losses from each class of financial instrument.

Nature and extent of risks arising from financial instruments

Qualitative disclosures

The qualitative disclosures describe:

- risk exposures for each type of financial instrument
- management's objectives, policies, and processes for managing those risks
- changes from the prior period.

Quantitative disclosures

The quantitative disclosures provide information about the extent to which the entity is exposed to risk, based on information provided internally to the entity's key management personnel. These disclosures include:

- summary quantitative data about exposure to each risk at the reporting date
- disclosures about credit risk, liquidity risk, and market risk as further described below
- concentrations of risk.

The key types of risk are outlined below.

Types of risk

There are four types of financial risk:

(1) **Market risk** – This refers to the possibility that the value of an asset (or burden of a liability) might go up or down. Market risk includes three types of risk: currency risk, interest rate risk and price risk.

   (a) **Currency risk** is the risk that the value of a financial instrument will fluctuate because of changes in foreign exchange rates.

   (b) Fair value **interest rate risk** is the risk that the value of a financial instrument will fluctuate due to changes in market interest rates. This is a common problem with fixed interest rate bonds. The price of these bonds goes up and down as interest rates go down and up.

   (c) Price risk refers to other factors affecting price changes. These can be specific to the enterprise (bad financial results will cause a share price to fall), relate to the sector as a whole (all Tech-Stocks boomed in the late nineties, and crashed in the new century) or relate to the type of security (bonds do well when shares are doing badly, and vice versa).

Market risk embodies not only the potential for a loss to be made but also a gain to be made.

(2) **Credit risk** – The risk that one party to a financial instrument fails to discharge its obligations, causing a financial loss to the other party. For example, a bank is exposed to credit risk on its loans, because a borrower might default on its loan.

(3) **Liquidity risk** – This is also referred to as funding risk. This is the risk that an enterprise will be unable to meet its commitments on its financial instruments. For example, a business may be unable to repay its loans when they fall due.

(4) **Cash flow interest rate risk** – This is the risk that future cash flows associated with a monetary financial instrument will fluctuate in amount due to changes in market interest rates. For example, the cash paid (or received) on floating rate loans will fluctuate in line with market interest rates.

14 Chapter summary

Classification of liabilities and equity:
- Liabilities include a contractual obligation to pay cash or issue a variable number of equity instruments
- Equity – no such obligations.

Financial assets:
- Measured at either
  - Fair value through profit or loss
  - Fair value through other comprehensive income
  - Amortised cost

Financial liabilities:
Measured at either:
- Fair value through profit or loss
- Amortised cost

Derivatives (assets and liabilities):
- Measured at fair value through profit or loss
- Volatility can be reduced by
  - fair value hedging
  - cash flow hedging

Impairment of financial assets:
- Loss allowances required for investments in debt measured at amortised cost or FVOCI

Disclosure requirements:
- Significance of financial instruments
- Nature and extents of risks
- Qualitative and quantitative issues

Test your understanding answers

Test your understanding 1 – Liabilities or equity?

1m preference shares

IAS 32 states that a financial liability is any contract that may be settled in the entity's own equity instruments and is a non-derivative for which the entity is obliged to deliver a variable number of its own equity instruments.

Therefore, a contract that requires the entity to deliver as many of the entity's own equity instruments as are equal in value to a certain amount should be treated as debt.

Coasters must redeem the first set of preference shares by issuing ordinary shares equal to the value of $3 million. The $3 million received from the preference share issue should be classified as a liability on the statement of financial position.

2m preference shares

A contract that will be settled by the entity receiving (or delivering) a fixed number of its own equity instruments in exchange for a fixed amount of cash or another financial asset is an equity instrument.

Coasters will redeem the second preference share issue with a fixed number of ordinary shares. Therefore, the $5.6 million from the second preference share issue should be classified as equity in the statement of financial position.

4m preference shares

A financial liability exists if there is an obligation to deliver cash or another financial asset.

There is no obligation for Coasters to repay the instrument.

Dividends are only payable if they are also paid on ordinary shares. There is no obligation to pay dividends on ordinary shares so there is no obligation to pay dividends on these preference shares.

The instrument is not a financial liability. The proceeds from the preference share issue should therefore be classified as equity in the statement of financial position.

Test your understanding 2 – Hoy

Hoy has a financial liability to be measured at amortised cost.

The financial liability is initially recorded at the fair value of the consideration received (the net proceeds of issue). This amount is then increased each year by interest at the effective rate and reduced by the actual repayments.

Hoy has no issue costs, so the net proceeds of issue were $9,500 ($10,000 less 5%). The annual cash payment is $200 (the 2% coupon rate multiplied by the $10,000 nominal value of the debt).

	Bal b/fwd	Finance costs (10%)	Cash paid	Bal c/fwd
Rep date	$	$	$	$
31 Dec X1	9,500	950	(200)	10,250
31 Dec X2	10,250	1,025	(200)	
			(11,075)	
		1,975		

Wiggins has a liability that will be classified and accounted for at amortised cost and thus initially measured at the fair value of consideration received less the transaction costs:

	$
Cash received ($20,000 × 90%)	18,000
Less the transaction costs	(1,000)
Initial recognition	17,000

The effective rate is used to determine the finance cost for the year – this is charged to profit or loss. The coupon rate is applied to the nominal value of the loan notes to determine the cash paid to the holder of the loan notes:

	Bal b/fwd	**Finance costs (12%)**	**Cash paid**	**Bal c/fwd**
Rep date	$	$	$	$
31 Dec X4	17,000	2,040	(1,200)	17,840
31 Dec X5	17,840	2,141	(1,200)	18,781
31 Dec X6	18,781	2,254	(1,200)	19,835
31 Dec X7	19,835	2,380	(1,200) (21,015)	
		8,815		

Cavendish has a financial liability to be measured at amortised cost.

It is initially recorded at the fair value of the consideration received. There is no discount on issue, nor is there any issue costs to deduct from the initial measurement.

The opening balance is increased each year by interest at the effective rate. The liability is reduced by the cash repayments – there are no interest repayments in this example because it is a zero rate bond.

	Bal b/fwd	**Finance costs (7%)**	**Cash paid**	**Bal c/fwd**
Rep date	$	$	$	$
31 Dec X5	10,000	700	Nil	10,700
31 Dec X6	10,700	749	(11,449)	

Test your understanding 3 – Bean

When a financial liability is designated to be measured at fair value through profit or loss to reduce an accounting mis-match, the fair value movement must be split into:

- fair value movement due to own credit risk, which is presented in other comprehensive income (OCI)
- the remaining fair value movement, which is presented in profit or loss.

The value of Bean's liability will be reduced by $30 million. A credit of $10 million will be recorded in OCI and a credit of $20 million will be recorded in profit or loss.

Test your understanding 4 – Craig

Up to 31 December 20X8, the accounting entries are the same under both scenarios.

(1) **Splitting the proceeds**

The cash payments on the bond should be discounted to their present value using the interest rate for a bond without the conversion rights, i.e. 8%.

Date		**Cash flow**	**Discount factor (8%)**	**Present value**
		$		$
31/12/X6	Interest	4,000	$1/1.08$	3,704
31/12/X7	Interest	4,000	$1/1.08^2$	3,429
31/12/X8	Interest and principal	104,000	$1/1.08^3$	82,559
				–––––––
Liability component			A	89,692
Net proceeds of issue were			B	100,000
Equity component			B – A	10,308

(2) **The annual finance costs and year end carrying amounts**

	Opening balance	Finance cost (8%)	Cash paid	Closing balance
	$	$	$	$
X6	89,692	7,175	(4,000)	92,867
X7	92,867	7,429	(4,000)	96,296
X8	96,296	7,704	(4,000)	100,000

(3) (a) **Conversion**

The carrying amounts at 31 December 20X8 are:

	$
Equity	10,308
Liability – bond	100,000
	110,308

If the conversion rights are exercised, then 50,000 ($100,000 ÷ 2) equity shares of $1 are issued and $60,308 is classified as share premium.

(b) **Redemption**

The carrying amounts at 31 December 20X8 are the same as under 3a. On redemption, the $100,000 liability is extinguished by cash payments. The equity component remains within equity, probably as a non-distributable reserve.

Test your understanding 5 – Ashes' financial assets

(1) Investments in equity held for short-term speculative purposes must be classified and accounted for as fair value through profit or loss. Such assets are initially recognised at fair value. Any transaction costs are expensed to profit or loss. The assets are remeasured to fair value at the reporting date with the gains and losses on remeasurement recognised in profit or loss.

(2) Investments in equity that, from the outset, are going to be held indefinitely may be irrevocably designated upon initial recognition as fair value through other comprehensive income. Such assets are initially recognised at fair value plus transaction costs. They are remeasured to fair value at the reporting date and gains and losses on remeasurement are recognised in other comprehensive income. If no such election on purchase is made then the investment must be classified and accounted for as fair value through profit or loss (see (1) above).

Test your understanding 6 – Paloma

A debt instrument can be held at amortised cost if

- the entity intends to hold the financial asset to collect contractual cash flows, rather than selling it to realise fair value changes.
- the contractual cash flows of the asset are solely payments of principal and interest based upon the principal amount outstanding.

Paloma's objective is to hold the financial assets and collect the contractual cash flows. Making some sales when cash flow deteriorates does not contradict that objective.

The bond pays a market level of interest, and therefore the interest payments received provide adequate compensation for the time value of money or the credit risk associated with the principal amount outstanding.

This means that the asset can be measured at amortised cost.

Test your understanding 7 – Tokyo

(a) The business model is to hold the asset until redemption. Therefore, the debt instrument will be measured at amortised cost.

The asset is initially recognised at its fair value plus transaction costs of $97,000 ($95,000 + $2,000).

Interest income will be recognised in profit or loss using the effective rate of interest.

	Bfd	Interest (8%)	Receipt	Cfd
	$	$	$	$
y/e 31/12/X1	97,000	7,760	(5,000)	99,760
y/e 31/12/X2	99,760	7,981	(5,000)	102,741
y/e 31/12/X3	102,741	8,219	(5,000) (105,960)	nil

In the year ended 31 December 20X1, interest income of $7,760 will be recognised in profit or loss and the asset will be held at $99,760 on the statement of financial position.

In the year ended 31 December 20X2, interest income of $7,981 will be recognised in profit or loss and the asset will be held at $102,741 on the statement of financial position.

In the year ended 31 December 20X3, interest income of $8,219 will be recognised in profit or loss.

(b) The business model is to hold the asset until redemption, but sales may be made to invest in other assets will higher returns. Therefore, the debt instrument will be measured at fair value through other comprehensive income.

The asset is initially recognised at its fair value plus transaction costs of $97,000 ($95,000 + $2,000).

Interest income will be recognised in profit or loss using the effective rate of interest.

The asset must be revalued to fair value at the year end. The gain will be recorded in other comprehensive income.

	Bfd	Interest (per (a))	Receipt	Total	Gain/ (loss)	Cfd
	$	$	$	$	$	$
y/e 31/12/X1	97,000	7,760	(5,000)	99,760	10,240	110,000
y/e 31/12/X2	110,000	7,981	(5,000)	112,981	(8,981)	104,000
y/e 31/12/X3	104,000	8,219	(5,000) (105,960)	1,259	(1,259)	nil

Note that the amounts recognised in profit or loss as interest income must be the same as if the asset was simply held at amortised cost. Therefore, the interest income figures are the same as in part (a).

In the year ended 31 December 20X1, interest income of $7,760 will be recognised in profit or loss and a revaluation gain of $10,240 will be recognised in other comprehensive income. The asset will be held at $110,000 on the statement of financial position.

In the year ended 31 December 20X2, interest income of $7,981 will be recognised in profit or loss and a revaluation loss of $8,981 will be recognised in other comprehensive income. The asset will be held at $104,000 on the statement of financial position.

In the year ended 31 December 20X3, interest income of $8,219 will be recognised in profit or loss and a revaluation loss of $1,259 will be recognised in other comprehensive income.

(c) The bond would be classified as fair value through profit or loss.

The asset is initially recognised at its fair value of $95,000. The transaction costs of $2,000 would be expensed to profit or loss.

In the year ended 31/12/X1, interest income of $5,000 ($100,000 × 5%) would be recognised in profit or loss. The asset would be revalued to $110,000 with a gain of $15,000 ($110,000 – $95,000) recognised in profit or loss.

On 1/1/X2, the cash proceeds of $110,000 would be recognised and the financial asset would be derecognised.

Test your understanding 8 – Magpie

The loan is a financial asset because Magpie has a contractual right to receive cash in two years' time.

Financial assets are initially recognised at fair value. Fair value is the price paid in an orderly transaction between market participants at the measurement date.

Market participants would receive 8% interest on loans of this type, whereas the loan made to the supplier is interest-free. It would seem that the transaction has not occurred on fair value terms.

The financial asset will not be recognised at the price paid of $2 million as this is not the fair value. Instead, the fair value must be determined. This can be achieved by calculating the present value of the future cash flows from the loan (discounted using a market rate of interest).

The financial asset will therefore be initially recognised at $1.71 million ($2m × 1/1.08^2). The entry required to record this is as follows:

Dr Financial asset	$1.71m
Dr Profit or loss	$0.29m
Cr Cash	$2.00m

The financial asset is subsequently measured at amortised cost:

	1 Jan X1	Interest (8%)	Receipt	31 Dec X1
	$m	$m	$m	$m
y/e 31/12/X1	1.71	0.14	–	1.85

Interest income of $0.14 million is recorded by posting the following:

Dr Financial asset	$0.14m
Cr Profit or loss	$0.14m

The loan is interest-free, so no cash is received during the period.

The financial asset will have a carrying amount of $1.85 million as at 31 December 20X1.

By 31 December 20X2, the financial asset will have a carrying amount of $2 million. This amount will then be repaid by the supplier.

Test you understanding 9 – Tahoe

Using available information, Tahoe needs to assess whether the credit risk on the bond has increased significantly since inception.

It would seem that San Fran's performance has declined and this may have an impact on its liquidity.

The review of San Fran's credit rating by external agencies is suggestive of wider concerns about the performance and position of San Fran.

The fact that market bond prices are static suggests that the decline in San Fran's bond price is entity specific. This is likely to be a response to San Fran's increased credit risk.

Based on the above, it would seem that the credit risk of the bond is no longer low. As a result, it can be concluded that credit risk has increased significantly since inception.

This means that Tahoe must recognise a loss allowance equal to lifetime expected credit losses on the bond.

Test your understanding 10 – Napa

The credit risk on the financial asset has not significantly increased. Therefore, a loss allowance should be made equal to 12-month expected credit losses. The loss allowance should factor in a range of possible outcomes, as well as the time value of money.

The credit loss on the asset is $586,777 (W1). This represents the present value of the difference between the contractual cash flows and the expected receipts if a default occurs.

The expected credit loss is $2,934 ($586,777 credit loss × 0.5% probability of occurrence). A loss allowance of $2,934 will be created and an impairment loss of $2,934 will be charged to profit or loss in the year ended 31 December 20X1.

The net carrying amount of the financial asset on the statement of financial position is $997,066 ($1,000,000 – $2,934).

Note: Interest in future periods will continue to be charged on the asset's gross carrying amount of $1,000,000.

Date of receipt	Expected cash shortfall	Discount rate	Present value
	$		$
31/12/X2	100,000	1/1.1	90,909
31/12/X3	100,000	$1/1.1^2$	82,645
31/12/X3	500,000	$1/1.1^2$	413,223
			586,777

Test your understanding 11 – Eve

Evidence about the significant financial difficulties of Fern mean that the asset is now credit impaired.

Expected losses on credit impaired assets are calculated as the difference between the asset's gross carrying amount and the present value of the expected future cash flows discounted using the original effective rate of interest.

Because the coupon and the effective interest rate are the same, the carrying amount of the asset will remain constant at $10,000.

The present value of the future cash flows discounted using the original effective rate is $5,660 ($6,000 × 1/1.06).

The expected losses are therefore $4,340 ($10,000 – $5,660) and so a loss allowance should be recognised for this amount. Therefore, the existing loss allowance must be increased by $3,340 ($4,340 – $1,000) with an expense charged to profit or loss.

The asset is credit impaired and so interest income will now be calculated on the net carrying amount of $5,660 (the gross amount of $10,000 less the loss allowance of $4,340). Consequently, in the last year of the loan, interest income of $340 (5,660 × 6%) will be recognised in profit or loss.

Test your understanding 12 – FVOCI and expected losses

A loss of $50 ($1,000 – $950) arising on the revaluation of the asset to fair value will be recognised in other comprehensive income.

Dr OCI	$50
Cr Financial asset	$50

The 12-month expected credit losses of $30 will be debited to profit or loss. The credit entry is not recorded against the carrying amount of the asset but rather against other comprehensive income:

Dr Impairment loss (P/L)	$30
Cr OCI	$30

There is therefore a cumulative loss in OCI of $20 (the fair value change of $50 offset by the impairment amount of $30).

Test your understanding 13 – Ming

The principle at stake with derecognition or otherwise of receivables is whether, under the factoring arrangement, the risks and rewards of ownership pass from Ming to the factor. The key risk with regard to receivables is the risk of bad debt.

In the first arrangement the $180,000 has been received as a one-off, non refundable sum. This is factoring without recourse for bad debts. The risk of bad debt has clearly passed from Ming to the factoring bank. Accordingly Ming should derecognise the receivable and there will be an expense of $20,000 recognised.

In the second arrangement the $70,000 is simply a payment on account. More may be received by Ming implying that Ming retains an element of reward. The monies received are refundable in the event of default and as such represent an obligation. This means that the risk of slow payment and bad debt remains with Ming who is liable to repay the monies so far received. Despite the passage of legal title the receivable should remain recognised in the accounts of Ming. In substance Ming has borrowed $70,000 and this loan should be recognised immediately. This will increase the gearing of Ming.

Test your understanding 14 – Case

An entity has transferred a financial asset if it has transferred the contractual rights to receive the cash flows of the asset.

IFRS 9 says that if an entity has transferred a financial asset, it must evaluate the extent to which it has retained the significant risks and rewards of ownership. If the entity transfers substantially all the risks and rewards of ownership, the entity must derecognise the financial asset.

Gains and losses on the disposal of a financial asset are recognised in the statement of profit or loss.

Case is under no obligation to buy back the shares and is therefore protected from future share price declines. Moreover, If Case does repurchase the shares, this will be at fair value rather than a pre-fixed price and therefore Case does not retain the risks and rewards related to price fluctuations.

The risks and rewards of ownership have been transferred and, as such, Case should derecognise the financial asset. A profit of $1m ($5m – $4m) should be recognised in profit or loss.

Test your understanding 15 – Jones

(a) On purchase the investment is recorded at the consideration paid. The asset is classified as fair value through other comprehensive income and, as such, transaction costs are included in the initial value:

Dr	Asset	41m
Cr	Cash	41m

At the reporting date the asset is remeasured to fair value and the gain of $19m ($60m – $41m) is recognised in other comprehensive income and taken to equity:

Dr	Asset	19m
Cr	Other components of equity	19m

On disposal, the asset is derecognised. The profit or loss on disposal, recorded in the statement of profit or loss, is determined by comparing disposal proceeds with the carrying value of the asset:

Dr	Cash	70m
Cr	Asset	60m
Cr	Profit or loss	10m

Note that the any gains or losses previously taken to equity are **not** recycled upon derecognition, although they may be reclassified within equity.

(b) If Jones had designated the investment as fair value through profit and loss, the transaction costs would have been recognised as an expense in profit or loss. The entry posted on the purchase date would have been:

Dr	Asset	40m
Cr	Cash	40m
Dr	Profit or loss	1m
Cr	Cash	1m

At the reporting date, the asset is remeasured to fair value and the gain of $20m ($60m – $40m) is recognised in the statement of profit or loss:

Dr	Asset	20m
Cr	Profit or loss	20m

On disposal the asset is derecognised and the profit on disposal is recorded in the statement of profit or loss:

Dr	Cash	70m
Cr	Asset	60m
Cr	Profit or loss	10m

Note that the reported profit on derecognition of $10 million is the same whether the asset was designated as fair value through profit or loss or fair value through other comprehensive income.

Test your understanding 16 – Hoggard

In all scenarios the cost of the derivative on 1 January 20X6 is $500 ($5 × 100) and an asset is recognised in the statement of financial position.

Dr	Asset – option	$500
Cr	Cash	$500

Outcome A

If the option is sold for $1,500 (100 × $15) before the exercise date, it is derecognised at a profit of $1,000.

Dr	Cash	$1,500
Cr	Asset – option	$500
Cr	Profit or loss	$1,000

Outcome B

If the option lapses unexercised, then it is derecognised and there is a loss to be taken to profit or loss:

Dr	Profit or loss	$500
Cr	Asset – option	$500

Outcome C

If the option is exercised then the option is derecognised, the entity records the cash paid upon exercise, and the investment in shares is recognised at fair value. An immediate profit is recognised:

Dr	Asset – investment (100 × $25)	$2,500
Cr	Cash (100 × $10)	$1,000
Cr	Asset – option	$500
Cr	Profit or loss	$1,000

Test your understanding 17 – Fair value hedge

The hedged item is an investment in equity that is measured at fair value through other comprehensive income (OCI). Therefore, the increase in the fair value of the derivative of $90,000 and the fall in fair value of the equity interest of $100,000 since the inception of the hedge are taken to OCI.

Dr Derivative	$90,000
Cr OCI	$90,000
Dr OCI	$100,000
Cr Equity investment	$100,000

The net result is a small loss of $10,000 in OCI.

Test your understanding 18 – Firm commitments

(a) The futures contract is a derivative and is measured at fair value with all movements being accounted for through profit or loss.

The fair value of the futures contract at 1 October 20X1 was nil. By the year end, it had risen to $95,000. Therefore, at 31 December 20X1, Chive will recognise an asset at $95,000 and a gain of $95,000 will be recorded in profit or loss.

(b) If the relationship had been designated as a fair value hedge then the movement in the fair value of the hedging instrument (the future) and the fair value of the hedged item (the firm commitment) since inception of the hedge are accounted for through profit or loss.

The derivative has increased in fair value from $nil at 1 October 20X1 to $95,000 at 31 December 20X1. Purchasing CU2 million at 31 December 20X1 would cost Chive $100,000 more than it would have done at 1 October 20X1. Therefore the fair value of the firm commitment has fallen by $100,000.

At year end, the derivative will be held at its fair value of $95,000, and the gain of $95,000 will be recorded in profit or loss.

The $100,000 fall in the fair value of the commitment will also be accounted for, with an expense recognised in profit or loss.

In summary, the double entries are as follows:

Dr Derivative	$95,000
Cr Profit or loss	$95,000
Dr Profit or loss	$100,000
Cr Firm commitment	$100,000

The gain on the derivative and the loss on the firm commitment largely net off. There is a residual $5,000 ($100,000 – $95,000) net expense in profit or loss due to hedge ineffectiveness. Nonetheless, financial statement volatility is far less than if hedge accounting had not been used.

Test your understanding 19 – Cash flow hedge

(a) The movement on the hedging instrument is less than the movement on the hedged item. Therefore, the instrument is remeasured to fair value and the gain is recognised in other comprehensive income.

Dr Derivative	$8,500
Cr OCI	$8,500

(b) The movement on the hedging instrument is more than the movement on the hedged item. The excess movement of $900 ($10,000 – $9,100) is recognised in the statement of profit or loss.

Dr Derivative	$10,000
Cr Profit or loss	$900
Cr OCI	$9,100

Test your understanding 20 – Bling

(a) Between 1 October 20X1 and 31 December 20X1, the fair value of the futures contract had fallen by $0.9m. Over the same time period, the hedged item (the estimated cash receipts from the sale of the inventory) had increased by $0.9m ($8.6m – $7.7m).

Under a cash flow hedge, the movement in the fair value of the hedging instrument is accounted for through other comprehensive income. Therefore, the following entry is required:

Dr Other comprehensive income	$0.9m
Cr Derivative	$0.9m

The loss recorded in other comprehensive income will be held within equity.

(b) The following entries are required:

Dr Cash	$8.6m
Cr Revenue	$8.6m
Dr Cost of sales	$6.4m
Cr Inventory	$6.4m

To record the sale of the inventory at fair value

Dr Derivative	$0.9m
Cr Cash	$0.9m

To record the settlement of the futures contract

Dr Profit or loss	$0.9m
Cr OCI	$0.9m

To recycle the losses held in equity through profit or loss in the same period as the hedged item affects profit or loss.

Test your understanding 21 – Grayton

The forward rate agreement has no fair value at its inception so is initially recorded at $nil.

This is a cash flow hedge. The derivative has fallen in value by $10,000 but the cash flows have increased in value by $10,000 (it is now $10,000 cheaper to buy the asset).

Because it has been designated a cash flow hedge, the movement in the value of the hedging instrument is recognised in other comprehensive income:

Dr	Other comprehensive income	$10,000
Cr	Derivative	$10,000

(Had this not been designated a hedging instrument, the loss would have been recognised immediately in profit or loss.)

The forward contract will be settled and closed when the asset is purchased.

Property, plant and equipment is a non-financial item. The loss on the hedging instrument held within equity is adjusted against the carrying amount of the plant.

The following entries would be posted:

Dr	Liability – derivative	$10,000
Dr	Plant	$90,000
Cr	Cash	$100,000

Being the settlement of the derivative and the purchase of the plant.

Dr	Plant	$10,000
Cr	Cash flow hedge reserve	$10,000

Being the recycling of the losses held within equity against the carrying amount of the plant. Notice that the plant will be held at $100,000 ($90,000 + $10,000) and the cash spent in total was $100,000. This was the position that the derivative guaranteed.

Test your understanding 21 – Solution

The forward rate agreement has no fair value at its inception so is initially recorded at $nil.

This is a cash flow hedge. The derivative has fallen in value by $10,000, but the cash flows have increased in value by $10,000 (it is now $10,000 cheaper to buy the asset).

Because it has been designated a cash flow hedge, the movement in the value of the hedging instrument is recognised in other comprehensive income.

Dr	Other comprehensive income	$10,000
Cr	Derivative	$10,000

(Had this not been designated a hedging instrument, the loss would have been recognised immediately in profit or loss.)

The forward contract will be settled and closed when the asset is purchased.

Property, plant and equipment is a non-financial item. The loss on the hedging instrument held within equity is adjusted against the carrying amount of the plant.

The following entries would be posted:

Dr	Liability – derivative	$10,000
Dr	Plant	$90,000
Cr	Cash	$100,000

Being the settlement of the derivative and the purchase of the plant.

Dr	Plant	$10,000
Cr	Cash flow hedge reserve	$10,000

Being the recycling of the losses held within equity against the carrying amount of the plant. Notice that the plant will be held at $100,000 ($90,000 + $10,000) and the cash spent in total was $100,000. This was the position that the derivative guaranteed.

chapter

12

Tax

Chapter learning objectives

Upon completion of this chapter you will be able to:

- apply and discuss the recognition and measurement of deferred tax liabilities and deferred tax assets
- determine the recognition of tax expense or income and its inclusion in the financial statements.

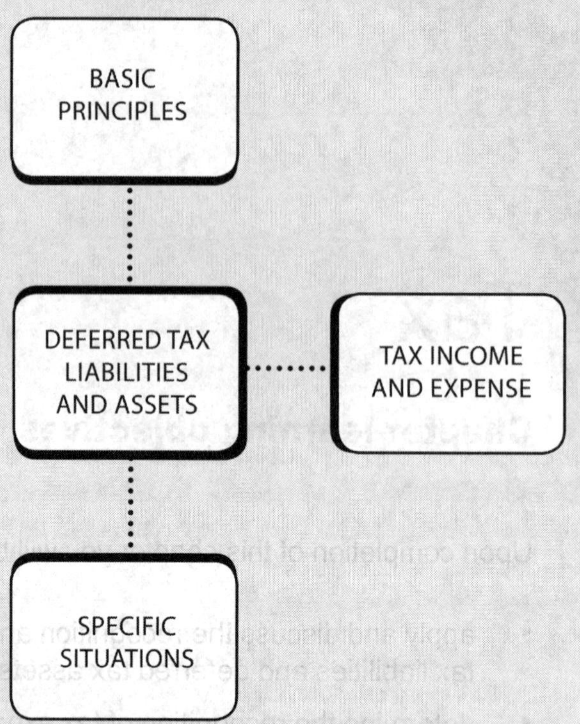

1 Basic principles of tax

Taxation

Taxation is a major expense for business entities. IAS 12 Income Taxes notes that there are two elements to tax that an entity must deal with:

- **Current tax** – the amount payable to the tax authorities in relation to the trading activities of the current period.
- **Deferred tax** – an accounting measure used to match the tax effects of transactions with their accounting treatment. It is not a tax that is levied by the government that needs to be paid, but simply an application of the accruals concept.

In summary, the tax expense for an entity is calculated as follows:

Tax expense = current tax +/– movement in deferred tax

2 Current tax

Accounting for current tax

Current tax is the amount expected to be paid to the tax authorities by applying the tax laws and tax rates in place at the reporting date.

Current tax is recognised in the financial statements by posting the following entry:

Dr Tax expense (P/L)
Cr Tax payable (SFP)

Current tax expense and income

IAS 12 contains the following requirements relating to current tax.

- Unpaid tax for current and prior periods should be recognised as a liability. Overpaid current tax is recognised as an asset.
- Current tax should be accounted for in profit or loss unless the tax relates to an item that has been accounted for in equity.
- If the item was disclosed as an item of other comprehensive income and accounted for in equity, then the tax should be disclosed as relating to other comprehensive income and allocated to equity.
- Tax is measured at the amount expected to be paid. Tax rates used should be those that have been enacted or substantively enacted by the reporting date.

3 Basic principles of deferred tax

The need to provide for deferred tax

There are generally differences between accounting standards (such as IFRS Standards) and the tax rules of a particular jurisdiction. This means that accounting profits are normally different from taxable profits.

Some differences between accounting and tax treatments are permanent:

- Fines, political donations and entertainment costs would be expensed to the statement of profit or loss but are normally disallowed by the tax authorities. Therefore, these costs are eliminated ('added back') in the company's tax computation.

Some differences between accounting and tax treatments are temporary:

- Capital assets might be written down at different rates for tax purposes than they are in the financial statements.

Temporary differences may mean that profits are reported in the financial statements before they are taxable. Conversely, it might mean that tax is payable even though profits have not yet been reported in the financial statements.

According to the accruals concept, the tax effect of a transaction should be reported in the same accounting period as the transaction itself. Therefore, an adjustment to the tax charge may be required. This gives rise to deferred tax.

Deferred tax only arises on temporary differences. It is not accounted for on permanent differences.

A **temporary difference** is the difference between the carrying amount of an asset or liability and its tax base.

The **tax base** is the **'amount attributed to an asset or liability for tax purposes'** (IAS 12, para 5).

Illustration 1 – Basic principles of deferred tax

Prudent prepares financial statements to 31 December each year. On 1 January 20X0, the entity purchased a non-current asset for $1.6 million that had an anticipated useful life of four years. This asset qualified for immediate tax relief of 100% of the cost of the asset.

For the year ending 31 December 20X0, the draft accounts showed a profit before tax of $2 million. The directors anticipate that this level of profit will be maintained for the foreseeable future.

Prudent pays tax at a rate of 30%. Apart from the differences caused by the purchase of the non-current asset in 20X0, there are no other differences between accounting profit and taxable profit or the tax base and carrying amount of net assets.

Required:

Compute the pre, and post-tax profits for Prudent for each of the four years ending 31 December 20X0–20X3 inclusive and for the period as a whole assuming:

(a) **that no deferred tax is recognised**

(b) **that deferred tax is recognised.**

Solution

(a) No deferred tax

First of all, it is necessary to compute the taxable profits of Prudent for each period and the current tax payable:

	Year ended 31 December				Total
	20X0	20X1	20X2	20X3	
	$000	$000	$000	$000	$000
Accounting profit	2,000	2,000	2,000	2,000	8,000
Add back Depreciation	400	400	400	400	1,600
Deduct Capital allowances	(1,600)	–	–	–	(1,600)
Taxable profits	800	2,400	2,400	2,400	8,000
Current tax at 30%	240	720	720	720	2,400

The differences between the accounting profit and the taxable profit that occur from one year to another, cancel out over the four years as a whole.

The statements of profit or loss for each period and for the four years as a whole, are given below:

	Year ended 31 December				Total
	20X0	20X1	20X2	20X3	
	$000	$000	$000	$000	$000
Profit before tax	2,000	2,000	2,000	2,000	8,000
Current tax	(240)	(720)	(720)	(720)	(2,400)
Profit after tax	1,760	1,280	1,280	1,280	5,600

Ignoring deferred tax produces a performance profile that suggests a declining performance between 20X0 and 20X1.

In fact the decline in profits is caused by the timing of the current tax charge on them.

In 20X0, some of the accounting profit escapes tax, but the tax is only postponed until 20X1, 20X2 and 20X3, when the taxable profit is more than the accounting profit.

(b) **Deferred tax is recognised**

The deferred tax figures that are required in the statement of financial position are given below:

	Year ended 31 December			
	20X0	**20X1**	**20X2**	**20X3**
	$000	$000	$000	$000
Carrying amount	1,200	800	400	Nil
Tax base	Nil	Nil	Nil	Nil
Temporary difference at year end	1,200	800	400	Nil
Closing deferred tax liability (30%)	360	240	120	Nil
Opening deferred tax liability	Nil	(360)	(240)	(120)
So charge/(credit) to P/L	360	(120)	(120)	(120)

The statements of profit or loss for the four year period including deferred tax are shown below:

	Year ended 31 December				Total
	20X0	**20X1**	**20X2**	**20X3**	
	$000	$000	$000	$000	$000
Profit before tax	2,000	2,000	2,000	2,000	8,000
Current tax	(240)	(720)	(720)	(720)	(2,400)
Deferred tax	(360)	120	120	120	Nil
Profit after tax	1,400	1,400	1,400	1,400	5,600

A more meaningful performance profile is presented.

Examples of temporary differences

Examples of temporary differences include (but are not restricted to):

- Tax deductions for the cost of non-current assets that have a different pattern to the write-off of the asset in the financial statements.
- Pension liabilities that are accrued in the financial statements, but are allowed for tax only when the contributions are made to the pension fund at a later date.
- Intra-group profits in inventory that are unrealised for consolidation purposes yet taxable in the computation of the group entity that made the unrealised profit.
- A loss is reported in the financial statements and the related tax relief is only available by carry forward against future taxable profits.
- Assets are revalued upwards in the financial statements, but no adjustment is made for tax purposes.
- Development costs are capitalised and amortised to profit or loss in future periods, but were deducted for tax purposes as incurred.
- The cost of granting share options to employees is recognised in profit or loss, but no tax deduction is obtained until the options are exercised.

Calculating temporary differences

Deferred tax is calculated by comparing the carrying amount of an asset or liability to its tax base. The tax base is the amount attributed to the asset or liability for tax purposes. To assist with determining the tax base, IAS 12 notes that:

- **'The tax base of an asset is the amount that will be deductible for tax purposes against any taxable economic benefits that will flow to an entity when it recovers the carrying amount of the asset. If those economic benefits will not be taxable, the tax base of the asset is equal to its carrying amount'** (IAS 12, para 7).
- **'The tax base of a liability is its carrying amount, less any amount that will be deductible for tax purposes in future periods. In the case of revenue which is received in advance, the tax base of the liability is its carrying amount, less any amount of the revenue that will not be taxable in future periods'** (IAS 12, para 8).

When looking at the difference between the carrying amount and the tax base of an asset or liability:

- If the carrying amount exceeds the tax base, the temporary difference is said to be a **taxable** temporary difference which will give rise to a deferred tax **liability**.
- If the tax base exceeds the carrying amount, the temporary difference is a **deductible** temporary difference which will give rise to a deferred tax **asset**.

Test your understanding 1 – Dive (temporary differences)

An entity, Dive, provides the following information regarding its assets and liabilities as at 31 December 20X1.

	Carrying amount	**Tax base**	**Temporary difference**
Assets			
A machine cost \$100,000. Depreciation of \$18,000 has been charged to date. Tax allowances of \$30,000 have been claimed.			
Interest receivable in the statement of financial position is \$1,000. The interest will be taxed when received.			
Trade receivables have a carrying amount of \$10,000. The revenue has already been included in taxable profit.			
Inventory has been written down by \$500 to \$4,500 in the financial statements. The reduction is ignored for tax purposes until the inventory is sold.			

Liabilities			
Current liabilities include accrued expenses of $1,000. This is deductible for tax on a cash paid basis.			
Accrued expenses have a carrying amount of $5,000. The related expense has been deducted for tax purposes.			

Required:

Complete the table with carrying amount, tax base and temporary difference for each of the assets and liabilities.

4 Deferred tax liabilities and assets

Recognition

IAS 12 Income Taxes states that deferred tax should be provided for on all taxable temporary differences, unless the deferred tax liability arises from:

- goodwill, for which amortisation is not tax deductible
- the initial recognition of an item that affects neither accounting profit nor taxable profit, and which does not result from a business combination.

Deferred tax assets should be recognised on all deductible temporary differences unless:

- the exceptions above apply
- insufficient taxable profits are expected to be available in the future against which the deductible temporary difference can be utilised.

Measurement

The tax rate in force (or expected to be in force) when the asset is realised or the liability is settled, should be applied to the temporary difference to calculate the deferred tax balance. IAS 12 specifies that this rate must be based on legislation enacted or substantively enacted by the reporting date.

Deferred tax assets and liabilities are **not** discounted to present value.

The entry to profit or loss and other comprehensive income in respect of deferred tax is the difference between the net liability (or asset) at the beginning of the year and the net liability (or asset) at the end of the year. It is important to note that:

- If the item giving rise to the deferred tax is dealt with in profit or loss, the related deferred tax should also be presented in profit or loss.
- If the item giving rise to the deferred tax is dealt with in other comprehensive income, the related deferred tax should also be recorded in other comprehensive income and held within equity.

Offsetting

IAS 12 notes that it is appropriate to offset deferred tax assets and liabilities in the statement of financial position as long as:

- the entity has a legally enforceable right to set off **current** tax assets and **current** tax liabilities
- the deferred tax assets and liabilities relate to tax levied by the same tax authority.

Test your understanding 2 – Dive (deferred tax calculation)

Required:

Using the information in 'test your understanding 1', calculate Dive's deferred tax balance as at 31 December 20X1. The applicable tax rate is 30%.

Test your understanding 3 – Brick

Brick is a company with a reporting date of 30 April 20X4. The company obtains tax relief for research and development expenditure on a cash paid basis. The recognition of a material development asset during the year, in accordance with IAS 38, created a significant taxable temporary difference as at 30 April 20X4.

The tax rate for companies as at the reporting period was 22%. On 6 June 20X4, the government passed legislation to lower the company tax rate to 20% from 1 January 20X5.

Required:

Explain which tax rate should have been used to calculate the deferred tax liability for inclusion in the financial statements for the year ended 30 April 20X4.

5 Specific situations

Revaluations

Deferred tax should be recognised on the revaluation of property, plant and equipment even if:

- there is no intention to sell the asset
- any tax due on the gain made on any sale of the asset can be deferred by being 'rolled over' against the cost of a replacement asset.

Revaluation gains are recorded in other comprehensive income and so any deferred tax arising on the revaluation must also be recorded in other comprehensive income.

Test your understanding 4 – Dodge

An entity, Dodge, owns property, plant and equipment that cost $100,000 when purchased. Depreciation of $40,000 has been charged up to the reporting date of 31 March 20X1. The entity has claimed total tax allowances on the asset of $50,000. On 31 March 20X1, the asset is revalued to $90,000. The tax rate is 30%.

Required:

Explain the deferred tax implications of this situation.

Investment properties and deferred tax

The deferred tax calculation must take into consideration how the asset is measured together with how the entity expects to recover its value. In some jurisdictions, trading profits are taxed at different rates than capital gains.

IAS 12 presumes that the carrying amount of investment properties measured at fair value will be recovered from a sales transaction, unless there is evidence to the contrary.

IAS 40 illustration

Melbourne has an investment property, which is measured using the fair value model in accordance with IAS 40, comprising the following elements:

	Cost	Fair value
	$000	$000
Land	800	1,200
Building	1,200	1,800
	2,000	3,000

Further information is as follows:

- Accumulated tax allowances claimed on the building to date are $600,000.
- Unrealised changes in the carrying value of investment property do not affect taxable profit.
- If an investment property is sold for more than cost, the reversal of accumulated tax allowances will be included in taxable profit and taxed at the standard rate.
- The standard rate of tax is 30%, but for asset disposals in excess of cost, the tax rate is 20%, unless the asset has been held for less than two years, when the tax rate is 25%.

Required:

Calculate the deferred tax liability required if:

(a) **Melbourne expects to hold the investment property for more than two years.**

(b) **Melbourne expects to sell the investment property within two years.**

Solution

A summary of cost, fair value, and accumulated allowances claimed to date, together with tax base and temporary difference is as follows:

	(a)	(b)	(c)	(a) – (c) = (d)	(b) – (d) = (e)
	Cost	**Fair value**	**Tax allowances claimed**	**Tax base**	**Temp. diff**
	$000	$000	$000	$000	$000
Land	800	1,200	–	800	400
Building	1,200	1,800	(600)	600	1,200
	2,000	3,000	(600)	1,400	1,600

Note that the tax rate to apply in each situation will be the tax rate expected to apply when the investment property is sold.

(a) **If Melbourne expects to hold the investment property for more than two years:**

The reversal of the accumulated tax allowances claimed on the building element will be charged at the standard rate of 30%, whilst the proceeds in excess of cost will be charged at 20% as follows:

		$000
Accumulated tax allowances	(600 × 30%)	180
Proceeds in excess of cost	(1,000 × 20%)	200
Deferred tax liability		380

(b) **If Melbourne expects to sell the investment property within two years:**

The reversal of the accumulated tax allowances claimed on the building element will be charged at the standard rate of 30%, whilst the proceeds in excess of cost will be charged at 25% as follows:

		$000
Accumulated tax allowances	(600 × 30%)	180
Proceeds in excess of cost	(1,000 × 25%)	250
Deferred tax liability		430

Share option schemes

Accounting for share option schemes involves recognising an annual remuneration expense in profit or loss throughout the vesting period. Tax relief is not normally granted until the share options are exercised. The amount of tax relief granted is based on the intrinsic value of the options (the difference between the market price of the shares and the exercise price of the option).

This delayed tax relief means that equity-settled share-based payment schemes give rise to a deferred tax asset.

The following pro-forma can be used to calculate the deferred tax asset arising on an equity-settled share-based payment scheme:

	$	$
Carrying amount of share-based payment	Nil	
Less:		
Tax base of the share-based payment*	(X)	
	–––	
× Tax rate %	X	
	–––	–––
Deferred tax asset		X
		–––

* The tax base is the expected future tax relief (based on the intrinsic value of the options) that has accrued by the reporting date.

Where the amount of the estimated future tax deduction exceeds the accumulated remuneration expense, this indicates that the tax deduction relates partly to the remuneration expense and partly to equity. Therefore, the deferred tax must be recognised partly in profit or loss and partly in equity.

Test your understanding 5 – Splash

An entity, Splash, established a share option scheme for its four directors. This scheme commenced on 1 July 20X8. Each director will be entitled to 25,000 share options on condition that they remain with Splash for four years, from the date the scheme was introduced.

Information regarding the share options is provided below:

Fair value of option at grant date	$10
Exercise price of option	$5

The fair value of the shares at 30 June 20X9 was $17 per share.

A tax deduction is only given for the share options when they are exercised. The allowable deduction will be based on the intrinsic value of the options. Assume a tax rate of 30%.

Required:

Calculate and explain the amounts to be included in the financial statements of Splash for the year ended 30 June 20X9, including explanation and calculation of any deferred tax implications.

Unused tax losses

Where an entity has unused tax losses, IAS 12 allows a deferred tax asset to be recognised only to the extent that it is probable that future taxable profits will be available against which the unused tax losses can be utilised.

IAS 12 advises that the deferred tax asset should only be recognised after considering:

- whether an entity has sufficient taxable temporary differences against which the unused tax losses can be offset.
- whether it is probable the entity will make taxable profits before the tax losses expire.
- whether the cause of the tax losses can be identified and whether it is likely to recur (otherwise, the existence of unused tax losses is strong evidence that future taxable profits may not be available).
- whether tax planning opportunities are available.

Test you understanding 6 – Red

As at 31 December 20X1, Red has tax adjusted losses of $4m which arose from a one-off restructuring exercise. Under tax law, these losses may be carried forward to relieve taxable profits in the future. Red has produced forecasts that predict total future taxable profits over the next three years of $2.5m. However, the accountant of Red is not able to reliably forecast profits beyond that date.

The tax rate for profits earned during the year ended 31 December 20X1 is 30%. However, the government passed legislation during the reporting period that lowered the tax rate to 28% from 1 January 20X2.

Required:

Explain the deferred tax implications of the above.

6 Business combinations and deferred tax

Accounting for a business combination, such as the consolidation of a subsidiary, can have several deferred tax implications.

Fair value adjustments

The identifiable assets and liabilities of the acquired subsidiary are consolidated at fair value but the tax base derives from the values in the subsidiary's individual financial statements. A temporary difference is created, giving rise to deferred tax in the consolidated financial statements.

The deferred tax recognised on this difference is treated as part of the net assets acquired and, as a result, impacts upon the amount of goodwill recognised on the acquisition of the subsidiary.

The goodwill itself does not give rise to deferred tax because IAS 12 specifically excludes it.

Test your understanding 7 – Tom

On 30 June 20X1 Tom acquired 100% of the shares of Jones for $300,000. At this date, the carrying amount of the net assets of Jones were $250,000. Included in this net asset figure is inventory which cost $50,000 but which had a replacement cost of $55,000. The applicable tax rate is 30%.

Required:

Explain the deferred tax implications of the above in the consolidated financial statements of the Tom group.

Provisions for unrealised profit

When one company within a group sells inventory to another group company, unrealised profits remaining within the group at the reporting date must be eliminated. The following adjustment is required in the consolidated financial statements:

Dr Cost of sales (P/L)
Cr Inventory (SFP)

This adjustment reduces the carrying amount of inventory in the consolidated financial statements but the tax base of the inventory remains as its cost in the individual financial statements of the purchasing company.

This creates a **deductible temporary difference**, giving rise to a **deferred tax asset** in the consolidated financial statements.

Note: you may find it easier to think of this adjustment in terms of profits. The unrealised profit on the intra-group transaction is removed from the consolidated financial statements and therefore the tax charge on this profit must also be removed.

Test your understanding 8 – Mug

Mug has owned 80% of the ordinary shares of Glass for many years. During the current year, Mug sold inventory to Glass for $250,000 making a gross profit margin of 40%. One quarter of this inventory remains unsold by Glass at the reporting date.

The tax rate is 20%.

Required:

Discuss the deferred tax implications of the above transaction.

Unremitted earnings

A temporary difference arises when the carrying amount of investments in subsidiaries, associates or joint ventures is different from the tax base.

- The carrying amount in consolidated financial statements is the investor's share of the net assets of the investee, plus purchased goodwill. The tax base is usually the cost of the investment. The difference is the unremitted earnings (i.e. undistributed profits) of the subsidiary, associate or joint venture.
- IAS 12 says that deferred tax should be recognised on this temporary differences except when:
  - the investor controls the timing of the reversal of the temporary difference and
  - it is probable that the profits will not be distributed in the foreseeable future.
- An investor can control the dividend policy of a subsidiary, but not always that of other types of investment. This means that deferred tax does not arise on investments in subsidiaries, but may arise on investments in associates and joint ventures.

Financial assets may give rise to deferred tax if they are revalued.

7 Other issues

Arguments for recognising deferred tax

If a deferred tax liability is ignored, profits are inflated and the obligation to pay an increased amount of tax in the future is also ignored. The arguments for recognising deferred tax are summarised below.

- The accruals concept requires tax to be matched to profits as they are earned.
- The deferred tax will eventually become an actual tax liability.
- Ignoring deferred tax overstates profits, which may result in:
  - over-optimistic dividend payments based on inflated profits
  - distortion of earnings per share and of the price/earnings ratio, both important indicators of an entity's performance
  - shareholders being misled.

Arguments for not recognising deferred tax

Some people believe that the 'temporary difference' approach is conceptually wrong. The framework for the preparation and presentation of financial statements defines a liability as an obligation to transfer economic benefits, as the result of a past event. In practice, a liability for deferred tax is often recognised before the entity actually has an obligation to pay the tax.

For example, suppose that an entity revalues a non-current asset and recognises a gain. It will not be liable for tax on the gain until the asset is sold. However, IAS 12 requires that deferred tax is recognised immediately on the revaluation gain, even if the entity has no intention of selling the asset (and realising the gain) for several years.

As a result, the IAS 12 approach could lead to the build-up of liabilities that may only crystallise in the distant future, if ever.

8 Chapter summary

Basic principles
- Temporary differences
- Examples
- Calculations

Deferred tax liabilities and assets
- Recognition
- Measurement

Tax income andexpense
- Current tax
- Deferred tax

Specific situations
- Revaluations
- Business combinations
- Unremitted earnings
- Losses

Test your understanding answers

Test your understanding 1 – Dive (temporary differences)

	Carrying amount	Tax base	Temp. difference
	$	$	$
Non-current asset	82,000	70,000	12,000
Interest receivable	1,000	Nil	1,000
Receivables	10,000	10,000	Nil
Inventory	4,500	5,000	(500)
Accrual (cash basis for tax)	(1,000)	Nil	(1,000)
Accrual (already had tax relief)	(5,000)	(5,000)	Nil

Test your understanding 2 – Dive (deferred tax calculation)

The net temporary difference as at the reporting date is as follows:

	$
Non-current assets	12,000
Interest receivable	1,000
Receivables	–
Inventory	(500)
Accrual (cash basis for tax)	(1,000)
Accrual (already had tax relief)	–
	11,500

There will be a deferred tax liability because the carrying value of the net assets and liabilities exceeds their net tax base. The deferred tax liability is calculated by applying the relevant tax rate to the temporary difference.

The deferred tax liability is therefore $3,450 ($11,500 × 30%).

Assuming that there is no opening deferred tax liability, the following accounting entry is required:

Dr Tax expense (P/L)	$3,450
Cr Deferred tax liability (SFP)	$3,450

Test your understanding 3 – Brick

Deferred tax liabilities and assets should be measured using the tax rates expected to apply when the asset is realised. This tax rate must have been enacted or substantively enacted by the end of the reporting period.

The government enacted the 20% tax rate after the period end. Therefore, it should not be used when calculating the deferred tax liability for the year ended 30 April 20X4. The current 22% rate should be used instead.

Per IAS 10, changes in tax rates after the end of the reporting period are a non-adjusting event. However, if the change in the tax rate is deemed to be material then Brick should disclose this rate change and an estimate of the financial impact.

Test your understanding 4 – Dodge

The carrying value of the asset is $90,000 and the tax base is $50,000 ($100,000 – 50,000). The carrying value exceeds the tax base by $40,000 ($90,000 – $50,000).

This temporary difference will give rise to a deferred tax liability of $12,000 ($40,000 × 30%).

Prior to the revaluation, the carrying amount of the asset was $60,000. The asset was then revalued to $90,000. Therefore, $30,000 ($90,000 – $60,000) of the temporary difference relates to the revaluation. Revaluation gains are recorded in other comprehensive income and so the deferred tax charge relating to this gain should also be recorded in other comprehensive income. This means that the tax charged to other comprehensive income is $9,000 ($30,000 × 30%).

The following accounting entry is required:

Dr Other comprehensive income	$9,000
Dr Profit or loss (bal. fig.)	$3,000
Cr Deferred tax liability	$12,000

The balance on the revaluation reserve within other components of equity will be $21,000 ($30,000 revaluation gain – $9,000 deferred tax).

Test your understanding 5 – Splash

The expense recognised for an equity-settled share-based payment scheme is calculated based on the fair value of the options at the grant date. This expense is spread over the vesting period. At each reporting date, the entity should reassess the number of options expected to vest.

The expense for the scheme in the year ended 30 June 20X9 is $250,000 (4 × 25,000 × $10 × 1/4).

For tax purposes, tax relief is allowed based on the intrinsic value of the options at the date they are exercised.

At the reporting date, the shares have a market value of $17 but the options allow the holders to purchase these shares for $5. The options therefore have an intrinsic value of $12 ($17 – $5).

The deferred tax asset is calculated as follows:

	$	$
Carrying value of share-based payment	Nil	
Tax base of the share-based payment (4 × 25,000 × ($17 – $5) × 1/4)	(300,000)	
× Tax rate 30%	(300,000)	
Deferred tax asset		90,000

Where the amount of the estimated future tax deduction exceeds the accumulated remuneration expense, this indicates that the tax deduction relates partly to the remuneration expense and partly to equity.

In this case, the estimated future tax deduction is $300,000 whereas the accumulated remuneration expense is $250,000. Therefore, $50,000 of the temporary difference is deemed to relate to an equity item, and the deferred tax relating to this should be credited to equity.

The following entry is required:

Dr Deferred tax asset	$90,000
Cr Equity ($50,000 × 30%)	$15,000
Cr Profit or loss ($250,000 × 30%)	$75,000

If the deferred tax asset is to be recognised, it must be capable of reliable measurement and also be regarded as recoverable.

Test you understanding 6 – Red

A deferred tax asset can be recognised if it is deemed probable that future taxable profits will be available against which the unused losses can be utilised.

The tax losses have arisen from an exceptional event, suggesting that the entity will return to profitability. Forecasts produced by the accountant confirm this.

Red is only able to reliably forecast future profits of $2.5m. This limits the deferred tax asset that can be recognised.

Deferred tax should be calculated using the tax rate that is expected to be in force when the temporary difference reverses based on the rates enacted by the reporting date. This means that the 28% rate should be used.

The deferred tax asset that can be recognised is therefore $700,000 ($2.5m × 28%). There will be a corresponding credit to the tax expense in the statement of profit or loss.

Test your understanding 7 – Tom

According to IFRS 3, the net assets of the subsidiary at the acquisition date must be consolidated at fair value. The carrying amount of the inventory in the group financial statements will be $55,000. The tax base of the inventory is based on its carrying amount of $50,000 in the individual financial statements. Therefore, there is a temporary difference of $5,000 that arises on consolidation.

A deferred tax liability must be recognised in the consolidated financial statements for $1,500 ($5,000 × 30%). This is treated as a reduction in the subsidiary's net assets at the acquisition date, which will increase the goodwill arising on acquisition.

	$	$
Consideration		300,000
Net assets:		
Carrying amount	250,000	
Fair value uplift	5,000	
Deferred tax liability	(1,500)	
		(253,500)
Goodwill at acquisition		46,500

Test your understanding 8 – Mug

There has been an intra-group sale and some of the inventory remains within the group at the reporting date. The profits held within this unsold inventory must therefore be removed from the consolidated statements.

The profit on the sale was $100,000 ($250,000 × 40%). Of this, $25,000 ($100,000 × 25%) remains within the inventory of the group.

The adjustment required to eliminate the unrealised profits is:

Dr Cost of sales	$25,000
Cr Inventory	$25,000

The carrying amount of inventory in the consolidated financial statements is now $25,000 lower than its tax base, creating a deductible temporary difference of $25,000. This gives rise to a deferred tax asset of $5,000 ($25,000 × 20%) in the consolidated statement of financial position as well as a corresponding reduction to the tax expense in the consolidated statement of profit or loss.

The adjustment required to account for the deferred tax is:

Dr Deferred tax asset	$5,000
Cr Tax expense	$5,000

chapter

13

Segment reporting

Chapter learning objectives

Upon completion of this chapter you will be able to:

- determine the nature and extent of reportable segments
- specify and discuss the nature of segment information to be disclosed.

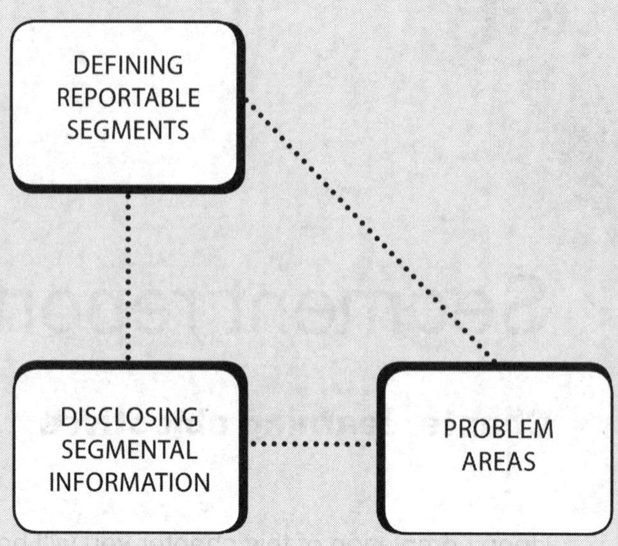

1 Defining reportable segments

Introduction

Segmental reports are designed to reveal significant information that might otherwise be hidden by the process of presenting a single statement of profit or loss and other comprehensive income and statement of financial position for an entity.

IFRS 8 Operating Segments requires certain entities to disclose information about each of its operating segments that will enable users of the financial statements to evaluate the nature and financial effects of the business activities in which it engages and the economic environments in which it operates.

IFRS 8 applies to entities which trade debt or equity instruments in a public market.

An **operating segment** is defined as a component of an entity:

- **'that engages in business activities from which it may earn revenues and incur expenses**
- **whose operating results are regularly reviewed by the entity's chief operating decision maker to make decisions about resources to be allocated to the segment and assess its performance**
- **for which discrete financial information is available'** (IFRS 8, para 5).

How to define reportable segments

Under IFRS 8, an operating segment is a component whose results are regularly reviewed by the entity's chief operating decision maker. This means that the segments reported in the financial statements are the same as those that are disclosed and reviewed in internal management reports.

Management may use more than one set of segment information. For example, they might analyse information by classes of business (different products or services) and by geographical areas. If this is the case then management must identify a **single** set of components on which to base the segmental disclosures. The basis of reporting information should be the one that best enables users to understand the business and the environment in which it operates.

Not every part of an entity is necessarily an operating segment or part of an operating segment:

- Corporate headquarters and other similar departments do not earn revenue and are therefore not operating segments.
- An entity's pension plan is not an operating segment.

IFRS 8 says that two or more operating segments can be aggregated and reported as a single operating segment provided that they have similar economic characteristics, and are similar in the following respects:

- products and services
- production processes
- classes of customer
- distribution methods.

Test your understanding 1 – E–Games

E-Games is a UK based company that sells computer games and hardware. Sales are made through the E-Games website as well as through high street stores. The products sold online and in the stores are the same. E-Games sells new releases for $40 in its stores, but for $30 online.

Internal reports used by the chief operating decision maker show the results of the online business separately from the stores. However, they will be aggregated together for disclosure in the financial statements.

Required:

Should the online business and the high street stores be aggregated into a single segment in the operating segments disclosure?

Quantitative thresholds

An entity must separately report information about an operating segment that meets any of the following quantitative thresholds:

- **'its reported revenue, including both sales to external customers and inter-segment sales, is ten per cent or more of the combined revenue of all operating segments**
- **its reported profit or loss is ten per cent or more of the greater, in absolute amount, of:**
  - **the combined reported profit of all operating segments that did not report a loss and**
  - **the combined reported loss of all operating segments that reported a loss.**
- **its assets are ten per cent or more of the combined assets of all operating segments'** (IFRS 8, para 13).

At least 75% of the entity's external revenue must be included in reportable segments. Other segments should be identified as reportable segments until 75% of external revenue is reported.

Information about other business activities and operating segments that are not reportable are combined into an 'all other segments' category.

Test your understanding 2 – Identifying reportable segments

The management of a company have identified operating segments based on geographical location. Information for these segments is provided below:

Segment	Total revenue	External revenue	Internal revenue	Profit/ (loss)	Assets
	$000	$000	$000	$000	$000
Europe	260	140	120	98	3,400
Middle East	78	33	45	(26)	345
Asia	150	150	–	47	995
North America	330	195	135	121	3,800
Central America	85	40	45	(15)	580
South America	97	54	43	12	880
	1,000	612	388	237	10,000

Required:

According to IFRS 8, which segments must be reported?

2 Disclosing reportable segments

General information

IFRS 8 requires disclosure of the following:

- Factors used to identify reportable segments
- The types of products and services sold by each reportable segment.

Information about profit or loss and other segment items

For each reportable segment an entity should report:

- a measure of profit or loss
- a measure of total assets.

Other information should be disclosed if regularly provided to the chief operating decision maker.

IFRS 8 requires segmental reports to be based on the information reported to and used by management, even where this is prepared on a different basis from the rest of the financial statements. Therefore, an entity must provide explanations of the measurement of segment profit or loss, segment assets and segment liabilities.

Example of a segmental report

	Segment A	**Segment B**	**Segment C**	**All other**	**Totals**
	$000	$000	$000	$000	$000
Revenues from external customers	5,000	9,500	12,000	800	27,300
Revenues from inter-segment transactions	–	3,000	1,500	–	4,500
Interest revenue	800	1,000	1,500	–	3,300
Interest expense	600	700	1,100	–	2,400
Depreciation and amortisation	100	50	1,500	–	1,650
Exceptional costs	200	–	–	–	200
Segment profit	70	900	2,300	100	3,370
Impairment of assets	200	–		–	200
Segment assets	5,000	3,000	12,000	400	20,400
Additions to non-current assets	700	500	800	–	2,000
Segment liabilities	3,000	1,800	8,000	–	12,800

Notes

(1) The 'all other' column shows amounts relating to segments that fall below the quantitative thresholds.

(2) Impairment of assets is disclosed as a material non-cash item.

(3) Comparatives should be provided. These should be restated if an entity changes the structure of its internal organisation so that its reportable segments change, unless the information is not available and the cost of preparing it would be excessive.

3 Problem areas in segmental reporting

Problems with IFRS 8

Segmental reports provide useful information, but they also have limitations.

- Trading between segments may distort the results of each operating segment, particularly if the transactions do not occur at fair value.
- IFRS 8 states that segments should reflect the way in which the entity is managed. This means that segments information is only useful for comparing the performance of the same entity over time, not for comparing the performance of different entities.
- The segmentation process is based on management's perspective, and some users lack trust in management's intentions. For example, management may attempt to conceal loss-making areas of the business within a larger, profitable reportable segment.
- The guidance around the aggregation of segments is vague, and may lead to entities over-aggregating segments to reduce the level of detail that they are required to report.
- Common costs may be allocated to different segments on whatever basis the directors believe is reasonable. This can lead to arbitrary allocation of these costs.

4 Chapter summary

Defining reportable segments
- Managerial approach
- Ten per cent thresholds

Disclosing segmental information
- General information
- Information about profit or loss and other segment items
- Entity wide disclosures
- Measurement
- Reconciliations

Problem areas
- Subjectivity
- Common costs
- Inter-segment sales

Test your understanding answers

Test your understanding 1 – E-Games

IFRS 8 says that two or more operating segments may be aggregated into a single segment if they have similar economic characteristics and the segments are similar in the following respects:

- The nature of products or services.
- The types of customer.
- Distribution methods.

The standard says that segments with similar economic characteristics would have similar long-term gross margins.

The E-Games stores and online business sell the same types of product, and there are likely to be no major differences in the types of customer (individual consumers). Therefore, in these respects, the segments are similar.

However, customers will collect their goods from the stores, but E-Games will deliver the products sold online. This means that distribution methods are different.

Moreover, there are different sales prices between the stores and the online business, giving rise to significant differences in gross margin. This suggests dissimilarity in terms of economic characteristics.

This means that it might be more appropriate to disclose these two segments separately.

Note:

There is no 'right' or 'wrong' answer here. There are numerous retailers who do not disclose their online operations as a separate segment. However, the International Accounting Standards Board notes in its post-implementation review of IFRS 8 that many companies are over-aggregating segments. For exam purposes, it is important to state the relevant recognition criteria and then to apply these to the information given in the question.

Test your understanding 2 – Identifying reportable segments

The 10% tests

Segment	**10% total revenue (W1)**	**10% results test (W2)**	**10% assets (W3)**	**Report?**
Europe	Y	Y	Y	Y
Middle East	N	N	N	N
Asia	Y	Y	N	Y
North America	Y	Y	Y	Y
Central America	N	N	N	N
South America	N	N	N	N

Based on the 10% tests, Europe, Asia and North America are reportable. However, we must check whether they comprise at least 75% of the company's external revenue.

The 75% test

	External revenue
	$000
Europe	140
Asia	150
North America	195
Total	485

The external revenue of reportable segments is 79% ($485,000/ $612,000) of total external revenue. The 75% test is met and no other segments need to be reported.

Conclusion

The reportable segments are Europe, Asia and North America.

(W1) **10% of total sales**

10% × $1m = $100,000.

All segments whose total sales exceed $100,000 are reportable.

(W2) **10% of results**

10% of profit making segments:

10% × ($98,000 + $47,000 + $121,000 + $12,000) = $27,800

10% of loss making segments:

10% × ($26,000 + $15,000) = $4,100

Therefore, all segments which make a profit or a loss of greater than $27,800 are reportable.

(W3) **10% of total assets**

10% × $10m = $1m.

All segments whose assets exceed $1m are reportable.

chapter

14

Related parties

Chapter learning objectives

Upon completion of this chapter you will be able to:

- determine the parties considered to be related to an entity
- identify the implications of related party relationships and the need for disclosure.

1 The need for disclosure of related parties

A related party transaction is defined as **'the transfer of resources, services or obligations between related parties, regardless of whether a price is charged'** (IAS 24, para 6).

Transactions between related parties are a normal feature of business. However, users of the financial statements need to know about these transactions because they can distort the financial performance and position of an entity.

Illustration – The need for related party disclosures

Company A owns 75% of the equity shares of B. A sells goods to B at prices significantly above market rate. As a result, the profit of A is more than it would have been had it sold all of its goods to a third party.

Company A is therefore not comparable with that of similar companies. Its performance has been distorted because it trades with an entity over which it has control. This has enabled it to charge prices that are not equivalent to those in arm's length transactions.

Companies A and B are related parties. Users of the financial statements, such as investors and banks, need to be made aware of the transactions that have occurred between these two companies to enable them to make a proper assessment of the financial statements.

2 Definition of a related party

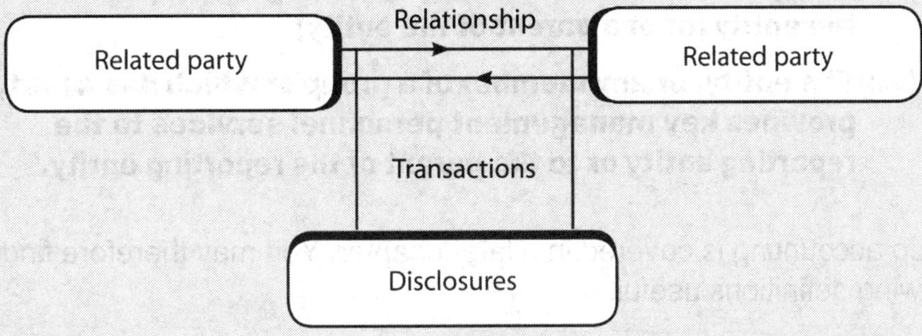

A related party is defined as **'a person or entity that is related to the entity that is preparing its financial statements'** (IAS 24, para 9).

IAS 24 (para 9) gives the following rules which should be used to determine the existence of related party relationships:

(a) **'A person or a close member of that person's family is related to a reporting entity if that person:**

- (i) **has control or joint control of the reporting entity**
- (ii) **has significant influence over the reporting entity**
- (iii) **is a member of the key management personnel of the reporting entity or of a parent of the reporting entity.**

(b) **An entity is related to a reporting entity if any of the following conditions apply:**

- (i) **The entity and the reporting entity are members of the same group (which means that each parent, subsidiary and fellow subsidiary is related to the others)**
- (ii) **One entity is an associate or joint venture of the other entity (or an associate or joint venture of a member of a group of which the other entity is a member)**
- (iii) **Both entities are joint ventures of the same third party**
- (iv) **One entity is a joint venture of a third entity and the other entity is an associate of the third entity**

(v) **The entity is a post-employment benefit plan for the benefit of employees of either the reporting entity or an entity related to the reporting entity. If the reporting entity is itself such a plan, the sponsoring employers are also related to the reporting entity**

(vi) **The entity is controlled or jointly controlled by a person identified in (a)**

(vii) **A person identified in (a)(i) has significant influence over the entity or is a member of the key management personnel of the entity (or of a parent of the entity)**

(viii) **The entity, or any member of a group of which it is a part, provides key management personnel services to the reporting entity or to the parent of the reporting entity.'**

Group accounting is covered in a later chapter. You may therefore find the following definitions useful:

- A **subsidiary** is an entity over which an investor has control.
- A **joint venture** is an entity over which an investor has joint control.
- An **associate** is an entity over which an investor has significant influence.

'In the definition of a related party, an associate includes subsidiaries of the associate and a joint venture includes subsidiaries of the joint venture' (IAS 24, para 12).

IAS 24 notes that the following should not be considered related parties:

- two entities just because they have a director or other member of key management personnel in common
- two joint venturers just because they share joint control of a joint venture
- a customer or supplier with whom an entity transacts a significant volume of business.

Substance over form should be applied when deciding if two parties are related.

Related parties summary

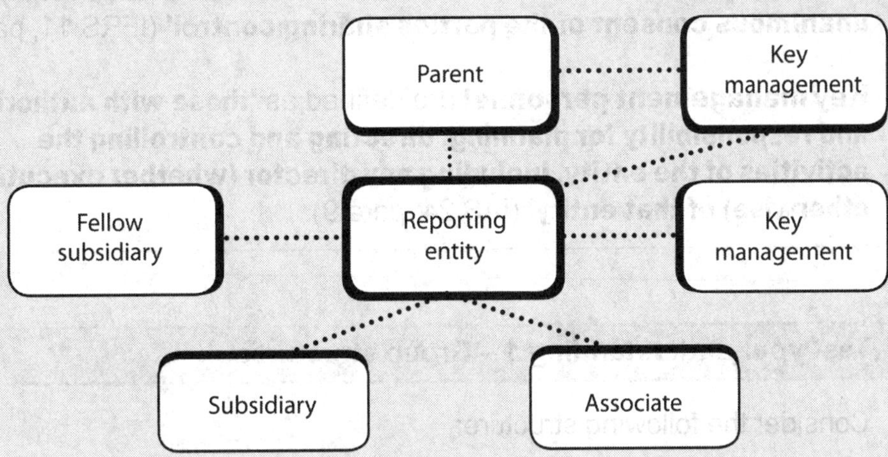

Further detail on definitions

'Close members of the family of a person are those family members who may be expected to influence, or be influenced by, that person in their dealings with the entity and include:

- **that person's children and spouse or domestic partner**
- **children of that person's spouse or domestic partner**
- **dependants of that person or that person's spouse or domestic partner' (IAS 24, para 9).**

Control is defined in IFRS 10. An investor **controls an investee** when:

- the investor has power over the investee, and
- the investor is exposed, or has rights, to variable returns from its involvement with the investee, and
- the investor has the ability to affect those returns through its power over the investee.

In simple terms, control is normally assumed when one entity owns more than half of the equity shares of another entity.

Significant influence is defined in IAS 28 Investments in Associates and Joint Ventures as the **'power to participate in, but not control, the financial and operating policy decisions of an entity'** (IAS 28, para 3). Significant influence is normally assumed when an entity owns between 20% and 50% of the equity shares of another entity.

Joint control is defined in IFRS 11 Joint Arrangements as **'the contractually agreed sharing of control of an arrangement, which exists only when decisions about the relevant activities require the unanimous consent of the parties sharing control'** (IFRS 11, para 7).

Key management personnel are defined as **'those with authority and responsibility for planning, directing and controlling the activities of the entity, including any director (whether executive or otherwise) of that entity'** (IAS 24, para 9).

Test your understanding 1 – Group structures

Consider the following structure:

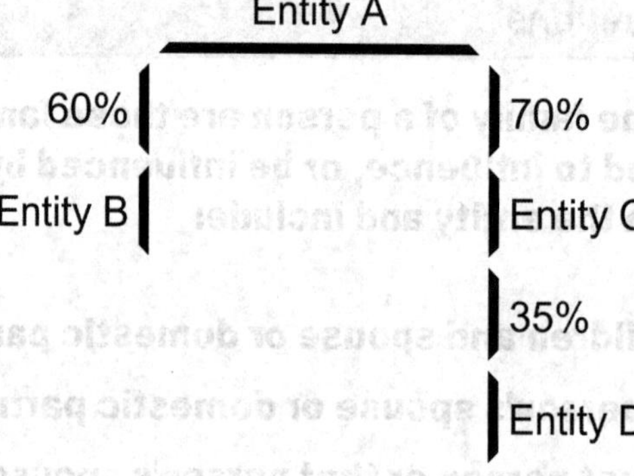

Required:

Identify the related party relationships within the above structure.

Test your understanding 2 – Individual shareholdings

Consider each of the following situations:

(a)

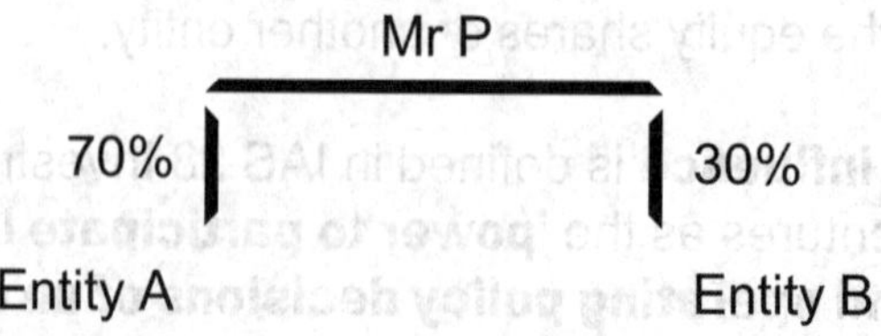

Mr P controls entity A and is able to exert significant influence over entity B.

(b)

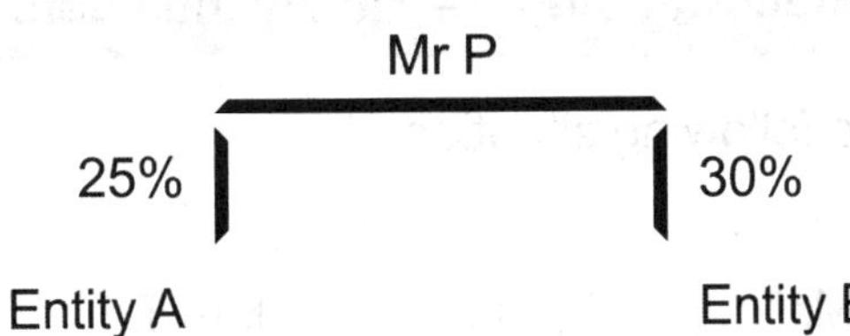

Mr P is able to exert significant influence over entity A and entity B.

Required:

For each situation explain whether or not entity A and entity B are related parties.

Test your understanding 3 – Key management personnel

Consider the following situation:

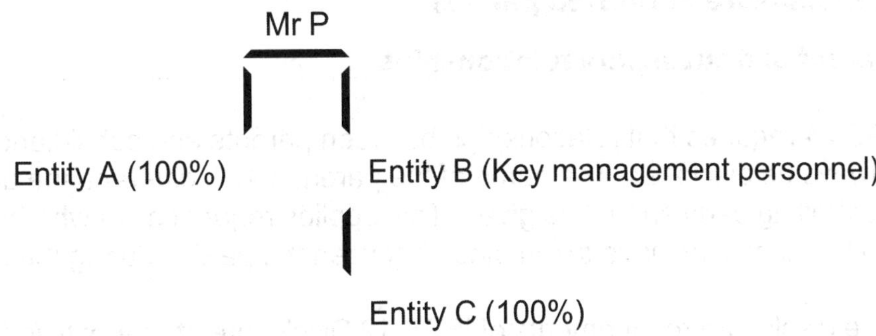

Mr P owns all of the issued share capital of entity A. He also is a member of the key management personnel of entity B which, in turn, owns all of the issued share capital of entity C.

Required:

Discuss the related party relationships arising from the above structure.

Test your understanding 4 – Family members

Consider the following situation:

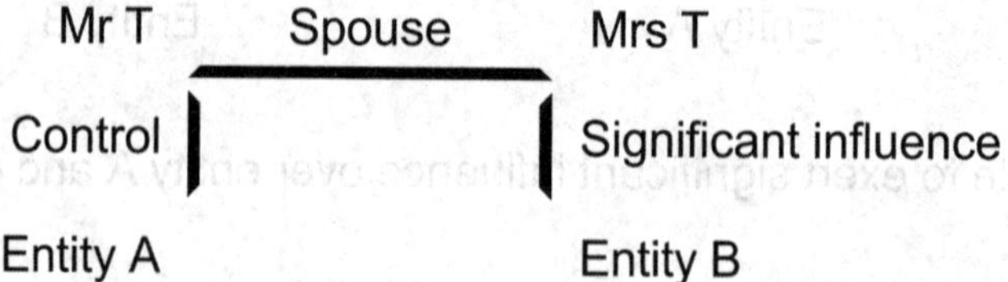

Mr T controls entity A. His spouse, Mrs T, exercises significant influence over entity B.

Required:

Discuss the related party relationships arising from the above.

3 Disclosure of related parties

Parent and subsidiary relationships

IAS 24 requires that relationships between parents and subsidiaries should always be disclosed. The name of the parent and, if different, the ultimate controlling party should be given. This applies regardless of whether or not any transactions have taken place between the parties during the period.

The disclosure requirements of IFRS 12 Disclosure of Interests in Other Entities (covered later in this text) also apply

Key management personnel

Total compensation granted to key management personnel should be disclosed. IAS 24 says that this should also be broken down into the following categories:

- short-term benefits
- pension benefits
- termination benefits
- share-based payment schemes.

Disclosure of transactions and balances

If there have been transactions between related parties, and if there are balances outstanding between the parties, the following should be disclosed:

- the nature of the related party relationship
- a description of the transactions
- the amounts of the transactions
- the amounts and details of any outstanding balances
- allowances for receivables in respect of the outstanding balances
- the irrecoverable debt expense in respect of outstanding balances.

Disclosure should be made whether or not a price was charged.

IAS 24 specifies that an entity may only disclose that related party transactions were made on terms equivalent to those that prevail in arm's length transactions if such terms can be substantiated.

Government-related entities

A reporting entity is exempt from the above disclosures in respect of transactions and balances that they have with a government that has control, joint control or significant influence over the reporting entity

If this exemption is applied, IAS 24 requires that the following disclosures are made instead:

- details of the government and a description of its relationship with the reporting entity
- details of individually significant transactions
- an indication of the extent of other transactions that are significant in aggregate.

Test your understanding 5 – Picture and Frame

Joanne Smith has owned 60% of the equity shares of Picture and 70% of the equity shares of Frame for many years. On 1 January 20X4, Picture entered into a lease agreement with Frame. Under the terms of the lease, Picture would lease one of its unused warehouses, with a remaining useful life of 20 years, to Frame for five years. Consideration payable by Frame would be $10,000 a year in arrears. Market rentals for similar sized warehouses tend to be around $100,000 per year.

Required:

Discuss the correct treatment of the above transaction in Picture's financial statements for the year ended 30 June 20X4.

4 Chapter summary

The need for disclosure of related parties

- Users need to be aware of related party relationships because transactions may not have happened at normal market rates.

Disclosure of related parties

- Parent/subsidiary relationships
- Disclosure of transactions and balances
- Key management compensation

Test your understanding answers

Test your understanding 1 – Group structures

Entity A:

Entities that are within the same group are related to one another. Entities B and C are therefore related parties of A.

D is an associate of C. C is a member of A's group. This means that D is a related party of A.

Entity B:

Entities that are within the same group are related to one another. Entities A and C are therefore related parties of B.

D is an associate of C. C is a member of the same group as B. This means that D is a related party of B

Entity C:

Entities that are within the same group are related to one another. Entities A and B are therefore related parties of C.

Entities are related if one is an associate of another. C and D are therefore related parties.

Entity D:

Entities are related if one is an associate of another. D and C are therefore related parties.

Entities are related if one is an associate of a member of a group of which the other entity is also a member. D is an associate of C. Companies A and B are in the same group as C. This means that D is also a related party of A and B.

Test your understanding 2 – Individual shareholdings

Situation A:

Mr P is a related party of both entity A and entity B as he is able to exercise either control or significant influence over each entity.

Mr P controls entity A and has significant influence over entity B. Therefore, A and B are related parties.

Situation B:

Mr P is a related party of both entity A and entity B as he is able to exercise significant influence over each entity.

Mr P does not control either entity A or entity B. Therefore, A and B are not related parties.

Test your understanding 3 – Key management personnel

Mr P has control over entity A, meaning that Mr P is a related party of A.

Mr P is a member of key management personnel of B, so is a related party of B.

A and B are related parties, because Mr P controls A and is a member of key management personnel of B.

Entity B controls entity C so B and C are related parties.

Mr P is a member of key management personnel of the parent of C, so Mr P and C are related parties.

This means that entities A and C are also related parties (Mr P controls A and is a member of key management personnel of the parent company of C).

Test your understanding 4 – Family members

Mr T and Mrs T are close family.

Mr T controls entity A. Mr T and Mrs T are related parties of entity A.

Mrs T has significant influence over entity B. Mrs T and Mr T are related parties of entity B.

Mr and Mrs T control entity A and have significant influence over entity B. A and B are related parties.

Test your understanding 5 – Picture and Frame

According to IFRS 16 Leases, a finance lease is a lease where the risks and rewards of ownership transfer to the lessee. The lease between Picture and Frame is only for a fraction of the asset's remaining useful life and the lease payments are insignificant. The lease is therefore an operating lease. Picture should recognise lease income on a straight line basis over the lease term. Therefore, \$5,000 (\$10,000 × 6/12) should be recognised in the current year's statement of profit or loss, as well as a corresponding entry to accrued income on the statement of financial position.

Picture and Frame are under joint control of Joanne Smith, so this means that they are related parties. Disclosure is required of all transactions between Picture and Frame during the financial period. Picture must disclose details of the leasing transaction and the income of \$5,000 from Frame during the year.

Disclosures that related party transactions were made on terms equivalent to an arm's length transaction can only be made if they can be substantiated. The lease rentals are only 10% of normal market rate meaning that this disclosure cannot be made.

chapter

15

Adoption of International Financial Reporting Standards

Chapter learning objectives

Upon completion of this chapter you will be able to:

- apply and discuss the accounting implications of the first time adoption of a body of new accounting standards
- evaluate the implications of worldwide convergence with International Financial Reporting Standards
- Discuss the influence of national regulators on International Financial Reporting Standards.

1 IFRS 1: First time adoption of International Financial Reporting Standards

Adoption of International Financial Reporting Standards

Although not as significant as they once were, differences remain between IFRS Standards and national standards. Therefore, there is an accounting issue when a company adopts IFRS Standards for the first time.

An entity may adopt IFRS Standards for a number of reasons:

- An entity may be seeking a listing, and listing rules may require the use of IFRS Standards.
- Unlisted multinational corporate groups may choose to adopt IFRS Standards as the basis for financial reporting throughout the group. This may save time and resources in the preparation of management information throughout the group, and streamline group annual financial reporting requirements.
- Entities may believe that adoption of IFRS Standards could assist in their efforts to raise capital, particularly if potential capital providers are familiar with IFRS Standards.
- Entities may believe that they are 'doing the right thing' by adopting IFRS Standards as they are already used by many other large entities.

IFRS 1 First Time Adoption of IFRS

IFRS 1 First-time Adoption of International Financial Reporting Standards sets out the procedures to follow when an entity adopts IFRS Standards in its published financial statements for the first time.

IFRS 1 defines a **first-time adopter** an entity that, for the first time, makes an explicit and unreserved statement that its annual financial statements comply with IFRS Standards.

There are five issues that need to be addressed when adopting IFRS Standards:

(1) The date of transition to IFRS Standards

(2) Which IFRS Standards should be adopted

(3) How gains or losses arising on adopting IFRS Standards should be accounted for

(4) The explanations and disclosures to be made in the year of transition

(5) What exemptions are available.

Date of transition

The **date of transition** is the **'beginning of the earliest period for which an entity presents full comparative information under IFRS Standards in its first financial statements produced using IFRS Standards'** (IFRS 1, Appendix A).

If an entity adopts IFRS Standards for the first time for the year ended 31 December 20X8 and presents one year of comparative information then the date of transition is 1 January 20X7 (i.e. the first day of the comparative period).

An opening IFRS statement of financial position should be produced as at the date of transition. This statement need not be published, but it will provide the opening balances for the comparative period.

Which IFRS Standards should be adopted?

- The entity should use the same accounting policies for all the periods presented. These policies should be based solely on IFRS Standards in force at the reporting date.
- A major problem for entities preparing for the change-over is that IFRS Standards keep changing. Therefore an entity may apply an IFRS Standard that is not yet mandatory if that standard permits early application.
- IFRS 1 states that the opening IFRS statement of financial position must:
  - recognise all assets and liabilities required by IFRS Standards
  - not recognise assets and liabilities not permitted by IFRS Standards
  - reclassify all assets, liabilities and equity components in accordance with IFRS Standards
  - measure all assets and liabilities in accordance with IFRS Standards.
- An entity's estimates at the date of transition to IFRS Standards should be consistent with estimates made for the same date in accordance with previous GAAP unless evidence exists that those estimates were wrong.

Reporting gains and losses

Any gains or losses arising on the adoption of IFRS Standards should be recognised directly in retained earnings. In other words, they are not recognised in profit or loss.

Explanations and disclosures

- Entities must explain how the transition to IFRS Standards affects their reported financial performance, financial position and cash flows.
- When preparing its first statements under IFRS Standards, an entity may identify errors made in previous years. The correction of these errors must be disclosed separately.
- When preparing statements in accordance with IFRS Standards for the first time, the fair value of property, plant and equipment, intangible assets and investment properties can be used as the 'deemed cost'. If so, the entity must disclose the aggregate of those fair values and the adjustment made to their carrying values under the previous GAAP.

Exemptions

IFRS 1 grants limited exemptions in situations where the cost of compliance would outweigh the benefits to the user. For example:

- Previous business combinations do not have to be restated.
- An entity can choose to deem past translation gains and losses on an overseas subsidiary to be nil.
- An entity need not restate the borrowing cost component that was capitalised under previous GAAP at the date of transition.
- Under IAS 32, the proceeds of convertible debt are split into a liability component and an equity component. If the debt had been repaid by the date of transition, no adjustment is needed to recognise the equity component upon adopting IFRS Standards for the first time.
- If a subsidiary adopts IFRS Standards later than its parent, then the subsidiary may value its assets and liabilities either at its own transition date or its parent's transition date (which would normally be easier).

Test your understanding 1 – Nat

Nat is a company that used to prepare financial statements under local national standards. Their first financial statements produced in accordance with IFRS Standards are for the year ended December 20X5 and these will include comparative information for the previous financial year. Its previous GAAP financial statements are for the years ended 31 December 20X3 and 20X4. The directors are unsure about the following issues:

(i) Nat received $5 million in advance orders for a new product on 31 December 20X3. These products were not dispatched until 20X4. In line with its previous GAAP, this $5m was recognised as revenue.

(ii) A restructuring provision of $1 million relating to head office activities was recognised at 31 December 20X3 in accordance with previous GAAP. This does not qualify for recognition as a liability in accordance with IAS 37.

(iii) Nat made estimates of accrued expenses and provisions at 31 December 20X3. Some of these estimates turned out to be under-stated. Nat believes that the estimates were reasonable and in line with the requirements of both its previous GAAP and IFRS Standards.

Required:

In accordance with IFRS 1, how should the above issues be dealt with?

Implications of adopting International Financial Reporting

There are a number of considerations to be made when adopting IFRS Standards for the first time. The key considerations are discussed below.

Initial evaluation

The transition to IFRS Standards requires careful and timely planning. Initially there are a number of questions that must be asked to assess the current position within the entity.

(a) Is there appropriate knowledge within the entity?

(b) Are there any agreements (such as bank covenants) that are dependent on local GAAP?

(c) Will there be a need to change the information systems?

(d) Which IFRS Standards will affect the entity?

(e) Is this an opportunity to improve the accounting systems?

Once the initial evaluation of the current position has been made, the entity can determine the nature of any assistance required.

They may need to:

- engage experts in IFRS Standards for assistance
- inform key stakeholders of the impact that IFRS Standards could have on reported performance
- produce a project plan that incorporates the resource requirements, training needs, management teams and timetable with a timescale that ensures there is enough time to produce the first financial statements in accordance with IFRS Standards.
- investigate the impact of the change on computer systems and establish if the current system can easily be changed.

Other considerations

Aside from the practical aspect of implementing the move to IFRS Standards, there are a number of other factors to consider:

(i) Debt covenants

- The entity will have to consider the impact of the adoption of IFRS Standards on debt covenants and other legal contracts.
- Covenants based on financial position ratios (for example the gearing ratio) and profit or loss measures (such as interest cover) will probably be affected significantly by the adoption of a different set of accounting standards.
- Debt covenants may need to be renegotiated and rewritten, as it would not seem to be sensible to retain covenants based on a local GAAP if this is no longer to be used.

(ii) Performance related pay

- There is a potential impact on income of moving to IFRS Standards, which causes a problem in designing an appropriate means of determining executive bonuses, employee performance related pay and long-term incentive plans.
- With the increase in the use of fair values and the potential recycling of gains and losses under IFRS Standards (e.g. IAS 21 The Effects of Changes in Foreign Exchange Rates), the identification of relevant measures of performance will be quite difficult.
- There may be volatility in the reported figures, which will have little to do with financial performance but could result in major differences in the pay awarded to a director from one year to another.

(iii) Views of financial analysts

- It is important that the entity considers how to communicate the effects of a move to IFRS Standards with the markets and analysts.
- The focus of the communication should be to provide assurance about the process and to quantify the changes expected. Unexpected changes in ratios and profits could adversely affect share prices.

2 Harmonisation

Reasons for differences in accounting practices

The reasons why accounting practices may differ from one country to another include the following:

- **Legal systems.** In some countries, financial statements are prepared according to a strict code imposed by the government. This is often because the accounts are being prepared primarily for tax purposes rather than for investment.
- **Professional traditions.** In contrast to countries where accounting standards are embedded in legislation, other countries have a strong and influential accounting profession and can rely on the profession to draft relevant standards.
- **User groups.** As mentioned above, in some countries the tax authorities are the main users of accounts, and so a standardised, rule-based approach to accounting emerges. Quite often, depreciation rates will be set by law rather than being based upon useful lives. In countries where businesses are generally financed by loans (rather than by equity) then financial statements will focus on a business' ability to service and pay back its debts. In the UK and the US, businesses are generally financed through equity. In these countries, the shareholders share the risks of profits and losses, and so they demand full disclosure of a business' financial affairs.
- **Nationalism.** Individual countries believe that their own standards are the best.
- **Culture.** Differences in culture can lead to differences in the objective and method of accounting.

Culture and local custom

Financial reporting practice may be influenced by cultural factors in a number of ways.

- Religion may affect accounting practices. For example, Islamic law forbids the charging or accepting of interest.
- Different nationalities have different attitudes to risk. For example, in Japan high gearing is usual and is a sign of confidence in an entity.

- In the UK and the USA, the main objective of management and shareholders is generally to maximise profit in the short term. However, in other countries, investors and management may have different or wider objectives, such as long-term growth, stability, benefiting the community and safeguarding the interests of employees.

Benefits of harmonisation

There are a number of reasons why the harmonisation of accounting standards would be beneficial. Businesses operate on a global scale and investors make investment decisions on a worldwide basis. There is thus a need for financial information to be presented on a consistent basis. The advantages are as follows.

(1) **Multi-national entities**

Multi-national entities would benefit from closer harmonisation for the following reasons.

(a) Access to international finance would be easier as financial information is more understandable if it is prepared on a consistent basis.

(b) In a business that operates in several countries, the preparation of financial information would be easier as it would all be prepared on the same basis.

(c) There would be greater efficiency in accounting departments.

(d) Consolidation of financial statements would be easier.

(2) **Investors**

If investors wish to make decisions based on the worldwide availability of investments, then better comparisons between entities are required. Harmonisation assists this process, as financial information would be consistent between different entities from different regions.

(3) **International economic groupings**

International economic groupings, e.g. the EU, could work more effectively if there were international harmonisation of accounting practices. Part of the function of international economic groupings is to make cross-border trade easier. Similar accounting regulations would improve access to capital markets and therefore help this process.

The role of standard setters

National standard setters

The harmonisation process has gathered pace in the last few years. From 2005 all European listed entities were required to adopt IFRS Standards in their group financial statements. Many other countries including Australia, Canada and New Zealand decided to follow a similar process. National standard setters are committed to a framework of accounting standards based on IFRS Standards.

National standard setters and the Board

In February 2005, the Board issued a memorandum setting out its responsibilities and those of national standard setters:

- The Board has a responsibility to ensure that it makes information available on a timely basis so that national standard setters can be informed of its plans. Sufficient time should be allowed in relation to consultative documents so that national standard setters have sufficient time to prepare the information in their own context and to receive comments from their own users.
- The national standard setters should deal with domestic barriers to adopting or converging with IFRS Standards. They should avoid amending an IFRS Standard when adopting it in their own jurisdiction. They should encourage their own constituents to communicate their technical views to the Board. They should also make known any differences of opinion that they have with a project as early as possible in the process.

Chapter summary

First time adoption of IFRS

- Five points to consider are:
  - the date of transition to IFRS
  - which IFRS should be adopted
  - how gains or losses arising on adopting IFRS should be accounted for
  - the explanations and disclosures to be made in the year of transition
  - what exemptions are available

Implications of adoption of IFRS

- Consider practical implications – training, IT systems, planning project
- Also consider terms in debt covenants, calculation of performance-related pay and anything that is based on the profit figure
- Communicate with analysts on the expected changes to the financial statements

Differences in accounting practices

- There are historical reasons for differences in accounting systems such as legal, professional, culture
- Some accounting differences remain, but the harmonisation process is taking place
  Many countries are adopting IFRS
- The IASB is aiming to converge with the US standard-setter the FASB to harmonise IFRS with US GAAP

Test your understanding answers

Test your understanding 1 – Nat

Comparative figures prepared under IFRS Standards for year ended 31 December 20X4 must be presented. Nat's date of transition is therefore 1 January 20X4 and an opening IFRS statement of financial position must be produced as at this date.

Some of the accounting policies that Nat uses in its opening IFRS statement of financial position differ from those that it used for the same date using its previous GAAP. The resulting adjustments arise from events and transactions before the date of transition to IFRS Standards. Therefore, Nat should recognise those adjustments directly in retained earnings.

Transaction (i)
The sale does not meet the revenue recognition criteria per IFRS 15 Revenue from Contracts with Customers because control of the asset has not transferred from the seller to the customer. In the opening IFRS statement of financial position as at 1 January 20X4, a contract liability should be recognised. The $5 million loss on recognition of this liability will be accounted for in retained earnings.

Transaction (ii)
The provision does not meet the criteria in IAS 37. In the opening IFRS statement of financial position as at 1 January 20X4, the provision should be derecognised. The $1 million gain on derecognition of this provision will be accounted for in retained earnings.

Transaction (iii)
Although some of the accruals and provisions turned out to be under-estimates, Nat concluded that its estimates were reasonable and, therefore, no error has occurred. In accordance with IAS 8, this issue should be accounted for prospectively. Therefore the additional expense will be recognised within the profit or loss figures prepared in accordance with IFRS Standards for the year ended 31 December 20X4.

chapter

16

Specialised entities and specialised transactions

Chapter learning objectives

Upon completion of this chapter you will be able to:

- account for transactions and events occurring in not- for-profit and public sector entities
- discuss the accounting treatments not allowable under the SMEs Standard including the revaluation model for certain assets
- discuss and apply the simplifications introduced by the SMEs Standard including accounting for goodwill and intangible assets, financial instruments, defined benefit schemes, exchange differences and associates and joint ventures
- identify when an entity may no longer be viewed as a going concern and outline circumstances when a reconstruction may be an alternative to corporate liquidation
- outline the appropriate accounting treatment required relating to reconstructions.

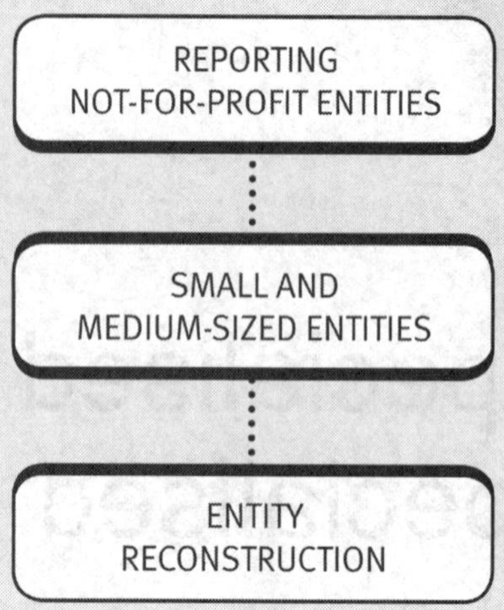

1 Not-for-profit entities

Reporting not-for-profit entities

A **not-for-profit entity** is one that does not carry on its activities for the purposes of profit or gain to particular persons and does not distribute its profits or assets to particular persons.

The main types of not-for-profit entity are:

- clubs and societies
- charities
- public sector organisations (including central government, local government and National Health Service bodies).

The objectives of a not-for-profit entity

- The main objective of public sector organisations is to provide services to the general public. Their long-term aim is normally to break even, rather than to generate a surplus.
- Most public sector organisations aim to provide value for money, which is usually analysed into the three Es – economy, efficiency and effectiveness.
- Other not-for-profit entities include charities, clubs and societies whose objective is to carry out the activities for which they were created.

Assessing performance in a not-for-profit entity

- It can be difficult to monitor and evaluate the success of a not-for-profit organisation as the focus is not on a resultant profit as with a traditional business entity.
- The success of the organisation should be measured against the key indicators that reflect the visions and values of the organisation. The strategic plan will identify the goals and the strategies that the organisation needs to adopt to achieve these goals.
- The focus should be the measures of output, outcomes and their impact on what the charity is trying to achieve.

Accounting in a not-for-profit entity

The financial statements of a public sector entity or a charity are set out differently from those of a profit making entity, because their purpose is different. A public sector organisation is not reporting a profit; it is reporting on its income and how it has spent that income in achieving its aims.

The financial statements include a statement of financial position or balance sheet, but the statement of profit or loss and other comprehensive income is usually replaced with a statement of financial activities or an income and expenditure account showing incoming resources and resources expended.

Example of not-for-profit accounts

An example of a statement of financial activities for a charity is shown below.

The Toytown Charity, Statement of Financial Activities for the year ended 31 March 20X7

	$
Incoming resources	
Resources from generated funds	
Grants	10,541,000
Legacies	5,165,232
Donations	1,598,700
Activities for generating funds	
Charity shop sales	10,052,693
Investment income	3,948,511
Total incoming resources	31,306,136

Resources expended	
Cost of generating funds	
Fund raising	(1,129,843)
Publicity	(819,828)
Charity shop operating costs	(6,168,923)
Charitable activities	
Supporting local communities	(18,263,712)
Elderly care at home	(4,389,122)
Pride in Toytown campaign	(462,159)
Total resources expended	(31,233,587)
Net incoming resources for the year	72,549
Funds brought forward at 1 March 20X6	21,102
Funds carried forward at 31 March 20X7	93,651

The statement of financial position or balance sheet of a not-for-profit entity only differs from that of a profit making entity in the reserves section, where there will usually be an analysis of the different types of reserve, as shown below:

Toytown Charity, Balance sheet as at 31 March 20X7

	$
Non-current assets	
Tangible assets	80,500
Investments	12,468
	92,968
Current assets	
Inventory	2,168
Receivables	10,513
Cash	3,958
	16,639
Total assets	109,607
Reserves	
Restricted fund	20,200
Unrestricted funds	73,451
	93,651

Non-current liabilities	
Pension liability	9,705
Current liabilities	
Payables	6,251
Total funds	109,607

The reserves are separated into restricted and unrestricted funds.

- Unrestricted funds are funds available for general purposes.
- Restricted funds are those that have been set aside for a specific purpose or in a situation where an individual has made a donation to the charity for a specific purpose, perhaps to replace some equipment, so these funds must be kept separate.

2 Small and medium sized entities

The SMEs Standard

Definition

A small or medium entity may be defined or characterised as follows:

- they are usually owner-managed by a relatively small number of individuals such as a family group, rather than having an extensive ownership base
- they are usually smaller entities in financial terms such as revenues generated and assets and liabilities under the control of the entity
- they usually have a relatively small number of employees
- they usually undertake less complex or difficult transactions which are normally the focus of a financial reporting standard.

One of the underlying requirements for financial reporting is that the cost and burden of producing financial reporting information for shareholders and other stakeholders should not outweigh the benefits of making that information available.

IFRS for small and medium-sized entities (the SMEs Standard) has been issued for use by entities that have no public accountability. This means that debt or equity instruments are not publicly traded. The SMEs Standard reduces the burden of producing information that is not likely to be of interest to the stakeholders of a small or medium company.

The problem of differential reporting

- It can be difficult to define a small or medium entity.
- If a company ceases to qualify as a small or medium entity then there will be a cost and time burden in order to comply with full IFRS and IAS Standards.
- There may be comparability problems if one company applies full IFRS and IAS Standards whilst another applies the SMEs Standard.

What is the effect of introducing the SMEs Standard?

The SMEs Standard will be updated approximately every three years. In contrast, companies that use full IFRS and IAS Standards have to incur the time cost of ensuring compliance with regular updates.

Accounting under full IFRS and IAS Standards necessitates compliance with approximately 3,000 disclosure points. In contrast, the SMEs Standard comprises approximately 300 disclosure points all contained within the one document. This significantly reduces the time spent and costs incurred in producing financial statements.

Key omissions from the SMEs Standard

The subject matter of several reporting standards has been omitted from the SMEs Standard, as follows:

- Earnings per share (IAS 33)
- Interim reporting (IAS 34)
- Segmental reporting (IFRS 8)
- Assets held for sale (IFRS 5).

Omission of subject matter from the SMEs Standard is usually because the cost of preparing and reporting information exceeds the expected benefits which users would expect to derive from that information.

Accounting choices disallowed under the SMEs Standard

There are a number of accounting policy choices allowed under full IFRS and IAS Standards that are not available to companies that apply the SMEs Standard. Under the SMEs Standard:

- Goodwill is always recognised as the difference between the cost of the business combination and the fair value of the net assets acquired. In other words, the fair value method for measuring the non-controlling interest is not available.

- Intangible assets must be accounted for at cost less accumulated amortisation and impairment. The revaluation model is not permitted for intangible assets.
- After initial recognition, investment property is remeasured to fair value at the year end with gains or losses recorded in profit or loss. The cost model can only be used if fair value cannot be measured reliably or without undue cost or effort.

Key simplifications in the SMEs Standard

The subject matter of other reporting standards has been simplified for inclusion within the SMEs Standard. Key simplifications to be aware of are as follows:

- Borrowing costs are always expensed to profit or loss.
- Whilst associates and jointly controlled entities can be accounted for using the equity method in the consolidated financial statements, they can also be held at cost (if there is no published price quotation) or fair value. Therefore, simpler alternatives to the equity method are available.
- Depreciation and amortisation estimates are not reviewed annually. Changes to these estimates are only required if there is an indication that the pattern of an asset's use has changed.
- Expenditure on research and development is always expensed to profit or loss.
- If an entity is unable to make a reliable estimate of the useful life of an intangible asset, then the useful life is assumed to be ten years.
- Goodwill is amortised over its useful life. If the useful life cannot be reliably established then management should use a best estimate that does not exceed ten years.
- On the disposal of an overseas subsidiary, cumulative exchange differences that have been recognised in other comprehensive income are not recycled to profit or loss.
- When measuring defined benefit obligations, the entity is permitted to:
  - **'ignore estimated future salary increases**
  - **ignore future service of current employees**
  - **ignore possible in-service mortality of current employees between the reporting date and the date employees are expected to begin receiving post-employment benefits'** (SMEs Standard, para 28.19).

- There are numerous simplifications with regards to financial instruments. These include:
  - Measuring most debt instruments at amortised cost.
  - Recognising most investments in shares at fair value with changes in fair value recognised in profit or loss. If fair value cannot be measured reliably then the shares are held at cost less impairment.

Advantages and disadvantages of the SMEs Standard

Advantages

- There will be time and cost savings due to simplifications and omissions, particularly with regards to disclosure.
- The SMEs Standard is worded in an accessible way.
- All standards are located within one document so it is therefore easier and quicker to find the information required.

Disadvantages

- There are issues of comparability when comparing one company that uses full IFRS and IAS Standards and another which uses the SMEs Standard.
- The SMEs Standard is arguably still too complex for many small companies. In particular, the requirements with regards to leases and deferred tax could be simplified.

3 Entity reconstruction schemes

The purpose of an entity reconstruction

If an entity is in financial difficulty it may have no recourse but to accept liquidation as the final outcome. However it may be in a position to survive, and indeed flourish, by taking up some future contract or opportunities. The only hindrance to this may be that any future operations may need a prior cash injection. This cash injection cannot be raised because the present structure and status of the entity may not be attractive to current and outside investors.

A typical corporate profile of an entity in this situation could be as follows:

- Accumulated trading losses
- Arrears of unpaid debenture and loan interest

- No payment of equity dividends for several years
- Market value of equity shares below their nominal value
- Lack of investor and market confidence in the entity.

To get a cash injection the entity will need to undergo a reorganisation or reconstruction.

A reconstruction of the entity's capital may help to alleviate these problems and may involve one or more of the following procedures:

- Write off the accumulated losses.
- Write off arrears of repayment of loan finance.
- Write down the nominal value of the equity capital.

How is this achieved?

To do this the entity must ask all or some of its existing stakeholders to surrender existing rights and amounts owing in exchange for new rights under a new or reformed entity.

Why would stakeholders be willing to do this?

The main reason is that a reconstruction may result in an outcome preferable to any other alternative as follows:

- Providers of loan finance and other creditors may be left with little or no prospect of repayment.
- Providers of equity finance may be left with little or no prospect of a return (dividends and capital growth) on their investment.
- Corporate liquidation may provide some return to providers of loan finance, but is unlikely to provide any return to equity holders, depending upon the financial position of the entity.

How could this be agreed between the various stakeholders?

It may be helpful to review the situation faced by each group of stakeholders as follows:

- Equity shareholders are the last group to be allocated funds in a corporate liquidation, and therefore have a high chance of receiving no return at all. It would therefore seem appropriate that they should bear most of the losses from the present situation, in exchange for potential future benefits if the entity is profitable following reconstruction.

- Trade creditors and payables may have some prospect of recovery of at least part of the amounts due to them as they rank ahead of equity holders for repayment upon corporate liquidation. Some trade creditors may also protect themselves from the risk of non-recovery by including the right to retain legal title or ownership of goods delivered to customers until they are paid for. In the event of non-recovery of amounts due to them, they will have the right to take repossession of their inventory.
- Debenture holders often have a better chance of recovery of capital under liquidation than other stakeholders because such loans are often secured against entity assets. However, even in this situation, the full amount outstanding of such loans may not be recovered. In this case, any amount not recovered from the assets used as security (or collateral) would then normally be regarded as an unsecured creditor in the same way as trade payables.

It may therefore be in the best interests of all stakeholders to agree to a scheme of reconstruction. In effect, they give up existing rights and amounts owing (which are unlikely to be recovered) for the opportunity to share in the future profitability which may arise from the extra cash which can be generated as a consequence of their actions. This can only be achieved if all stakeholders are willing to compromise by waiving some or all of their existing rights, and if they can be convinced that there is an improved prospect of future returns as a result of a reconstruction scheme.

Capital reduction schemes

Under a capital reduction scheme, an entity may:

- write off unpaid equity capital – this situation may arise, for example, if there are partly-paid shares in issue. The entity is effectively reducing the nominal value of its equity share capital by the amount not yet called up and paid by the equity holders.
- write off any equity capital which is lost or not represented by available assets – in this situation, the entity has a deficit on retained earnings due to accumulated losses, preventing the payment of an equity dividend and depressing the share price.
- write off any paid up equity capital which is in excess of requirements – in this situation, the entity uses surplus cash to repay its equity holders.

This scheme does not really affect creditors as the equity holders have reduced their capital stake in the entity, either by reducing the nominal value of the shares in issue, or by reducing the total number of shares in issue, or a combination of both.

This scheme is normally regulated by formalised procedures detailed in law, such as the Companies Act 2006 s641 in the United Kingdom. In examination questions, it is unlikely that there will be questions set which require a specific and detailed knowledge of law from any particular jurisdiction.

Illustration – Struggler

Struggler has the following statement of financial position at 30 June 20X8:

	$000
Assets	500
	500
Equity and liabilities:	$000
Issued equity shares ($1 each)	600
Share premium	100
Retained earnings/(deficit)	(300)
Liabilities	100
	500

Struggler has the following problems:

- Accumulated losses which prevent payment of a dividend should the entity become profitable at some future date.
- Issued equity capital of $600,000 which is only backed by assets to the extent of $500,000.
- Difficulty in attracting new sources of equity and loan finance.

Required:

Apply a capital reduction scheme and restate the statement of financial position at 30 June 20X8.

Solution

Using the reduction of capital scheme, the deficit on retained earnings could be cleared by reducing both the share premium and issued equity capital accounts. Any balance on share premium account should be utilised first to minimise the reduction of equity capital as follows:

	$000	$000
Dr Share premium	100	
Dr Equity share capital	200	
Cr Retained earnings		300

The resulting statement of financial position would be:

	$000
Assets	500
	500

Equity and liabilities:	$000
Issued equity shares	400
Share premium	nil
Retained earnings/(deficit)	nil
Liabilities	100
	500

The equity holders have effectively recognised the financial reality of their situation by reducing the nominal value of the issued share capital. If the entity begins to make profits following the reconstruction, there is no longer a deficit on retained earnings to clear before a dividend can be paid. Potential equity and/or loan finance providers may also be encouraged by this situation.

The reduction in equity capital could be reflected by either a reduction in the nominal value per share (from $1 down to approximately (400/600) $0.67, or by converting and reducing shareholdings on a pro-rata basis. For example, if a person previously owned thirty shares with a nominal value of $1 each, following conversion and reduction, they would now own only twenty shares with a nominal value of $1 each. In either situation, the total equity share capital would be $400,000.

Reconstruction schemes

Reconstruction schemes extend the principles of the capital reduction schemes by including the various creditors within the scheme. In addition to reducing equity share capital, reconstruction schemes may also include:

- writing off debenture loan interest arrears
- replacement of debenture loans with new loans having different interest and capital repayment terms
- write off amounts owing to unsecured or trade payables.

In practical terms, this can only be achieved if all stakeholders agree to forego some of their current legal and commercial rights. For those in the weakest position, usually the equity holders, they would be expected to sacrifice more than others.

In the United Kingdom, these schemes are governed by the Companies Act 2006 s895. As with the capital reduction scheme considered earlier, it is unlikely that an examination question will be set which requires a detailed knowledge of specific law from any one jurisdiction.

Illustration – Machin

Consider the statement of financial position of Machin at 30 June 20X9:

	$000
Non-current assets:	
Intangible – brand	50,000
Tangible	220,000
	270,000
Current assets:	
Inventory	20,000
Receivables	30,000
	320,000

Equity and liabilities:	$000
Equity share capital ($1)	100,000
Share premium	75,000
Retained earnings	(100,000)
	75,000
Non-current liabilities: Debenture loan	125,000
Current liabilities:	
Bank overdraft	20,000
Trade payables	100,000
	320,000

The following reconstruction scheme is to be applied:

(1) The equity shares of $1 nominal value currently in issue will be written off and will be replaced on a one-for-one basis by new equity shares with a nominal value of $0.25.

(2) The debenture loan will be replaced by the issue of new equity shares – four new equity shares with a nominal value of $0.25 each for every $1 of debenture loan converted.

(3) Existing equity holders will be offered the opportunity to subscribe for three new equity shares with a nominal value of $0.25 each for every one equity share currently held. The shares are to be issued at nominal value. It is expected that all current equity holders will take up this opportunity.

(4) The share premium account is to be eliminated.

(5) The brand is considered to be impaired and must be written off.

(6) Retained earnings deficit is to be eliminated.

Required:

Prepare the statement of financial position of Machin immediately after the scheme has been put into effect. Show any workings required to arrive at the solution.

Solution

Begin by opening a reconstruction account:

All adjustments to the statement of financial position as a result of the reconstruction scheme must be accounted for within this account. Any balance remaining on this account will be used to either write down assets or create a capital reserve.

Reconstruction account

	$000		$000
New equity shares (100,000 × $0.25) (Note 1)	25,000	Equity shares ($1) (Note 1)	100,000
New equity shares (125,000 × 4 × $0.25) (Note 2)	125,000	Debenture loan (Note 2)	125,000
Brand impaired (Note 5)	50,000	Share premium (Note 4)	75,000
Retained earnings (Note 6)	100,000		
	300,000		300,000

The note references refer to the details of the reconstruction scheme.

The debenture holders may be prepared to sacrifice their rights as a creditor if they believe that Machin will trade profitably following the reconstruction scheme. They will forego the rights of a creditor in exchange for the rights of an equity holder – i.e. future dividends plus growth in the capital value of their equity shares.

The resulting statement of financial position for Machin will be:

	$000
Non-current assets:	
Intangible – brand	nil
Tangible	220,000
Current assets:	
Inventory	20,000
Receivables	30,000
Bank ((20,000) + 75,000) (Note 3)	55,000
	325,000
Share capital (W1)	225,000
Share premium	nil
Retained earnings	nil
	225,000
Non-current liabilities: Debenture loan	nil
Current liabilities:	
Bank overdraft (eliminated by cash receipt from share issue)	nil
Trade payables	100,000
	325,000

(W1) **Confirmation of equity share capital following reorganisation:**

		No
Note 1	Issue of one new equity share for one old equity share	100,000
Note 2	Convert debenture loan into new equity shares: 125,000 × 4	500,000
Note 3	Issue of new equity shares for cash	300,000
		900,000

Share capital is therefore $225,000 (900,000 × $0.25).

Illustration – Bentham

Bentham has been making losses for several years, principally due to severe competition, which has put downward pressure on revenues whilst costs have increased.

The statement of financial position for Bentham at 30 June 20X1 is as follows:

	$000
Non-current assets	7,200
Current assets	10,550
	17,750
Equity and liabilities	$000
Equity share capital ($1 shares)	20,000
Retained earnings (deficit)	(17,250)
	2,750
Non-current liabilities:	
11% debentures 20X3 (secured)	7,000
8% debentures 20X4 (secured)	5,000
Current liabilities	3,000
	17,750

The entity has changed its marketing strategy and, as a result, it is expected that annual profit before interest and tax will be $3,000,000 for the next five years. Bentham incurs tax at 25% on profit before tax.

The directors are proposing to reconstruct Bentham and have produced the following proposal for discussion:

(1) The existing $1 equity shares are to be cancelled and replaced by equity shares of $0.25.

(2) The 8% debentures are to be replaced by 8,000,000 equity shares of $0.25 each, regarded as fully paid up, plus $3,000,000 6% debentures 20X9.

(3) Existing shareholders will have their $1 equity shares replaced by 11,000,000 $0.25 equity shares, regarded as fully paid up.

(4) The 11% debentures are to be redeemed in exchange for:
   - $6,000,000 6% debentures 20X9, and
   - 4,000,000 equity shares of $0.25, regarded as fully paid up.

In the event of a liquidation, it is estimated that the net realisable value of the assets would be $6,200,000 for the non-current assets and $10,000,000 for the current assets.

Required:

- **Prepare a statement of financial position for Bentham at 1 July 20X1, immediately after the reconstruction scheme has been implemented.**
- **Prepare computations to show the effect of the proposed reconstruction scheme on each of the equity shareholders, 11% debenture holders and 8% debenture holders.**
- **Comment on the potential outcome of the scheme from the perspective of a shareholder who currently owns 10% of the equity share capital on whether to agree to the reconstruction scheme as proposed.**

Solution

Bentham – the revised statement of financial position at 1 July 20X1 following reconstruction would be:

	$000
Non-current assets	7,200
Current assets	10,550
	17,750

Equity and liabilities:	$000
Equity share capital (23 million shares × $0.25) (W1)	5,750
Retained earnings	nil
	5,750
Non-current liabilities:	
6% debentures 20X9 (W1)	9,000
Current liabilities	3,000
	17,750

(W1) The reconstruction account would be as follows:

Reconstruction account

	$000		$000
New 6% debentures	6,000	11% Debentures redeemed	7,000
New equity shares: 4m × $0.25	1,000	8% Debenture redeemed	5,000
New equity shares: 11m × $0.25	2,750	Equity cancelled	20,000
New equity shares: 8m × $0.25	2,000		
New 6% debentures	3,000		
Deficit on retained earnings	17,250		
	32,000		32,000

If Bentham was to be put into liquidation, rather than undergo the reconstruction, the following could be the consequence:

	$000
Net realisable value of non-current assets	6,200
Net realisable value of current assets	10,000
	16,200
Repayment of 11% secured debenture loan	(7,000)
Repayment of 8% secured debenture loan	(5,000)
Available for unsecured creditors	4,200
Unsecured creditors	(3,000)
Available for equity holders	1,200

It can be seen that, whilst secured creditors will be paid off, and there should then be sufficient assets available for payment of unsecured creditors, equity shareholders would not fully recover the nominal value of their shareholding. The equity holders would receive only (1,200/20,000) $0.06 for each $1 equity share held. Note that this does not include any legal and professional fees that may be payable to implement such a scheme.

If the scheme is implemented, the debenture holders would forego part of their prior claim for repayment in exchange for equity shares. If they are to agree to this, they must be satisfied regarding the reliability of the profit forecast for future trading, so that they can receive future dividends and enjoy capital growth on the value of their shares. Additionally, they will have a significant equity holding of 12 million out of 23 million equity shares. This is just enough to give them a majority of the equity capital; they could then use their voting power to appoint or remove directors as they see appropriate.

If the reconstruction scheme is implemented, the revised capital structure results in significantly more equity shares in issue, with reduced long term liabilities in the form of secured debenture loans. It can be seen that the current debenture loan holders have deferred the repayment date of their loans from 20X3 and 20X4 respectively to 20X9, and accepted a reduced rate of interest on their loans. In addition, they have received some equity shares which will give them the opportunity to share in the future prosperity of Bentham if it becomes profitable following the reconstruction.

From the perspective of someone who holds 10% of the equity before the reconstruction takes place, the following comments can be made:

- The gearing ratio has reduced as follows:

Before:	$000		After:	$000	
Gearing ratio	12,000 / 14,750	= 81.3%		9,000 / 14,750	= 61.0%

  The reduction in gearing will be regarded as a decrease in financial risk for the equity holders.

- If the forecast regarding expected profit before interest and tax is reliable, then the following will result:

	$000
Profit before interest and tax	3,000
Less: debenture interest (9,000 × 6%)	540
Profit before tax	2,460
Tax (× 25%)	(615)
Profit after tax available to equity holders	1,845

  Potentially, there are retained profits available for payment of an equity dividend. Whilst it may not be advisable to distribute all profit after tax in the form of a dividend, it is a positive step to have retained earnings within the entity. Additionally, interest cover of (3,000/540) 5.5 may be regarded as reasonable in the circumstances.

- One further factor is the change in proportionate voting power if the reconstruction scheme is implemented. Previously, someone who owned 10% of the equity share capital would have 10% × 11 million = 1.1 million equity shares in the restructured entity out of 23 million equity shares – i.e. 4.7% of the equity shares. This is a significant dilution of voting power, but it may be a reasonable thing to give up in exchange for the future prospect of the continuation of Bentham, together with the potential receipt of a dividend if the forecast is realistic.

Test your understanding 1 – Wire

Wire has suffered from poor trading conditions over the last three years. Its statement of financial position at 30 June 20X1 is as follows:

	$	$
Non-current assets:		
Land and buildings		193,246
Plant and equipment		60,754
Investment in Cord		27,000
		281,000
Current assets:		
Inventory	120,247	
Receivables	70,692	
		190,939
		471,939
Equity and liabilities:		$
Equity shares ($1)		200,000
Retained earnings (deficit)		(39,821)
		160,179
Non-current liabilities:		
8% debenture 20X4	80,000	
5% debenture 20X5	70,000	
		150,000
Current liabilities:		
Trade payables	112,247	
Interest payable	12,800	
Overdraft	36,713	
		161,760
		471,939

It has been difficult to generate revenues and profits in the current year and inventory levels are very high. Interest has not been paid to the debenture holders for two years. Although the debentures are secured against the land and buildings, the debenture holders have demanded either a scheme of reconstruction or the liquidation of Wire.

During a meeting of directors and representatives of the shareholders and debenture holders, it was decided to implement a scheme of reconstruction.

The following scheme has been agreed in principle:

(1) Each $1 equity share is to be redesignated as an equity share of $0.25.

(2) The existing 5% debenture is to be exchanged for a new issue of $35,000 9.5% loan stock, repayable in 20X9, plus 140,000 equity shares of $0.25 each. In addition, they will subscribe for $9,000 debenture stock, repayable 20X9, at par value. The rate of interest on this new debenture is 9.5%.

(3) The equity shareholders are to accept a reduction in the nominal value of their shares from $1 to $0.25 per share, and subscribe for a new issue on the basis of one-for-one at a price of $0.30 per share.

(4) The 8% debenture holders, who have received no interest for two years, are to receive 20,000 equity shares of $0.25 each in lieu of the interest payable. It is agreed that the value of the interest liability is equivalent to the fair value of the shares to be issued. In addition, they have agreed to defer repayment of their loan until 20X9, subject to an increased rate of interest of 9.5%.

(5) The deficit on retained earnings is to be written off.

(6) The investment in Cord has been subject to much speculation as Cord has just obtained the legal rights to a new production process. As a result, the value of the investment has increased to $60,000. This investment is to be sold as part of the reconstruction scheme.

(7) The bank overdraft is to be repaid.

(8) 10% of the receivables are regarded as non-recoverable and are to be written off.

(9) The remaining assets were independently valued, and should now be recognised at the following amounts:

	$
Land	80,000
Buildings	80,000
Equipment	30,000
Inventory	50,000

If the reconstruction goes ahead, the following is expected to happen:

(1) It is expected that, due to the refinancing, operating profits will be earned at the rate of $50,000 after depreciation, but before interest and tax.

(2) Wire will be subject to tax on its profit before tax at 25%.

Required:

- **Prepare the statement of financial position of Wire immediately after the reconstruction.**
- **Advise the equity holders and debenture holders whether or not they should support the reconstruction scheme.**

External reconstructions

External reconstruction schemes normally involve the assets and liabilities of the current entity being transferred to a new entity on an agreed basis. Typically, this will require information regarding the following:

- details of purchase consideration to acquire the business as a whole, or specified assets and liabilities – this may give rise to goodwill for the purchaser.
- details of what will happen to assets and liabilities currently belonging to the entity which are to be sold, transferred, written off or realised as appropriate – this will lead to a profit or loss on realisation for the vendor.
- how repayment or settlement of capital of the selling entity is to be arranged.

Illustration – Smith

Smith has agreed to acquire the net assets, excluding the bank balance, and the debenture liability which is to be paid off in cash, of Thompson. The purchase consideration comprises the following:

	$000
50,000 $1 equity shares at a fair value of $1.04	52,000
$30,000 debenture loan issued at par value	30,000
Cash	18,000
	100,000

When determining the consideration to be paid, the directors of Smith valued the land and buildings of Thompson at $40,000, inventory at $15,000 and receivables at carrying value, subject to a 3% write off for bad debts.

After the sale, Thompson is liquidated.

The statement of financial position of Thompson immediately before the acquisition is as follows:

	$
Non-current assets:	
Land and buildings	24,000
Plant and machinery	22,000
	46,000
Current assets:	
Inventory	19,000
Receivables	20,000
Bank	5,000
	90,000

	$
Equity and liabilities:	
Equity shares ($1)	30,000
Share premium	10,000
Retained earnings	16,000
	56,000
Non-current liabilities:	
6% debentures	20,000
Current liabilities:	
Trade payables	14,000
	90,000

Required:

- **Prepare the closing entries for Thompson**
- **Prepare the opening statement of financial position for Smith.**

Solution

Closing accounting for Thompson

(W1) **Realisation account**

	$	$
Carrying values:		
Land and buildings	24,000	
Plant and equipment	22,000	
Inventory	19,000	
Receivables	20,000	
Creditors		14,000
Purchase consideration		100,000
Profit on realisation (bal fig) (W3)	29,000	
	114,000	114,000

(W2) **Bank and cash**

	$	$
Balance b/fwd	5,000	
Cash received for sale of business	18,000	
Debenture stock paid off		20,000
Cash to shareholders as part of winding up (W3)		3,000
	23,000	23,000

(W3) **Capital settlement on winding up**

	$	$
Equity shares received at FV	52,000	
Debenture received	30,000	
Cash return to equity holders (W2)	3,000	
Share capital		30,000
Share premium		10,000
Retained earnings		16,000
Profit on realisation (W1)		29,000
	85,000	85,000

(W4) **Receivable Account – Smith**

	$	$
Purchase consideration due		
Equity shares	100,000	
Shares at FV		52,000
Debenture loan		30,000
Cash		18,000
	100,000	100,000

Smith – Statement of Financial Position

Assets	$
Goodwill*	17,600
Land and buildings	40,000
Plant and equipment	22,000
	79,600
Current assets:	
Inventory	15,000
Receivables	19,400
	114,000
Equity and liabilities	$
Equity share capital ($1)**	50,000
Share premium**	2,000
Non-current liabilities: Debenture loan	30,000
Current liabilities:	
Trade payables	14,000
Bank overdraft	18,000
	114,000

Notes:

* Goodwill is the difference between the consideration paid and the net assets acquired:

	$	$
Consideration		100,000
Land and buildings	40,000	
Plant and equipment	22,000	
Inventory	15,000	
Receivables ($20,000 × 97%)	19,400	
Trade payables	(14,000)	
		(82,400)
Goodwill		17,600

** The fair value of equity shares issued is $52,000 (50,000 × $1.04).

Of this the nominal value will be $50,000 (50,000 × $1) giving rise to a share premium of $2,000 (50,000 × ($1.04 – $1)).

4 Chapter summary

Reporting not-for-profit entities
- Includes clubs, charities and public sector organisations
- Their main objective is to provide a service, rather than to return a profit

Small and medium sized entities
- Full IFRS is too detailed
- IFRS for SME omits some standards and simplifies others

Entity reconstructions
- An alternative to liquidation
- May involve writing off share capital, loan arrears, and accumulated losses

Test your understanding answers

Test your understanding 1 – Wire

Wire – statement of financial position at 30 June 20X1 (after reconstruction)

	$
Non-current assets:	
Land and buildings at valuation	160,000
Equipment	30,000
Financial asset – investment in Cord	nil
	190,000
Current assets:	
Inventory	50,000
Receivables (70,692 × 90%)	63,623
Bank (W2)	92,287
	395,910

	$
Equity and liabilities:	
Equity shares ($0.25 each) (W3)	140,000
Share premium (W3)	17,800
Retained earnings	nil
Capital reserve (W1)	1,863
	159,663
Non-current liabilities:	
9.5% debentures (W4)	124,000
Current liabilities:	
Trade payables	112,247
	395,910

Wire – workings:

(W1) **Reconstruction account**

	$	$
Carrying values:		
Land and buildings	193,246	
Equipment	60,754	
Investment in Cord	27,000	
Inventory	120,247	
Receivables written off (70,962 × 10%)	7,069	
Deficit on retained earnings written off	39,821	
Revised valuations:		
Land and buildings		160,000
Equipment		30,000
Investment in Cord		60,000
Inventory		50,000
Share capital reduced (200,000 @ $0.75)		150,000
Capital reserve (bal fig)	1,863	
	450,000	450,000

(W2) **Bank account**

		$
Overdraft		(36,713)
New equity share issue	200,000 × $0.30	60,000
New debenture issue	9,000 at par value	9,000
Sale of investment – Cord		60,000
		92,287

(W3) **Shareholdings**

	Equity shares		Share premium
	Number	**$**	**$**
Redesignated existing shares ($0.25 each)	200,000	50,000	
New issue ($0.30 each)	200,000	50,000	10,000
Part-exchange of 5% debenture	140,000	35,000	
Debenture interest (12,800 – 5,000)**	20,000	5.000	7,800
	560,000	140,000	17,800

**8% deb interest on $80,000 p.a. for 2 years = $12,800 – $5,000 (20,000 × $0.25) = $7,800 share premium.

(W4) **Debenture loan**

	$
8% debenture 20X4 deferred to 20X9 with 9.5% interest rate	80,000
New 9.5% debentures 20X9 – nominal value	9,000
New 9.5% debentures 20X9 – part conversion of 5% debenture	35,000
	124,000

Advice to equity and debt holders:

Based upon the situation at 30 June 20X1 before the reconstruction scheme was devised, the following can be ascertained:

(1) There are sufficient assets to repay the secured debentures and perhaps most of the arrears of interest.

(2) Unsecured creditors would be unlikely to receive payment in full for amounts owed.

(3) Equity shareholders are unlikely to receive anything upon liquidation.

If a reconstruction scheme is to be agreed between the various parties, those who are in the strongest position (secured creditors) would expect to give up the least. Those in the weakest position (unsecured creditors and equity holders), would be expected to sacrifice more of their current entitlement to have any chance of recovery in the future.

The position of Wire if it was to go into liquidation is as follows:

		$
Land and buildings		160,000
Plant and equipment		30,000
Investment		60,000
Inventory		50,000
Receivables (70,962 × 90%)		63,623
Assets available		363,263
Secured liabilities (80,000 + 70,000)		(150,000)
		213,623
Current liabilities:		
Overdraft	36,713	
Interest	12,800	
Trade payables	112,247	
		(161,760)
Available to equity holders		51,863

The above summary identifies the position of the various stakeholders if there was no reconstruction scheme and Wire was liquidated. The debenture holders would be sure to receive their loan repayment, together with probably all of the arrears of interest, depending upon realised values of the assets and no other significant liabilities being uncovered.

The equity holders would not receive a full return of the nominal value of their capital, receiving only approximately (51,863/200,000) $0.26 per share.

Consequently, if the reconstruction scheme is implemented:

(1) The debenture holders are to be offered an increased rate of interest, but must also accept extension of the lending period to 20X9. It continues to be secured against land and buildings. Their position is relatively strong and safe.

(2) Some of the debenture holders have exchanged some of their legal rights as creditors for rights as equity holders. They must hope that Wire becomes profitable so that they can receive dividends in future years and that the share price increases. In addition, they must hope that, even if Wire gets into financial difficulties at a later date, there are still sufficient assets available to repay them, after the secured creditors have been repaid.

(3) It would appear that Wire will make profit after tax if the reconstruction goes ahead. If the profit forecast is reliable, this will be as follows:

	$
Profit before tax and interest	50,000
Less: debenture interest (9.5% × $124,000)	11,780
Profit before tax	38,220
Tax (× 25%)	(9,555)
Profit available to equity holders	28,665

Earnings per share would therefore be: $28,665/560,000 = 5.1 cents per share (i.e. $0.051 per share).

chapter

17

Non-financial reporting

Chapter learning objectives

Upon completion of this chapter you will be able to:

- discuss the increased demand for transparency in corporate reports, and the emergence of non-financial reporting standards
- discuss why entities might include disclosures relating to the environment and society
- appraise the impact of environmental, social and ethical factors on performance measurement
- evaluate current reporting requirements in the areas of environmental and social reporting, including the development of integrated reporting
- discuss the progress towards a framework for integrated reporting.

1 Non-financial reporting

Non-financial reporting

Non-financial information, in the form of additional information provided alongside the financial information in the annual report, has become more important in recent years.

While financial information remains important, stakeholders are interested in other aspects of an entity's performance.

For example:

- how the business is managed
- its future prospects
- the entity's policy on the environment
- its attitude towards social responsibility.

Although these activities do have an impact upon financial position and performance, some users of financial statements may have a particular interest in these activities. For example, potential shareholders may be attracted to invest in a particular entity (or not), based upon their environmental or social policies, in addition to their financial performance. Regulators or consumer pressure groups may also have a particular interest in such policies and disclosures to manage their activities or monitor the effectiveness of their activities.

Additional reports and disclosures go some way towards providing transparency for evaluation of entity financial performance, position and strategy. Transparency fosters confidence in the information which is made available to investors and other stakeholders who may be interested in both financial and non-financial information.

2 Management commentary

Management commentary

Purpose of the Management Commentary

The IFRS Practice Statement (PS) Management Commentary provides a framework for the preparation and presentation of management commentary on a set of financial statements.

Management commentary provides users with more context through which to interpret the financial position, financial performance and cash flows of an entity.

It is not mandatory for entities to produce a management commentary.

Framework for presentation of management commentary

The purpose of a management commentary is:

- to provide management's assessment of the entity's performance, position and progress
- to supplement information presented in the financial statements, and
- to explain the factors that might impact performance and position in the future.

This means that the management commentary should include information which is forward-looking.

Elements of management commentary

Management commentary should include information that is essential to an understanding of:

- the nature of the business
- management's objectives and strategies
- the entity's resources, risks and relationships
- the key performance measures that management use to evaluate the entity's performance.

3 Environmental reporting

Environmental reporting

Environmental reporting is the disclosure of information in the published annual report or elsewhere, of the effect that the operations of the business have on the natural environment.

Environmental reporting in practice

There are two main vehicles that companies use to publish information about the ways in which they interact with the natural environment:

(a) The published annual report (which includes the financial statements)

(b) A separate environment report (either as a paper document or simply posted on the company website).

IAS 1 points out that any statement or report presented outside financial statements is outside the scope of IFRS Standards. This means there are no mandatory requirements governing the production or content of separate environmental reports.

The content of environment reports

The content of an environment report may cover the following areas.

(a) **Environmental issues pertinent to the entity and industry**

– The entity's policy towards the environment and any improvements made since first adopting the policy.

- Whether the entity has a formal system for managing environmental risks.
- The identity of the director(s) responsible for environmental issues.
- The entity's perception of the risks to the environment from its operations.
- The extent to which the entity would be capable of responding to a major environmental disaster and an estimate of the full economic consequences of such a future major disaster.
- The effects of, and the entity's response to, any government legislation on environmental matters.
- Details of any significant infringement of environmental legislation or regulations.
- Material environmental legal issues in which the entity is involved.
- Details of any significant initiatives taken, if possible linked to amounts in financial statements.
- Details of key indicators (if any) used by the entity to measure environmental performance. Actual performance should be compared with targets and with performance in prior periods.

(b) **Financial information**

- The entity's accounting policies relating to environmental costs, provisions and contingencies.
- The amount charged to profit or loss during the accounting period in respect of expenditure to prevent or rectify damage to the environment caused by the entity's operations. This could be analysed between expenditure that the entity was legally obliged to incur and other expenditure.
- The amount charged to profit or loss during the accounting period in respect of expenditure to protect employees and society in general from the consequences of damage to the environment caused by the entity's operations. Again, this could be analysed between compulsory and voluntary expenditure.
- Details (including amounts) of any provisions or contingent liabilities relating to environmental matters.
- The amount of environmental expenditure capitalised during the year.
- Details of fines, penalties and compensation paid during the accounting period in respect of non-compliance with environmental regulations.

4 Social reporting

Social reporting

Corporate social reporting is the process of communicating the social and environmental effects of organisations' economic actions to particular interest groups within society and to society at large.

Social responsibility

A business interacts with society in several different ways as follows.

- It employs human resources in the form of management and other employees.
- Its activities affect society as a whole, for example, it may:
  - be the reason for a particular community's existence
  - produce goods that are helpful or harmful to particular members of society
  - damage the environment in ways that harm society as a whole
  - undertake charitable works in the community or promote particular values.

If a business interacts with society in a responsible manner, the needs of other stakeholders should be taken into account and performance may encompass:

- providing fair remuneration and an acceptable working environment
- paying suppliers promptly
- minimising the damage to the environment caused by the entity's activities
- contributing to the community by providing employment or by other means.

Reasons for social reporting

There are a number of reasons why entities publish social reports:

(a) They may have deliberately built their reputation on social responsibility (e.g. Body Shop) in order to attract a particular customer base.

(b) They may perceive themselves as being under particular pressure to prove that their activities do not exploit society as a whole or certain sections of it (e.g. Shell International and large utility companies).

(c) They may be genuinely convinced that it is in their long-term interests to balance the needs of the various stakeholder groups.

(d) They may fear that the government will eventually require them to publish socially oriented information if they do not do so voluntarily.

5 Sustainability

Sustainability

Sustainability is the process of conducting business in such a way that it enables an entity to meet its present needs without compromising the ability of future generations to meet their needs.

Introduction

A sustainability report is a report published by a company or organisation about the economic, environmental and social impacts caused by its everyday activities.

More and more business entities are reporting their approach to sustainability in addition to the financial information reported in the annual report. There are increased public expectations for business entities and industries to take responsibility for the impact their activities have on the environment and society.

Reporting sustainability

Reports include highlights of non-financial performance such as environmental, social and economic reports during the accounting period. The report may be included in the annual report or published as a stand alone document, possibly on the entity's website. The increase in popularity of such reports highlights the growing trend that business entities are taking sustainability seriously and are attempting to be open about the impact of their activities.

Framework for sustainability reporting

There is no framework for sustainability reporting within IFRS Standards. This lack of regulation leads to several problems:

(a) Because disclosure is largely voluntary, not all businesses disclose information. Those that do tend to do so either because they are under particular pressure to prove their 'green' credentials (for example, large public utility companies whose operations directly affect the environment) or because they have deliberately built their reputation on environmental friendliness or social responsibility.

(b) The information disclosed may not be complete or reliable. Many businesses see environmental reporting largely as a public relations exercise and therefore only provide information that shows them in a positive light.

(c) The information may not be disclosed consistently from year to year.

(d) Some businesses, particularly small and medium sized entities, may believe that the costs of preparing and circulating additional information outweigh the benefits of doing so.

However, the benefits of sustainability reporting are widely known. In particular, shareholders, banks and the public are more likely to see the rewards of long-term sustainable behaviour rather than short-term profit seeking.

6 Integrated reporting

Integrated reporting and the IIRC

What is the IIRC?

The International Integrated Reporting Council (IIRC) was created to respond to the need for a concise, clear, comprehensive and comparable integrated reporting framework.

The IIRC define an integrated report (IR) as 'a concise communication about how an organisation's strategy, governance, performance and prospects, in the context of its external environment, lead to the creation of value in the short, medium and long term.'

The IIRC believe that integrated reporting will contribute towards a more stable economy and a more sustainable world.

What is the role of the IIRC?

At present a range of standard-setters and regulatory bodies are responsible for individual elements of reporting. No single body has the oversight or authority to bring together these different elements that are essential to the presentation of an integrated picture of an organisation and the impact of environmental and social factors on its performance. In addition, globalisation means that an accounting and reporting framework needs to be developed on an international basis. At present, there is a risk that, as individual regulators respond to the risks faced, multiple standards will emerge.

The role of the IIRC is to:

- raise awareness of this issue and develop a consensus among governments, listing authorities, business, investors, accounting bodies and standard setters for the best way to address it
- develop an overarching integrated reporting framework setting out the scope of integrated reporting and its key components
- identify priority areas where additional work is needed and provide a plan for development
- consider whether standards in this area should be voluntary or mandatory and facilitate collaboration between standard-setters and convergence in the standards needed to underpin integrated reporting; and
- promote the adoption of integrated reporting by relevant regulators and report preparers.

Who are the members?

The IIRC brings together a powerful cross section of representatives from the corporate, accounting, securities, regulatory, and standard-setting sectors. Membership will comprise international representation from the following stakeholder groups: companies, investors, regulators, standard-setters, inter-governmental organisations, non-governmental organisations, the accounting profession, civil society and academia.

Further information on the IIRC can be found at www.integratedreporting.org

The International Integrated Reporting Framework

The International Integrated Reporting (IR) Framework is an examinable document for P2.

Objective of the Framework

The IR Framework establishes 'guiding principles' and 'content elements' that govern the overall content of an integrated report. This will help organisations to report their value creation in ways that are understandable and useful to the users.

The IR Framework is aimed at the private sector, although could be adapted for use by charities and the public sector.

The key users of an integrated report are deemed to be the providers of financial capital. However, the report will also benefit employees, suppliers, customers, local communities and policy makers.

The Framework is principles based and therefore does not prescribe specific KPIs that must be disclosed. Senior management need to use judgement to identify which issues are material. These decisions should be justified to the users of the report.

Those charged with governance are not required to acknowledge their responsibility for the integrated report. It was felt that such disclosures might increase legal liability in some jurisdictions and therefore deter some companies from applying the IR Framework.

Fundamental concepts in the IR framework

An integrated report concerns how value is created over the short-, medium- and long-term. To this extent, a number of fundamental concepts underpin the IR framework. These are:

- The capitals
- The organisation's business model
- The creation of value over time.

The **capitals** are stocks of value that are inputs to an organisation's business model. The capitals identified by the IR are financial, manufactured, intellectual, human, social and relationship, and natural.

- The capitals will increase, decrease or be transformed through an organisation's business activities.
  - The use of natural resources will decrease natural capital, making a profit will increase financial capital.
  - Employment could increase human capital through training, or reduce human capital through unsafe or exploitative working practices.

Central to integrated reporting is the overall impact that a business has on the full range of capitals through its business model.

The **business model** is a business' chosen system of inputs, business activities, outputs and outcomes that aims to create value over the short, medium and long term.

- An integrated report must identify key **inputs**, such as employees, or natural resources. It is important to explain how secure the availability, quality and affordability of components of natural capital are.

- At the centre of the **business model** is the conversion of inputs into outputs through business activities, such as planning, design, manufacturing and the provision of services.
- An integrated report must identify an organisation's key **outputs**, such as products and services. There may be other outputs, such as chemical by-products or waste. These need to be discussed within the business model disclosure if they are deemed to be material.
- **Outcomes** are defined as the consequences (positive and negative) for the capitals as a result of an organisation's business activities and outputs. Outcomes can be internal (such as profits or employee morale) or external (impacts on the local environment).

Value is created over time and for a range of stakeholders. IR is based on the belief that the increasing financial capital (e.g. profit) at the expense of human capital (e.g. staff exploitation) is unlikely to maximize value in the longer term. IR thus helps users to establish whether short-term value creation can be sustained into the medium- and long-term.

The content of an integrated report

An integrated report should include all of the following content elements:

- **Organisational overview and external environment** – 'What does the organisation do and what are the circumstances under which it operates?'
- **Governance** – 'How does the organisation's governance structure support its ability to create value in the short, medium and long term?'
- **Opportunities and risks** – 'What are the specific opportunities and risks that affect the organisation's ability to create value over the short, medium and long term, and how is the organisation dealing with them?'
- **Strategy and resource allocation** – 'Where does the organisation want to go and how does it intend to get there?'
- **Business model** – 'What is the organisation's business model and to what extent is it resilient?'
- **Performance** – 'To what extent has the organisation achieved its strategic objectives and what are its outcomes in terms of effects on the capitals?'
- **Future outlook** – 'What challenges and uncertainties is the organisation likely to encounter in pursuing its strategy, and what are the potential implications for its business model and future performance?'
- **Basis of presentation** – 'How does the organisation determine what matters to include in the integrated report and how are such matters quantified or evaluated?'

Including this content will help companies shift the focus of their reporting from historical financial performance to longer-term value creation.

Illustration – Integrated reports

AA is a UK-based public limited company that purchases shoes directly from manufacturers and then sells them through its own UK-based shops. AA has been profitable for many years and has continued to expand, financing this through bank loans.

AA's shoes sell particularly well amongst lower income families and AA has therefore specifically targeted this demographic. AA offers a discount of 50% on school shoes if the child is entitled to free school meals. This discount is partly subsidised by a government grant.

AA maximises its profits by buying its inventory from overseas. In the past year there have been several press reports about poor working conditions and pay in factories where AA products are manufactured. AA is conscious that it needs to monitor its supplier's employment conditions more closely.

AA has also been criticised in the press for the quality of its products. Some customers have complained that the shoes are not well-made and that they must be regularly replaced. A major consumer magazine has strongly argued that AA products are a 'false economy' and that customers would save money in the long-term if they bought slightly more expensive but better quality shoes

Staff who work in AA's shops are paid the national minimum wage. Training is minimal and staff turnover is extremely high.

AA does not fully engage with local or national recycling initiatives. The directors of the company believe these initiatives would increase operating costs, thus reducing the affordability of its products for its target demographic.

The success of the AA business model has led to an increased number of competitors. Although these competitors do not yet have the same high street presence as AA, some of them have invested more money into developing online stores. Although AA has a website, its products cannot be purchased online.

Required:

Why would an Integrated Report provide useful information about AA?

Solution

An integrated report might highlight a number of positive issues about AA:

- AA's financial capital has increased as a result of its profitable current business activities.
- Financial capital has increased due to the receipt of government grants and this will help AA to repay its debts in the short and also, potentially, the medium term.
- AA's has a positive impact on social capital by helping low income families to buy essential items of clothing. This is likely to foster brand loyalty from these customers, as well as generating good publicity. This may lead to a further increase in financial capital in the future.

However, it could be argued that the AA business model will not create value in the long-term. An integrated report might refer to the following issues:

- The government grants may not continue indefinitely. This could be due to government budget cuts, increasing competition or, perhaps, as a result of ongoing quality issues with AA products.
- AA does not invest highly in human capital. Unskilled and untrained staff are unlikely to foster brand loyalty and could lead to a loss of custom over time.
- AA uses cheap labour from overseas. Although this is likely to increase financial capital, it may lead to a net decrease in other capitals
  - AA may be criticised for not investing in local communities, or for exploiting overseas workers. By not investing in human capital there may also be a negative impact on social and relationship capital.
  - AA's recognition of the need to increasingly monitor its suppliers indicates that current economic benefits may not be sustainable in the longer-term.

- Purchasing goods from overseas will increase AA's carbon footprint. Moreover, AA does not widely recycle. Its activities thus place an overall drain on natural capital and this may deter some investors and consumers.
- A focus on high street expansion may leave AA vulnerable to online competitors, who will be able to offer the same products more cheaply. AA's lack of investment in staff may compound this because the retail stores are unlikely to offer a greater experience or level of service than can be obtained online. The current business model may therefore not be resilient in the medium or long term.

Summary

AA's business model is currently profitable. Such information could be obtained from the historical financial statements. However, an integrated report that looks at value creation and stability in the medium and longer term may offer a more pessimistic outlook. Banks are more likely to invest in companies who have sustainable business models and therefore integrated reports will help them to make stronger investment decisions. Other investors, such as potential or current shareholders, would also be able to make more informed decisions.

Producing an Integrated report is not mandatory. Businesses which have a detrimental net impact on capitals (particularly non-financial capitals) are unlikely to voluntarily produce an integrated report. In contrast, companies who create value in sustainable ways are more likely to want to disclose this to users. However, if the production of an integrated report was mandatory, then it might motivate a company like AA to shift its focus from increasing short term financial capital to the generation of an array of capitals over the medium and long-term.

7 Chapter summary

Non-financial reporting

Management commentary
- Provides management's view of the entity's performance, the reasons, and the implications.

Environmental reporting
- Details the effect of the business on the environment

Social reporting
- Details the organisation's impact on society

Sustainability reporting
- Details actions and policies towards helping future generations meet their needs.

Integrated reporting
- Communication about how value is created in the short, medium and long term
- Aimed at investors

chapter

18

Current issues

Chapter learning objectives

Upon completion of this chapter you will be able to:

- discuss current issues in corporate reporting, including:
  - recent IFRS Standards
  - practice and regulatory issues
  - proposed changes to IFRS Standards
  - problems with extant standards
- identify the issues and deficiencies that have led to a proposed change to an accounting standard
- apply and discuss the implications of a proposed change to an accounting standard on the performance and statement of financial position of an entity.

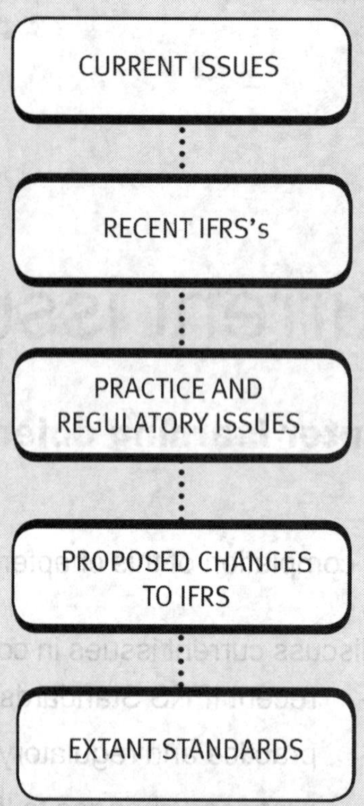

1 Introduction

What is meant by a 'current issue'?

In relation to 'current issues', the ACCA P2 study guide says that candidates need to be able to discuss:

- recent IFRS Standards
- practice and regulatory issues
- proposed changes to IFRS Standards
- problems with extant standards.

2 Recent IFRS Standards

Recently issued standards

IFRS 16 Leases was issued recently. This standard is covered in Chapter 7.

3 Practice and regulatory issues

Key issues for regulators

The European Securities and Markets Authority (ESMA) regularly highlights areas of focus for European national regulators when they review financial statements. The financial reporting topics identified by ESMA in recent years are:

- financial instruments
- impairment of non-financial assets
- defined benefit obligations
- provisions
- preparation and presentation of consolidated financial statements
- joint arrangements
- deferred tax assets
- fair values
- cash flows.

Financial instruments

Transparency of information relating to financial instruments is important for users of the financial statements, particularly as a result of the financial crisis. The disclosure requirements of IFRS 7 are therefore a key area for concern. Entities must include relevant quantitative and qualitative disclosures that reflect the nature of their risk exposure.

Impairment of non-financial assets

The current economic environment increases the likelihood that the carrying amount of assets will exceed their recoverable amounts. Therefore, users must be provided with sufficient information, in accordance with IAS 36, about impairment reviews conducted during a reporting period.

When calculating value-in-use, ESMA emphasises the need to use realistic assumptions. Disclosures should include entity-specific information related to assumptions used when preparing discounted cash flows (such as growth rates, discount rate and consistency of such rates with past experience) and sensitivity analyses.

Defined benefit obligations

A defined benefit obligation should be discounted using the yield on high-quality corporate bonds. However, if a country does not have a deep market in such bonds then the market yields on government bonds should be used instead. As a result of the economic crisis, some entities will need to change their approach. ESMA emphasises the need for entities to be transparent about the yields used and the reasons for using them.

Provisions

Information about provisions is key because it highlights the risks and uncertainties that an entity is subject to. Yet the information provided is often over-aggregated and overly standardised in nature. ESMA emphasises that, in accordance with IAS 37, entities should disclose descriptions of the nature of the obligations concerned, the expected timing of outflows of economic benefits, uncertainties related to the amount and timing of those outflows as well as major assumptions about future events. This should be done for each class of provision and should reflect the risks specific to the entity.

Preparation and presentation of consolidated financial statements

ESMA notes that entities must consult the application guidance in IFRS 10 Consolidated Financial Statements when assessing whether control exists. Such assessments require significant judgement and so entities must carefully explain these judgements in the financial statement disclosures.

ESMA has also stressed the importance of disclosing whether there are restrictions on the use of cash and cash equivalent balances within the group.

Joint arrangements

The classification of a joint arrangement is based on the rights and obligations of the parties to the arrangement. ESMA notes that joint arrangements with similar characteristics may need to be classified in different ways depending on their structure. As such, it is vital that entities adequately disclose the significant judgements and assumptions made regarding the nature of interests in joint arrangements.

Deferred tax assets

In accordance with IAS 12 Income Taxes, the recognition of a deferred tax asset is limited to the extent that future taxable profits will be available against which the deductible temporary differences can be utilised. Recent losses provide strong evidence that future profits may be lacking and therefore the recognition of deferred tax assets should be conditional on convincing evidence. ESMA notes that entities should disclose the nature of the evidence used when assessing deferred tax asset recognition, the period used for the assessment, and any key judgements or assumptions made.

Fair values

ESMA believes that there is room for improvement with regards to the measurement and disclosure of the fair values of non-financial assets. Fair value measurement should maximise observable inputs.

Cash flows

ESMA notes that entities need to provide greater disclosure of the reasoning behind the classification of cash flows, particularly when this is judgemental. Entities also need to assess more carefully whether their financial instruments meet the definition of a 'cash equivalent'.

4 Proposed changes to IFRS Standards

The change process

The International Accounting Standards Board (the Board) is continually engaged in projects to update and improve existing standards and introduce new ones.

At any time there are a number of discussion papers (DPs) and exposure drafts (EDs) in issue as part of these projects.

A good source of up to date information is the current projects page of the Board's website at www.iasb.org.

Proposed changes

The following table outlines documents, other than issued IAS and IFRS Standards, that are examinable in P2 and indicates where these are covered in this text.

Statement/Document	Textbook chapter
IFRS Practice Statement: Application of Materiality in Financial Statements	1
ED 2015/3 Conceptual Framework for Financial Reporting	1
ED 2015/1 Classification of Liabilities – proposed amendments to IAS 1	3
Practice Statement on Management Commentary	17
The International <IR> Framework	17
ED 2014/4 Measuring Quoted Investments in Subsidiaries, Joint Ventures and Associates at Fair Value	19

5 Extant standards

Critiques of existing standards

Although knowledge of developments in the accountancy profession and upcoming standards are a central part of the P2 syllabus, the Examiner has also noted the importance of being able to critique existing accounting standards. Critiques of existing standards can be found within the relevant chapters in this text. For example:

- The Conceptual Framework for Financial Reporting – Chapter 1
- IAS 1 Presentation of Financial Statements – Chapter 3
- IFRS 15 Revenue from Contracts with Customers – Chapter 4
- IFRS 2 Share-based payments – Chapter 9
- IAS 37 Provisions, Contingent Liabilities and Contingent Assets – Chapter 10
- IAS 12 Income Taxes – Chapter 12
- IFRS 8 Operating Segments – Chapter 13
- IFRS 3 Business Combinations – Chapter 19
- IAS 7 Statement of Cash Flows – Chapter 24

Test your understanding 1 – Mineral

Mineral owns a machine that is central to its production process. At the reporting date, the machine's carrying amount exceeds its tax base. This difference is due to the revaluation of the asset to fair value in the financial statements. Due to its importance, it is extremely unlikely that the machine will be sold.

At the year-end, Mineral received $10 million. In return, Mineral must issue ordinary shares in 12 months' time. The number of shares to be issued will be determined based on the quoted price of Mineral's shares at the issue date.

Required:

For each of the transactions above:

(i) **Briefly explain how it should be accounted for in accordance with International Financial Reporting Standards**

(ii) **Discuss why the accounting treatment could be argued to contradict the definition of the elements given by the Framework.**

Chapter summary

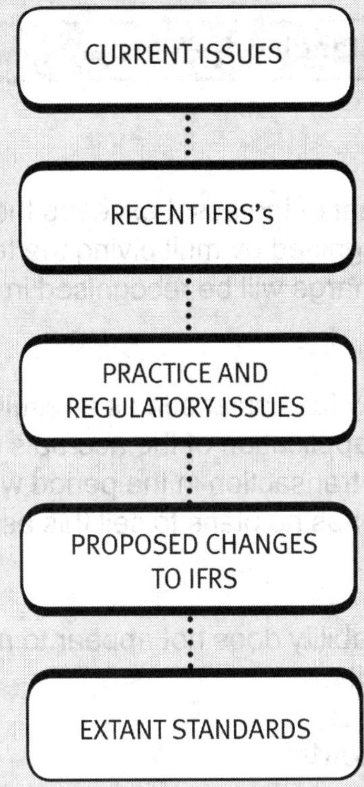

Test your understanding answers

Test your understanding 1 – Mineral

Deferred tax

The carrying amount of the asset exceeds the tax base. A deferred tax liability will be recognised by multiplying the temporary difference by the tax rate. The tax charge will be recognised in other comprehensive income.

No obligation to pay tax has arisen as a result of the revaluation. Rather, deferred tax is an application of the accruals concept in that it recognises the tax effects of a transaction in the period when the transaction occurs. Moreover, Mineral has no plans to sell this asset so the payment of this tax is not probable.

The deferred tax liability does not appear to meet the Framework's definition of a liability.

Financial instruments

IAS 32 states that a financial liability is **'any contract that may be settled in the entity's own equity instruments and is a non-derivative for which the entity is obliged to deliver a variable number of its own equity instruments'** (IAS 32, para 11).

The contract requires that Mineral delivers as many of its own equity instruments as are equal in value to a certain amount. Per IAS 32, this contract should be classified as a financial liability.

An equity instrument is not a resource of an entity. This contract does not therefore represent an obligation to transfer a resource.

The financial liability does not satisfy the Framework's definition of a liability.

chapter

19

Group accounting – basic groups

Chapter learning objectives

Upon completion of this chapter you will be able to:

- apply the method of accounting for business combinations
- apply the principles in determining the cost of a business combination
- apply the recognition and measurement criteria for identifiable acquired assets and liabilities and goodwill
- apply and discuss the criteria used to identify a subsidiary and an associate
- determine and apply appropriate procedures to be used in preparing group financial statements
- Identify and outline:
  - the circumstances in which a group is required to prepare consolidated financial statements
  - the circumstances when a group may claim an exemption from the preparation of consolidated financial statements
  - why directors may not wish to consolidate a subsidiary and where this is permitted
- apply the equity method of accounting for associates
- outline and apply the key definitions and accounting methods which relate to interests in joint arrangements.

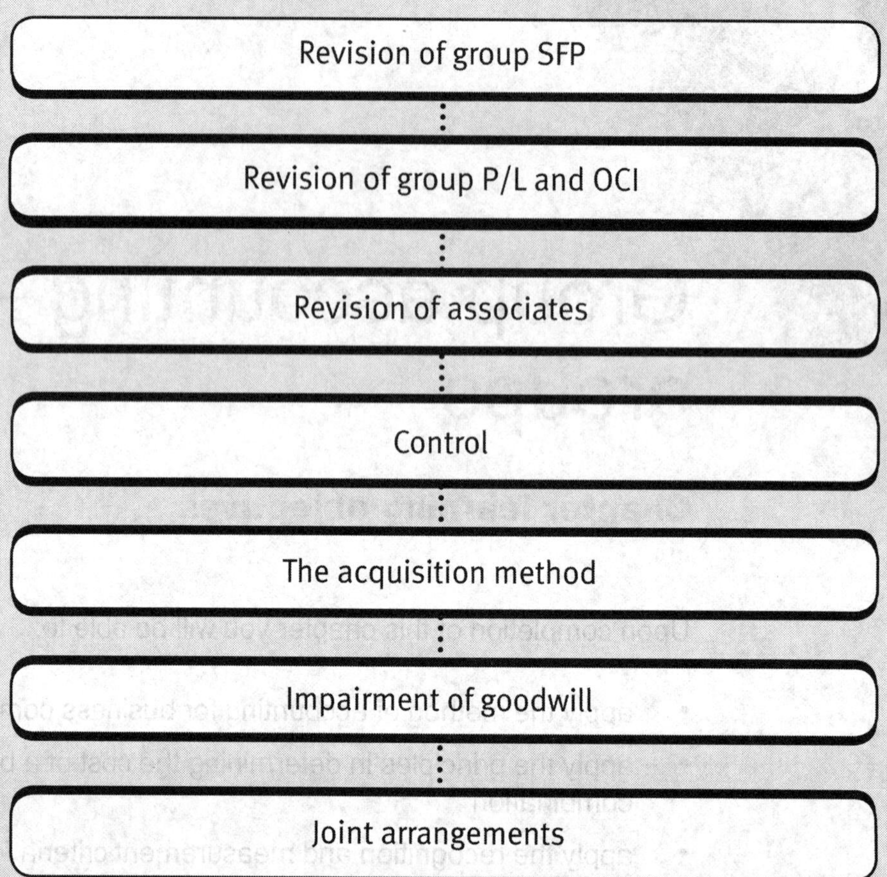

1 Overview of interests in other entities

The following diagram presents an overview of the varying types of interests in other entities, together with identification of applicable reporting standards.

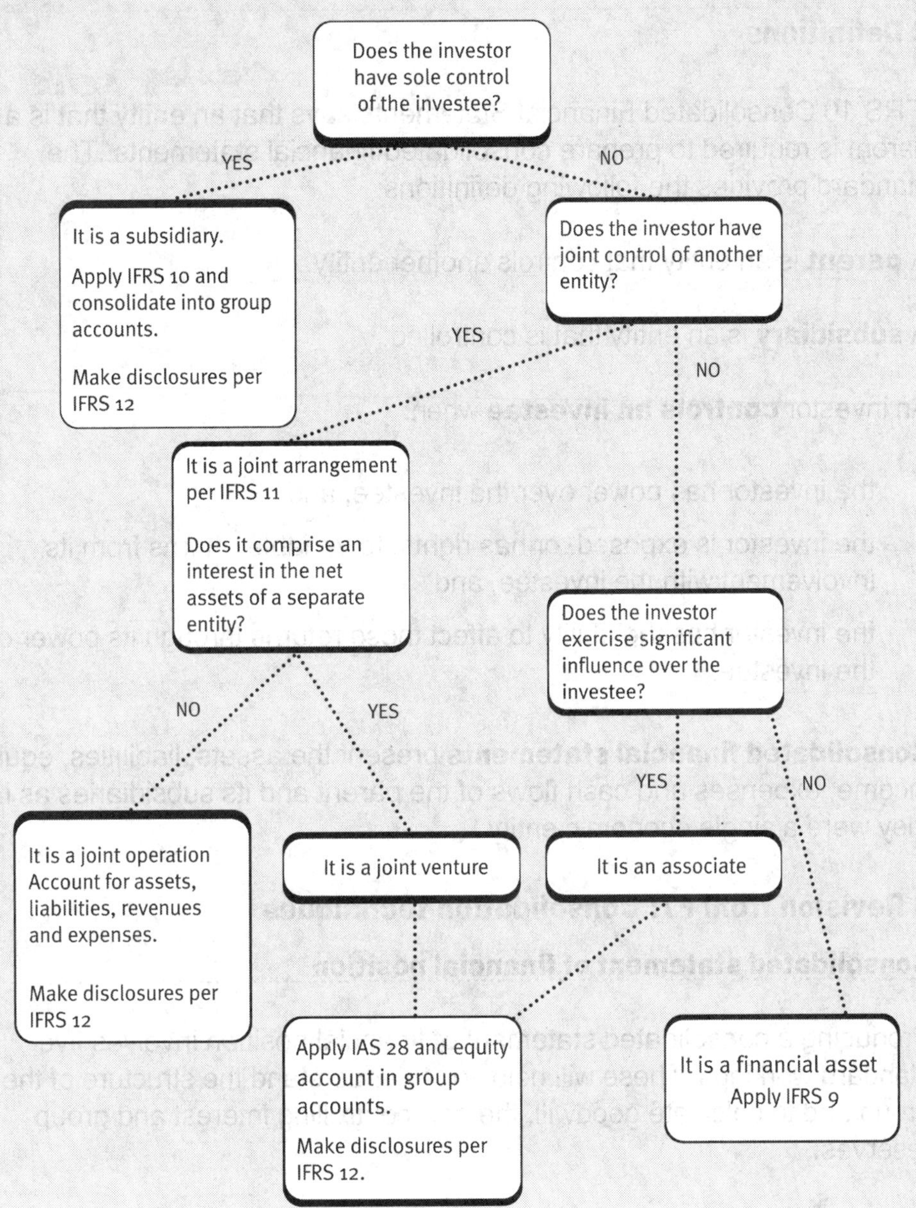

The standards referred to in the diagram above cover a range of group accounting issues:

- IFRS 10 Consolidated Financial Statements
- IFRS 11 Joint Arrangements
- IFRS 12 Disclosure of Interests in Other Entities
- IAS 28 Investments in Associates and Joint Ventures

These standards, as well as IFRS 3 Business Combinations, are covered in this chapter. IFRS 9 Financial Instruments was dealt with earlier in the publication.

2 Definitions

IFRS 10 Consolidated Financial Statements says that an entity that is a parent is required to prepare consolidated financial statements. The standard provides the following definitions:

A **parent** is an entity that controls another entity.

A **subsidiary** is an entity that is controlled.

An investor **controls an investee** when:

- the investor has power over the investee, and
- the investor is exposed, or has rights, to variable returns from its involvement with the investee, and
- the investor has the ability to affect those returns through its power over the investee.

Consolidated financial statements present the assets, liabilities, equity, income, expenses and cash flows of the parent and its subsidiaries as if they were a single economic entity.

3 Revision from F7: Consolidation techniques

Consolidated statement of financial position

Producing a consolidated statement of financial position involves five standard workings. These will help you to understand the structure of the group and to calculate goodwill, the non-controlling interest and group reserves.

The first step in any examination question should be to determine the group structure.

(W1) **Group structure**

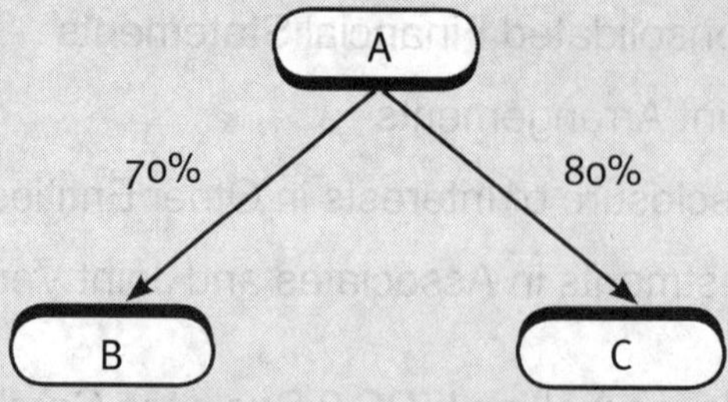

This working is useful to decide the status of any investments. If one entity is controlled by another entity then it is a subsidiary and must be consolidated.

In numerical exam questions, control is normally presumed to exist if one company owns more than half of the voting capital of another entity.

Once the group structure has been determined, set up a proforma statement of financial position.

Group statement of financial position as at the reporting date

	$000
Goodwill (W3)	X
Assets (P + S)	X
Total assets	X
Equity capital (Parent's only)	X
Retained earnings (W5)	X
Other components of equity (W5)	X
Non-controlling interest (W4)	X
Total equity	X
Liabilities (P + S)	X
Total equity and liabilities	X

You will need to do the following:

- Eliminate the carrying amount of the parent's investments in its subsidiaries (these will be replaced by goodwill)
- Add together the assets and liabilities of the parent and its subsidiaries in full
- Include only the parent's balances within share capital and share premium
- Set up and complete standard workings 2 – 5 to calculate goodwill, the non-controlling interest and group reserves.

(W2) **Net assets of each subsidiary**

This working sets out the fair value of the subsidiary's identifiable net assets at acquisition date and at the reporting date.

	At acquisition	**At reporting date**
	$000	$000
Equity capital	X	X
Share premium	X	X
Other components of equity	X	X
Retained earnings	X	X
Goodwill in the accounts of the sub.	(X)	(X)
Fair value adjustments (FVA)	X	X
Post acq'n dep'n/amort. on FVA		(X)
PURP if the sub is the seller		(X)
	X	X
	(to W3)	

Remember to update the face of the statement of financial position for adjustments made to the net assets at the reporting date (such as fair value uplifts and provisions for unrealised profits (PURPS)).

The fair value of the subsidiary's net assets at the acquisition date are used in the calculation of goodwill.

The movement in the subsidiary's net assets since acquisition is used to calculate the non-controlling interest and group reserves.

(W3) **Goodwill**

	$000
Fair value of purchase consideration	X
NCI at acquisition**	X
	X
Less: fair value of identifiable net assets at acquisition (per net assets working)	(X)
Goodwill at acquisition	X
Less: impairment to date	(X)
Goodwill to consolidated SFP	X

**if full goodwill method adopted, NCI value = FV of NCI at date of acquisition. This will normally be given in a question.

**if proportionate goodwill method adopted, NCI value = NCI % of the fair value of the net assets at acquisition (per W2).

(W4) **Non-controlling interest**

	$000
NCI value at acquisition (W3)	X
NCI % of post-acquisition movement in net assets (W2)	X
Less: NCI % of goodwill impairment (fair value method only)	(X)
NCI to consolidated SFP	X

(W5) **Group reserves**

Retained earnings

	$000
Parent's retained earnings (100%)	X
For each subsidiary: group share of post-acquisition retained earnings (W2)	X
Add: gain on bargain purchase (W3)	X
Less: goodwill impairment** (W3)	(X)
Less: PURP if the parent was the seller	(X)
Retained earnings to consolidated SFP	X

** If the NCI was valued at fair value at the acquisition date, then only the parent's share of the goodwill impairment is deducted from retained earnings.

Other components of equity

	$000
Parent's other components of equity (100%)	X
For each subsidiary: group share of post-acquisition other components of equity (W2)	X
Other components of equity to consolidated SFP	X

Consolidated statement of profit or loss and other comprehensive income

Step 1: Group structure

This working is useful to decide the status of any investments. If one entity is controlled by another entity then it is a subsidiary and must be consolidated.

In numerical exam questions, control is normally presumed to exist if one company owns more than half of the voting capital of another entity.

Step 2: Pro-forma

Once the group structure has been determined, set up a proforma statement of profit or loss and other comprehensive income.

Remember to leave space at the bottom to show the profit and total comprehensive income (TCI) attributable to the owners of the parent company and the profit and TCI attributable to the non-controlling interest.

Group statement of profit or loss and other comprehensive income for the year ended 30 June 20X8

	$000
Revenue (P + S)	X
Cost of sales (P + S)	(X)
Gross profit	X
Operating costs (P + S)	(X)
Profit from operations	X
Investment income (P + S)	X
Finance costs (P + S)	(X)
Profit before tax	X
Income tax (P + S)	(X)
Profit for the period	X
Other comprehensive income (P + S)	X
Total comprehensive income	X

Profit attributable to:	
Equity holders of the parent (bal. fig)	X
Non-controlling interest (Step 4)	X
Profit for the period	X

Total comprehensive income attributable to:	
Equity holders of the parent (bal. fig)	X
Non-controlling interest (Step 4)	X
Total comprehensive income for the period	X

Step 3: Complete the pro-forma

Add together the parent and subsidiary's incomes and expenses and items of other comprehensive income on a line-by-line basis.

- If the subsidiary has been acquired mid-year, make sure that you pro-rate the results of the subsidiary so that only post-acquisition incomes, expenses and other comprehensive income are consolidated.
- Ensure that you eliminate intra-group incomes and expenses, unrealised profits on intra-group transactions, as well as any dividends received from the subsidiary.

Step 4: Calculate the profit/TCI attributable to the non-controlling interest

Remember, profit for the year and TCI for the year must be split between the group and the non-controlling interest. The following proforma will help you to calculate the profit and TCI attributable to the non-controlling interest.

	Profit $000	**TCI** $000
Profit/TCI of the subsidiary for the year (pro-rated for mid-year acquisition)	X	X
PURP (if S is the seller)	(X)	(X)
Excess depreciation/amortisation	(X)	(X)
Goodwill impairment (under FV model only)	(X)	(X)
× NCI %	X	X
Profit/TCI attributable to the NCI	X	X

Associates

Definitions

An **associate** is defined as **'an entity over which the investor has significant influence and which is neither a subsidiary nor a joint venture of the investor'** (IAS 28, para 3).

Significant influence is the power to participate in, but not control, the financial and operating policy decisions of an entity. IAS 28 states that:

- Significant influence is usually evidenced by representation on the board of directors, which allows the investing entity to participate in policy decisions.
- A holding between 20% and 50% of the voting power is presumed to give significant influence, unless it can be clearly demonstrated that this is not the case.
- It is presumed that a holding of less than 20% does not give significant influence, unless such influence can be clearly demonstrated.

Accounting for associates

Associates are not consolidated because the parent does not have control. Instead they are accounted for using the **equity method**.

Statement of financial position

IAS 28 requires that the carrying amount of the associate is determined as follows:

	$000
Cost	X
Add: P% of increase in reserves	X
Less: impairment losses	(X)
Less: P% of unrealised profits if P is the seller	(X)
Less: P% of excess depreciation on fair value adjustments	(X)
Investment in associate	X

The investment in the associate is shown in the non-current assets section of the consolidated statement of financial position.

Statement of profit or loss and other comprehensive income

For an associate, a single line item is presented in the statement of profit or loss below operating profit. This is made up as follows:

	$000
P% of associate's profit after tax	X
Less: Current year impairment loss	(X)
Less: P% of unrealised profits if associate is the seller	(X)
Less: P% of excess depreciation on fair value adjustments	(X)
Share of profit of associate	X

Within consolidated other comprehensive income, the group should present its share of the associate's other comprehensive income (if applicable).

Adjustments

Dividends received from the associate must be removed from the consolidated statement of profit or loss.

Transactions and balances between the associate and the parent company are not eliminated from the consolidated financial statements because the associate is not a part of the group.

The group share of any unrealised profit arising on transactions between the group and the associate must be eliminated.

- If the associate is the seller:
  - Dr Share of the associate's profit (P/L)/Retained earnings (SFP)
  - Cr Inventories (SFP)
- If the associate is the purchaser:
  - Dr Cost of sales (P/L)/Retained earnings (SFP)
  - Cr Investment in the associate (SFP)

General points and disclosures

IAS 28 notes the following:

- The financial statements used to equity account for the associate should be drawn up to the investor's reporting date. If this is not possible, then the difference in reporting dates should be less than three months.

- The associate's accounting policies should be harmonised with those of its investor.
- The investor should disclose its share of the associate's contingencies.
- A list and description of significant associates should be disclosed. This will note the ownership interests and voting interests for each associate.

Note that the equity method is not used in the following situations:

- the investment is classified as held for sale in accordance with IFRS 5 Non-current Assets Held for Sale and Discontinued Operations
- the investor is itself a subsidiary, its owners do not object to the equity method not being applied and its debt and equity securities are not publicly traded. In this case, the investor's parent must present consolidated financial statements that do use the equity method.

Illustration 1 – Consolidated statement of financial position

Summarised financial statements for three entities for the year ended 30 June 20X8 are as follows:

Statements of financial position

	Borough	**High**	**Street**
Assets	$	$	$
Property, plant and equipment	100,000	80,000	60,000
Investments	121,000	–	–
Inventories	22,000	30,000	15,000
Receivables	70,000	10,000	2,000
Cash and cash equivalents	47,000	25,000	3,000
	360,000	145,000	80,000

Equity and liabilities			
Equity capital ($1 shares)	100,000	75,000	35,000
Retained earnings	200,000	50,000	40,000
Other components of equity	10,000	5,000	–
Liabilities	50,000	15,000	5,000
	360,000	145,000	80,000

On 1 July 20X7, Borough purchased 45,000 shares in High for $100,000. At that date, High had retained earnings of $30,000 and no other components of equity. High's net assets had a fair value of $120,000 and the fair value of the non-controlling interest was $55,000. It is group policy to value the non-controlling interest at acquisition at fair value.

The excess of the fair value of High's net assets over their carrying amounts at the acquisition date relates to property, plant and equipment. This had a remaining estimated useful life of five years at the acquisition date. Goodwill has been subject to an impairment review and it was determined to be impaired by $7,000.

On 1 July 20X7, Borough purchased 10,500 equity shares in Street for $21,000. At that date, Street had retained earnings of $25,000 and no other components of equity.

During the year Borough sold goods too High for $10,000 at a margin of 50%. By the reporting date, High had only sold 80% of these goods. Included in the receivables of Borough and the liabilities of High are intra-group balances of $5,000.

On 5 July 20X8, Borough received notification that an employee was claiming damages against them as a result of a work-place accident that took place on 30 April 20X8. Lawyers have advised that there is a 60% chance that Borough will lose the case and will be required to pay damages of $30,000.

Required:

Prepare the consolidated statement of financial position as at 30 June 20X8.

Solution

Borough Group statement of financial position as at 30 June 20X8

	$
Non Current Assets	
Goodwill (W3)	28,000
Property, plant and equipment ($100,000 + $80,000 + $15,000 (W2) – $3,000 (W2))	192,000
Investment in Associate (W7)	25,500
Current Assets	
Inventories ($22,000 + $30,000 – $1,000 (W6))	51,000
Receivables ($70,000 + $10,000 – $5,000 inter.co)	75,000
Cash and cash equivalents ($47,000 + $25,000)	72,000
	443,500
Equity capital	100,000
Retained earnings (W5)	179,500
Other components of equity (W5)	13,000
Non-controlling interest (W4)	61,000
Total equity	353,500
Liabilities ($50,000 + $15,000 – $5,000 inter.co + $30,000 (W8))	90,000
	443,500

(W1) **Group structure**

Borough is the parent

High is a 60% subsidiary (45/75)

Street is a 30% associate (10.5/35)

Both acquisitions took place a year ago

(W2) **Net assets of High**

	Acq	Rep date
	$	$
Equity capital	75,000	75,000
Other components of equity	–	5,000
Retained earnings	30,000	50,000
Fair value adjustment (FVA)	15,000*	15,000
Depreciation on FVA ($15,000/5)	–	(3,000)
*bal fig	120,000	142,000

(W3) **Goodwill**

	$
Consideration	100,000
FV of NCI at acquisition	55,000
	155,000
FV of net assets at acquisition (W2)	(120,000)
Goodwill at acquisition	35,000
Impairment	(7,000)
Goodwill at the reporting date	28,000

(W4) **Non-controlling interest**

	$
Fair value of NCI at acquisition (given)	55,000
NCI % of post-acquisition net assets (40% × ($142,000 – $120,000) (W2))	8,800
NCI share of goodwill impairment (40% × $7,000)	(2,800)
	61,000

(W5) **Group reserves**

Group retained earnings

	$
Parent	200,000
Provision (W8)	(30,000)
Share of post-acquisition retained earnings:	
High: 60% × (($50,000 – $3,000) – $30,000) (W2)	10,200
Street: 30% × ($40,000 – $25,000)	4,500
Group share of goodwill impairment (60% × $7,000)	(4,200)
PURP (W6)	(1,000)
	179,500

Other components of equity

	$
Parent	10,000
Share of post-acquisition other components of equity:	
High: 60% × ($5,000 – $nil) (W2)	3,000
	13,000

(W6) **Provision for unrealised profit**

The profit on the intra-group sale was $5,000 (50% × $10,000).

The unrealised profit still in inventory is $1,000 (20% × $5,000).

The parent was the seller, so retained earnings is adjusted in (W5)

Dr Retained earnings	$1,000
Cr Inventories	$1,000

(W7) **Investment in the associate**

	$
Cost	21,000
Share of increase in retained earnings (30% × ($40,000 – $25,000))	4,500
	25,500

(W8) **Provision**

The obligating event, the accident, happened during the reporting period. This means that there is an obligation from a past event, and a probable outflow of resources that can be measured reliably. A provision is therefore required for the best estimate of the amount payable, which is $30,000. This is charged to the statement of profit or loss so will reduce retained earnings in (W5).

Dr Retained earnings	$30,000
Cr Provisions	$30,000

Illustration 2 – Consolidated statement of profit or loss

H has owned 80% of the ordinary shares of S and 30% of the ordinary shares of A for many years. The information below is required to prepare the consolidated statement of profit or loss for the year ended 30 June 20X8.

Statements of profit or loss for the year ended 30 June 20X8

	H	**S**	**A**
	$	$	$
Revenue	500,000	200,000	100,000
Cost of sales	(100,000)	(80,000)	(40,000)
Gross profit	400,000	120,000	60,000
Distribution costs	(160,000)	(20,000)	(10,000)
Administrative expenses	(140,000)	(40,000)	(10,000)
Profit from operations	100,000	60,000	40,000
Tax	(23,000)	(21,000)	(14,000)
Profit after tax	77,000	39,000	26,000

Note: There were no items of other comprehensive income in the year.

At the date of acquisition, the fair value of S's plant and machinery, which at that time had a remaining useful life of ten years, exceeded the book value by $10,000.

During the year S sold goods to H for $10,000 at a margin of 25%. By the year-end H had sold 60% of these goods.

The group accounting policy is to measure non-controlling interests using the proportion of net assets method. The current year goodwill impairment loss was $1,200, and this should be charged to administrative expenses.

By 30 June 20X8 the investment in A had been impaired by $450, of which the current year loss was $150.

On 1 January 20X8, H signed a contract to provide a customer with support services for the following twelve months. H received the full fee of $30,000 in advance and recognised this as revenue.

Required:

Prepare the consolidated statement of profit or loss for the year ended 30 June 20X8.

Solution

Group statement of profit or loss for the year ended 30 June 20X8

	$
Revenue ($500,000 + $200,000 – $10,000 (W3) – $15,000 (W4))	675,000
Cost of sales ($100,000 + $80,000 + $1,000 (W2) – $10,000 (W3) + $1,000 (W3))	(172,000)
Gross profit	503,000
Distribution costs ($160,000 + $20,000)	(180,000)
Administrative expenses ($140,000 + $40,000 + $1,200 GW imp)	(181,200)
Profit from operations	141,800
Share of profit of associate ((30% × $26,000) – $150 impairment)	7,650
Profit before tax	149,450
Tax ($23,000 + $21,000)	(44,000)
Profit for the period	105,450

Attributable to:	
Equity holders of the parent (bal. fig)	98,050
Non-controlling interest (W5)	7,400
Profit for the period	105,450

Workings

(W1) **Group structure**

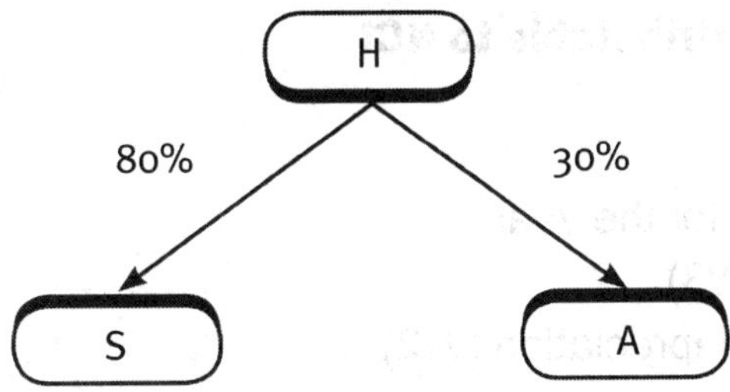

(W2) **Excess depreciation**

$10,000/10 years = $1,000.

The adjusting entry is:

Dr Cost of sales	$1,000
Cr PPE	$1,000

(W3) **Intra-group trading**

The $10,000 trading between S and H must be eliminated:

Dr Revenue	$10,000
Cr Cost of sales	$10,000

The profit on the sale was $2,500 (25% × $10,000). Of this, $1,000 ($2,500 × 40%) remains within the inventories of the group. The PURP adjustment is therefore:

Dr Cost of sales	$1,000
Cr Inventories	$1,000

(W4) **Revenue**

The performance obligation is satisfied over time. Based on the passage of time, the contract is 50% (6/12) complete so only 50% of the revenue should be recognised by the reporting date. Therefore $15,000 ($30,000 × 50%) should be removed from revenue and held as a liability on the SFP.

Dr Revenue	$15,000
Cr Contract liability	$15,000

(W5) **Profit attributable to NCI**

	$	$
S's profit for the year	39,000	
PURP (W3)	(1,000)	
Excess depreciation (W2)	(1,000)	
	37,000	
× 20%		
Profit attributable to NCI		7,400

Note: If the parent had sold goods to the subsidiary then the PURP adjustment would not be included when calculating the profit attributable to the NCI.

Goodwill has been calculated using the share of net assets method. Therefore, none of the impairment loss is attributable to the NCI.

Illustration 3 – Associates

Paint has several investments in subsidiary companies. On 1 July 20X1, it acquires 30% of the ordinary shares of Animate for $2m. This holding gives Paint significant influence over Animate.

At the acquisition date, the fair value of Animate's net assets approximate to their carrying values with the exception of a building. This building, with a remaining useful life of 10 years, had a carrying value of $1m but a fair value of $1.8m.

Between 1 July 20X1 and 31 December 20X1, Animate sold goods to Paint for $1 million making a profit of $100,000. All of these goods remain in the inventory of Paint. This sale was made on credit and the invoice has not yet been settled.

Animate made a profit after tax of $800,000 for the year ended 31 December 20X1. At 31 December 20X1, the directors of Paint believe that the investment in the associate needs impairing by $50,000.

Required:

Prepare extracts from the consolidated statement of financial position and the consolidated statement of profit or loss showing the treatment of the associate for the year ended 31 December 20X1.

Solution

Consolidated statement of financial position	$
Investment in associate (W1)	2,058,000
Consolidated statement of profit or loss	
Share of profit of associate (W2)	28,000

Note: No adjustment is required for receivables and payables held between Paint and Animate.

(W1) **Investment in associate**

	$
Cost	2,000,000
Share of post-acquisition profit (30% × $800,000 × 6/12)	120,000
Share of excess depreciation (30% × (($1.8m – $1m)/10 years) × 6/12)	(12,000)
Impairment	(50,000)
Investment in associate	2,058,000

The inventory is held within the group so the parent's share of the PURP is credited against inventory rather than the investment in the associate.

(W2) **Share of associate's profit**

	$
P's share of A's profit after tax (30% × $800,000 × 6/12)	120,000
Impairment	(50,000)
P's share of excess depreciation (30% × (($1.8m – $1m)/10 years) × 6/12)	(12,000)
P's share of PURP (30% × $100,000)	(30,000)
Share of profit of associate	28,000

4 Control

Consolidated statements are produced if one entity controls another entity. It is often presumed that control exists if a company owns more than 50% of the ordinary shares of another company. However, in section B of the P2 exam, the examiner may test the definition of control in more detail.

According to IFRS 10, an investor **controls an investee** when:

- the investor has power over the investee, and
- the investor is exposed, or has rights, to variable returns from its involvement with the investee, and
- the investor has the ability to affect those returns through its power over the investee.

IFRS 10 identifies a range of circumstances that may need to be considered when determining whether or not an investor has power over an investee, such as:

- exercise of the majority of voting rights in an investee
- contractual arrangements between the investor and other parties
- holding less than 50% of the voting shares, with all other equity interests held by a numerically large, dispersed and unconnected group
- holding potential voting rights (such as convertible loans) that are currently capable of being exercised
- the nature of the investor's relationship with other parties that may enable that investor to exercise control over an investee.

It is therefore possible to own less than 50% of the ordinary shares of another entity and to still exercise control over it.

Application of IFRS 10 control definition

An investor has 48 per cent of the voting rights of another entity. The remaining 52 per cent of the voting rights are held by thousands of other shareholders, none of whom individually hold more than 1 per cent of the voting rights. These other shareholders have no relationship with one another.

Due to the size of its holding and the relative size of the other shareholdings, the investor believes that it controls the investee.

Test your understanding 1 – Control

Parsley has a 40% holding in the ordinary shares of Oregano. Another investor has a 10% shareholding in Oregano whilst the remaining voting rights are held by thousands of shareholders, none of whom individually hold more than 1 per cent of the voting rights. Parsley also holds debt instruments that, as at 30 April 20X4, are convertible into ordinary shares of Oregano at a price of $4 per share. At 30 April 20X4, the shares of Oregano trade at $3.80 per share. If the debt was converted into ordinary shares, Parsley would hold 60% of the voting rights in Oregano. Parsley and Oregano undertake similar activities and would benefit from synergies.

Required:

Discuss how Parsley's investment in the ordinary shares of Oregano should be treated in the consolidated financial statements for the year ended 30 April 20X4.

Exemptions from consolidation

Intermediate parent companies

An intermediate parent entity is an entity which has a subsidiary but is also itself a subsidiary of another entity. For example:

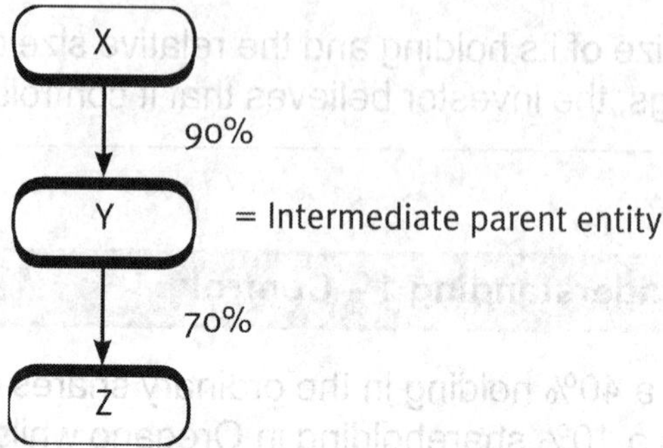

IFRS 10 permits a parent entity not to present group financial statements provided all of the following conditions apply:

- it is a wholly-owned, or partially-owned subsidiary where owners of the non-controlling interest do not object to the non-preparation
- its debt or equity instruments are not currently traded in a domestic or foreign market
- it is not in the process of having any of its debt or equity instruments traded on a domestic or foreign market
- the ultimate parent entity produces consolidated financial statements that comply with IFRS Standards and which are available to the public.

If this is the case, IAS 27 Separate Financial Statements requires that the following disclosures are made:

- the fact that consolidated financial statements have not been presented
- a list of significant investments (subsidiaries, joint ventures and associates) including percentage shareholdings, principal place of business and country of incorporation
- the bases on which those investments listed above have been accounted for in its separate financial statements.

Investment entities

An investment entity is defined by IFRS 10 as an entity that:

(a) obtains funds from investors and provides them with investment management services, and

(b) invests those funds to earn returns from capital appreciation, investment income, or both, and

(c) measures the performance of its investments on a fair value basis.

Investment entities do not consolidate an investment over which they have control. Instead, the investment is measured at fair value at each reporting date with gains and losses recorded in profit or loss.

Invalid reasons to exclude a subsidiary from consolidation

In addition to the valid reasons to exclude a subsidiary from consolidation considered earlier, directors of the parent entity may seek to exclude a subsidiary from group accounts for several invalid reasons, including:

- **Long-term restrictions on the ability to transfer funds to the parent**. This exclusion from consolidation is not permitted as it may still be possible to control a subsidiary in such circumstances.
- The **subsidiary undertakes different activities** and/or operates in different locations, thus being distinctive from other members of the group. This is not a valid reason for exclusion from consolidation. Indeed it could be argued that inclusion within the group accounts of such a subsidiary will enhance the relevance and reliability of the information contained within the group accounts.
- The **subsidiary has made losses or has significant liabilities** which the directors would prefer to exclude from the group accounts to improve the overall reported financial performance and position of the group. This could be motivated, for example, by determination of directors' remuneration based upon group financial performance. This is not a valid reason for exclusion from consolidation.
- The directors may seek to **disguise the true ownership of the subsidiary**, perhaps to avoid disclosure of particular activities or events, or to avoid disclosure of ownership of assets. This could be motivated, for example, by seeking to avoid disclosure of potential conflicts of interest which may be perceived adversely by users of financial statements.

- The directors may seek to exclude a subsidiary from consolidation in order for the group to **disguise its true size and extent**. This could be motivated, for example, by trying to avoid legal and regulatory compliance requirements applicable to the group or individual subsidiaries. This is not a valid reason for exclusion from consolidation.

5 The acquisition method

IFRS 3 applies to business combinations. A business combination is where an acquirer obtains control of a business.

IFRS 3 defines a business as **'an integrated set of activities and assets that is capable of being conducted and managed to provide a return in the form of dividends, lower costs, or other economic benefits' benefits'** (IFRS 13, Appendix A). Therefore:

- if the assets acquired are not a business, the transaction should be accounted for as the purchase of an asset
- if the assets acquired do constitute a business, the transaction is accounted for by applying the acquisition method outlined in IFRS 3.

The acquisition method has the following requirements:

- Identifying the acquirer
- Determining the acquisition date
- Recognising and measuring the subsidiary's identifiable assets and liabilities
- Recognising goodwill (or a gain from a bargain purchase) and any non-controlling interest.

Although you will be aware of many of these requirements from your previous studies, as well as from the illustrations earlier in this chapter, you are expected to have a more detailed knowledge of each of these elements for the P2 exam.

Identifying the acquirer

The acquirer is the entity that has assumed control over another entity.

In a business combination, it is normally clear which entity has assumed control.

The acquirer

Lyra pays $1 million to obtain 60% of the ordinary shares of Pan.

Lyra is the acquiring company.

However, sometimes it is not clear as to which entity is the acquirer. For these cases, IFRS 3 provides guidance:

- The acquirer is normally the entity that has transferred cash or other assets within the business combination
- If the business combination has not involved the transfer of cash or other assets, the acquirer is usually the entity that issues its equity interests.

Other factors to consider are as follows:

- The acquirer is usually the entity whose (former) management dominates the combined entity
- The acquirer is usually the entity whose owners have the largest portion of voting rights in the combined entity
- The acquirer is normally the bigger entity.

Test your understanding 2 – Identifying the acquirer

Abacus and Calculator are two public limited companies. The fair values of the net assets of these two companies are $100 million and $60 million respectively.

On 31 October 20X1, Abacus incorporates a new company, Phone, in order to effect the combination of Abacus and Calculator. Phone issues its shares to the shareholders of Abacus and Calculator in return for their equity interests.

After this, Phone is 60% owned by the former shareholders of Abacus and 40% owned by the former shareholders of Calculator. On the board of Phone are 4 of the former directors of Abacus and 2 of the former directors of Calculator.

Required:

With regards to the above business combination, identify the acquirer.

The acquisition date

The acquisition date is the date on which the acquirer obtains control over the acquiree. This will be the date at which goodwill must be calculated and from which the incomes and expenses of the acquiree will be consolidated.

Identifiable assets and liabilities

The acquirer must measure the identifiable assets acquired and the liabilities assumed at their fair values at the acquisition date.

Remember, when completing a consolidated statement of financial position, these fair value uplifts are adjusted in the net assets table (W2).

Goodwill in the subsidiary's individual financial statements is not an identifiable asset because it cannot be separately disposed of.

Fair value of the identifiable net assets of the acquiree

Identifiable assets

IFRS 3 says that an asset is identifiable if:

- It is capable of disposal separately from the business owning it, or
- It arises from contractual or other legal rights, regardless of whether those rights can be sold separately.

The identifiable assets and liabilities of the subsidiary should be recognised at fair value where:

- they meet the definitions of assets and liabilities in the Conceptual Framework for Financial Reporting, and
- they are exchanged as part of the business combination rather than a separate transaction.

Items that are not identifiable or do not meet the definitions of assets or liabilities are subsumed into the calculation of purchased goodwill.

Contingent liabilities

Contingent liabilities that are present obligations arising from past events and that can be measured reliably are recognised at fair value at the acquisition date. This is true even where an economic outflow is not probable. The fair value will incorporate the probability of an economic outflow.

Provisions

A provision for future operating losses cannot be created as this is a post-acquisition item. Similarly, restructuring costs are only recognised to the extent that a liability actually exists at the date of acquisition.

Fair value – exceptions

There are some exceptions to the requirement to measure the subsidiary's net assets at fair value when accounting for business combinations. Assets and liabilities falling within the scope of the following standards should be valued according to those standards:

- IAS 12 Income Taxes
- IAS 19 Employee Benefits
- IFRS 2 Share-based Payment
- IFRS 5 Non-current Assets Held for Sale and Discontinued Operations.

Test your understanding 3 – Fair value of identifiable net assets

P purchased 60% of the shares of S on 1 January 20X1. At the acquisition date, S had share capital of $10,000 and retained earnings of $190,000.

The property, plant and equipment of S includes land with a carrying value of $10,000 but a fair value of $50,000.

Included within the intangible assets of S is goodwill of $20,000 which arose on the purchase of the trade and assets of a sole-trader business. S has an internally generated brand that is not recognised (in accordance with IAS 38). The directors of P believe that this brand has a fair value of $150,000.

In accordance with IAS 37, the financial statements of S disclose the fact that a customer has initiated legal proceedings against them. If the customer wins, which lawyers have advised is unlikely, estimated damages would be $1m. The fair value of this contingent liability has been assessed as $100,000 at the acquisition date.

The directors of P wish to close one of the divisions of S. They estimate that this will cost $200,000 in redundancy payments.

Required:

What is the fair value of S's identifiable net assets at the acquisition date?

Goodwill

Goodwill should be recognised on a business combination. This is calculated as the difference between:

(1) The aggregate of the fair value of the consideration transferred and the non-controlling interest in the acquiree at the acquisition date, and

(2) The fair value of the acquiree's identifiable net assets and liabilities.

Purchase consideration

When calculating goodwill (W3), purchase consideration transferred to acquire control of the subsidiary must be measured at fair value.

When determining the fair value of the consideration transferred, remember that:

- Contingent consideration is included even if payment is not deemed probable. Its fair value will incorporate the probability of payment occurring.
- Acquisition costs are excluded from the calculation of purchase consideration.
  - Legal and professional fees are expensed to profit or loss as incurred
  - Debt or equity issue costs are accounted for in accordance with IFRS 9 Financial Instruments.

Contingent consideration

IFRS 3 says that contingent consideration is an obligation of the acquirer to transfer additional assets or equity interests if specified future events occur or conditions are met.

In an examination question the acquisition date fair value of any contingent consideration (or details of how to calculate it) would be given.

The payment of contingent consideration may be in the form of equity or a liability (issuing a debt instrument or cash) and should be recorded as such under the rules of IAS 32 Financial Instruments: Presentation (or other applicable standard).

Changes in the fair value of any contingent consideration after the acquisition date are dealt with in IFRS 3.

- Changes due to additional information obtained after the acquisition date that affects the facts or circumstances as they existed at the acquisition date are accounted for retrospectively. This means that the liability (and goodwill) are remeasured. This further information must have been obtained within twelve months of the acquisition date.
- Changes due to events after the acquisition date (for example, meeting an earnings target which triggers a higher payment than was provided for at acquisition) are treated as follows:
  - Contingent consideration classified as equity shall not be remeasured. Its subsequent settlement shall be accounted for within equity (e.g. Cr share capital/share premium Dr retained earnings).
  - Contingent consideration classified as an asset or a liability shall be remeasured at fair value with the movement recognised in profit or loss.

Note: Although contingent consideration is usually a liability, it may be an asset if the acquirer has the right to a return of some of the consideration transferred if certain conditions are met.

Test your understanding 4 – Purchase consideration

Following on from TYU 3, the purchase consideration transferred by P in exchange for the shares in S was as follows:

- Cash paid of $300,000
- Cash to be paid in one year's time of $200,000

- 10,000 shares in P. These had a nominal value of $1 and a fair value at 1 January 20X1 of $3 each
- $250,000 to be paid in one year's time if S makes a profit before tax of more than $2m. There is a 50% chance of this happening. The fair value of this contingent consideration can be measured as the present value of the expected value.

Legal fees associated with the acquisition were $10,000.

Where required, a discount rate of 10% should be used.

Required:

Per IFRS 3, what is the fair value of the consideration transferred to acquire control of S?

Goodwill and the non-controlling interest

The calculation of goodwill will depend on the method chosen to value the non-controlling interest at the acquisition date.

IFRS 3 provides a choice in valuing the non-controlling interest at acquisition:

EITHER:	OR:
Method 1 – The proportionate share of net assets method	**Method 2 – The fair value method**
NCI % × Fair value of the net assets of the subsidiary at the acquisition date	Fair value of NCI at date of acquisition. This is usually given in the question.

If the NCI is valued at acquisition as their proportionate share of the acquisition net assets, then only the acquirer's goodwill will be calculated.

- Where an exam question requires the use of this method, it will state that 'it is group policy to value the non-controlling interest at its proportionate share of the fair value of the subsidiary's identifiable net assets'.

If the NCI is valued at acquisition at fair value, then goodwill attributable to both the acquirer and the NCI will be calculated. This is known as the 'full goodwill method'.

- Where an exam question requires the use of this method, it will state that 'it is group policy to value the non-controlling interest using the full goodwill method' or that 'the non-controlling interest is measured at fair value'.

Test your understanding 5 – Goodwill

Following on from 'Test your understandings' 3 and 4, the fair value of the non-controlling interest at the acquisition date is $160,000.

Required:

Calculate the goodwill arising on the acquisition of S if the non-controlling interest at the acquisition date is valued at:

(a) **fair value**

(b) **its proportion of the fair value of the subsidiary's identifiable net assets.**

Non-controlling interest – choice of method

The method used to measure the NCI should be decided on a transaction by transaction basis. This means that, within the same group, the NCI in some subsidiaries may have been measured at fair value at acquisition, whilst the NCI in other subsidiaries may have been measured at acquisition using the proportionate basis.

Measurement period

During the measurement period, IFRS 3 requires the acquirer in a business combination to retrospectively adjust the provisional amounts recognised at the acquisition date to reflect new information obtained about facts and circumstances that existed as of the acquisition date.

This would result in goodwill arising on acquisition being recalculated.

The measurement period ends no later than twelve months after the acquisition date.

Measurement period illustration

P bought 100% of the shares of S on 31 December 20X1 for $60,000. On the acquisition date, it was estimated that the fair value of S's net assets were $40,000.

For the year ended 31 December 20X1, P would consolidate S's net assets of $40,000 and would also show goodwill of $20,000 ($60,000 – $40,000).

However, P receives further information on 30 June 20X2 which indicates that the fair value of S's net assets at the acquisition date was actually $50,000. This information was determined within the measurement period and so is retrospectively adjusted for.

Therefore, the financial statements for the year ended 31 December 20X1 will be adjusted. P will now consolidate S's net assets of $50,000 and will show goodwill of $10,000 ($60,000 – $50,000).

Bargain purchases

If the share of net assets acquired exceeds the consideration given, then a gain on bargain purchase ('negative goodwill') arises on acquisition. The accounting treatment for this is as follows:

- IFRS 3 says that negative goodwill is rare and therefore it may mean that an error has been made in determining the fair values of the consideration and the net assets acquired. The figures must be reviewed for errors.
- If no errors have been made, the negative goodwill is credited immediately to profit or loss.

6 Impairment of goodwill

IAS 36 Impairment of Assets requires that goodwill is tested for impairment annually.

Goodwill does not generate independent cash inflows. Therefore, it is tested for impairment as part of a cash generating unit.

A cash generating unit is the **'smallest identifiable group of assets that generates cash inflows that are largely independent of the cash inflows from other assets or groups of assets'** (IAS 36, para 6).

For exam purposes, a subsidiary is normally designated as a cash generating unit.

Accounting for an impairment

An **impairment loss** is the amount by which the carrying amount of an asset or a cash generating unit exceeds its recoverable amount.

Recoverable amount is the higher of fair value less costs to sell and value in use.

Impairment losses on a subsidiary will firstly be allocated against goodwill and then against other assets on a pro-rata basis.

Accounting for an impairment with a non-controlling interest

Full method of valuing NCI

Goodwill calculated under the fair value method represents full goodwill. It can therefore be added together with the other net assets of the subsidiary and compared to the recoverable amount of the subsidiary's net assets on a like for like basis.

Any impairment of goodwill is allocated between the group and the NCI based upon their respective shareholdings.

Proportionate method of valuing NCI

If the NCI is valued at acquisition at its share of the subsidiary's net assets then only the goodwill attributable to the group is calculated. This means that the NCI share of goodwill is not reflected in the group accounts. As such, any comparison between the carrying amount of the subsidiary (including goodwill) and the recoverable amount of its net assets will not be on a like-for-like basis.

- In order to address this problem, goodwill must be grossed up to include goodwill attributable to the NCI prior to conducting the impairment review. This grossed up goodwill is known as **total notional goodwill**.
- As only the parent's share of the goodwill is recognised in the group accounts, only the parent's share of the goodwill impairment loss should be recognised.

Illustration 4 – Impairment of goodwill

A owns 80% of B. At 31 October 20X6 the carrying amount of B's net assets is $60 million, excluding goodwill of $8 million that arose on the original acquisition.

The recoverable amount of the net assets of B is $64 million.

Calculate the impairment loss if:

(a) the NCI at acquisition was measured at fair value

(b) the NCI at acquisition was measured at its proportion of the fair value of the subsidiary's identifiable net assets.

Solution

(a) **Full goodwill method**

	$m
Goodwill	8
Net assets	60
Carrying amount	68
Recoverable amount	64
Impairment	4

The impairment loss will be allocated against goodwill, reducing it from $8m to $4m.

The $4m impairment expense will be charged to profit or loss. Of this, $3.2m ($4m × 80%) is attributable to the group and $0.8m ($4m × 20%) is attributable to the NCI.

(b) **Proportionate method**

	$m	$m
Goodwill	8	
Unrecognised NCI (20/80 × $8m)	2	
	–––	
Total notional goodwill		10
Net assets		60
		–––
Carrying amount		70
Recoverable amount		64
		–––
Impairment		6
		–––

The impairment loss is allocated against the total notional goodwill.

Only the group's share of goodwill has been recognised in the financial statements and so only the group's share (80%) of the impairment is recognised. The impairment charged to profit or loss is therefore $4.8m and goodwill will be reduced to $3.2m ($8m – $4.8m).

Test your understanding 6 – Happy

On 1 January 20X5, Lucky group purchased 80% of Happy for $500,000. The fair value of the identifiable net assets of Happy at the date of acquisition amounted to $590,000.

The carrying amount of Happy's net assets at 31 December is $520,000 (excluding goodwill). Happy is a cash-generating unit.

At 31 December 20X5 the recoverable amount of Happy's net assets is $530,000.

Required:

Calculate the impairment loss and explain how this would be dealt with in the financial statements of the Lucky group. if:

(a) **the NCI at acquisition was measured at its fair value of $130,000.**

(b) **the NCI at acquisition was measured at its share of the fair value of Happy's identifiable net assets.**

Impact on the financial statements

If goodwill is calculated using the fair value method (i.e. the non-controlling interest is valued at fair value at the acquisition date), then goodwill and the non-controlling interest will be higher than if the proportionate method was used. Although this will reduce the return on capital employed, it will also strengthen the gearing ratio.

The higher asset value reported when using the fair value method may lead to higher impairment losses being charged to profit or loss.

Test your understanding 7 – Pauline

On 1 April 20X7 Pauline acquired the following non-current investments:

- 6 million equity shares in Sonia by an exchange of two shares in Pauline for every four shares in Sonia plus $1.25 per acquired Sonia share in cash. The market price of each Pauline share at the date of acquisition was $6 and the market price of each Sonia share at the date of acquisition was $3.25.
- 30% of the equity shares of Arthur at a cost of $7.50 per share in cash.

Only the cash consideration of the above investments has been recorded by Pauline. In addition $1,000,000 of professional costs relating to the acquisition of Sonia is included in the cost of the investment.

The summarised draft statements of financial position of the three companies at 31 March 20X8 are presented below:

	Pauline	**Sonia**	**Arthur**
	$000	$000	$000
Assets			
Non-current assets			
Property, plant and equipment	36,800	20,800	36,000
Investments in Sonia and Arthur	26,500	–	–
Financial assets	13,000	–	–
	76,300	20,800	36,000

Current assets			
Inventories	13,800	12,400	7,200
Trade receivables	6,400	3,000	4,800
Total assets	96,500	36,200	48,000
Equity and liabilities			
Equity shares of $1 each	20,000	8,000	8,000
Retained earnings			
– at 31 March 20X7	32,000	12,000	22,000
– for year ended 31 March 20X8	18,500	5,800	10,000
	70,500	25,800	40,000
Non-current liabilities			
7% Loan notes	10,000	2,000	2,000
Current liabilities			
Trade payables	16,000	8,400	6,000
	96,500	36,200	48,000

The following information is relevant to the preparation of the consolidated statement of financial position:

(i) At the date of acquisition Sonia had an internally generated brand name. The directors of Pauline estimate that this brand name has a fair value of $2 million, an indefinite life and has not suffered any impairment.

(ii) On 1 April 20X7, Pauline sold an item of plant to Sonia at its agreed fair value of $5 million. Its carrying amount prior to the sale was $4 million. The estimated remaining life of the plant at the date of sale was five years.

(iii) During the year ended 31 March 20X8 Sonia sold goods to Pauline for $5.4 million. Sonia had marked up these goods by 50% on cost. Pauline had a third of the goods still in its inventory at 31 March 20X8. There were no intra-group payables or receivables at 31 March 20X8.

(iv) Pauline has a policy of valuing non-controlling interests at fair value at the date of acquisition. For this purpose the share price of Sonia at this date should be used. Impairment tests on 31 March 20X8 concluded that the recoverable amount of the net assets of Sonia were $34 million.

(v) The financial assets in Pauline's statement of financial position are classified as fair value through profit or loss. In the draft financial statements, they are held at their fair value as at 1 April 20X7. They have a fair value of $18 million as at 31 March 20X8.

Required:

Prepare the consolidated statement of financial position for the Pauline group as at 31 March 20X8.

7 IFRS 11 – Joint arrangements

IFRS 11 Joint Arrangements adopts the definition of control as included in IFRS 10 (see earlier within this chapter) as a basis for determining whether there is joint control.

Joint arrangements are defined **'as arrangements where two or more parties have joint control'** (IFRS 11, Appendix A). This will only apply if the relevant activities require unanimous consent of those who collectively control the arrangement.

Joint arrangements may take the form of either:

- joint operations
- joint ventures.

The key distinction between the two forms is based upon the parties' rights and obligations under the joint arrangement.

IFRS 11 Joint arrangements

Joint operations

Joint operations are defined as joint arrangements whereby **'the parties that have joint control have rights to the assets and obligations for the liabilities'** (IFRS 11, Appendix A). Normally, there will not be a separate entity established to conduct joint operations.

Example of a joint operation

A and B decide to enter into a joint operation to produce a new product. A undertakes one manufacturing process and B undertakes the other. A and B have agreed that decisions regarding the joint operation will be made unanimously and that each will bear their own expenses and take an agreed share of the sales revenue from the product.

Joint ventures

Joint ventures are defined as joint arrangements whereby **'the parties have joint control of the arrangement and have rights to the net assets of the arrangement'** (IFRS 11, Appendix A). This will normally be established in the form of a separate entity to conduct the joint venture activities.

Example of a joint venture

A and B decide to set up a separate entity, C, to enter into a joint venture. A will own 55% of the equity capital of C, with B owning the remaining 45%. A and B have agreed that decision-making regarding the joint venture will be unanimous. Neither party will have direct right to the assets, or direct obligation for the liabilities of the joint venture; instead, they will have an interest in the net assets of entity C set up for the joint venture.

Accounting for joint arrangements

Joint operations

If the joint operation meets the definition of a 'business' then the principles in IFRS 3 Business Combinations apply when an interest in a joint operation is acquired:

- Acquisition costs are expensed to profit or loss as incurred
- The identifiable assets and liabilities of the joint operation are measured at fair value
- The excess of the consideration transferred over the fair value of the net assets acquired is recognised as goodwill.

At the reporting date, the individual financial statements of each joint operator will recognise:

- its share of assets held jointly
- its share of liabilities incurred jointly
- its share of revenue from the joint operation
- its share of expenses from the joint operation.

The joint operator's share of the income, expenses, assets and liabilities of the joint operation are included in its individual financial statements and so they will automatically flow through to the consolidated financial statements.

Joint ventures

In the individual financial statements, an investment in a joint venture can be accounted for:

- at cost
- in accordance with IFRS 9 Financial Instruments, or
- by using the equity method.

In the consolidated financial statements, the interest in the joint venture entity will be accounted for using the equity method. The treatment of a joint venture in the consolidated financial statements is therefore identical to the treatment of an associate.

Test your understanding 8 – A, B, C and D

A, B and C establish a new entity, which is called D. A has 50 per cent of the voting rights in the new entity, B has 30 per cent and C has 20 per cent. The contractual arrangement between A, B and C specifies that at least 75 per cent of the voting rights are required to make decisions about the activities of entity D.

Required:

How should A account for its investment in D in its consolidated financial statements?

Illustration 5 – Joint operation – Blast

Blast has a 30% share in a joint operation. The assets, liabilities, revenues and costs of the joint operation are apportioned on the basis of shareholdings. The following information relates to the joint arrangement activity for the year ended 30 November 20X2:

- The manufacturing facility cost $30m to construct and was completed on 1 December 20X1 and is to be dismantled at the end of its estimated useful life of 10 years. The present value of this dismantling cost to the joint arrangement at 1 December 20X1, using a discount rate of 8%, was $3m.
- During the year ended 30 November 20X2, the joint operation entered into the following transactions:
  - goods with a production cost of $36m were sold for $50m
  - other operating costs incurred amounted to $1m
  - administration expenses incurred amounted to $2m.

Blast has only accounted for its share of the cost of the manufacturing facility, amounting to $9m. The revenue and costs are receivable and payable by the two other joint operation partners who will settle amounts outstanding with Blast after each reporting date.

Required:

Show how Blast will account for the joint operation within its financial statements for the year ended 30 November 20X2.

Solution – Blast

Profit or loss impact:	$m
Revenue ($50m × 30%)	15.000
Cost of sales ($36m × 30%)	(10.800)
Operating costs ($1m × 30%)	(0.300)
Depreciation (($30m + 3m) × 1/10 × 30%)	(0.990)
Administration expenses ($2m × 30%)	(0.600)
Finance cost ($3m × 8% × 30%)	(0.072)
Share of net profit re joint operation (include in retained earnings within SOFP)	2.238

Statement of financial position impact:	$m
Property, plant and equipment (amount paid = share of cost)	9.000
Dismantling cost ($3m × 30%)	0.900
Depreciation ($33m × 1/10 × 30%)	(0.990)
	8.910
Trade receivables (i.e. share of revenue due)	15.000
Non-current liabilities:	
Dismantling provision (($3m × 30%) + $0.072)	0.972
Current liabilities:	
Trade payables ($10.8m + $0.3m + $0.6m) (i.e. share of expenses to pay)	11.700

The amounts calculated above should be classified under the appropriate headings within the statement of profit or loss for the year or statement of financial position as appropriate.

Note also that where there are amounts owed to and from a joint operating partner, it may be acceptable to show just a net amount due to or from each partner.

8 Other issues in group accounting

IFRS 12 Disclosure of Interests in Other Entities

IFRS 12 is the single source of disclosure requirements for business combinations. Disclosure requirements include:

- disclosure of significant assumptions and judgements made in determining whether an investor has control, joint control or significant influence over an investee
- disclosure of the nature, extent and financial effects of its interests in joint arrangements and associates
- additional disclosures relating to subsidiaries with non-controlling interests, joint arrangements and associates that are individually material
- significant restrictions on the ability of the parent to access and use the assets or to settle the liabilities of its subsidiaries

- extended disclosures relating to "structured entities", previously referred to as special-purpose entities, to enable a full understanding of the nature of the arrangement and associated risks, such as the terms on which an investor may be required to provide financial support to such an entity.

IAS 27 Separate Financial Statements

IAS 27 applies when an entity has interests in subsidiaries, joint ventures or associates and either elects to, or is required to, prepare separate non-consolidated financial statements.

In separate financial statements, investments in subsidiaries, joint ventures or associates can be accounted for:

- at cost
- in accordance with IFRS 9 Financial Instruments, or
- by using the equity method.

In separate financial statements, dividends received from an investment are recognised in profit or loss unless the equity method is used. If the equity method has been used, then dividends received reduce the carrying amount of the investment.

Current issues – proposed amendments

The following exposure draft, relating to group accounting issues, is examinable in P2.

ED/2014/4 Measuring Quoted Investments in Subsidiaries, Joint Ventures and Associates at Fair Value

There are instances when investments in a subsidiary, joint venture or associate are required to be measured at fair value. For example:

- Investment entities do not consolidate entities over which they have control but instead measure them at fair value through profit or loss
- Investments in subsidiaries, joint ventures or associates may be held at fair value in individual (non-consolidated) financial statements.

Some users of IFRS Standards are unsure how fair value should be determined in these instances. The Board therefore wish to clarify that the fair value for quoted investments in subsidiaries, joint ventures and associates should be determined by multiplying the quoted price by the number of shares held.

Current issues – criticisms of IFRS 3

The Board has conducted a post-implementation review of IFRS 3 Business Combinations. Users of the standard raised the following issues.

Definition of a business

- More guidance is needed on when an asset acquisition is not a business.
- Some industries might consider a set of assets to be a business, whereas others might not. This limits comparability, because of the large differences between accounting for asset purchases and accounting for business combinations.
- Based on the difficulties involved in establishing whether a 'business' has been acquired, some have argued that the differences in the accounting treatment of asset purchases and business combinations are not justified and should be reduced.

Fair values

- The requirement to fair value the assets and liabilities of the acquired subsidiary at the acquisition date makes it difficult to compare entities that grow via acquisitions with those that grow organically.
- Recognising the inventory of a subsidiary at its acquisition date fair value will reduce profit margins in the next period, thus reducing comparability year-on-year.

Intangibles

- IFRS 3 requires entities to recognise separable intangibles at fair value at the acquisition date, but this proves difficult if no active market exists.

Contingent consideration

- The calculation of the fair value of contingent consideration is extremely subjective, increasing the risk of bias and reducing comparability.
- Contingent consideration may be linked to the success of a long-term development project. It has been argued that changes in the fair value of the consideration in such scenarios should be recorded against the development asset, rather than in profit or loss.

Goodwill

- Some have argued that a gain on a bargain purchase should not be recognised in profit or loss, but rather in other comprehensive income, because it distorts the performance profile of an entity.
- It is argued that goodwill impairment reviews are complex, subjective and time-consuming.
- It has been argued that the requirement to subject goodwill to annual impairment reviews, rather than to amortise it, increases volatility in profit or loss.
- Over time, purchased goodwill will be replaced by internally generated goodwill. Per IAS 38 Intangible Assets, internally generated goodwill should not be recognised as an asset and so some argue that the purchased goodwill should be amortised (rather than be subject to annual impairment review).

NCI

- Allowing a measurement choice for the NCI at acquisition reduces comparability between entities.
- Measuring the fair value of the NCI can be problematic, and highly judgemental, if the entity is not listed.

9 Chapter summary

Revision of group SFP:
- Group structure (W1)
- Proforma and adding
- Workings 2 – 5

Revision of group P/L and OCI:
- Group structure
- Proforma and adding
- Profit and TCI split

Revision of associates:
- Use the equity method

Control:
- Power
- Rights to variable returns
- The ability to use power to affect returns

The acquisition method:
- Identify the acquirer
- Identify the acquisition date
- Recognise net assets at fair value
- Recognise goodwill and the NCI

Impairment of goodwill:
- Goodwill calculated under the proportionate method must be grossed up.

Joint arrangements:
- Joint operations
- Joint ventures

Test your understanding answers

Test your understanding 1 – Control

An investor controls an investee if the investor has:

- **'power over the investee**
- **exposure, or rights, to variable returns from its involvement with the investee**
- **the ability to use its power over the investee to affect the amount of the investor's returns'** (IFRS 10, para 7).

When assessing control, an investor considers its potential voting rights. Potential voting rights are rights to obtain voting rights of an investee, such as those arising from convertible instruments or options.

Potential voting rights are considered if the rights are substantive. This would mean that the rights need to be currently exercisable. Other factors that should be considered in determining whether potential voting rights are substantive, according to IFRS 10, include:

- whether the exercise price creates a financial barrier that would prevent (or deter) the holder from exercising its rights
- whether the party or parties that hold the rights would benefit from the exercise of those rights.

Parsley has voting rights that are currently exercisable and these should be factored into an assessment of whether control exists. The fact that the exercise price on the convertible instrument is out of the money (i.e. the exercise price is higher than the current market price) could potentially deter Parsley from taking up these voting rights. However, these options are not deeply out of the money. This may also be compensated by the fact that synergies would arise on the acquisition. This would suggest that it is likely that Parsley will exercise the options. The potential voting rights should therefore be considered substantive.

Based on the above, Parsley has control over Oregano. Oregano should be treated as a subsidiary and consolidated.

Test your understanding 2 – Identifying the acquirer

If the business combination has not involved the transfer of cash or other assets, the acquirer is usually the entity that issues its equity interests. This might point towards Phone being the acquirer, since Phone has issued shares in exchange for the shares of Abacus and Calculator.

However, other circumstances must be considered:

- The acquirer is usually the entity whose (former) management dominates the management of the combined entity.
- The acquirer is usually the entities whose owners retain or receive the largest portion of the voting rights in the combined entity.
- The acquirer is normally the entity whose size is greater than the other entities.

All three of these circumstances would point towards Abacus being the acquirer. This would appear to reflect the substance of the transaction since Phone has been incorporated by Abacus as a way of enabling a business combination with Calculator.

Test your understanding 3 – Fair value of identifiable net assets

	$
Share capital	10,000
Retained earnings	190,000
Fair value uplift ($50,000 – $10,000)	40,000
Goodwill	(20,000)
Brand	150,000
Contingent liability	(100,000)
Fair value of identifiable net assets at acquisition	270,000

Goodwill in the subsidiary's own financial statements is not an identifiable asset because it cannot be disposed of separately from the rest of the business.

No adjustment is made to the fair value of the net assets for the estimated redundancy provision. This is because no obligation exists at the acquisition date.

Test your understanding 4 – Purchase consideration

	$
Cash paid	300,000
Deferred cash ($200,000 × (1/1.1))	181,818
Shares (10,000 × $3)	30,000
Contingent consideration ($250,000 × 50% × (1/1.1))	113,636
Fair value of consideration	625,454

The legal fees are expensed to the statement of profit or loss.

Test your understanding 5 – Goodwill

	Fair value method	**Net assets method**
	$	$
Consideration (TYU 4)	625,454	625,454
Add: NCI at acquisition (part b = 40% × $270,000)	160,000	108,000
	785,454	733,454
FV of identifiable net assets at acquisition (TYU 3)	(270,000)	(270,000)
	515,454	463,454

The fair value method calculates both the group's goodwill and the goodwill attributable to the non-controlling interest. Therefore, goodwill is higher under this method.

The proportion of net assets method only calculates the goodwill attributable to the group. Goodwill is lower under this method.

Test your understanding 6 – Happy

(a) **Full goodwill method**

Goodwill arising on acquisition:

	$000
Fair value of consideration paid	500
NCI at acquisition	130
	630
Less: fair value of net assets at acquisition	(590)
Goodwill	40

Impairment review:

	$000
Goodwill	40
Net assets	520
Carrying amount	560
Recoverable amount	(530)
Impairment	30

The impairment loss is allocated against goodwill, reducing it from $40,000 to $10,000.

The $30,000 impairment expense will be charged to the statement of profit or loss. Of this, $24,000 (80% × $30,000) is attributable to the group and $6,000 (20% × $30,000) is attributable to the NCI.

(b) **Proportionate method**

Goodwill arising on acquisition:

	$000
Fair value of consideration paid	500
NCI share of net assets at acquisition (20% × $590,000)	118
	618
Less: fair value of net assets at acquisition	(590)
Goodwill	28

Impairment review:

	$000	$000
Goodwill	28	
Unrecognised NCI (20/80 × $28,000)	7	
Total notional goodwill		35
Net assets		520
Carrying amount		555
Recoverable amount		(530)
Impairment		25

The impairment loss is firstly allocated to the notional goodwill. However, only the group's share of the goodwill was recognised in the financial statements and so only the group's share of the impairment is recognised.

The total impairment recognised is therefore $20,000 (80% × $25,000). This will be charged to the statement of profit or loss and is all attributable to the group.

Test your understanding 7 – Pauline

Consolidated statement of financial position as at 31 March 20X8

	$000
Assets	
Non-current assets	
Property, plant and equipment ($36,800 + $20,800 – $800 (W8))	56,800
Goodwill (W3)	6,800
Intangible assets (W2)	2,000
Investment in associate (W6)	21,000
Financial assets (W9)	18,000
	104,600
Current assets	
Inventories ($13,800 + $12,400 – $600 (W7))	25,600
Trade receivables ($6,400 + $3,000)	9,400
Total assets	139,600
Equity and liabilities	
Equity attributable to equity holders of the parent	
Equity shares of $1 each ($20,000 + $3,000 (W3))	23,000
Share premium (W3)	15,000
Retained earnings (W5)	58,200
	96,200
Non-controlling interest (W4)	7,000
Total equity	103,200
Non-current liabilities	
7% Loan notes ($10,000 + $2,000)	12,000
Current liabilities	
Trade payables ($16,000 + $8,400)	24,400
Total equity and liabilities	139,600

Workings

(W1) **Group structure**

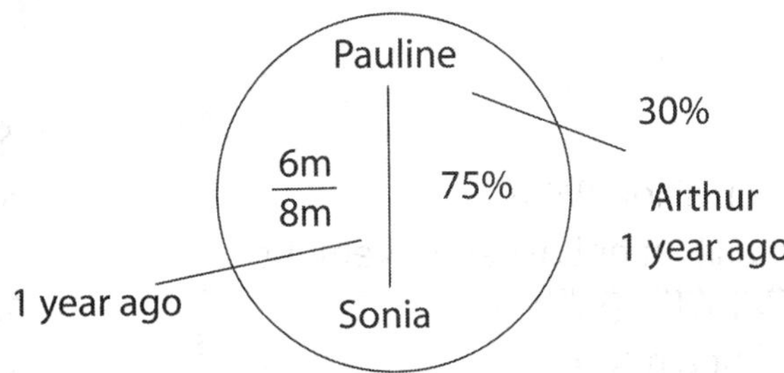

(W2) **Net assets – Sonia**

	At acquisition date	**At reporting date**
	$000	$000
Equity capital	8,000	8,000
Retained earnings	12,000	17,800
Fair value adj:		
Brand	2,000	2,000
PURP (W7)		(600)
	22,000	27,200

(W3) **Goodwill**

	Sonia
	$000
Fair value of consideration	
Share exchange (6m × 2/4 × $6)	18,000
Cash paid (6m × $1.25)	7,500
	25,500
FV of NCI at acquisition (2m × $3.25)	6,500
	32,000
Less FV of net assets at acquisition (W2)	(22,000)
Goodwill at acquisition	
	10,000
Impairment (W10)	(3,200)
Goodwill at reporting date	6,800

The 3 million shares issued by Pauline in the share exchange at a value of $6 each would be recorded as $1 per share in equity capital and $5 per share in share premium. This gives an increase in equity capital of $3 million and a share premium of $15 million.

(W4) **NCI**

	$000
Fair value of NCI at acquisition (W3)	6,500
NCI share of post-acquisition net asset movement (25% × ($27,200 – $22,000)) (W2)	1,300
NCI share of goodwill impairment (25% × $3,200) (W10)	(800)
	7,000

(W5) **Group retained earnings**

	$000
100% of Pauline's retained earnings ($32,000 + $18,500)	50,500
Professional costs written off	(1,000)
Gain on financial assets (W9)	5,000
P% of Sonia's post-acquisition retained earnings** (75% × (($17,800 – $600) – $12,000) (W2))	3,900
P% of Arthur's post-acquisition retained earnings (30% × $10,000)	3,000
PPE PURP (W8)	(800)
P% of goodwill impairment (75% × $3,200) (W10)	(2,400)
	58,200

** It is worth noting that, if the subsidiary has no 'other components of equity', then you could simply take P's share of the subsidiary's post-acquisition net assets movement:

75% × ($27,200 – $22,000 (W2)) = $3,900.

(W6) **Investment in associate**

	$000
Cost (8,000 × 30% × $7.50)	18,000
P's share post-acquisition reserves ($10,000 × 30%)	3,000
	21,000

(W7) **PURP in inventory**

Intra-group sales are $5.4 million on which Sonia made a profit of $1,800,000 ($5,400,000 × 50/150).

The unrealised profit still in inventory is therefore $600,000 ($1,800,000 × 1/3).

Sonia is the seller so the profit must be removed from Sonia's retained earnings in W2.

The adjusting entry is:

Dr Retained earnings (W2)	$600,000
Cr Inventories	$600,000

(W8) **PURP in PPE**

The carrying amount of the PPE is $4m ($5m – ($5m/5 years)).

If no group transfer had happened, then the carrying amount would have been $3.2m ($4m – ($4m/5 years).

PPE must therefore be reduced by $800,000 ($4m – $3.2m). Pauline is the seller so the profit impact must be adjusted against Pauline's retained earnings in W5. The adjusting entry is:

Dr Retained earnings (W5)	$800,000
Cr PPE	$800,000

(W9) **Financial assets**

The financial assets must be remeasured to fair value and the gain recorded through profit or loss.

The gain on revaluation to fair value is $5m ($18m – $13m). This will be recorded in profit or loss and will increase group retained earnings in W5.

(W10) **Impairment**

	$000
Goodwill (W3)	10,000
Net assets (W2)	27,200
Carrying amount	37,200
Recoverable amount	(34,000)
Impairment	3,200

The impairment loss will be charged against goodwill.

Full goodwill has been calculated so the impairment expense must be allocated between the NCI (W4) and retained earnings (W5).

Test your understanding 8 – A, B, C and D

A does not control the arrangement because it needs the agreement of B when making decisions. This would imply that A and B have joint control of the arrangement because decisions about the activities of the entity cannot be made without both A and B agreeing.

In the consolidated financial statements of the A Group, D should be treated as a joint venture. This is because it is a separate entity over which A has joint control. The joint venture will be accounted for using the equity method.

chapter

20

Complex groups

Chapter learning objectives

Upon completion of this chapter you will be able to:

- apply the method of accounting for business combinations, including complex group structures
- determine and apply appropriate procedures to be used in preparing group financial statements.

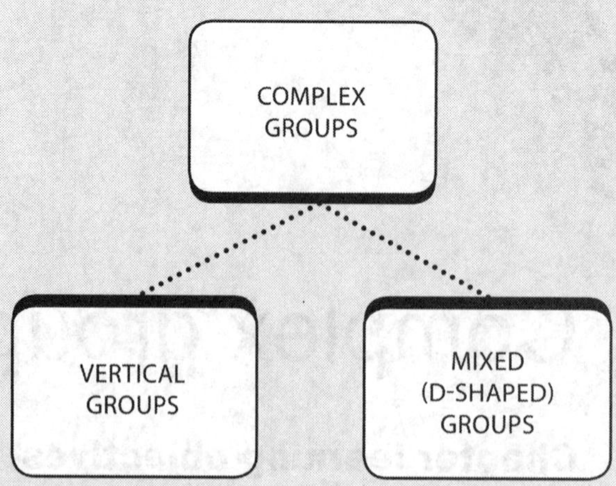

1 Complex group structures

Complex group structures exist where a subsidiary of a parent entity owns a shareholding in another entity which makes that other entity also a subsidiary of the parent entity.

Complex structures can be classified under two headings:

- Vertical groups
- Mixed groups.

2 Vertical groups

Definition

A **vertical group** arises where a subsidiary of the parent entity holds shares in a further entity such that control is achieved. The parent entity therefore controls both the subsidiary entity and, in turn, its subsidiary (often referred to as a sub-subsidiary entity).

Look at the following two situations:

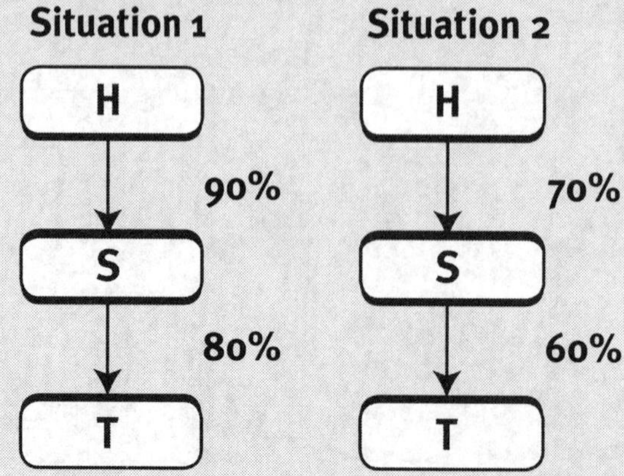

In both situations, H controls S, and S controls T. H is therefore able to exert control over T by virtue of its ability to control S. All three companies form a vertical group.

Both companies that are controlled by the parent are consolidated.

The basic techniques of consolidation are the same as seen previously, with some changes to the goodwill, NCI and group reserves calculations.

Approach to a question

When establishing the group structure, follow these steps:

- Control – which entities does the parent control directly or indirectly?
- Percentages – what are the effective ownership percentages for consolidation?
- Dates – when did the parent achieve control over the subsidiary and the sub-subsidiary?

Illustration 1 – Vertical group structure

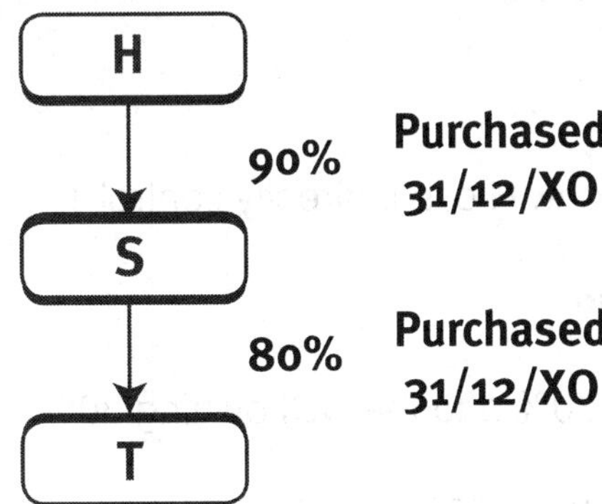

Control

H controls S and S controls T. Therefore, H can indirectly control T.

Effective consolidation percentage

S will be consolidated with H owning 90% and the NCI owning 10%.

T will be consolidated with H owning 72% (90% × 80%) and the NCI owning 28% (100% – 72%).

These effective ownership percentages will be used in standard workings (W4) and (W5).

Dates

S will be consolidated from 31 December 20X0.

When H acquires control of S, it also acquires indirect control over T. Therefore H will consolidate T from 31 December 20X0.

Illustration 2 – Vertical group structure

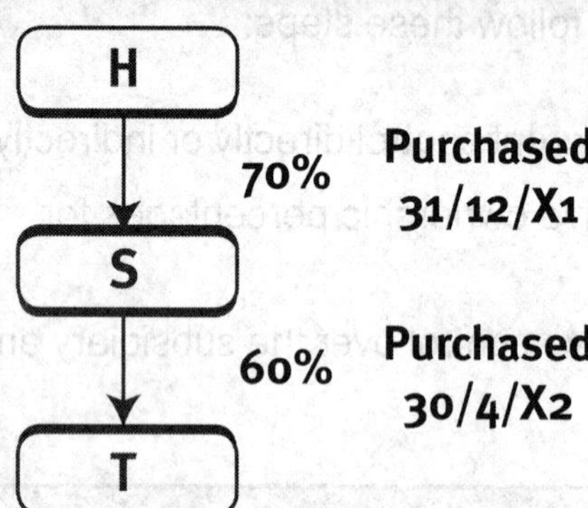

Control

H controls S and S controls T. Therefore, H can indirectly control T.

Effective consolidation percentage

S will be consolidated with H owning 70% and the NCI owning 30%.

T will be consolidated with H owning 42% (70% × 60%) and the NCI owning 58% (100% – 42%).

The effective ownership percentages will be used in standard workings (W4) and (W5).

Do not be put off by the fact that the effective group interest in T is less than 50%, and that the effective non-controlling interest in T is more than 50%.

Dates

S will be consolidated from 31 December 20X1.

However, S did not gain control of T until 30 April 20X2 meaning that H does not indirectly control T until this date. Therefore, T is consolidated into the H group from 30 April 20X2.

Indirect holding adjustment

Accounting for a sub-subsidiary requires an **indirect holding adjustment**.

- Goodwill in the sub-subsidiary is calculated from the perspective of the ultimate parent company. Therefore, the cost of the investment in the sub-subsidiary should be the parent's share of the amount paid by its subsidiary.
  - The NCI's share of the cost of the investment in the sub-subsidiary must be eliminated from the goodwill calculation.
- The value of the non-controlling interest in the subsidiary includes the NCI's share of the cost of the investment in the sub-subsidiary.
  - The NCI's share of the cost of the investment in the sub-subsidiary must be eliminated from the NCI calculation.

Illustration 3 – Indirect holding adjustment

On 31 December 20X1, A purchased 90% of the equity shares in B for $150,000 and B purchased 80% of the equity shares in C for $100,000.

At this date, the fair value of the net assets of B and C were $144,000 and $90,000 respectively. The fair value of the non-controlling interest in B and C was $17,000 and $15,000 respectively.

Required:

Calculate goodwill and the non-controlling interest for inclusion in the consolidated statement of financial position as at 31 December 20X1.

Solution

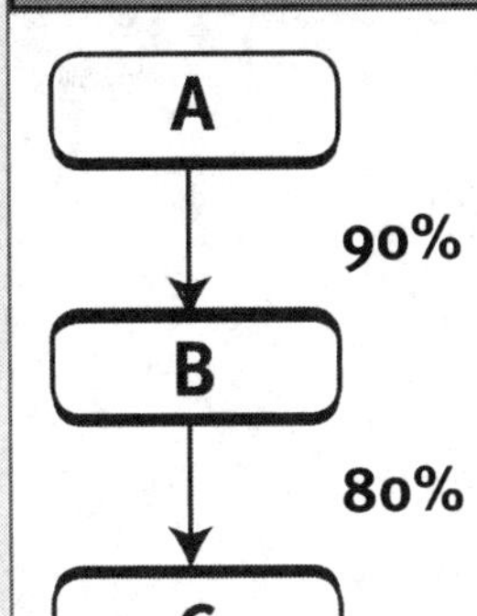

Goodwill

	B	C
	$	$
Consideration	150,000	100,000
Indirect holding adjustment (10% × $100,000)		(10,000)
Add: FV of non-controlling interest at acquisition	17,000	15,000
	167,000	105,000
Less: Net assets at acquisition	(144,000)	(90,000)
Goodwill at acquisition	23,000	15,000

Non-controlling interest

	$
B: NCI at acquisition (W3)	17,000
B: Indirect holding adjustment (W3)	(10,000)
C: NCI at acquisition (W3)	15,000
Non-controlling interest	22,000

Note: In subsequent years, the NCI will be adjusted for its share of the post-acquisition net asset movement of each subsidiary.

The NCI % in B is 10% (100% – 90%).

The NCI % in C is 28% (100% – (90% × 80%))

Illustration 4 – Vertical group 1

The draft statements of financial position of David, Colin and John, as at 31 December 20X4, are as follows:

	D	C	J
	$000	$000	$000
Sundry assets	280	180	130
Shares in subsidiary	120	80	
	400	260	130
Equity capital ($1 shares)	200	100	50
Retained earnings	100	60	30
Liabilities	100	100	50
	400	260	130

The following information is also available:

- David acquired 75,000 $1 shares in Colin on 1 January 20X4 when the retained earnings of Colin amounted to $40,000. At that date, the fair value of the non-controlling interest in Colin was valued at $38,000.
- Colin acquired 40,000 $1 shares in John on 30 June 20X4 when the retained earnings of John amounted to $25,000. The retained earnings of John had been $20,000 on the date of David's acquisition of Colin. On 30 June 20X4, the fair value of the non-controlling interest in John (both direct and indirect), based upon effective shareholdings, was $31,000.
- Goodwill has suffered no impairment. It is group policy to use the full goodwill method.

Required:

Produce the consolidated statement of financial position of the David group as at 31 December 20X4.

Solution

Statement of financial position for the David group at 31 December 20X4

	$000
Goodwill ($18 + $16) (W3)	34
Sundry assets ($280 + $180 + $130)	590
	624
Equity and liabilities:	
Equity capital	200
Retained earnings (W5)	118
	318
Non-controlling interest (W4)	56
Total equity	374
Liabilities ($100 + $100 + $50)	250
	624

(W1) **Group structure**

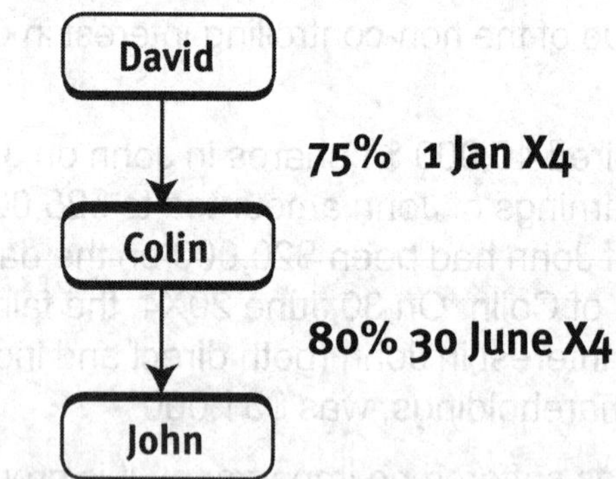

Control

David controls Colin and Colin controls John. Therefore, David can indirectly control John.

Effective consolidation percentage

Colin will be consolidated with David owning 75% and the NCI owning 25%.

John will be consolidated with David owning 60% (75% × 80%) and the NCI owning 40% (100% – 60%).

The effective ownership percentages will be used in standard workings (W4) and (W5).

Dates

Colin will be consolidated from 1 Jan 20X4.

However, Colin did not gain control of John until 30 June X4. Therefore, David does not indirectly control John until this date. As such, John is consolidated from 30 June 20X4.

(W2) **Net assets**

The acquisition date will be the date on which David (the parent company) gained control over each entity:

- Colin: 1 January 20X4
- John: 30 June 20X4

This means that the information given regarding John's retained earnings at 1 January 20X4 is irrelevant in this context.

Net assets of subsidiaries

	Colin		**John**	
	At acq'n	**At rep date**	**At acq'n**	**At rep date**
	$000	$000	$000	$000
Equity capital	100	100	50	50
Retained earnings	40	60	25	30
	140	160	75	80

(W3) **Goodwill**

A separate goodwill calculation is required for each subsidiary.

For the sub-subsidiary, goodwill is calculated from the perspective of the ultimate parent entity (David) rather than the immediate parent (Colin). Therefore, the effective cost of John is only David's share of the amount that Colin paid for John, i.e. $80,000 × 75% = $60,000.

	Colin	**John**
	$000	$000
Cost of investment in subsidiary	120	80
Indirect holding adjustment (25% × $80,000)	–	(20)
Fair value of NCI	38	31
	158	91
FV of net assets (W2)	(140)	(75)
	18	16

(W4) **Non-controlling interest**

	$000
Colin: NCI at acquisition (W3)	38
Colin: NCI share of post-acq'n net assets (25% × $20,000 (W2))	5
Less: Indirect holding adjustment (25% × 80,000)	(20)
John: NCI at acquisition (W3)	31
John NCI share of post acq'n net assets (40% × $5,000 (W2))	2
	56

(W5) **Group retained earnings**

	$000
David	100
Colin: 75% × $20,000 (W2)	15
John: 60% × $5,000 (W2)	3
	118

Note that only the group's effective share (60%) is taken of John's post-acquisition retained earnings.

Illustration 5 – Vertical group 2

The draft statements of financial position of Daniel, Craig and James as at 31 December 20X4 are as follows:

	D	C	J
	$000	$000	$000
Sundry assets	180	80	80
Shares in subsidiary	120	80	
	300	160	80
Equity capital	200	100	50
Retained earnings	100	60	30
	300	160	80

- Craig acquired 40,000 $1 shares in James on 1 January 20X4 when the retained earnings of James amounted to $25,000.
- Daniel acquired 75,000 $1 shares in Craig on 30 June 20X4 when the retained earnings of Craig amounted to $40,000 and those of James amounted to $30,000.

It is group policy to value the non-controlling interest using the proportion of net assets method.

Required:

Produce the consolidated statement of financial position of the Daniel group at 31 December 20X4.

Solution

Consolidated statement of financial position of the Daniel group at 31 December 20X4

	$000
Assets:	
Goodwill ($15 + $12) (W3)	27
Sundry assets ($180 + $80 + $80)	340
	367
Equity and liabilities:	
Equity capital	200
Retained earnings (W5)	115
Non-controlling interest (W4)	52
	367

(W1) **Group structure**

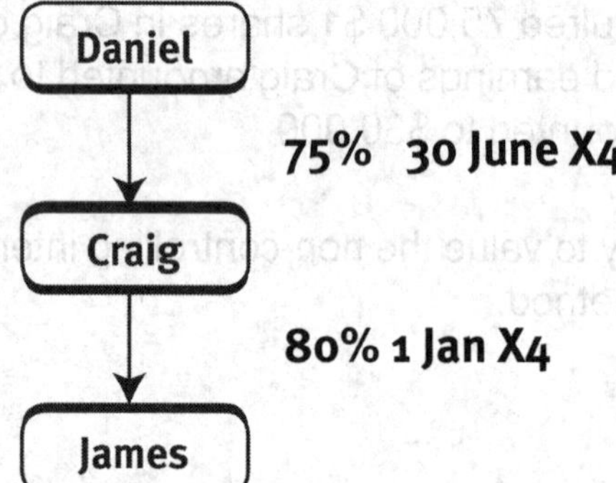

Control

Daniel controls Craig and Craig controls James. Therefore, Daniel can indirectly control James.

Effective consolidation percentage

Craig will be consolidated with Daniel owning 75% and the NCI owning 25%.

James will be consolidated with Daniel owning 60% (75% × 80%) and the NCI owning 40% (100% – 60%).

The effective ownership percentages will be used in standard workings (W4) and (W5). They will also be used in (W3) to calculate goodwill, as the group policy is to use the proportion of net assets method.

Dates

Craig will be consolidated from 30 June 20X4.

When Daniel acquires control of Craig, it also acquires indirect control over James. Therefore Daniel will consolidate James from 30 June 20X4.

(W2) **Net assets**

	Craig		**James**	
	Acq'n date	**Rep date**	**Acq'n date**	**Rep date**
	$000	$000	$000	$000
Share capital	100	100	50	50
Retained earnings	40	60	30	30
	140	160	80	80

(W3) **Goodwill**

	Craig	**James**
	$000	$000
Cost of investment	120	80
Indirect holding adjustment (25% × $80,000)	–	(20)
NCI at acquisition: Craig: 25% × $140,000 (W2) James: 40% × $80,000 (W2)	35	32
	155	92
FV of NA at acquisition (W2)	(140)	(80)
Goodwill	15	12

(W4) **Non-controlling interest**

	$000
Craig: NCI at acquisition (W3)	35
Craig: NCI % post-acq'n net assets (25% × ($160,000 – $140,000)) (W2)	5
Less: indirect holding adjustment (W3)	(20)
James: NCI at acquisition (W3)	32
James: NCI % post-acq'n net assets (40% × ($80,000 – $80,000)) (W2)	–
	52

(W5) **Group retained earnings**

	$000
Daniel	100
Craig: 75% × ($60,000 – $40,000) (W2)	15
James: 60% × ($30,000 – $30,000) (W2)	–
	115

Test your understanding 1 – H, S & T

The following are the statements of financial position at 31 December 20X7 for H group companies:

	H $	S $	T $
75% of the shares in S	65,000	–	–
60% of the shares in T	–	55,000	–
Sundry assets	280,000	133,000	100,000
	345,000	188,000	100,000
Equity share capital ($1 shares)	100,000	60,000	50,000
Retained earnings	45,000	28,000	25,000
Liabilities	200,000	100,000	25,000
	345,000	188,000	100,000

All the shareholdings were acquired on 1 January 20X1 when the retained earnings of S were $10,000 and those of T were $8,000. At that date, the fair value of the non-controlling interest in S was $20,000. The fair value of the total non-controlling interest (direct and indirect) in T was $50,000. It is group policy to value the non-controlling interest using the full goodwill method.

At the reporting date, the recoverable amount of the net assets of S were $93,000. It was deemed that goodwill arising on the acquisition of T was not impaired.

Required:

Prepare the consolidated statement of financial position for the H group at 31 December 20X7.

Test your understanding 2 – Grape, Vine and Wine

The statements of financial position of three entities at 30 June 20X6 were as follows:

	Grape	Vine	Wine
	$000	$000	$000
Investment	110	60	–
Sundry assets	350	200	120
	460	260	120
Equity share capital	100	50	10
Retained earnings	210	110	70
Liabilities	150	100	40
	460	260	120

Grape purchased 40,000 of the 50,000 $1 shares in Vine on 1 July 20X5, when the retained earnings of that entity were $80,000. At that time, Vine held 7,500 of the 10,000 $1 shares in Wine. These had been purchased on 1 January 20X5 when Wine's retained earnings were $65,000. On 1 July 20X5, Wine's retained earnings were $67,000.

At 1 July 20X5, the fair value of the non-controlling interest in Vine was $27,000, and that of Wine (both direct and indirect) was $31,500. It is group policy to value the non-controlling interest using the full goodwill method.

The equity share capital of Grape includes $20,000 received from the issue of 20,000 class B shares on 30 June 20X6. These shares entitle the holders to fixed annual dividends. The holders of these B shares can also demand the repayment of their capital from 30 June 20X9.

Included in the liabilities of Grape are $100,000 proceeds from the issue of a loan on 1 July 20X5. There are no annual interest payments and Grape therefore believes that no further accounting entries are required until the repayment date. The loan is repayable on 30 June 20X8 at a premium of 100%. The effective rate of interest on the loan is 26.0%.

Required:

Prepare the consolidated statement of financial position for the Grape group at 30 June 20X6.

3 Mixed (D-shaped) groups

Definition

In a mixed group situation the parent entity has a direct controlling interest in at least one subsidiary. In addition, the parent entity and the subsidiary together hold a controlling interest in a further entity.

For example:

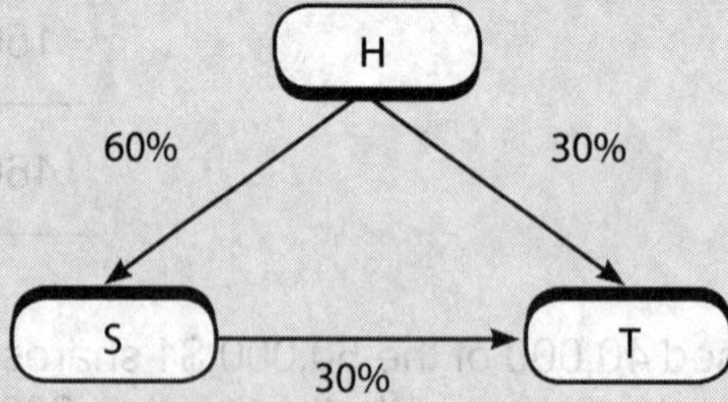

- H has 60% of the shares of S. S is therefore a subsidiary of H.
- H has a 30% direct holding in T. H also controls S, who has a 30% holding in T. H therefore controls T through its direct and indirect holdings. This means that T is part of H's group and must be consolidated.

Accounting for a mixed group is similar to accounting for a vertical group.

Approach to a question

Follow the same steps as with a vertical group when establishing group structure:

- Control
- Percentages of ownership
- Dates of acquisition

Illustration 6 – Mixed group structure

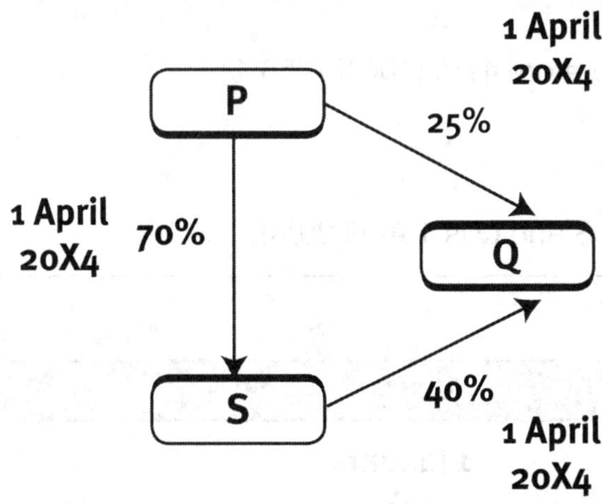

P acquired a 70% interest in S on 1 April 20X4, and acquired a 25% interest in Q on the same date.

S acquired a 40% interest in Q on 1 April 20X4.

Control

P controls S. This makes S a subsidiary of P.

P is able to direct 25% + 40% = 65% of the voting rights of Q. Q is a sub-subsidiary of P.

Effective consolidation percentage

S will be consolidated with P owning 70% and the NCI owning 30%.

P's effective interest in Q is calculated as follows:

Direct	25%
Indirect (70% × 40%)	28%
P's effective interest in Q	53%

The NCI interest in Q is therefore 47% (100% – 53%).

Dates

The date of acquisition for S and Q is 1 April 20X4.

Illustration 7 – Mixed group structure

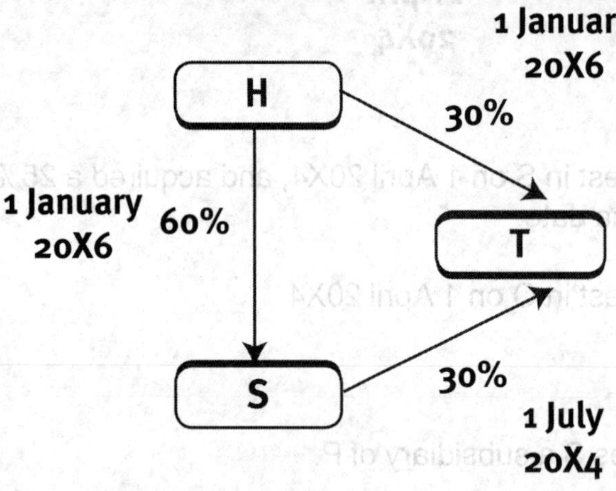

H acquired a 60% interest in S on 1 January 20X6, and acquired a 30% interest in T on the same date.

S acquired a 30% interest in T on 1 July 20X4.

Control

H controls S. This makes S a subsidiary of H.

H is able to direct 30% + 30% = 60% of the voting rights of T. T is a sub-subsidiary of H.

Effective consolidation percentage

S will be consolidated with H owning 60% and the NCI owning 40%.

H's effective interest in T is calculated as follows:

Direct	30%
Indirect (60% × 30%)	18%
H's effective interest in T	48%

The NCI interest in T is therefore 52% (100% – 48%).

Dates

The date of acquisition for S and T is 1 January 20X6.

Further detail on mixed groups

Note that the definition of a mixed group does not include the situation where the parent and an associate together hold a controlling interest in a further entity.

E.g.

H owns 35% of S, S owns 40% of W and H owns 40% of W.

This is **not** a mixed group situation. Neither S nor W is a member of the H group, although S and W may both be 'associates' of H.

H's interest in W might be calculated as before as (35% × 40%) + 40% = 54%. Although H has an arithmetic interest in W that is more than 50%, it does not have parent entity control of W, as it does not control S's 40% stake in W.

Consolidation

All consolidation workings are the same as those used in vertical group situations, with the exception of goodwill.

The goodwill calculation for the sub-subsidiary differs slightly from a vertical group. The cost of the sub-subsidiary must include the following:

- the cost of the parent's holding (the direct holding)
- the cost of the subsidiary's holding (the indirect holding)
- the indirect holding adjustment.

Illustration 8 – H, S, C

The statements of financial position of H, S and C as at 31 December 20X5 were as follows:

	H	S	C
	$	$	$
75% of shares in S	72,000	–	–
40% of shares in C	25,000	–	–
30% of shares in C	–	20,000	–
Sundry assets	125,000	120,000	78,000
	222,000	140,000	78,000
Equity share capital ($1 shares)	120,000	60,000	40,000
Retained earnings	95,000	75,000	35,000
Liabilities	7,000	5,000	3,000
	222,000	140,000	78,000

All shares were acquired on 31 December 20X2 when the retained earnings of S amounted to $30,000 and those of C amounted to $10,000.

It is group accounting policy to value the non-controlling interest on a proportionate basis.

Required:

Prepare the statement of financial position for the H group as at 31 December 20X5.

Solution

Group statement of financial position for H group as at 31 December 20X5

	$
Goodwill ($4,500 + $8.750) (W3)	13,250
Sundry assets ($125,000 + $120,000 + $78,000)	323,000
	336,250

Equity and liabilities:	$
Equity share capital	120,000
Retained earnings (W5)	144,375
Non-controlling interest (W4)	56,875
Total equity	321,250
Liabilities ($7,000 + $5,000 + $3,000)	15,000
	336,250

(W1) **Group structure**

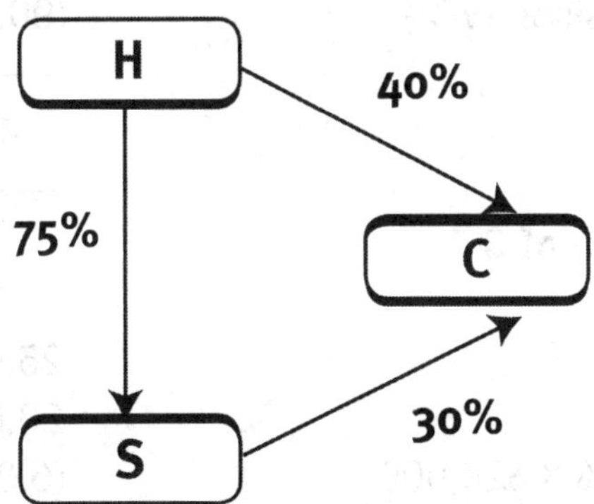

H's interest in S in 75%. The NCI interest in S is 25%.

H's effective interest in C:	
Direct	40.0%
Indirect (75% × 30%)	22.5%
	62.5%

The NCI interest in C is 37.5% (100% – 62.5%).

(W2) **Net assets**

S's net assets	**At acq'n**	**At rep date**
	$	$
Equity capital	60,000	60,000
Retained earnings	30,000	75,000
	90,000	135,000

C's net assets		
	$	$
Equity capital	40,000	40,000
Retained earnings	10,000	35,000
	50,000	75,000

(W3) **Goodwill**

Goodwill arising on acquisition of S	
	$
Cost of H's investment	72,000
NCI at acquisition (25% × $90,000 (W2))	22,500
	94,500
Less: FV of net assets at acquisition (W2)	(90,000)
Goodwill	4,500

Goodwill arising on acquisition of C	
	$
Cost of H's investment	25,000
Cost of S's investment	20,000
Indirect holding adjustment (25% × $20,000)	(5,000)
NCI at acquisition (37.5% × $50,000 (W2))	18,750
	58,750
Less: FV of net assets at acquisition (W2)	(50,000)
Goodwill	8,750

(W4) **Non-controlling interest**

	$
S – NCI at acquisition (W3)	22,500
S – NCI % of post acquisition net assets (25% × $45,000 (W2))	11,250
Indirect holding adjustment (W3)	(5,000)
C – NCI at acquisition (W3)	18,750
C – NCI % of post acquisition net assets (37.5% × $25,000 (W2))	9,375
	56,875

(W5) **Retained earnings**

	$
100% of H's retained earnings	95,000
Group share of S's post acquisition retained earnings (75% × $45,000 (W2))	33,750
Group share of C's post acquisition retained earnings (62.5% × $25,000 (W2))	15,625
	144,375

Test your understanding 3 – T, S & R

The following are the summarised statements of financial position of T, S and R as at 31 December 20X4.

	T	S	R
	$	$	$
Non-current assets	140,000	61,000	170,000
Investments	200,000	65,000	–
Current assets	30,000	28,000	15,000
	370,000	154,000	185,000
Equity shares of $1 each	200,000	80,000	100,000
Retained earnings	150,000	60,000	80,000
Other components of equity	10,000	8,000	–
Liabilities	10,000	6,000	5,000
	370,000	154,000	185,000

On 1 January 20X3 S acquired 35,000 ordinary shares in R at a cost of $65,000 when the retained earnings of R amounted to $40,000.

On 1 January 20X4 T acquired 64,000 shares in S at a cost of $120,000 and 40,000 shares in R at a cost of $80,000. On this date, the retained earnings of S and R amounted to $50,000 and $60,000 respectively. S also had other components of equity of $3,000. The fair value of the NCI in S on 1 January 20X4 was $27,000. The fair value of the NCI (direct and indirect) in R was $56,000. The non-controlling interest is measured using the full goodwill method. At the reporting date, goodwill has not been impaired.

On 1 January 20X4, T entered into a lease agreement. T is the lessor and is leasing a machine to a third party for two years. The machine has a useful economic life of ten years. No receipt was due during 20X4 so no accounting entries have been posted. T is due a receipt of $10,000 on 31 December 20X5.

On 1 January 20X4, T granted 100 share appreciation rights (SARs) to 60 managers. These entitle the holders to a cash bonus based on the share price of T. The SARs vest if the managers are still employed by T at 31 December 20X7. Five managers left during 20X4 and it is expected that another 15 will leave prior to 31 December 20X7. The fair value of each SAR was $10 on 1 January 20X4 and $14 on 31 December 20X4.

Required:

Prepare the consolidated statement of financial position of the T group as at 31 December 20X4.

4 Chapter summary

Complex Groups:
where a subsidiary of a parent entity owns all or part of a shareholding, which makes another entity also a subsidiary of the parent entity

Vertical groups:

- consolidate all companies from date P achieved control
- include the indirect holding adjustment in goodwill and NCI workings
- use effective group interest in subsidiary for reserves and NCI calculations

Mixed (D-shaped) groups:

- consolidate all companies from date P achieved control
- goodwill must include the cost of direct and indirect holdings. Include the indirect holding adjustment in Goodwill and NCI workings
- use effective group interest in subsidiary for reserves and NCI calculations

Test your understanding answers

Test your understanding 1 – H, S & T

Consolidated statement of financial position as at 31 December 20X7

	$
Goodwill ($5,000 + $33,250) (W3)	38,250
Sundry net assets ($280,000 + $133,000 + $100,000)	513,000
	551,250
Equity and liabilities	
Equity share capital	100,000
Retained earnings (W5)	58,650
NCI (W4)	67,600
Liabilities ($200,000 + $100,000 + $25,000)	325,000
	551,250

(W1) **Group structure**

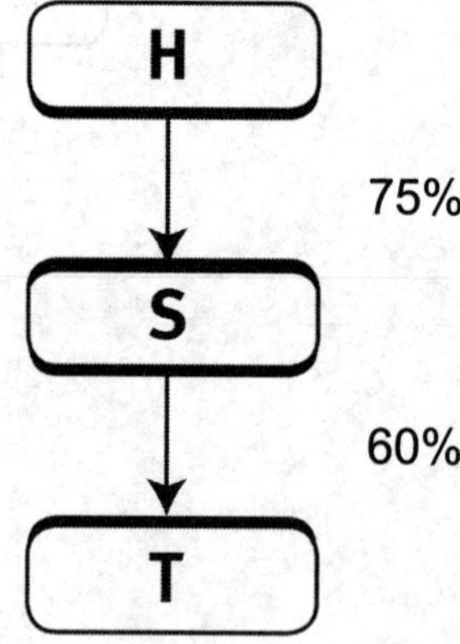

		%
S:	Group share	75
	NCI	25
T:	Group share (75% × 60%)	45
	NCI (100% – 45%)	55

(W2) **Net assets**

	S		T	
	acq'n	**rep date**	**acq'n**	**rep date**
	$	$	$	$
Equity capital	60,000	60,000	50,000	50,000
Retained earnings	10,000	28,000	8,000	25,000
	70,000	88,000	58,000	75,000

(W3) **Goodwill**

	S	T
	$	$
Consideration paid	65,000	55,000
FV of NCI	20,000	50,000
Indirect Holding Adjustment (25% × $55,000)	–	(13,750)
	85,000	91,250
FV of NA at acquisition	(70,000)	(58,000)
Goodwill at acquisition	15,000	33,250
Impairment (W5)	(10,000)	–
Goodwill at reporting date	5,000	33,250

(W4) **Non-controlling interest**

	$
S – FV at date of acquisition	20,000
S – NCI % of post-acq'n net assets (25% × $18,000 (W2))	4,500
Indirect Holding Adjustment (W3)	(13,750)
T – FV at date of acquisition	50,000
T – NCI % of post-acq'n net assets (55% × $17,000 (W2))	9,350
NCI % of S's goodwill impairment (25% × $10,000 (W3))	(2,500)
	67,600

(W5) **Consolidated retained earnings**

	$
Retained earnings of H	45,000
Group % of post-acquisition retained earnings:	
S – (75% × $18,000 (W2))	13,500
T – (45% × $17,000 (W2))	7,650
H's % of S's goodwill impairment (75% × $10,000 (W3))	(7,500)
	58,650

(W6) **Goodwill impairment**

	$
Goodwill in S before impairment review (W3)	15,000
Net assets of S at reporting date (W2)	88,000
	103,000
Recoverable amount	(93,000)
Goodwill impairment	10,000

Test your understanding 2 – Grape, Vine and Wine

Consolidated statement of financial position as at 30 June 20X6

	$
Goodwill ($7,000 + $2,500 (W3))	9,500
Sundry assets ($350,000 + $200,000 + $120,000)	670,000
	679,500
Equity and liabilities	$
Equity share capital ($100,000 – $20,000 (W6))	80,000
Retained earnings (W5)	209,800
Non-controlling interest (W4)	53,700
Liabilities ($150,000 + $100,000 + $40,000 + $20,000 (W6) + $26,000 (W7))	336,000
	679,500

(W1) **Group structure**

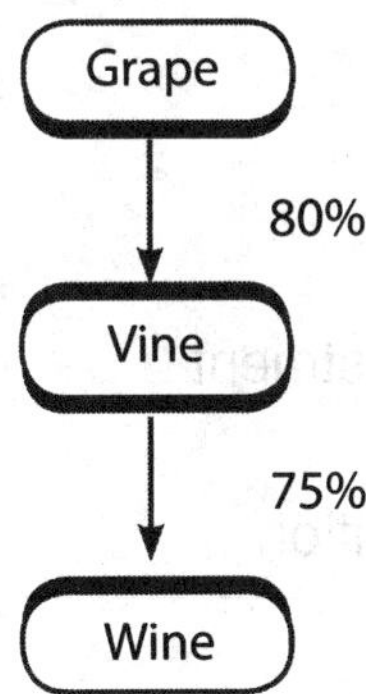

Effective consolidation percentage

Vine will be consolidated with Grape owning 80% and the NCI owning 20%.

Wine will be consolidated with Grape owning 60% (80% × 75%) and the NCI owning 40% (100% – 60%).

The effective ownership percentages will be used in standard workings (W4) and (W5).

Dates

Grape gained control over Vine and Wine on 1 July 20X5.

(W2) **Net assets**

	Vine		**Wine**	
	acq'n	**rep. date**	**acq'n**	**rep. date**
	$	$	$	$
Equity capital	50,000	50,000	10,000	10,000
Retained earnings	80,000	110,000	67,000	70,000
	130,000	160,000	77,000	80,000

The acquisition date for both entities is the date they joined the Grape group, i.e. 1 July 20X5.

(W3) **Goodwill**

	Vine	Wine
	$	$
Consideration paid	110,000	60,000
Indirect holding adjustment (20% × $60,000)		(12,000)
FV of NCI at acquisition	27,000	31,500
	137,000	79,500
FV of net assets at acquisition (W2)	(130,000)	(77,000)
Goodwill	7,000	2,500

(W4) **Non-controlling interest**

	$
V – NCI at acquisition (W3)	27,000
V – NCI share of post acq'n net assets (20% × $30,000 (W2))	6,000
Indirect holding adjustment (W3)	(12,000)
W – NCI at acquisition (W3)	31,500
W – NCI share of post acq'n net assets (40% × $3,000 (W2))	1,200
	53,700

(W5) **Consolidated retained earnings**

	$
Retained earnings of Grape	210,000
Interest on liability (W7)	(26,000)
Group share of post-acquisition retained earnings	
V (80% × $30,000 (W2))	24,000
W (60% × $3,000 (W2))	1,800
	209,800

(W6) **Shares**

A financial liability exists if there is an obligation to deliver cash.

The class B shares are a financial liability and must be reclassified:

Dr Equity share capital	$20,000
Cr Liabilities	$20,000

(W7) **Loan**

The loan will be measured at amortised cost. A finance cost must be charged using the effective rate. The finance cost for the year is $26,000 ($100,000 × 26%).

Dr Finance costs/retained earnings (W5)	$26,000
Cr Liabilities	$26,000

Test your understanding 3 – T, S & R

T consolidated statement of financial position as at 31 December 20X4

	$
Goodwill ($14,000 + $28,000 (W3))	42,000
Non-current assets ($140,000 + $61,000 + $170,000)	371,000
Current assets ($30,000 + $28,000 + $15,000 + $5,000 (W6))	78,000
	491,000
	$
Equity share capital	200,000
Retained earnings (W5)	162,600
Other components of equity (W5)	14,000
	376,600
Non-controlling interest (W4)	79,400
Liabilities ($10,000 + $6,000 + $5,000 + $14,000 (W7))	35,000
	491,000

(W1) **Group structure**

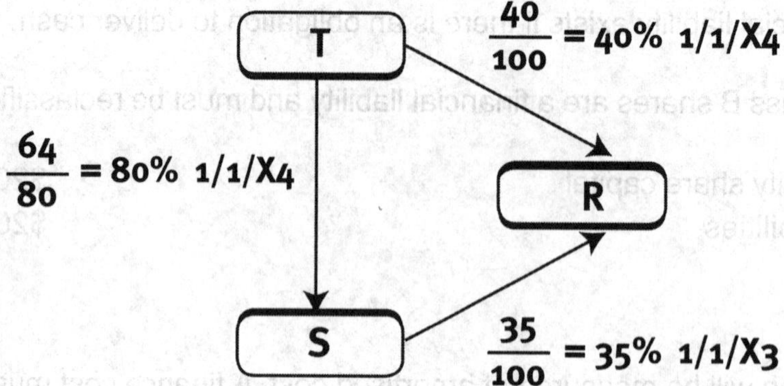

T has an 80% holding in S. The NCI holding is 20%.

T's effective holding in R is calculated as follows:

Direct	40%
Indirect (80% × 35%)	28%
	68%

The NCI holding in R is 32% (100% – 68%).

T's acquisition date for both entities is 1 January 20X4.

(W2) **Net assets**

S's Net assets	**At acq'n**	**At rep date**
	$	$
Equity share capital	80,000	80,000
Retained earnings	50,000	60,000
Other components of equity	3,000	8,000
	133,000	148,000

R's Net assets		
	$	$
Equity share capital	100,000	100,000
Retained earnings	60,000	80,000
	160,000	180,000

(W3) **Goodwill**

Goodwill arising on the acquisition of S

	$
Consideration paid	120,000
FV of NCI	27,000
	147,000
FV of net assets at acquisition (W2)	(133,000)
Goodwill	14,000

Goodwill arising on the acquisition of R

	$
Cost of T's investment	80,000
Cost of S's investment	65,000
Indirect holding adjustment (20% × 65,000)	(13,000)
Fair value of NCI at acquisition	56,000
	188,000
FV of net assets at acquisition (W2)	(160,000)
Goodwill	28,000

(W4) **Non-controlling interest**

	$
S – FV of NCI at acquisition	27,000
NCI share of S's post acquisition net assets (20% × ($148,000 – $133,000) (W2))	3,000
Indirect holding adjustment (W3)	(13,000)
R – FV of NCI at acquisition	56,000
NCI share of R's post acquisition net assets (32% × ($180,000 – $160,000) (W2))	6,400
	79,400

(W5) **Group retained earnings**

	$
100% of T's retained earnings	150,000
Operating lease (W6)	5,000
Share-based payment (W7)	(14,000)
Group share of S's post acquisition retained earnings (80% × ($60,000 – $50,000) (W2))	8,000
Group share of R's post acquisition retained earnings (68% × ($80,000 – $60,000) (W2))	13,600
	162,600

Other components of equity

	$
100% of T's other components of equity	10,000
Group share of S's post acquisition other components (80% × ($8,000 – $3,000) (W2))	4,000
Group share of R's post acquisition other components (68% × nil (W2))	–
	14,000

(W6) **Operating lease**

The lease term is much shorter than the useful life of the asset so it appears to be an operating lease. The total lease receipts should be recognised as income in the statement of profit or loss on a straight line basis.

The annual operating lease income is $5,000 ($10,000/2 years).

The adjusting entry is:

Dr Current assets	$5,000
Cr Profit or loss/Retained earnings (W5)	$5,000

(W7) **Share-based payments**

This is a cash-settled share-based payment scheme.

The expense should be spread across the vesting period. The expense to be recognised is based on the fair value of the scheme at the period end and the number of SARs that are expected to vest.

(60 employees – 5 – 15) × 100 × \$14 × 1/4 = \$14,000

The adjusting entry is:

Dr Profit or loss/Retained earnings (W5)	\$14,000
Cr Liabilities	\$14,000

chapter

21

Change in a group structure

Chapter learning objectives

Upon completion of this chapter you will be able to:

- prepare group financial statements where activities have been discontinued, or have been acquired or disposed of in the period
- apply and discuss the treatment of a subsidiary which has been acquired exclusively with a view to subsequent disposal.

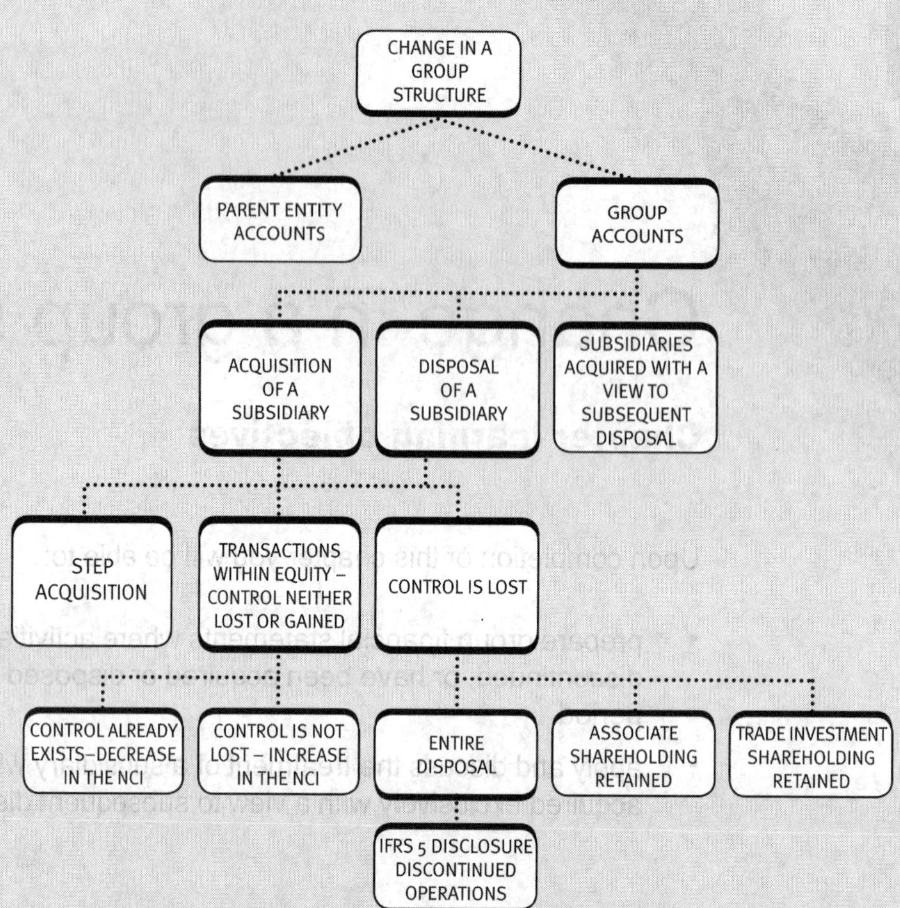

1 Acquisition of a subsidiary

There are two acquisition scenarios that need to be considered in more detail:

- mid-year acquisitions
- step acquisitions.

Mid-year acquisitions

A parent entity consolidates a subsidiary from the date that it achieves control. If this happens partway through the reporting period then it will be necessary to pro-rate the results of the subsidiary so that only the post-acquisition incomes and expenses are consolidated into the group statement of profit or loss.

Illustration 1 – Tudor – mid-year acquisition of a subsidiary

On 1 July 20X4 Tudor purchased 1,600,000 of the 2,000,000 $1 equity shares of Windsor for $10,280,000. On the same date it also acquired 1,000,000 of Windsor's $1 10% loan notes. At the date of acquisition the retained earnings of Windsor were $6,150,000.

The statements of profit or loss for each entity for the year ended 31 March 20X5 were as follows.

	Tudor	**Windsor**
	$000	$000
Revenue	60,000	24,000
Cost of sales	(42,000)	(20,000)
Gross profit	18,000	4,000
Distribution costs	(2,500)	(50)
Administrative expenses	(3,500)	(150)
Profit from operations	12,000	3,800
Investment income	75	–
Finance costs	–	(200)
Profit before tax	12,075	3,600
Tax	(3,000)	(600)
Profit for the year	9,075	3,000
Retained earnings bfd	16,525	5,400

There were no items of other comprehensive income in the year.

The following information is relevant:

(1) The fair values of Windsor's net assets at the date of acquisition were equal to their carrying values with the exception of plant and equipment, which had a carrying value of $2,000,000 but a fair value of $5,200,000. The remaining useful life of this plant and equipment was four years at the date of acquisition. Depreciation is charged to cost of sales and is time apportioned on a monthly basis.

(2) During the post-acquisition period Tudor sold goods to Windsor for $12 million. The goods had originally cost $9 million. During the remaining months of the year Windsor sold $10 million (at cost to Windsor) of these goods to third parties for $13 million.

(3) Incomes and expenses accrued evenly throughout the year.

(4) Tudor has a policy of valuing non-controlling interests using the full goodwill method. The fair value of non-controlling interest at the date of acquisition was $2,520,000.

(5) The recoverable amount of the net assets of Windsor at the reporting date was $14,150,000. Any goodwill impairment should be charged to administrative expenses.

Required:

Prepare a consolidated statement of profit or loss for Tudor group for the year ended 31 March 20X5.

Solution

Tudor group statement of profit or loss for the year ended 31 March 20X5

	$000
Revenue ($60,000 + (9/12 × $24,000) – $12,000)	66,000
Cost of sales ($42,000 + (9/12 × $20,000) – $12,000 + $600 (W6) + $500 (W5))	(46,100)
Gross profit	19.900
Distribution costs ($2,500 + (9/12 × $50))	(2,538)
Administrative expenses ($3,500 + (9/12 × $150) + $300 (W3))	(3,912)
Profit from operations	13,450
Investment income ($75 – $75)	–
Finance costs ((9/12 × $200) – $75)	(75)
Profit before tax	13,375
Tax ($3,000 + (9/12 × $600))	(3,450)
Profit after tax for the year	9,925
Profit attributable to:	
Owners of the parent (bal. fig)	9,655
Non-controlling interest (W7)	270
	9,925

There were no items of other comprehensive income in the year.

(W1) **Group structure – Tudor owns 80% of Windsor**

- the acquisition took place three months into the year
- nine months is post-acquisition

(W2) **Goodwill impairment**

	$000
Net assets of the subsidiary (W3)	13,000
Goodwill (W4)	1,450
	14,450
Recoverable amount	(14,150)
Impairment	300

The impairment will be allocated against goodwill and charged to the statement of profit or loss.

Goodwill has been calculated using the fair value method so the impairment needs to be factored in when calculating the profit attributable to the NCI (W7).

(W3) **Net assets**

	Acq'n date	**Rep. date**
	$000	$000
Equity capital	2,000	2,000
Retained earnings (Rep date = $5,400 bfd + $3,000)	6,150	8,400
Fair value adjustment – PPE ($5.2m – $2.0m)	3,200	3,200
Depreciation on FVA (W6)	–	(600)
	11,350	13,000

(W4) **Goodwill**

	$000
Consideration	10,280
FV of NCI at acquisition	2,520
	12,800
FV of net assets at acquisition (W3)	(11,350)
Goodwill pre-impairment review (W2)	1,450

(W5) **PURP**

$2 million ($12m – $10m) of the $12 million intra-group sale remains in inventory.

The profit that remains in inventory is $500,000 (($12m – $9m) × 2/12).

(W6) **Excess depreciation**

Per W3, there has been a fair value uplift in respect of PPE of $3,200,000.

This uplift will be depreciated over the four year remaining life.

The depreciation charge in respect of this uplift in the current year statement of profit or loss is $600,000 (($3,200,000/4 years) × 9/12).

(W7) **Profit attributable to the NCI**

	$000	$000
Profit of Windsor (9/12 × $3,000)	2,250	
Excess depreciation (W6)	(600)	
Goodwill impairment (W2)	(300)	
	1,350	
× 20%		
Profit attributable to the NCI		270

Step acquisitions

A step acquisition occurs when the parent company acquires control over the subsidiary in stages. This is achieved by buying blocks of shares at different times. Acquisition accounting is only applied at the date when control is achieved.

- Any pre-existing equity interest in an entity is accounted for according to:
  - IFRS 9 in the case of simple investments
  - IAS 28 in the case of associates and joint ventures
  - IFRS 11 in the case of joint arrangements other than joint ventures
- At the date when the equity interest is increased and control is achieved:
  (1) re-measure the previously held equity interest to fair value
  (2) recognise any resulting gain or loss in profit or loss for the year
  (3) calculate goodwill and the non-controlling interest on either a partial or full basis.

  For the purposes of the goodwill calculation, the consideration will be the fair value of the previously held equity interest plus the fair value of the consideration transferred for the most recent purchase of shares at the acquisition date. You may wish to use the following proforma:

	$
Fair value of previously held interest	X
Fair value of consideration for additional interest	X
NCI at acquisition	X
	X
Less: FV of net assets at acquisition	(X)
Goodwill at acquisition	X

- If there has been re-measurement of any previously held equity interest that was recognised in other comprehensive income, any changes in value recognised in earlier years are now reclassified to retained earnings.
- Purchasing further shares in a subsidiary after control has been acquired (for example taking the group interest from 60% to 75%) is regarded as a transaction between equity holders. Goodwill is not recalculated. This situation is dealt with separately within this chapter.

Illustration 2 – Ayre, Fleur and Byrne

Ayre has owned 90% of the ordinary shares of Fleur for many years. Ayre also has a 10% investment in the shares of Byrne, which was held in the consolidated statement of financial position as at 31 December 20X6 at $24,000 in accordance with IFRS 9. On 30 June 20X7, Ayre acquired a further 50% of Byrne's equity shares at a cost of $160,000.

The draft statements of profit or loss for the three companies for the year ended 31 December 20X7 are presented below:

Statements of profit or loss for the year ended 31 December 20X7

	Ayre	**Fleur**	**Byrne**
	$000	$000	$000
Revenue	500	300	200
Cost of sales	(300)	(70)	(120)
Gross profit	200	230	80
Operating costs	(60)	(80)	(60)
Profit from operations	140	150	20
Income tax	(28)	(30)	(4)
Profit for the period	112	120	16

The non-controlling interest is calculated using the fair value method. On 30 June 20X7, fair values were as follows:

- Byrne's identifiable net assets – $200,000
- The non-controlling interest in Byrne – $100,000
- The original 10% investment in Byrne – $26,000

Required:

Prepare the consolidated statement of profit or loss for the Ayre Group for the year ended 31 December 20X7 and calculate the goodwill arising on the acquisition of Byrne.

Solution

Group statement of profit or loss for the year ended 31 December 20X7

	$000
Revenue ($500 + $300 + (6/12 × $200))	900
Cost of sales ($300 + $70 + (6/12 × $120))	(430)
Gross profit	470
Operating costs ($60 + $80 + (6/12 × $60))	(170)
Profit from operations	300
Profit on derecognition of equity investment (W1)	2
	302
Income tax ($28 + $30 + (6/12 × $4))	(60)
Profit for the period	242
Profit attributable to:	
Equity holders of the parent (bal. fig)	226.8
Non-controlling interest (W2)	15.2
Profit for the period	242

Goodwill calculation

	$000
FV of previously held interest	26
FV of consideration for additional interest	160
NCI at acquisition date	100
	286
FV of net assets at acquisition	(200)
Goodwill	86

(W1) **Group Structure**

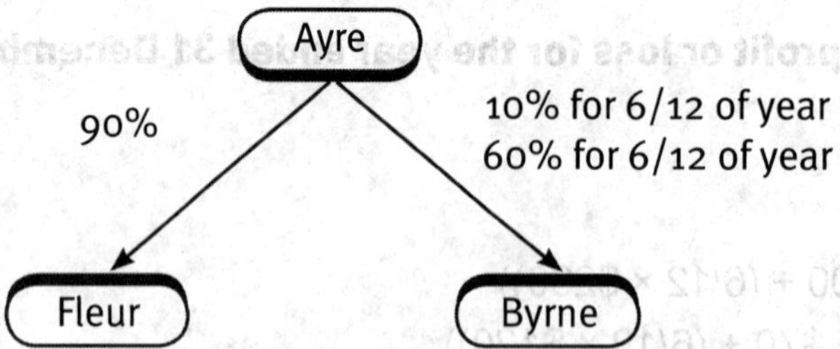

This is a step acquisition. The previous investment in shares must be revalued to fair value with the gain on revaluation recorded in the statement of profit or loss.

Dr Investment ($26,000 – $24,000)	2,000
Cr Profit or loss	2,000

The investment, now held at $26,000, is included in the calculation of goodwill.

Ayre had control over Byrne for 6/12 of the current year. Therefore 6/12 of the incomes and expenses of Byrne are consolidated in full.

(W2) **Profit attributable to the NCI**

	$000	$000
Profit of Fleur in consolidated profit or loss	120	
× 10%		12
Profit of Byrne in consolidated profit or loss (6/12 × $16)	8	
× 40%		3.2
Profit attributable to NCI		15.2

Test your understanding 1 – Major and Tom

The statements of financial position of two entities, Major and Tom, as at 31 December 20X6 are as follows:

	Major	Tom
	$000	$000
Investment	160	
Sundry assets	350	250
	510	250
Equity share capital	200	100
Retained earnings	250	122
Liabilities	60	28
	510	250

Major acquired 40% of Tom on 31 December 20X1 for $90,000. At this time, the retained earnings of Tom stood at $76,000. A further 20% of shares in Tom was acquired by Major three years later for $70,000. On this date, the fair value of the existing holding in Tom was $105,000. Tom's retained earnings were $100,000 on the second acquisition date. The NCI should be valued using the proportion of net assets method.

Required:

Prepare the consolidated statement of financial position for the Major group as at 31 December 20X6.

2 Disposal scenarios

During the year, one entity may sell some or all of its shares in another entity causing a loss of control.

Possible situations include:

(1) the disposal of all the shares held in the subsidiary

(2) the disposal of part of the shareholding, leaving a residual holding after the sale, which is regarded as an associate

(3) the disposal of part of the shareholding, leaving a residual holding after the sale, which is regarded as a trade investment.

The accounting treatment of all of these situations is very similar.

Disposals in the individual financial statements

In all of the above scenarios, the profit on disposal in the investing entity's individual financial statements is calculated as follows:

	$
Sales proceeds	X
Carrying amount (usually cost) of shares sold	(X)
Profit/(loss) on disposal	X/(X)

The profit or loss may need to be reported as an exceptional item. If so, it must be disclosed separately on the face of the parent's statement of profit or loss for the year.

There may be tax to pay on this gain, depending on the tax laws in place in the parent's jurisdiction. This would result in an increase to the parent company's tax expense in the statement of profit or loss.

Disposals in the consolidated financial statements

If the sale of shares causes control over a subsidiary to be lost, then the treatment in the consolidated financial statements is as follows:

- Consolidate the incomes and expenses of the subsidiary up until the disposal date
- On disposal of the subsidiary, derecognise its assets, liabilities, goodwill and non-controlling interest and calculate a profit or loss on disposal
- Recognise any remaining investment in the shares of the former subsidiary at fair value and subsequently account for this under the relevant accounting standard
  - A holding of 20–50% of the shares would probably mean that the remaining investment is an associate, which should be accounted for using the equity method
  - A holding of less than 20% of the shares would probably mean that the remaining investment should be accounted for under IFRS 9 Financial Instruments.

Where control of a subsidiary has been lost, the following template should be used for the calculation of the profit or loss on disposal:

	$	$
Disposal proceeds		X
Fair value of retained interest		X
		X
Less interest in subsidiary disposed of:		
Net assets of subsidiary at disposal date	X	
Goodwill at disposal date	X	
Less: Carrying amount of NCI at disposal date	(X)	
		(X)
Profit/(loss) to the group		X/(X)

Illustration 3 – Rock

Rock has held a 70% investment in Dog for two years. Goodwill has been calculated using the full goodwill method. There have been no goodwill impairments to date.

Rock disposes of all of its shares in Dog. The following information has been provided:

	$
Cost of investment	2,000
Dog – Fair value of net assets at acquisition	1,900
Dog – Fair value of the non-controlling interest at acquisition	800
Sales proceeds	3,000
Dog – Net assets at disposal	2,400

Required:

Calculate the profit or loss on disposal in:

(a) **Rock's individual financial statements**

(b) **the consolidated financial statements.**

Solution

(a) **Rock's individual financial statements**

	$
Sales proceeds	3,000
Cost of shares sold	(2,000)
Profit on disposal	1,000

(b) **Consolidated financial statements**

	$	$
Sales proceeds		3,000
Interest in subsidiary disposed of:		
Net assets at disposal	2,400	
Goodwill at disposal (W1)	900	
Carrying amount of NCI at disposal (W2)	(950)	
		(2,350)
Profit on disposal		650

(W1) **Goodwill**

	$
Consideration	2,000
FV of NCI at acquisition	800
	2,800
FV of net assets at acquisition	(1,900)
Goodwill	900

(W2) **NCI at disposal date**

	$
NCI at acquisition	800
NCI % of post acquisition net assets (30% × ($2,400 – $1,900))	150
	950

Illustration 4 – Thomas and Percy

Thomas disposed of a 25% holding in Percy on 30 June 20X6 for $125,000. A 70% holding in Percy had been acquired five years prior to this. Thomas uses the full goodwill method. Goodwill was impaired and written off in full prior to the year of disposal.

Details of Percy are as follows:

	$
Net assets at disposal date	340,000
Fair value of a 45% holding at 30 June 20X6	245,000

The carrying value of the NCI is $80,000 at the disposal date.

Required:

What is the profit or loss on disposal for inclusion in the consolidated statement of profit or loss for the year ended 31 December 20X6?

Solution

The group's holding in Percy has reduced from 70% to 45%. Control over Percy has been lost and a profit or loss on disposal must be calculated.

The profit on disposal to be included in the consolidated statement of profit or loss is calculated as follows:

	$	$
Proceeds		125,000
FV of retained interest		245,000
		370,000
Net assets recognised at disposal	340,000	
Goodwill at disposal	–	
Less: NCI at disposal date	(80,000)	
		(260,000)
Profit on disposal		110,000

On 30 June 20X6, the remaining investment in Percy will be recognised at its fair value of $245,000. From that date, it will be accounted for using the equity method in the consolidated financial statements.

Test your understanding 2 – Padstow

Padstow purchased 80% of the shares in St Merryn four years ago for $100,000. On 30 June it sold all of these shares for $250,000. The net assets of St Merryn at the acquisition date were $69,000 and at the disposal date were $88,000. Fifty per cent of the goodwill arising on acquisition had been written off in an earlier year. The fair value of the non-controlling interest in St Merryn at the date of acquisition was $15,000. It is group policy to account for goodwill using the full goodwill method.

Tax is charged at 30%.

Required:

(a) **Calculate the profit or loss arising to the parent entity on the disposal of the shares**.

(b) **Calculate the profit or loss arising to the group on the disposal of the shares.**

Test your understanding 3 – Hague

Hague has held a 60% investment in Maude for several years, using the full goodwill method to value the non-controlling interest. Half of the goodwill has been impaired prior to the date of disposal of shares by Hague. Details are as follows:

	$000
Cost of investment	6,000
Maude – Fair value of net assets at acquisition	2,000
Maude – Fair value of a 40% investment at acquisition date	1,000
Maude – Net assets at disposal	3,000
Maude – Fair value of a 25% investment at disposal date	3,500

Required:

(a) **Assuming a full disposal of the holding and proceeds of $10 million, calculate the profit or loss arising:**

(i) **in Hague's individual financial statements**

(ii) **in the consolidated financial statements.**

Tax is 25%.

(b) **Assuming a disposal of a 35% holding and proceeds of $5 million:**

   (i) **calculate the profit or loss arising in the consolidated financial statements**

   (ii) **explain how the residual shareholding will be accounted for.**

Ignore tax.

Presentation of disposed subsidiary in the consolidated financial statements

There are two ways of presenting the results of the disposed subsidiary:

(i) Time-apportionment line-by-line

In the consolidated statement of profit or loss, the income and expenses of the subsidiary are consolidated up to the date of disposal. The traditional way is to time apportion each line of the disposed subsidiary's results.

The profit or loss on disposal of the subsidiary would be presented as an exceptional item.

(ii) Discontinued operation

If the subsidiary qualifies as a discontinued operation in accordance with IFRS 5 then its results are aggregated into a single line on the face of the consolidated statement of profit or loss. This is presented immediately after profit for the period from continuing operations.

This single figure comprises:

- the profit or loss of the subsidiary up to the disposal date
- the profit or loss on the disposal of the subsidiary.

Test your understanding 4 – Kathmandu

The statements of profit or loss and extracts from the statements of changes in equity for the year ended 31 December 20X9 are as follows:

Statements of profit or loss for the year ended 31 December 20X9

	Kathmandu group	Nepal
	$	$
Revenue	553,000	450,000
Operating costs	(450,000)	(400,000)
Operating profits	103,000	50,000
Investment income	8,000	–
Profit before tax	111,000	50,000
Tax	(40,000)	(14,000)
Profit for the period	71,000	36,000

Extracts from SOCIE for year ended 31 December 20X9

	Kathmandu group	Nepal
	$	$
Retained earnings b/f	100,000	80,000
Profit for the period	71,000	36,000
Dividend paid	(25,000)	(10,000)
Retained earnings c/f	146,000	106,000

There were no items of other comprehensive income during the year.

Additional information

- The accounts of the Kathmandu group do not include the results of Nepal.
- On 1 January 20X5 Kathmandu acquired 70% of the shares of Nepal for $100,000 when the fair value of Nepal's net assets was $110,000. Nepal has equity capital of $50,000. At that date, the fair value of the non-controlling interest was $40,000. It is group policy to measure the NCI at fair value at the date of acquisition.
- Nepal paid its 20X9 dividend in cash on 31 March 20X9.
- Goodwill has not been impaired.

Required:

(a) Prepare the group statement of profit or loss for the year ended 31 December 20X9 for the Kathmandu group on the basis that Kathmandu plc sold its holding in Nepal on 1 July 20X9 for $200,000. This disposal is not yet recognised in any way in Kathmandu group's statement of profit or loss. Assume that Nepal does not represent a discontinued operation per IFRS 5.

(b) Explain and illustrate how the presentation of the group statement of profit or loss would differ from part (a) if Nepal represented a discontinued activity per IFRS 5.

(c) Prepare the group statement of profit or loss for the year ended 31 December 20X9 for the Kathmandu group on the basis that Kathmandu sold half of its holding in Nepal on 1 July 20X9 for $100,000 This disposal is not yet recognised in any way in Kathmandu group's statement of profit or loss. The residual holding of 35% has a fair value of $100,000 and leaves the Kathmandu group with significant influence over Nepal.

3 Control to control scenarios

In this chapter, we have looked at:

- share purchases that have led to control over another company being obtained
- share sales that have led to control over another company being lost.

However, some share purchases will simply increase an entity's holding in an already existing subsidiary (e.g. increasing a holding from 80% to 85%). Similarly, some share sales will not cause an entity to lose control over a subsidiary (e.g. decreasing a holding from 80% to 75%).

These 'control to control' scenarios will now be considered in more detail.

Increasing a shareholding in a subsidiary (e.g. 80% to 85%)

When a parent company increases its shareholding in a subsidiary, this is not treated as an acquisition in the group financial statements. For example, if the parent holds 80% of the shares in a subsidiary and buys 5% more then the relationship remains one of a parent and subsidiary. However, the NCI holding has decreased from 20% to 15%.

The accounting treatment of the above situation is as follows:

- The NCI within equity decreases
- The difference between the consideration paid for the extra shares and the decrease in the NCI is accounted for within equity (normally, in 'other components of equity').

Note that **no profit or loss** arises on the purchase of the additional shares. Goodwill is **not recalculated.**

The following proforma will help to calculate the adjustments required to NCI and other components of equity:

	$	
Cash paid	X	Cr
Decrease in NCI	(X)	Dr
Decrease/(increase) to other components of equity	X/(X)	Dr/Cr (bal. entry)

The decrease in NCI will represent the proportionate reduction in the carrying amount of the NCI at the date of the group's additional purchase of shares

- For example, if the NCI shareholding reduces from 30% to 20%, then the carrying amount of the NCI must be reduced by one-third.

Test your understanding 5 – Gordon and Mandy

Gordon has owned 80% of Mandy for many years.

Gordon is considering acquiring more shares in Mandy. The NCI of Mandy currently has a carrying amount of $20,000, with the net assets and goodwill having a carrying amount of $125,000 and $25,000 respectively.

Gordon is considering the following two scenarios:

(i) Gordon could buy 20% of the Mandy shares leaving no NCI for $25,000, or

(ii) Gordon could buy 5% of the Mandy shares for $4,000 leaving a 15% NCI.

Required:

Calculate the adjustments required to NCI and other components of equity.

Sale of shares without losing control (e.g. 80% to 75%)

From the perspective of the group accounts, a sale of shares which results in the parent retaining control over the subsidiary is simply a transaction between shareholders. If the parent company holds 80% of the shares of a subsidiary but then sells a 5% holding, a relationship of control still exists. As such, the subsidiary will still be consolidated in the group financial statements. However, the NCI has risen from 20% to 25%.

The accounting treatment of the above situation is as follows:

- The NCI within equity is increased
- The difference between the proceeds received and the increase in the non-controlling interest is accounted within equity (normally, in 'other components of equity').

Note that **no profit or loss** arises on the sale of the shares. Goodwill is **not recalculated.**

The following proforma will help to calculate the adjustments required to NCI and other components of equity:

	$	
Cash proceeds received	X	Dr
Increase in NCI	(X)	Cr
Increase/(Decrease) to other components of equity	X/ (X)	Cr/Dr (bal. entry)

The increase in the NCI will be the share of the net assets (always) and goodwill (fair value method only) of the subsidiary at the date of disposal which the parent has effectively sold to the NCI.

- For example, if the NCI shareholding increases from 20% to 30%, then the carrying amount of the NCI must be increased by 10% of the subsidiary's net assets and, if using the fair value method, goodwill.

Illustration 5 – No loss of control – Juno

Until 30 September 20X7, Juno held 90% of Hera. On that date it sold a 10% interest in the equity capital for $15,000. At the date of the share disposal, the carrying amount of net assets and goodwill of Juno were $100,000 and $20,000 respectively. At acquisition, the NCI was valued at fair value.

Required:

How should the sale of shares be accounted for in the Juno Group's financial statements?

Solution

	$	
Cash proceeds	15,000	Dr
Increase in NCI: 10% × ($100,000 + $20,000)	(12,000)	Cr
Increase in other components of equity (bal. fig)	3,000	Cr

There is no gain or loss to the group as there has been no loss of control. Note that, depending upon the terms of the share disposal, there could be either an increase or decrease in equity.

Test your understanding 6 – David and Goliath

David has owned 90% of Goliath for many years and is considering selling part of its holding, whilst retaining control of Goliath.

At the date of considering disposal of part of the shareholding in Goliath, the NCI has a carrying amount of $7,200 and the net assets and goodwill have a carrying amount of $70,000 and $20,000 respectively. The NCI was valued at fair value at the acquisition date.

(i) David could sell 5% of the Goliath shares for $5,000 leaving it holding 85% and increasing the NCI to 15%, or

(ii) David could sell 25% of the Goliath shares for $20,000 leaving it holding 65% and increasing the NCI to 35%.

Required:

How would these share sales be accounted for in the consolidated financial statements of the David group?

Test your understanding 7 – Pepsi

Statements of financial position for three entities at the reporting date are as follows:

	Pepsi	**Sprite**	**Tango**
	$000	$000	$000
Assets	1,000	800	500
Investment in Sprite	326	–	–
Investment in Tango	165	–	–
Total assets	1,491	800	500
Equity			
Ordinary share capital ($1)	500	200	100
Retained earnings	391	100	200
	891	300	300
Liabilities	600	500	200
Total equity and liabilities	1,491	800	500

Pepsi acquired 80% of Sprite when Sprite's retained earnings were $25,000, paying cash consideration of $300,000. It is group policy to measure NCI at fair value at the date of acquisition. The fair value of the NCI holding in Sprite at acquisition was $65,000.

At the reporting date, Pepsi purchased an additional 8% of Sprite's equity shares for cash consideration of $26,000. This amount has been debited to Pepsi's investment in Sprite.

Pepsi acquired 75% of Tango when Tango's retained earnings were $60,000, paying cash consideration of $200,000. The fair value of the NCI holding in Tango at the date of acquisition was $50,000.

At the reporting date, Pepsi sold 10% of the equity shares of Tango for $35,000. The cash proceeds have been credited to Pepsi's investment in Tango.

Required:

Prepare the consolidated statement of financial position of the Pepsi group.

4 Subsidiaries acquired exclusively with a view to resale

Subsidiaries acquired exclusively with a view to subsequent

A subsidiary acquired exclusively with a view to resale is not exempt from consolidation. However, if it meets the 'held for sale' criteria in IFRS 5 Non-current Assets Held for Sale and Discontinued Operations:

- it is presented in the financial statements as a disposal group classified as held for sale. This is achieved by amalgamating all its assets into one line item and all its liabilities into another
- it is measured, both on acquisition and at subsequent reporting dates, at fair value less costs to sell. (IFRS 5 sets down a special rule for such subsidiaries, requiring the deduction of costs to sell. Normally, it requires acquired assets and liabilities to be measured at fair value).

The 'held for sale' criteria in IFRS 5 include the requirements that:

- the subsidiary is available for immediate sale
- the sale is highly probable
- it is likely to be disposed of within one year of the date of its acquisition.

A newly acquired subsidiary which meets these held for sale criteria automatically meets the criteria for being presented as a discontinued operation.

Illustration: IFRS 5

David acquires Rose on 1 March 20X7. Rose is a holding entity with two wholly-owned subsidiaries, Mickey and Jackie. Jackie is acquired exclusively with a view to resale and meets the criteria for classification as held for sale. David's year-end is 30 September.

On 1 March 20X7 the following information is relevant:

- the identifiable liabilities of Jackie have a fair value of $40m
- the acquired assets of Jackie have a fair value of $180m
- the expected costs of selling Jackie are $5m.

On 30 September 20X7, the assets of Jackie have a fair value of $170m.

The liabilities have a fair value of $35m and the selling costs remain at $5m.

Discuss how Jackie will be treated in the David Group financial statements on acquisition and at 30 September 20X7.

Solution

On acquisition the assets and liabilities of Jackie are measured at fair value less costs to sell in accordance with IFRS 5:

	$m
Assets	180
Less selling costs	(5)
	175
Liabilities	(40)
Fair value less costs to sell	135

At the reporting date, the assets and liabilities of Jackie are remeasured to update the fair value less costs to sell.

	$m
Assets	170
Less selling costs	(5)
	165
Liabilities	(35)
Fair value less costs to sell	130

The fair value less costs to sell has decreased from $135m on 1 March to $130m on 30 September. This $5m reduction in fair value must be presented in the consolidated statement of profit or loss as part of the single line item entitled 'discontinued operations'. Also included in this line is the post-tax profit or loss earned/incurred by Jackie in the March – September 20X7 period.

The assets and liabilities of Jackie must be disclosed separately on the face of the statement of financial position. Jackie's assets will appear below the subtotal for the David group's current assets:

	$m
Non-current assets classified as held for sale	165

Jackie's liabilities will appear below the subtotal for the David group's current liabilities:

	$m
Liabilities directly associated with non-current assets classified as held for sale	35

No other disclosure is required.

5 Chapter summary

DISPOSALS

Parent entity accounts
Gain:

Proceeds	X
Cost	(X)
	X

Group accounts gain
- No gain or loss where no loss of control
- If control is lost, calculate gain as:

proceeds		X
FV of any interest retained		X
Net assets of sub at disposal	X	
Goodwill at disposal	X	
NCI at disposal	(X)	
		(X)
		(X)

Whole shareholding disposal of P/L: consolidate to disposal and show group gain
SFP: subsidiary's net assets not included

IFRSs Disclosure discontinued operations

No loss of control
P/L: consolidate for full year, calculate NCI pre and post disposal
SFP: consolidate as normal with NCI based on year end holding, account for gain or loss to NCI in equity

Associate shareholding retained
P/L: consolidate to date of disposal, then equity account, show gain
SFP: equity account at year end based on FV of associate shareholding at disposal

Trade investment shareholding retained
P/L: consolidate to date of disposal, then include dividend income, show gain
SFP: Record retained investment at fair value at disposal date

Subsidiaries acquired with a view to subsequent disposal must consolidate present as disposal group; measure at lower of CV and FV - selling costs

Step Acquisitions:
Parent acquires control over subsidiary in stages.

At date of acquiring control, revalue existing equity holding to FV and recognise gain or loss in profit or loss. Goodwill calculated as normal at date control is acquired

Acquisition of further shares after control is acquired are accounted for in equity. Goodwill is not remeasured.

Test your understanding answers

Test your understanding 1 – Major and Tom

Consolidated statement of financial position for Major as at 31 December 20X6

	$
Goodwill (W3)	55,000
Sundry assets ($350,000 + $250,000)	600,000
	655,000
Equity and liabilities	$
Equity share capital	200,000
Retained earnings (W5)	278,200
Non-controlling interest (W4)	88,800
Liabilities ($60,000 + $28,000)	88,000
	655,000

(W1) **Group structure**

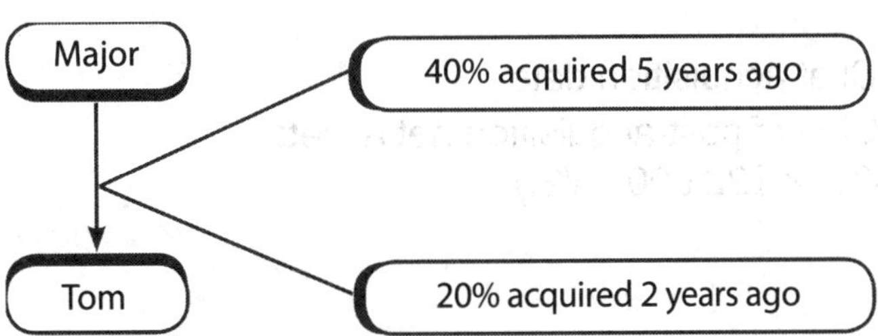

Tom becomes a subsidiary of Major from December 20X4.

The previously held investment must be revalued to fair value with the gain or loss recorded in the statement of profit or loss.

Dr Investment	
($105,000 – $90,000)	15,000
Cr Profit or loss	15,000

(W2) **Net assets**

	At Acquisition 20X4	At Reporting date
	$	$
Share capital	100,000	100,000
Retained earnings	100,000	122,000
	200,000	222,000

(W3) **Goodwill**

	$
Fair value of previously held interest	105,000
Fair value of consideration for additional interest	70,000
	175,000
NCI at acquisition (40% × $200,000)	80,000
Less: FV of net assets at acquisition (W2)	(200,000)
	55,000

(W4) **Non-controlling interest**

	$
NCI at acquisition date	80,000
NCI % of post-acquisition net assets (40% × $22,000 (W2))	8,800
	88,800

(W5) **Group Retained earnings**

	$
Major	250,000
Gain on revaluation of investment (W1)	15,000
Tom (60% × $22,000 (W2))	13,200
	278,200

Test your understanding 2 – Padstow

(a) **Profit to Padstow**

	$000
Sales proceeds	250
Cost of shares sold	(100)
Profit on disposal	150

The tax due on the profit on disposal is: ($150,000 × 30%)	45

The profit on disposal will be disclosed as an exceptional item in the statement of profit or loss.

The tax on the gain will be charged to the statement of profit or loss as part of the year's current tax charge.

(b) **Consolidated accounts**

	$000	$000
Sales proceeds		250
Net assets at disposal date	88.0	
Goodwill at disposal date (W1)	23.0	
Less: NCI at disposal date (W2)	(14.2)	
		(96.8)
Profit on disposal		153.2

The tax of $45,000 that arose on the disposal in the parent's financial statements will be consolidated into the group financial statements.

(W1) **Goodwill**

	$000
Consideration	100.0
NCI at acquisition	15.0
	115.0
FV of net assets at acquisition	(69.0)
Goodwill at acquisition	46.0
Impairment ($46 × 50%)	(23.0)
Goodwill at disposal date	23.0

(W2) **NCI at disposal date**

	$000
NCI at acquisition	15.0
NCI % of post-acq'n net assets movement (20% × ($88.0 – $69.0))	3.8
NCI % of impairment (20% × $23.0 (W1))	(4.6)
	14.2

Test your understanding 3 – Hague

(a) **Full disposal**

(i) **Profit in Hague's individual financial statements**

	$000
Sale proceeds	10,000
Cost of shares	(6,000)
Profit on disposal	4,000
Tax charge on disposal: (25% × $4,000)	(1,000)

(ii) **Profit in consolidated financial statements**

	$000	$000
Sale proceeds		10,000
FV of retained interest		nil
CV of subsidiary at disposal:		
Net assets at disposal:	3,000	
Goodwill at disposal (W1)	2,500	
Less: NCI at disposal date (W2)	(400)	
		(5,100)
Profit on disposal		4,900

(W1) **Goodwill**

	$000
Consideration	6,000
NCI at acquisition	1,000
	7,000
FV of NA at acquisition (given)	(2,000)
Goodwill at acquisition	5,000
Impaired (50%)	(2,500)
Goodwill at disposal	2,500

(W2) **NCI at disposal date**

	$000
NCI at acquisition	1,000
NCI share of post-acquisition net assets (40% × ($3,000 – $2,000))	400
Less: NCI share of goodwill impairment (40% × $2,500) (W1)	(1,000)
	400

(b) **Disposal of a 35% shareholding**

(i) **Profit in consolidated financial statements**

	$000	$000
Disposal proceeds		5,000
FV of retained interest		3,500
		8,500
CV of subsidiary at disposal date:		
Net assets at disposal	3,000	
Goodwill at disposal (W1)	2,500	
Less: NCI at disposal date (W2)	(400)	
		(5,100)
Profit on disposal		3,400

(ii) After the date of disposal, the residual holding will be accounted for using the equity method in the consolidated financial statements:

– The statement of profit or loss will show the group's share of the current year profit earned by the associate from the date significant influence was obtained.

– The statement of financial position will show the carrying value of the investment in the associate. This will be the fair value of the retained shareholding at the disposal date plus the group's share of the increase in reserves from this date.

Test your understanding 4 – Kathmandu

(a) **Consolidated statement of profit or loss – full disposal**

	$
Revenue ($553,000 + (6/12 × $450,000))	778,000
Operating costs ($450,000 + (6/12 × $400,000))	(650,000)
Operating profit	128,000
Investment income ($8,000 – ($10,000 × 70%))	1,000
Profit on disposal (W1)	80,400
Profit before tax	209,400
Tax ($40,000 + (6/12 × $14,000))	(47,000)
Profit for the period	162,400
Attributable to:	
Equity holders of Kathmandu (bal. fig)	157,000
Non-controlling interest (W5)	5,400
	162,400

There were no items of other comprehensive income during the year.

(b) **Group statement of profit or loss – discontinued operations presentation**

	$
Revenue	553,000
Operating costs	(450,000)
Operating profit	103,000
Investment income ($8,000 – (70% × $10,000))	1,000
Profit before tax	104,000
Tax	(40,000)
Profit for the period from continuing operations	64,000
Profit from discontinued operations (($36,000 × 6/12)+ $80,400 (W1))	98,400
	162,400
Attributable to:	
Equity holders of Kathmandu (bal. fig)	157,000
Non-controlling interest (W5)	5,400
	162,400

There were no items of other comprehensive income during the year.

Notice that the post-tax results of the subsidiary up to the date of disposal are presented as a one-line entry in the group statement of profit or loss. There is no line-by-line consolidation of results when this method of presentation is adopted.

(c) **Consolidated statement of profit or loss – partial disposal**

	$
Revenue ($553,000 + (6/12 × $450,000)	778,000
Operating costs ($450,000 + (6/12 × $400,000))	(650,000)
Operating profit	128,000
Investment income ($8,000 – (70% × $10,000)	1,000
Income from associate (35% × $36,000 × 6/12)	6,300
Profit on disposal (W6)	80,400
Profit before tax	215,700
Tax ($40,000 + (6/12 × $14,000))	(47,000)
Profit for the period	168,700

There were no items of other comprehensive income during the year.

Attributable to:	
Equity holders of Kathmandu (bal. fig)	163,300
Non-controlling interest (W5)	
	5,400
	168,700

(W1) **Profit on full disposal (part a)**

	$	$
Proceeds		200,000
Interest in subsidiary disposed of:		
Net assets at disposal (W2)	138,000	
Goodwill at disposal (W3)	30,000	
NCI at date of disposal (W4)	(48,400)	
		(119,600)
Profit on disposal		80,400

(W2) Net assets of Nepal at disposal

	$
Share capital	50,000
Retained earnings b/f	80,000
Profit up to disposal date (6/12 × $36,000)	18,000
Dividend paid prior to disposal	(10,000)
Net assets at disposal	138,000

(W3) Goodwill

	$
Consideration	100,000
FV of NCI at date of acquisition	40,000
	140,000
FV of net assets at date of acquisition	(110,000)
Goodwill	30,000

(W4) NCI at disposal date

FV of NCI at date of acquisition	40,000
NCI share of post-acquisition net assets (30% × ($138,000 (W2) – $110,000)	8,400
	48,400

(W5) Profit attributable to NCI

	$	$
Profit of Nepal (6/12 × $36,000)	18,000	
× 30%	18,000	
Profit attributable to NCI		5,400

(W6) **Profit on part disposal (part c)**

	$	$
Proceeds		100,000
FV of retained interest (per question)		100,000
		200,000
Net assets at disposal (W2)	138,000	
Unimpaired goodwill at disposal date (W3)	30,000	
	168,000	
NCI at date of disposal (W4)	(48,400)	
		(119,600)
Profit on disposal		80,400

Test your understanding 5 – Gordon and Mandy

(i) **Purchase of 20% of Mandy shares**

	$
Cash paid	25,000 Cr
Decrease in NCI ((20%/20%) × 20,000)	(20,000) Dr
Decrease in other components of equity	5.000 Dr

(ii) **Purchase of 5% of Mandy shares**

	$
Cash paid	4,000 Cr
Decrease in NCI ((5%/20%) × 20,000)	(5,000) Dr
Increase in other components of equity	(1,000) Cr

Test your understanding 6 – David and Goliath

(i) **Sale of 5% of Goliath shares**

	$
Cash proceeds	5,000 Dr
Increase in NCI (5% × ($70,000 + $20,000)	(4,500) Cr
Increase in other components of equity	500 Cr

(ii) **Sale of 25% of Goliath shares**

	$
Cash proceeds	20,000 Dr
Increase in NCI (25% × ($70,000 + $20,000)	(22,500) Cr
Decrease in other components of equity	(2,500) Dr

Note that in both situations, Goliath remains a subsidiary of David after the sale of shares. There is no gain or loss to the group – the difference arising is taken to equity. Goliath would continue to be consolidated within the David Group like any other subsidiary. There is no change to the carrying value of goodwill. The only impact will be the calculation of NCI share of retained earnings for the year – this would need to be time-apportioned based upon the NCI percentage pre- and post-disposal during the year.

Test your understanding 7 – Pepsi

Consolidated statement of financial position

	$000
Assets ($1,000 + $800 + $500)	2,300
Goodwill ($140 + $90) (W3)	230
Total assets	2,530
Equity	
Ordinary share capital ($1)	500
Retained earnings (W5)	556
Other components of equity ($6 – $4) (W6, W7)	2
	1,058
Non-controlling interests ($48 + $124) (W4)	172
	1,230
Liabilities ($600 + $500 + $200)	1,300
Total equity and liabilities	2,530

Workings

(W1) **Group structure**

Pepsi

Sprite Tango

Initial holding:	80%	Initial holding	75%
Acquisition:	8%	Disposal	(10%)
Reporting date	88%	Reporting date	65%

(W2) **Net Assets of subsidiaries**

Sprite	**Acquisition date**	**Reporting date**
	$000	$000
Share capital	200	200
Retained earnings	25	100
	225	300

Tango	**Acquisition date**	**Reporting date**
	$000	$000
Share capital	100	100
Retained earnings	60	200
	160	300

(W3) **Goodwill**

Sprite	$000
Consideration	300
FV of NCI at acquisition	65
Fair value of net assets at acquisition (W2)	(225)
	140

Tango	$000
Consideration	200
FV of NCI at acquisition	50
Fair value of net assets at acquisition (W2)	(160)
	90

(W4) **Non-controlling interest**

Sprite	$000
NCI at acquisition (W3)	65
NCI% × post acquisition net assets (20% × $75 (W2))	15
NCI before control to control adjustment	80
Decrease in NCI (W6)	(32)
	48

Tango	$000
NCI at acquisition (W3)	50
NCI% × post acquisition net assets (25% × $140 (W2))	35
NCI before control to control adjustment	85
Increase in NCI (W7)	39
	124

(W5) **Retained earnings**

	$000
Pepsi's retained earnings	391
Pepsi's % of Sprite's post acquisition retained earnings (80% × $75 (W2))	60
Pepsi's % of Tango's post acquisition retained earnings (75% × $140 (W2))	105
	556

(W6) **Control to control adjustment – Sprite**

	$000	
Cash paid	26	Cr
Decrease in NCI (8/20 × $80 (W4))	(32)	Dr
Increase to other components of equity	(6)	Cr

(W7) **Control to control adjustment – Tango**

	$000	
Cash received	35	Dr
Increase in NCI (10% × ($300 (W2) + $90 (W3))	(39)	Cr
Decrease to other components of equity	(4)	Dr

chapter

22

Group accounting – foreign currency

Chapter learning objectives

Upon completion of this chapter you will be able to:

- account for the consolidation of foreign operations and their disposal.

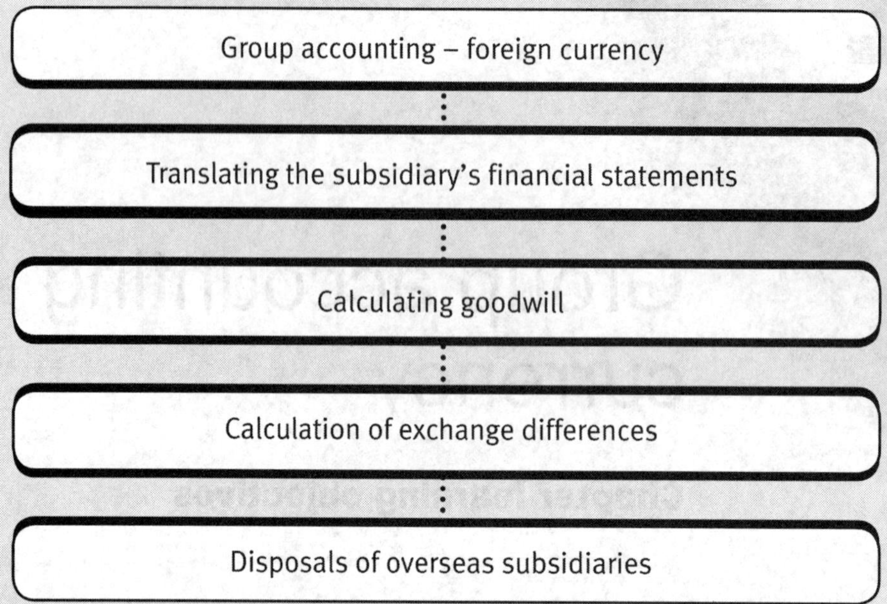

1 Key definitions

Foreign currency transactions in the individual financial statements of a company were covered earlier in this text.

Below is a reminder of some key definitions:

The **functional currency** is the currency of the **'primary economic environment where the entity operates'** (IAS 21, para 8). In most cases this will be the local currency.

The **presentation currency** is the **'currency in which the entity presents its financial statements'** (IAS 21, para 8).

2 Consolidation of a foreign operation

The functional currency used by a subsidiary to prepare its own individual accounting records and financial statements may differ from the presentation currency used for the group financial statements. Therefore, prior to adding together the assets, liabilities, incomes and expenses of the parent and subsidiary, the financial statements of an overseas subsidiary must be translated.

Translating the subsidiary's financial statements

The rules for translating an overseas subsidiary into the presentation currency of the group are as follows:

- **Incomes, expenses and other comprehensive income** are translated at the rate in place at the date of each transaction. The average rate for the year may be used as an approximation.
- **Assets and liabilities** are translated at the closing rate.

Illustration 1 – Dragon

This example runs through the chapter and is used to illustrate the basic steps involved in consolidating an overseas subsidiary.

Dragon bought 90% of the ordinary shares of Tattoo for DN180 million on 31 December 20X0. The retained earnings of Tattoo at this date were DN65 million. The fair value of the non-controlling interest at the acquisition date was DN14 million.

The financial statements of Dragon and Tattoo for the year ended 31 December 20X1 are presented below:

Statements of profit or loss for year ended 31 December 20X1

	Dragon	**Tattoo**
	$m	DNm
Revenue	1,200	600
Costs	(1,000)	(450)
Profit	200	150

Statements of financial position as at 31 December 20X1

	Dragon	**Tattoo**
	$m	DNm
Property, plant and equipment	290	270
Investments	60	–
Current assets	150	130
	500	400

Share capital	10	5
Retained earnings	290	215
Liabilities	200	180
	500	400

There has been no intra-group trading. Goodwill arising on the acquisition of Tattoo is not impaired. The presentation currency of the consolidated financial statements is the dollar ($).

Exchange rates are as follows:

	DN to $
31 December 20X0	3.0
31 December 20X1	2.0
Average for year to 31 December 20X1	2.6

Required:

For inclusion in the consolidated statement of profit or loss and other comprehensive income for the year ended 31 December 20X1, calculate:

- **Revenue**
- **Costs**

For inclusion in the consolidated statement of financial position as at 31 December 20X1, calculate:

- **Property, plant and equipment**
- **Investments**
- **Current assets**
- **Share capital**
- **Liabilities**

Solution

	$m
Revenue ($1,200 + (DN600/2.6))	1,430.8
Costs ($1,000 + (DN450/2.6))	(1,173.1)
PPE ($290 + (DN270/2))	425.0
Investments (eliminated on consolidation)	–
Current assets ($150 + (DN130/2))	215.0
Share capital (Dragon only)	10.0
Liabilities ($200 + (DN180/2))	290.0

Remember, the incomes and expenses of an overseas subsidiary are translated at the average rate. The assets and liabilities are translated at the closing rate.

Translating goodwill

Goodwill should be calculated in the functional currency of the subsidiary.

According to IAS 21, goodwill should be treated like other assets of the subsidiary and therefore translated at the reporting date using the closing rate.

As with all consolidated statement of financial position questions, it may be helpful to produce a table showing the subsidiary's net assets (at fair value) at both the year end and acquisition date ('Working 2'). This should be completed in the functional currency of the subsidiary.

Illustration 2 – Goodwill

Required:

Using the information in illustration 1, calculate goodwill for inclusion in the consolidated statement of financial position for the Dragon group as at 31 December 20X1.

Solution

Goodwill calculation

	DNm
Consideration	180
NCI at acquisition	14
Net assets at acquisition (W)	(70)
	124
Goodwill impairments	–
	124

Goodwill is translated at the closing rate to give a value of $62m (DN124/2).

(W) **Net assets of Tattoo**

	Acquisition date	Reporting date	Post-acquisition
	DNm	DNm	DNm
Share capital	5	5	
Retained earnings	65	215	
	70	220	150

Exchange differences

The process of translating an overseas subsidiary gives rise to exchange gains and losses. These gains and losses arise for the following reasons:

- **Goodwill**: Goodwill is retranslated each year-end at the closing rate. It will therefore increase or decrease in value simply because of exchange rate movements.
- **Opening net assets**: At the end of the prior year, the net assets of the subsidiary were translated at the prior year closing rate. This year, those same net assets are translated at this year's closing rate. Therefore, opening net assets will have increased or decreased simply because of exchange rate movements.

- **Profit**: The incomes and expenses (and, therefore, the profit) of the overseas subsidiary are translated at the average rate. However, making a profit increases the subsidiary's assets which are translated at the closing rate. This disparity creates an exchange gain or loss.

Current year exchange gains or losses on the translation of an overseas subsidiary and its goodwill are recorded in other comprehensive income.

Goodwill translation

The proforma for calculating the current year gain or loss on the retranslation of goodwill is as follows:

	DN	Exchange Rate	$
Opening goodwill	X	Opening rate	X
Impairment loss in year	(X)	Average rate	(X)
Exchange gain/(loss)	–	**Bal fig.**	X/(X)
Closing goodwill	X	Closing rate	X

If the subsidiary was purchased part-way through the current year, then substitute 'opening goodwill' for 'goodwill at acquisition'. This would then be translated at the rate of exchange on the acquisition date.

It is important to pay attention to the method of goodwill calculation:

- If the full goodwill method has been used, gain and losses will need to be apportioned between the group and the non-controlling interest.
- If the proportionate goodwill method has been used, then all of the exchange gain or loss on goodwill is attributable to the group.

Illustration 3 – Translating goodwill

Required:

Using the information in illustration 1, calculate the exchange gain or loss arising on the translation of the goodwill that will be credited/charged through other comprehensive income in the year ended 31 December 20X1.

Who is this gain or loss attributable to?

Solution

	DNm	Exchange Rate	$m
Opening goodwill	124.0	3.0	41.3
Impairment loss in year	–	2.6	–
Exchange gain	–	**Bal fig.**	20.7
Closing goodwill	124.0	2.0	62.0

The total translation gain of $20.7m will be credited to other comprehensive income.

This is then allocated to the group and NCI based on their respective shareholdings:

Group: $20.7m × 90% = $18.6m
NCI: $20.7m × 10% = $2.1m

Opening net assets and profit

The exchange gains or losses arising on the translation of opening net assets and profit for the year are generally calculated together.

The proforma for calculating the current year exchange gain or loss on the translation of the opening net assets and profit is as follows:

	DN	Exchange Rate	$
Opening net assets	X	Opening rate	X
Profit/(loss) for the year	X/(X)	Average rate	X/(X)
Exchange gain/(loss)	–	**Bal fig.**	X/(X)
Closing net assets	X	Closing rate	X

If the subsidiary was purchased part-way through the current year, then substitute 'opening net assets' and 'opening rate' for 'acquisition net assets' and 'acquisition rate'.

The gain or loss on translation of the opening net assets and profit is apportioned between the group and non-controlling interest based on their respective shareholdings.

Illustration 4 – Opening net assets and profit

Required:

Using the information in illustration 1, calculate the exchange gain or loss arising on the translation of the opening net assets and profit of Tattoo that will be credited/charged through other comprehensive income in the year ended 31 December 20X1.

Who are these gains or losses attributable to?

Solution

	DNm	Exchange Rate	$m
Opening net assets*	70	3.0	23.3
Profit/(loss) for the year*	150	2.6	57.7
Exchange gain/(loss)	–	**Bal fig.**	29.0
Closing net assets*	220	2.0	110.0

*These figures are taken from the net assets working, which can be found in the solution to illustration 2.

The total translation gain of $29.0m will be credited to other comprehensive income.

This is then allocated to the group and NCI based on their respective shareholdings:

Group: 29.0 × 90% = $26.1m
NCI: 29.0 × 10% = $2.9m

Exchange differences on the statement of financial position

Exchange gains and losses arising from the translation of goodwill and the subsidiary's opening net assets and profit which are attributable to the group are normally held in a translation reserve, a separate component within equity.

Illustration 5 – Reserves

Required:

Using the information in illustration 1, calculate the non-controlling interest, retained earnings and the translation reserve for inclusion in the consolidated statement of financial position as at 31 December 20X1.

Solution

Non-controlling interest

	$m
NCI at acquisition (DN14/3 opening rate)	4.7
NCI % of Tattoo's post-acquisition profits (10% × (DN150/2.6 average rate))	5.7
NCI % of goodwill translation (illustration 3)	2.1
NCI % of net assets and profit translation (illustration 4)	2.9
	15.4

Retained earnings

	$m
100% of Dragon	290.0
90% of Tattoo's post-acquisition profits (90% × (DN150/2.6))	51.9
	341.9

Translation reserve

	$m
Group share of goodwill forex (illustration 3)	18.6
Group share of net assets and profit forex (illustration 4)	26.1
	44.7

Illustration 6 – Completing the financial statements

Required:

Using the information in illustration 1, complete the consolidated statement of financial position and the statement of profit or loss and other comprehensive income for the Tattoo group for the year ended 31 December 20X1.

Solution

Statement of profit or loss and other comprehensive income for year ended 31 December 20X1

	$m
Revenue (illustration 1)	1,430.8
Costs (illustration 1)	(1,173.1)
Profit for the year	257.7
Other comprehensive income – items that may be classified to profit or loss in future periods	
Exchange differences on translation of foreign subsidiary ($20.7 (illustration 3) + $29.0 (illustration 4))	49.7
Total comprehensive income for the year	307.4
Profit attributable to:	
Owners of Dragon (bal. fig.)	251.9
Non-controlling interest (10% × (DN150/2.6 avg. rate))	5.8
Profit for the year	257.7
Total comprehensive income attributable to:	
Owners of Dragon (bal. fig.)	296.6
Non-controlling interest ($5.8 (profit) + $2.1 (illustration 3) + $2.9 (illustration 4))	10.8
Total comprehensive income for the year	307.4

Statement of financial position as at 31 December 20X1

	$m
Property, plant and equipment (illustration 1)	425.0
Goodwill (illustration 2)	62.0
Current assets (illustration 1)	215.0
	702.0
Share capital (illustration 1)	10.0
Retained earnings (illustration 5)	341.9
Translation reserve (illustration 5)	44.7
	396.6
Non-controlling interest (illustration 5)	15.4
	412.0
Liabilities (illustration 1)	290.0
	702.0

Test your understanding 1 – Parent and Overseas

Parent is an entity that owns 80% of the equity shares of Overseas, a foreign entity that has the Shilling as its functional currency. The subsidiary was acquired at the start of the current accounting period on 1 January 20X7 when its retained earnings were 6,000 Shillings.

At that date the fair value of the net assets of the subsidiary was 20,000 Shillings. This included a fair value adjustment in respect of land of 4,000 Shillings that the subsidiary has not incorporated into its accounting records and still owns.

Goodwill, which is unimpaired at the reporting date, is to be accounted for using the full goodwill method. At the date of acquisition, the non-controlling interest in Overseas had a fair value of 5,000 Shillings.

Statements of financial position:

	Parent	Overseas
	$	Shillings
Investment (20,999 shillings)	3,818	
Assets	9,500	40,000
	13,318	40,000
Equity and liabilities		
Equity capital	5,000	10,000
Retained earnings	6,000	8,200
Liabilities	2,318	21,800
	13,318	40,000

Statement of profit or loss for the year:

	Parent	Overseas
	$	Shillings
Revenue	8,000	5,200
Costs	(2,500)	(2,600)
Profit before tax	5,500	2,600
Tax	(2,000)	(400)
Profit for the year	3,500	2,200

Neither entity recognised any other comprehensive income in their individual financial statements during the reporting period.

Relevant exchange rates (Shillings to $1) are:

Date	Shillings: $1
1 January 20X7	5.5
31 December 20X7	5.0
Average for year to 31 December 20X7	5.2

Required:

Prepare the consolidated statement of financial position at 31 December 20X7, together with a consolidated statement of profit or loss and other comprehensive income for the year ended 31 December 20X7.

Test your understanding 2 – Saint and Albans

On the 1 July 20X1 Saint acquired 60% of Albans, whose functional currency is Ds. The presentation currency of the Saint group is the dollar ($). The financial statements of both entities are as follows.

Statements of financial position as at 30 June 20X2

	Saint	Albans
Assets	$	D
Investment in Albans	5,000	–
Loan to Albans	1,400	–
Property, plant and equipment	10,000	15,400
Inventories	5,000	4,000
Receivables	4,000	500
Cash and cash equivalents	1,600	560
	27,000	20,460
Equity and liabilities	$	D
Equity capital ($1/D1)	10,000	1,000
Share premium	3,000	500
Retained earnings	4,000	12,500
Non-current liabilities	5,000	5,460
Current liabilities	5,000	1,000
	27,000	20,460

Statements of profit or loss for the year ended 30 June 20X2

	Saint	Albans
	$	D
Revenue	50,000	60,000
Cost of sales	(20,000)	(30,000)
Gross profit	30,000	30,000
Distribution and Administration expenses	(20,000)	(12,000)
Profit before tax	10,000	18,000
Tax	(8,000)	(6,000)
Profit for the year	2,000	12,000

Note: There were no items of other comprehensive income within the individual financial statements of either entity.

The following information is applicable.

(i) Saint purchased the shares in Albans for D10,000 on the first day of the accounting period. At the date of acquisition the retained earnings of Albans were D500 and there was an upward fair value adjustment of D1,000. The fair value adjustment is attributable to plant with a remaining five-year life as at the date of acquisition. This plant remains held by Albans and has not been revalued.

(ii) Just before the year-end Saint acquired some goods from a third party at a cost of $800, which it sold to Albans for cash at a mark up of 50%. At the reporting date all these goods remain in the inventories of Albans.

(iii) On 1 June X2 Saint lent Albans $1,400. The liability is recorded at the historic rate within the non-current liabilities of Albans.

(iv) No dividends have been paid.

(v) Goodwill is to be accounted using the full goodwill method. An impairment review was performed and goodwill had reduced in value by 10% at 30 June 20X2. Impairment is to be charged to cost of sales. The fair value of the non-controlling interest at the date of acquisition was D5,000.

(vi) On 1 July 20X1, Saint received a government grant for $4,000. This grant was provided as a contribution towards the costs of training employees over the next two years. Saint has reduced its administrative expenses by the full $4,000.

(vii) On 30 June 20X2, Saint sold $2,000 of receivables to a factor for $1,500. Saint must reimburse the factor with any amounts not collected by 31 December 20X2. Saint has credited the proceeds received against receivables.

(viii) Exchange rates are as follows:

	D: $1
1 July 20X1	2.00
Average rate	3.00
1 June 20X2	3.90
30 June 20X2	4.00

Required:

Prepare the group statement of financial position as at 30 June 20X2 and the group statement of profit or loss and other comprehensive income for the year ended 30 June 20X2.

3 Disposals

On the disposal of a foreign subsidiary, the cumulative exchange differences recognised as other comprehensive income and accumulated in a separate component of equity become realised.

IAS 21 requires that these exchanges differences are recycled (i.e. reclassified) on the disposal of the subsidiary as part of the profit/loss on disposal.

Test your understanding 3 – LUMS Group

The LUMS group has sold its entire 100% holding in an overseas subsidiary for proceeds of $50,000. The net assets at the date of disposal were $20,000 and the carrying value of goodwill at that date was $10,000. The cumulative balance on the group foreign currency reserve is a gain of $5,000.

Required:

Calculate the gain arising on the disposal of the foreign subsidiary in the consolidated statement of profit or loss.

4 Other issues

Shortcomings in IAS 21

In relation to IAS 21, the following criticisms have been made:

Lack of theoretical underpinning

It is not clear why foreign exchange gains and losses on monetary items are recorded in profit or loss, yet foreign exchange gains and losses arising on consolidation of a foreign operation are reported in other comprehensive income (OCI).

It is argued that recording foreign exchange gains or losses on monetary items in profit or loss increases the volatility of reported profits. As such, it has been suggested that foreign exchange gains or losses should be recorded in OCI if there is a high chance of reversal.

Long-term items

It is argued that retranslating long-term monetary items using the closing rate does not reflect economic substance. This is because a current exchange rate is being used to translate amounts that will be repaid in the future.

Foreign exchange gains and losses on long-term items are highly likely to reverse prior to repayment/receipt, suggesting that such gains and losses are unrealised. This provides further weight to the argument that foreign exchange gains and losses on at least some monetary items should be recorded in OCI.

The average rate

IAS 21 does not stipulate how to determine the average exchange rate in the reporting period. This increases the potential for entities to manipulate their net assets or total comprehensive income.

The use of different average rates will limit comparability between reporting entities.

Monetary/non-monetary

The distinction between monetary and non-monetary items can be ambiguous and would benefit from further clarification.

Foreign operations

IAS 21 uses a restrictive definition of a 'foreign operation' – a subsidiary, associate, joint venture or branch whose activities are based in a country or currency other than that of the reporting entity. It is argued that IAS 21 should instead use a definition of a foreign operation that is based on substance, rather than legal form.

5 Chapter summary

Group accounting – foreign currency

Translating the subsidiary's financial statements
- Assets and liabilities at the closing rate
- Incomes, expenses and OCI at the average rate

Calculating goodwill
- Calculate in the subsidiary's currency
- Translate at the closing rate

Calculation of exchange differences on:
- Goodwill
- Opening net assets and profit

Current year gains and losses are recorded in OCI and held within equity.

Disposals of overseas subsidiaries
- Recycle cumulative foreign exchange gains and losses held in equity to profit or loss

Test your understanding answers

Test your understanding 1 – Parent and Overseas

Group statement of financial position

Note: The assets and liabilities of Overseas have been translated at the closing rate.

	$
Goodwill (W3)	1,200
Assets ($9,500 + ((Sh40,000 + Sh4,000 FVA)/5.0))	18,300
	19,500
Equity and liabilities	$
Equity capital	5,000
Retained earnings (W5)	6,338
Translation reserve (W6)	392
	11,730
Non-controlling interest (W4)	1,092
Total equity	12,822
Liabilities ($2,318 + (Sh21,800/5.0))	6,678
	19,500

Group statement of profit or loss and other comprehensive income for the year

Note: The income and expenses for Overseas have been translated at the average rate.

	$
Revenue ($8,000 + (Sh5,200/5.2))	9,000
Costs ($2,500 + (Sh2,600/5.2))	(3,000)
Profit before tax	6,000
Tax ($2,000 + (Sh400/5.2))	(2,077)
Profit for the year	3,923

Other comprehensive income	
Items that may be reclassified to profit or loss in future periods	
Exchange differences on translation of foreign subsidiary ($109 (W3) + $381 (W6))	490
Total comprehensive income for the year	4,413
Profit for the year attributable to:	
Owners of Parent (bal. fig.)	3,838
Non-controlling interest (20% × (Sh2,200/5.2))	85
	3,923
Total comprehensive income attributable to:	
Owners of Parent (bal. fig.)	4,230
Non-controlling interest $85 (profit) + $22(W3) + $76(W7)	183
	4,413

Workings

(W1) **Group structure**

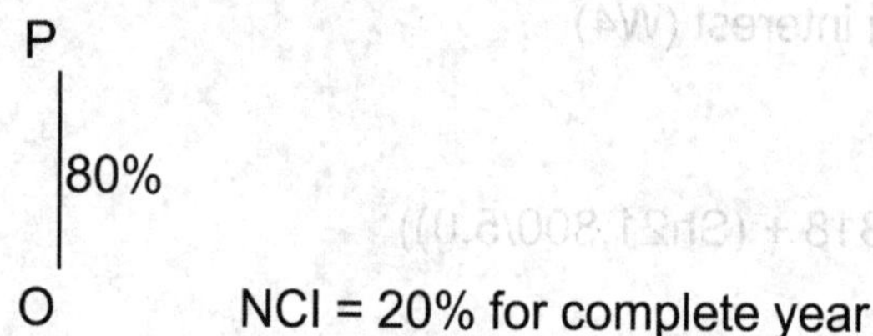

(W2) **Net assets of subsidiary in functional currency**

	Acq'n date	Rep date	
	Shillings	Shillings	Shillings
Share capital	10,000	10,000	
Retained earnings	6,000	8,200	
Fair value adjustment – land	4,000	4,000	
	20,000	22,200	2,200

(W3) **Goodwill calculation and forex**

Calculation of goodwill

Full goodwill:	**Shillings**
Cost of investment ($3,818 × 5.5)	20,999
FV of NCI at acquisition	5,000
	25,999
FV of NA at acquisition (W2)	(20,000)
Full goodwill at acquisition	5,999
Translate at closing rate (Sh5,999/5)	$1,200

Goodwill forex

	Shillings	**Exchange rate**	$
Goodwill at acquisition	5,999	5.5	1,091
Impairment	–		–
Exchange gain		**bal. fig**	**109**
Closing goodwill	5,999	5.0	1,200

The exchange gain on the retranslation of goodwill is allocated between the group and NCI based upon their respective shareholdings:

Group: 80% × $109 = $87 (W7)
NCI: 20% × $109 = $22 (W4)

(W4) **Non-controlling interest**

	$
NCI fair value at acquisition (Sh5,000/5.5 op. rate)	909
NCI share of post-acquisition profit (20% × (Sh2,200 (W2)/5.2 avg rate))	85
NCI share of exchange gain on retranslation of goodwill (W3)	22
NCI share of exchange gain on retranslation of net assets (W7)	76
	1,092

(W5) **Retained earnings**

	$
Parent	6,000
Group share of post-acquisition profit (80% × (2,200(W2)/5.2 avg. rate))	338
	6,338

(W6) **Translation reserve**

	$
Group share of goodwill forex (W3)	87
Group share of net assets and profit forex (W7)	305
	392

(W7) **Forex on net assets and profit**

	Shillings	**Rate**	$
Net assets at acquisition (W2)	20,000	5.5	3,636
Retained profit for the year (W2)	2,200	5.2	423
Exchange gain	**bal fig**		**381**
Closing net assets	22,200	5.0	4,440

Note that the total exchange gain on retranslation of the opening net assets and profit must be allocated between the group and NCI based upon their respective shareholdings as follows:

Group: 80% × $381 = $305 (W6)
NCI: 20% × $381 = $76 (W4)

Test your understanding 2 – Saint and Albans

Saint Group

Note: The assets and liabilities of Albans have been translated at the closing rate.

Group statement of financial position at 30 June 20X2

	$
Goodwill (W3)	2,700
Loan to Albans ($1,400 – $1,400 interco)	Nil
Property, plant and equipment ($10,000 + D14,500/4 + D1,000 (W2)/4 – D200 (W2)/4)	14,050
Inventories ($5,000 + D4,000/4 – $400 (W8))	5,600
Receivables ($4,000 + D500/4 + $1,500 (W10))	5,625
Cash and cash equivalents ($1,600 + D560/4)	1,740
	29,715

	$
Equity capital	10,000
Share premium	3,000
Retained earnings (W5)	3,692
Translation reserve (W7)	(2,773)
	13,919
Non-controlling interest (W4)	2,046
Total equity	15,965
Non-current liabilities ($5,000 + D5,460/4 + D140/4 – $1,400 interco)	5,000
Current liabilities ($5,000 + D1,000/4 + $2,000 (W9) + $1,500 (W10))	8,750
	29,715

Note: The income and expenses of Albans have been translated at the average rate for the year.

Group statement of profit or loss and other comprehensive income for the year ended 30 June 20X2

	$
Revenue ($50,000 + D60,000/3 – $1,200 interco)	68,800
Cost of sales ($20,000 + D30,000/3 + D200/3 (W2) + $400 (W3) + $400 (W8) – $1,200 interco)	(29,667)
Gross profit	39,133
Admin expenses ($20,000 + D12,000/3 + D140/3 (W2) + $2,000 (W9))	(26,047)
Profit before tax	13,086
Tax ($8,000 + D6,000/3)	(10,000)
Profit for the year:	3,086
Other comprehensive income – items that may be reclassified to profit or loss in future periods:	
Exchange loss on translation of foreign subsidiary (($2,900) (W3) + ($1,722) (W6))	(4,622)
Total comprehensive income for the year	(1,536)
Profit for the year:	
Attributable to Group (bal fig.)	1,691
Attributable to NCI ((40% × (D11,660 (W2)/3 avg. rate)) – $160 GW impairment (W3))	1,395
	3,086
Total comprehensive income for the year:	$
Attributable to Group (bal fig.)	(1,082)
Attributable to NCI ($1,395 profit – $1,160 (W3) – $689 (W6))	(454)
	(1,536)

Workings

(W1) **Group structure**

S
|60%
A NCI = 40% for complete year

(W2) **Net assets of subsidiary in functional currency**

	At acquisition	Rep date	Post-acq'n
	D	D	D
Equity capital	1,000	1,000	
Share premium	500	500	
Retained earnings	500	12,500	
Fair value adjustment – plant	1,000	1,000	
FVA – dep'n on plant (1/5)		(200)	
Exchange loss on loan*		(140)	
Post acquisition movement	3,000	14,660	11,660

***Exchange loss on loan received by Albans**

The loan was initially recorded at D5,460 ($1,400 × 3.9)

The loan needs to be retranslated using the closing rate to D5,600 ($1,400 × 4.0)

There is therefore an exchange loss of D140 (D5,600 – D5,460).

Dr Profit or loss/retained earnings (W2)	D140
Cr Non-current liabilities	D140

(W3) **Goodwill**

Goodwill calculation

	D
Cost to parent ($5,000 × 2.0)	10,000
FV of NCI at acquisition	5,000
	15,000
FV of NA at acquisition (W2)	(3,000)
Full goodwill at acquisition	12,000
Impairment – 10%	(1,200)
Unimpaired goodwill at reporting date	10,800

Exchange gain (loss) on retranslation of goodwill

	D	Rate	$
Goodwill at acquisition	12,000	2.0	6,000
Impairment	(1,200)	3.0	(400)
Exchange gain (loss)		**Bal fig**	**(2,900)**
Goodwill at reporting date	10,800	4.0	2,700

The impairment loss on the goodwill is allocated between the group and NCI based on their respective shareholdings:

Group: 60% × $400 = $240 (W5)
NCI: 40% × $400 = $160 (W4)

The exchange loss on retranslation of goodwill is allocated between the group and NCI based on their respective shareholdings:

Group: 60% × $2900 = $1,740 (W7)
NCI: 40% × $2900 = $1,160 (W4)

(W4) **Non-controlling interest**

	$
FV at acquisition per question (D5,000/2)	2,500
NCI % of post-acquisition profit 40% × (D11,660/3 avg rate) (W2)	1,555
NCI % of goodwill impairment (W3)	(160)
NCI % of retranslation loss on goodwill (W3)	(1,160)
NCI % of retranslation loss on net assets (W6)	(689)
	2,046

(W5) **Group retained earnings**

	$
Parent retained earnings	4,000
Government grant (W9)	(2,000)
Group share of goodwill impairment (W3)	(240)
Group share of post-acq'n profit 60% × (D11,660/3 avg. rate) (W2)	2,332
PURP (W8)	(400)
	3,692

(W6) **Exchange differences on retranslation of net assets**

	D	Rate	$
Acquisition net assets	3,000	2.0	1,500
Profit for year	11,660	3.0	3,887
Exchange gain/(loss)		**bal fig**	**(1,722)**
Closing net assets	14,660	4.0	(3,665)

The exchange loss is allocated between the group and NCI based upon respective shareholdings:

Group: 60% × $1,722 = $1,033 (W7)
NCI: 40% × $1,722 = $689 (W4)

(W7) **Translation reserve**

	$
Group share of forex on net assets and profit (W6)	(1,033)
Group share of forex on goodwill (W3)	(1,740)
	(2,773)

(W8) **PURP**

The profit on the intra-group sale is $400 ((50/100) × $800).

All of these items remain in group inventory. Therefore the adjustment required is:

Dr Cost of sales/retained earnings	$400
Cr Inventories	$400

(W9) **Government grant**

This is a revenue grant. It should be recognised in profit or loss on a systematic basis. The grant is intended to cover training costs over a two year period and so it should be recognised in profit or loss over two years.

Saint should increase its expenses by $2,000 (1/2 × $4,000) and record the balance as deferred income on the SFP.

Dr Administrative expenses/retained earnings	$2,000
Cr Current liabilities	$2,000

(W10) **Receivables factoring**

The risks and rewards of ownership have not transferred from Saint to the factor so the receivable should not be derecognised. The proceeds received should instead be shown as a liability.

The correcting entry is:

Dr Receivables	$1,500
Cr Liabilities	$1,500

Test your understanding 3 – LUMS Group

		$
Proceeds		50,000
Net assets recorded prior to disposal:		
Net assets	20,000	
Goodwill	10,000	
		(30,000)
Recycling of forex gains to P/L		5,000
		25,000

chapter

23

Group reorganisations

Chapter learning objectives

Upon completion of this chapter you will be able to:

- discuss the reasons behind a group reorganisation
- evaluate and assess the principal terms of a proposed group reorganisation.

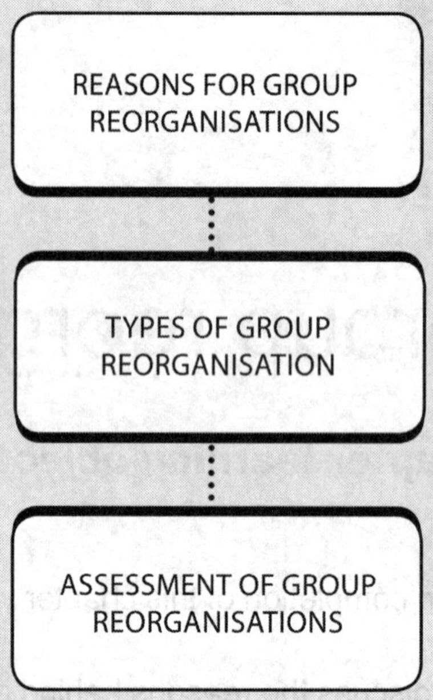

Definition of a group reorganisation

A group reorganisation (or restructuring) is any of the following:

(a) the transfer of shares in a subsidiary from one group entity to another

(b) the addition of a new parent entity to a group

(c) the transfer of shares in one or more subsidiaries of a group to a new entity that is not a group entity but whose shareholders are the same as those of the group's parent

(d) the combination into a group of two or more companies that before the combination had the same shareholders

(e) the acquisition of the shares of another entity that itself then issues sufficient shares so that the acquired entity has control of the combined entity.

Reasons for a reorganisation

There are a number of reasons why a group may wish to reorganise. These include the following.

- A group may wish to list on a public stock exchange. This is usually facilitated by creating a new holding company and keeping the business of the group in subsidiary entities.
- The ownership of subsidiaries may be transferred from one group company to another. This is often the case if the group wishes to sell a subsidiary, but retain its trade.
- The group may decide to transfer the assets and trades of a number of subsidiaries into one entity. This is called divisionalisation and is undertaken in order to simplify the group structure and save costs. The details of divisionalisation are not examinable at P2.
- There may be corporate tax advantages to reorganising a group structure, particularly if one or more subsidiaries within the group is loss-making.
- The group may split into two or more parts; each part is still owned by the same shareholders but is not related to the other parts. This is a demerger and is often done to enhance shareholder value. By splitting the group, the value of each part is realised whereas previously the stock market may have undervalued the group as a whole. The details of demergers are not examinable at P2.
- An unlisted entity may purchase a listed entity with the aim of achieving a stock exchange listing itself. This is called a reverse acquisition.

Types of group reorganisation

There are a number of ways of effecting a group reorganisation. The type of reorganisation will depend on what the group is trying to achieve.

New holding company

A group might set up a new holding entity for an existing group in order to improve co-ordination within the group or as a vehicle for flotation.

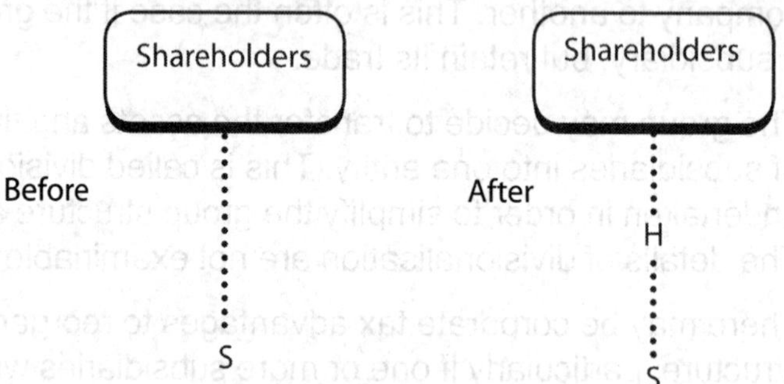

- H becomes the new holding entity of S.
- Usually, H issues shares to the shareholders of S in exchange for shares of S, but occasionally the shareholders of S may subscribe for shares in H and H may pay cash for S.

IFRS 3 excludes from its scope any business combination involving entities or businesses under 'common control', which is where the same parties control all of the combining entities/businesses both before and after the business combination.

As there is no mandatory guidance in accounting for these items, the acquisition method should certainly be used in examination questions.

Change of ownership of an entity within a group

This occurs when the internal structure of the group changes, for example, a parent may transfer the ownership of a subsidiary to another of its subsidiaries.

The key thing to remember is that the reorganisation of the entities within the group should not affect the group accounts, as shareholdings are transferred from one company to another and no assets will leave the group.

The individual accounts of the group companies will need to be adjusted for the effect of the transfer.

The following are types of reorganisation:

(a) **Subsidiary moved up**

Before

H

S

T

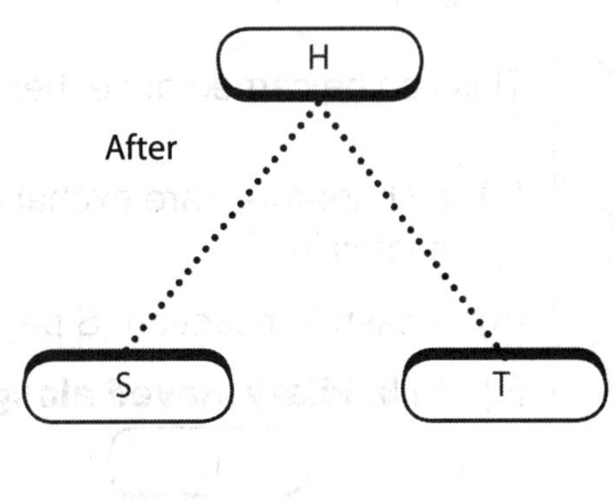

This can be achieved in one of two ways.

(a) S transfers its investment in T to H as a dividend in specie. If this is done then S must have sufficient distributable profits to pay the dividend.

(b) H purchases the investment in T from S for cash. In practice the purchase price often equals the fair value of the net assets acquired, so that no gain or loss arises on the transaction.

Usually, it will be the carrying value of T that is used as the basis for the transfer of the investment, but there are no legal rules confirming this.

A share-for-share exchange cannot be used as in many jurisdictions it is illegal for a subsidiary to hold shares in the parent company.

(b) **Subsidiary moved down**

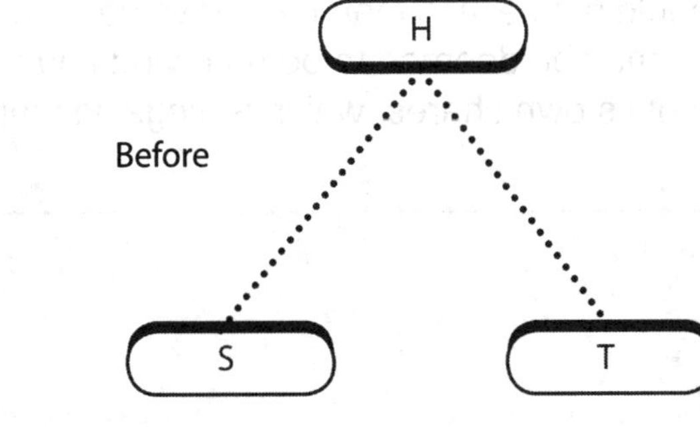

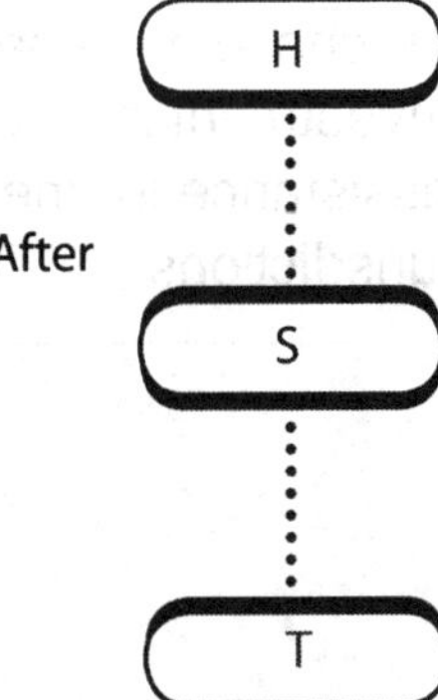

This reorganisation may be carried out where there are tax advantages in establishing a 'sub-group', or where two or more subsidiaries are linked geographically.

This can be carried out either by:

(a) a share-for-share exchange (S issues shares to H in return for the shares in T)

(b) a cash transaction (S pays cash to H).

(c) 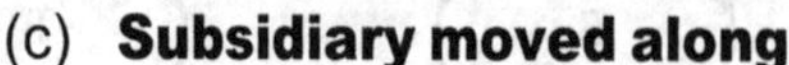
Subsidiary moved along

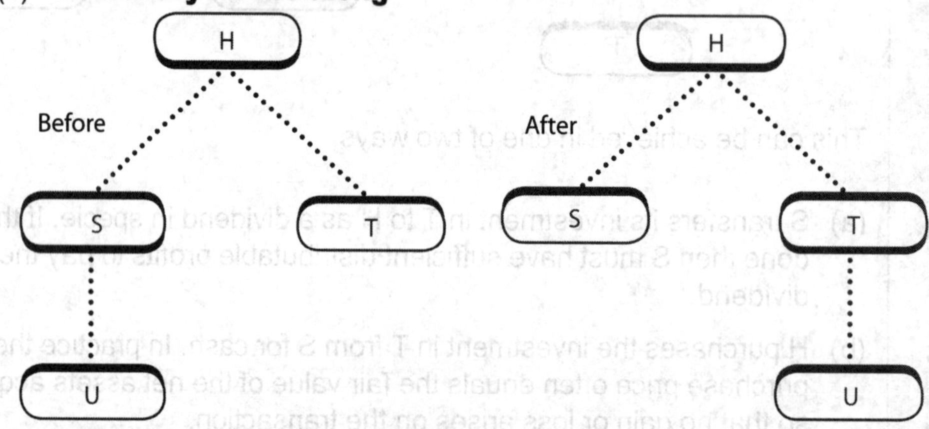

This is carried out by T paying cash (or other assets) to S. The consideration would not normally be in the form of shares because a typical reason for such a reconstruction would be to allow S to be managed as a separate part of the group or even disposed of completely. This could not be achieved effectively were S to have a shareholding in T.

If the purpose of the reorganisation is to allow S to leave the group, the purchase price paid by T should not be less than the fair value of the investment in U, otherwise S may be deemed to be receiving financial assistance for the purchase of its own shares, which is illegal in many jurisdictions.

Reverse acquisitions

Definition

A **reverse acquisition** occurs when an entity obtains ownership of the shares of another entity, which in turn issues sufficient shares so that the acquired entity has control of the combined entity.

Reverse acquisitions are a method of allowing unlisted companies to obtain a stock exchange quotation by taking over a smaller listed company.

For example, a private company arranges to be acquired by a listed company. This is effected by the public entity issuing shares to the private company so that the private company's shareholders end up controlling the listed entity. Legally, the public entity is the parent, but the substance of the transaction is that the private entity has acquired the listed entity.

Assessment of group reorganisations

Previous examination questions testing group reorganisations have provided a scenario with a group considering a number of reorganisation options. The questions have then asked for an evaluation and recommendation of a particular proposal.

In order to do this, you will need to consider the following:

- the impact of the proposal on the individual accounts of the group entities
- the impact of the proposal on the group accounts
- the purpose of the reorganisation
- whether there is any impairment of any of the group's assets
- whether any impairment loss should be recognised in relation to the investment in subsidiaries in the parent company accounts.

Group reorganisations and separate financial statements

IAS 27 Separate Financial Statements details the accounting treatment of investments in subsidiaries, associates and joint ventures when separate (non-consolidated) financial statements are produced.

In separate financial statements, investments in subsidiaries, associates and joint ventures can be measured:

- at cost
- in accordance with IFRS 9 Financial Instruments
- using the equity method.

A parent may reorganise the structure of its group by establishing a new entity as its parent. In this case, as long as certain criteria are met, the new parent records the cost of the original parent in its separate financial statements as the carrying amount of **'its share of the equity items shown in the separate financial statements of the original parent at the date of the reorganisation'** (IAS 27, para 13). The criteria that must be met are as follows:

- **'The new parent obtains control of the original parent by issuing equity instruments in exchange for existing equity instruments of the original parent**
- **The assets and liabilities of the new group and the original group are the same immediately before and after the reorganisation**
- **The owners of the original parent before the reorganisation have the same absolute and relative interests in the net assets of the original group and the new group immediately before and after the reorganisation'** (IAS 27, para 13).

The above rule also applies when an entity that is not a parent establishes a new entity as its parent.

1 Chapter summary

Reasons for group reorganisations

- Transfer of shares in a subsidiary from one group entity to another
- Addition of a new parent entity to a group
- Transfer of shares in one or more subsidiaries of a group to a new entity that is not a group entity, but whose shareholders are the same as those of the group's parent
- Combination into a group of two or more companies that before the combination had the same shareholders

Types of group reorganisations

- New holding company
- Change of ownership of an entity within the group
- Reverse acquisition

Assessment of group reorganisations

- Look for the effect on the group and individual financial statements
- Look for any impairment of assets in the group
- Look for any impairment of investments in the parent company

chapter

24

Group statement of cash flows

Chapter learning objectives

Upon completion of this chapter you will be able to:

- prepare and discuss group statements of cash flows.

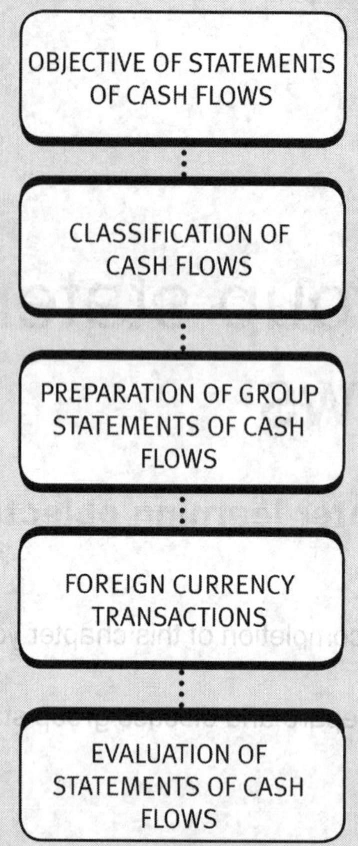

1 Objective of statements of cash flows

IAS 7 Statement of Cash Flows provides guidance on the preparation of a statement of cash flows. The objective of a statement of cash flows is to provide information on an entity's changes in cash and cash equivalents during the period.

The statement of financial position and statement of profit or loss are prepared on an accruals basis and do not show how the business has generated and used cash in the reporting period. The statement of profit or loss may show profits even though the company is suffering severe cash flow problems. A statement of cash flows is therefore important because it enables users of the financial statements to assess the liquidity, solvency and financial adaptability of the business.

Definitions

- **Cash** consists of cash in hand and deposits repayable upon demand, less overdrafts. This includes cash held in a foreign currency.
- **Cash equivalents** are **'short-term, highly liquid investments that are readily convertible to known amounts of cash and are subject to an insignificant risk of changes in value'** (IAS 7, para 6).
- **Cash flows** are **'inflows and outflows of cash and cash equivalents'** (IAS 7, para 6).

2 Classification of cash flows

IAS 7 does not prescribe a specific format for the statement of cash flows, although it requires that cash flows are classified under one of three headings:

- **cash flows from operating activities,** defined as the entity's principal revenue earning activities and other activities that do not fall under the next two headings
- **cash flows from investing activities,** defined as the acquisition and disposal of long-term assets and other investments (excluding cash equivalents)
- **cash flows from financing activities,** defined as activities that change the size and composition of the entity's equity and borrowings.

Proforma statement of cash flow per IAS 7

	$	$
Cash flows from operating activities		
Profit before tax	X	
Add: finance costs	X	
Less: investment income	(X)	
Less: income from associate	(X)	
Adjust for non-cash items dealt with in arriving at operating profit:		
Add: depreciation	X	
Less: gain on disposal of subsidiary	(X)	
Add: loss on disposal of subsidiary	X	
Add: loss on impairment charged to P/L	X	
Add: loss on disposal of non-current assets	X	
Add: increase in provisions	X	
	X/(X)	
Changes in working capital:		
Increase in inventory	(X)	
Increase in receivables	(X)	
Decrease in payables	(X)	
Cash generated/used from operations	X/(X)	
Interest paid	(X)	
Taxation paid	(X)	
Net cash Inflow/(outflow) from operating activities		X/(X)

Cash flows from investing activities		
Payments to purchase NCA	(X)	
Receipts from NCA disposals	X	
Net cash paid to acquire subsidiary	(X)	
Net cash proceeds from subsidiary disposal	X	
Cash paid to acquire associates	(X)	
Dividend received from associate	X	
Interest received	X	
Net cash inflow/(outflow) from investing activities		
		X/(X)
Cash flows from financing activities		
Proceeds from share issue	X	
Proceeds from loan or debenture issue	X	
Cash repayment of loans or debentures	(X)	
Lease liability repayments	(X)	
Equity dividend paid by parent	(X)	
Dividend paid to NCI	(X)	
Net cash inflow/(outflow) from financing activities		
		X/(X)
Increase/(decrease) in cash and equivalents		X/(X)
Cash and equivalents brought forward		X/(X)
Cash and equivalents carried forward		X/(X)

Classification of cash flows

Cash flows from operating activities

The key figure within cash flows from operating activities is 'cash generated from operations'. There are two methods of calculating cash generated from operations:

- The **direct method** shows operating cash receipts and payments, such as cash receipts from customers, cash payments to suppliers and cash payments to and on behalf of employees.

- The **indirect method** (used in the proforma statement of cash flows presented earlier in the chapter) starts with profit before tax and adjusts it for non-cash charges and credits, deferrals or accruals of past or future operating cash receipts and payments, as well as for items that relate to investing and financing activities. The most frequently occurring adjustments required are:
  - finance costs and investment incomes
  - depreciation or amortisation charges in the year
  - impairment charged to profit or loss in the year
  - profit or loss on disposal of non-current assets
  - change in inventories
  - change in trade receivables
  - change in trade payables.

IAS 7 permits either method, although encourages the use of the direct method. The methods differ only in respect of how the item 'cash generated from operating activities' is derived. A comparison between the direct and indirect method to arrive at cash generated from operations is shown below:

Direct method:	$m	**Indirect method:**	$m
Cash receipts from customers	15,424	Profit before tax	6,022
Cash payments to suppliers	(5,824)	Depreciation charges	899
Cash payments to and on behalf of employees	(2,200)	Increase in inventories	(194)
Other cash payments	(511)	Increase in receivables	(72)
		Increase in payables	234
	–––––		–––––
Cash generated from operations	6,889	Cash generated from operations	6,889
	–––––		–––––

The principal advantage of the direct method is that it discloses operating cash receipts and payments. Knowledge of the specific sources of cash receipts and the purposes for which cash payments have been made in past periods may be useful in assessing and predicting future cash flows.

Cash flows from investing activities

Cash flows to appear under this heading include:

- cash paid for property, plant and equipment and other non-current assets

- cash received on the sale of property, plant and equipment and other non-current assets
- cash paid for investments in or loans to other entities (excluding movements on loans from financial institutions, which are shown under financing)
- cash received for the sale of investments or the repayment of loans to other entities (again excluding loans from financial institutions).

Cash flows from financing activities

Financing cash flows mainly comprise receipts or repayments of principal from or to external providers of finance.

Financing cash inflows include:

- receipts from issuing shares or other equity instruments
- receipts from issuing debentures, loans, notes and bonds and from other long-term and short-term borrowings (other than overdrafts, which are normally included in cash and cash equivalents).

IAS 7 says that financing cash outflows include:

- repayments of amounts borrowed (other than overdrafts)
- the capital element of lease payments
- payments to reacquire or redeem the entity's shares.

Interest and dividends

IAS 7 allows interest and dividends, whether received or paid, to be classified under any of the three headings, provided the classification is consistent from period to period.

The practice adopted in this text is to classify:

- interest received as a cash flow from investing activities
- interest paid as a cash flow from operating activities
- dividends received as a cash flow from investing activities
- dividends paid as a cash flow from financing activities.

3 Cash and cash equivalents

The statement of cash flows reconciles cash and cash equivalents at the start of the reporting period to the end of the reporting period.

- Cash equivalents are **'short-term, highly liquid investments that are readily convertible to known amounts of cash and are subject to an insignificant risk of changes in value'** (IAS 7, para 6).
- 'Cash equivalents' are held in order to meet short-term cash commitments. They are not held for investment purposes.
- IAS 7 does not define 'readily convertible' but notes that an investment would qualify as a cash equivalent if it had a short maturity of **'three months or less from the date of acquisition'** (IAS 7, para 7).
- Equity investments are generally excluded from being included in cash equivalents because there is a significant risk of a change in value. IAS 7 makes an exception for preference shares with a short period to maturity and a specified redemption date.

Test your understanding 1 – Cash and cash equivalents

The accountant for Minted, a company, is preparing a statement of cash flows. She would like advice about whether the following items can be included within 'cash and cash equivalents'.

- An overdraft of $100,000.
- A balance of $500,000 held in a high-interest account. Minted must give 28 days' notice in order to access this money, which is held with the intention of meeting working capital shortages.
- An investment in the ordinary shares of Moolah. The shares are listed and therefore could be sold immediately. The shares have a fair value of $1m.

Required:

Advise the accountant of Minted whether the above items qualify as 'cash and cash equivalents'.

Unusual items and non-cash transactions

Unusual cash flows

Where cash flows are unusual because of their size or incidence, sufficient disclosure should be given to explain their cause and nature.

For a cash flow to be unusual on the grounds of its size alone, it must be unusual in relation to cash flows of a similar nature.

Discontinued activities

Cash flows relating to discontinued activities are required by IFRS 5 to be shown separately, either on the face of the statement of cash flows or in a disclosure note.

Major non-cash transactions

Material transactions not resulting in movements of cash should be disclosed in the notes to the statement of cash flows if disclosure is necessary for an understanding of the underlying transactions.

4 Individual statements of cash flows

For your F3 and F7 exams, you will have learned how to prepare statements of cash flows for individual companies. It may be worthwhile taking some time to revise this knowledge using the following exercises.

Test your understanding 2 – Extracts

Calculate the required cash flows in each of the following scenarios:

(1)

	20X1	**20X0**
	$	$
Property, plant and equipment (PPE)	250	100

During the year depreciation charged was $20, a revaluation surplus of $60 was recorded, and PPE with a carrying amount of $15 was disposed of. The carrying amount of assets recognised through lease agreements and classified as PPE was $30.

Required:

How much cash was spent on property, plant and equipment in the period?

(2)

	20X1	20X0
	$	$
Deferred tax liability	100	50
Income tax liability	120	100

The income tax charge in the statement of profit or loss was $180.

Required:

How much tax was paid in the period?

(3)

	20X1	20X0
	$	$
Retained earnings	300	200

The statement of profit or loss showed a profit for the period of $150.

Required:

How much was the cash dividend paid during the period?

Illustration – Single entity statements of cash flows

Below are the financial statements of Single for the year ended 30 September 20X2:

Statement of financial position as at 30 September 20X2 (including comparatives)

	20X2	20X1
	$m	$m
Non-current assets		
Property, plant and equipment	90	60
Current assets		
Inventories	32	20
Trade receivables	20	27
Cash and cash equivalents	8	12
	150	119

Equity and liabilities		
Share capital ($1 shares)	30	5
Retained earnings	60	35
	90	40
Non-current liabilities:		
Loans	10	29
Deferred tax	15	14
Current liabilities:		
Trade payables	23	25
Tax payable	12	11
	150	119

Statement of profit or loss for the year ended 30 September 20X2

	$m
Revenue	450
Operating expenses	(401)
Profit from operations	49
Finance cost	(3)
Profit before tax	46
Tax	(12)
Profit for the period	34

Notes

(1) Property, plant and equipment with a carrying amount of $9 million was disposed of for cash proceeds of $13 million. Depreciation for the year was $17 million.

(2) Trade payables as at 30 September 20X2 includes accruals for interest payable of $4 million (20X1: $5 million).

Required:

Prepare the statement of cash flows for Single for the year ended 30 September 20X2.

Solution

Statement of cash flows

	$m	$m
Cash flows from operating activities		
Profit before tax	46	
Finance cost	3	
Depreciation	17	
Profit on disposal of PPE ($13 – $9)	(4)	
Increase in inventories ($32 – $20)	(12)	
Decrease in receivables ($20 – $27)	7	
Decrease in payables (($23 – $4) – ($25 – $5))	(1)	
	56	
Interest paid (W1)	(4)	
Tax paid (W2)	(10)	
		42
Cash flows from investing activities		
Proceeds from sale of PPE	13	
Purchases of PPE (W3)	(56)	
		(43)
Cash flows from financing activities		
Proceeds from shares ($30 – $5)	25	
Repayment of loans ($10 – $29)	(19)	
Dividends paid (W4)	(9)	
		(3)
Decrease in cash and cash equivalents		(4)
Opening cash and cash equivalents		12
Closing cash and cash equivalents		8

Workings

(W1) **Interest**

	$m
Balance b/fwd	5
Profit or loss	3
Cash paid (bal. fig.)	(4)
Balance c/fwd	4

(W2) **Tax**

	$m
Balance b/fwd ($14 + $11)	25
Profit or loss	12
Cash paid (bal. fig.)	(10)
Balance c/fwd ($15 + $12)	27

(W3) **PPE**

	$m
Balance b/fwd	60
Depreciation	(17)
Disposal	(9)
Cash paid (bal. fig)	56
Balance c/fwd	90

(W4) **Retained earnings**

	$m
Balance b/fwd	35
Profit or loss	34
Cash dividends paid (bal. fig.)	(9)
Balance c/fwd	60

5 Preparation of a consolidated statement of cash flows

A consolidated statement of cash flows shows the cash flows between a group and third parties. It is prepared using the consolidated statement of financial position and the consolidated statement of profit or loss. This means that intra-group transactions have already been eliminated.

When producing a consolidated statement of cash flows, there are three extra elements that need to be considered:

- acquisitions and disposals of subsidiaries
- cash paid to non-controlling interests
- associates.

Acquisitions and disposals of subsidiaries

Acquisitions

- In the statement of cash flows we must record the actual cash flow for the purchase of the subsidiary net of any cash held by the subsidiary that is now controlled by the group.
- The assets and liabilities of the acquired subsidiary must be included in any workings to calculate the cash movement for an item during the year.

Illustration – Acquisition of a subsidiary

Sparkling buys 70% of the equity shares of Still for $500,000 in cash. At the acquisition date, Still had cash and cash equivalents of $25,000.

Although Sparkling paid $500,000 for the shares, it also gained control of Still's cash of $25,000. In the consolidated statement of cash flows, this would be presented as follows:

Cash flows from investing activities

	$000
Acquisition of subsidiary, net of cash acquired ($500,000 – $25,000)	(475)

Disposals

- The statement of cash flows will show the cash received from the sale of the subsidiary, net of any cash held by the subsidiary that the group has lost control over.
- The assets and liabilities of the disposed subsidiary must be included in any workings to calculate the cash movement for an item during the year.

Illustration – Disposal of a subsidiary

Sparkling owned 80% of the equity shares of Fizzy. During the period, these shares were sold for $800,000 in cash. At the disposal date, Fizzy had cash and cash equivalents of $70,000.

Although Sparkling received $800,000 for the shares, it lost control of Fizzy's cash of $70,000. In the consolidated statement of cash flows, this would be presented as follows:

Cash flows from investing activities

	$000
Disposal of subsidiary, net of cash disposed of ($800,000 – $70,000)	730

Illustration 1 – Acquisitions and disposals

Extracts from a group statement of financial position are presented below:

	20X8	**20X7**
	$000	$000
Inventories	74,666	53,019
Trade receivables	58,246	62,043
Trade payables	93,678	86,247

During 20X8, Subsidiary A was acquired and all shares in Subsidiary B were disposed of.

Details of the working capital balances of these two subsidiaries are provided below:

	Working capital of Subsidiary A at acquisition	Working capital of Subsidiary B at disposal
	$000	$000
Inventories	4,500	6,800
Trade receivables	7,900	6,700
Trade payables	8,250	5,740

Required:

Calculate the movement in inventories, trade receivables and trade payables for inclusion in the group statement of cash flows.

Solution

The net assets of Subsidiary A are being consolidated at the end of the year, but they were not consolidated at the start of the year. Conversely, the net assets of Subsidiary B are not consolidated at the end of the year, but they were consolidated at the start of the year. The working capital balances brought forward and carried forward are therefore not directly comparable.

Comparability can be achieved by calculating the movement between the closing and opening figures and then:

- Deducing the subsidiary's balances at the acquisition date for a subsidiary acquired during the year.
- Adding the subsidiary's balances at the disposal date for a subsidiary disposed of during the year.

	Inventories	Trade receivables	Trade payables
	$000	$000	$000
Bal c/fwd	74,666	58,246	93,678
Bal b/fwd	(53,019)	(62,043)	(86,247)
	21,647	(3,797)	7,431
Less: Sub acquired in year	(4,500)	(7,900)	(8,250)
Add: Sub disposed in year	6,800	6,700	5,740
Movement in the year	inc 23,947	dec (4,997)	inc 4,921
Impact on cash flow	Outflow	Inflow	Inflow

Cash paid to non-controlling interests

- When a subsidiary that is not wholly owned pays a dividend, some of that dividend is paid outside of the group to the non-controlling interest.
- Dividends paid to non-controlling interests should be disclosed separately in the statement of cash flows.
- To calculate the dividend paid, reconcile the non-controlling interest in the statement of financial position from the opening to the closing balance. You can use a T-account or a schedule to do this.

Illustration 2 – Cash paid to NCI

The following information has been extracted from the consolidated financial statements of WG, which has a year end of the 31 December:

	20X7	20X6
	$000	$000
Statement of financial position		
Equity:		
Non-controlling interest	780	690
Statement of profit or loss		
Profit for the period attributable to the non-controlling interest	120	230

During the year, WG bought a 70% shareholding in CC. WG uses the full goodwill method for all subsidiaries. The fair value of the non-controlling interest in CC at the acquisition date was $60,000.

During the year, WG disposed of its 60% holding in TT. At the acquisition date, the fair value of the NCI and the fair value of TT's net assets were $35,000 and $70,000 respectively. The net assets of TT at the disposal date were $100,000.

Required:

What is the dividend paid to non-controlling interest in the year ended 31 December 20X7?

Solution

	$000
NCI b/fwd	690
NCI re sub acquired in year	60
NCI share of profit for the year	120
NCI derecognised due to subsidiary disposal (W1)	(47)
Cash dividend paid in year (bal. fig)	(43)
NCI c/fwd	780

(W1) **NCI at date of TT disposal**

	$000
FV of NCI at acquisition	35
NCI % of post-acquisition net assets 40% × ($100,000 – $70,000)	12
	47

Alternatively, a T account can be used:

Non-controlling interests

	$000		$000
NCI derecognised re sub disposal (W1)	47	NCI Balance b/fwd	690
Dividends paid (bal fig)	43	NCI recognised re acq'n of sub	60
NCI Balance c/fwd	780	Share of profits in year	120
	870		870

Associates

An associate is a company over which an investor has significant influence. Associates are not part of the group and therefore cash flows between the group and the associate must be reported in the statement of cash flows.

Cash flows relating to associates that need to be separately reported within the statement of cash flows are as follows:

- dividends received from an associate
- loans made to associates
- cash payments to acquire associates
- cash receipts from the sale of associates.

These cash flows should be presented as cash flows from investing activities.

Remember, associates are accounted for using the equity method. This means that, in the consolidated statement of profit or loss, the group records its share of the associate's profit for the year. This is a non-cash income and so must be deducted in the reconciliation between profit before tax and cash generated from operations.

Illustration 3 – Associates

The following information is from the consolidated financial statements of H:

Extract from consolidated statement of profit or loss for year ended 31 December 20X1

	$000
Profit from operations	734
Share of profit of associate	48
Profit before tax	782
Tax	(304)
Profit for the year	478

Extracts from consolidated statement of financial position as at 31 December 20X1 (with comparatives)

	20X1	20X0
	$000	$000
Non-current assets		
Investment in associate	466	456
Loan to associate	380	300

Required:

Calculate the relevant figures to be included in the group statement of cash flows for the year ended 31 December 20X1.

Solution

Extracts from statement of cash flows

	$000
Cash flows from operating activities	
Profit before tax	782
Share of profit of associate	(48)
Investing activities	
Dividend received from associate (W1)	38
Loan to associate (380 – 300)	(80)

(W1) **Dividend received from associate**

When dealing with the dividend from the associate, the process is the same as we have already seen with the non-controlling interest.

Set up a schedule or T account and include all the balances that relate to the associate. The balancing figure will be the cash dividend received from the associate.

	$000
Balance b/fwd	456
Share of profit of associate	48
Cash dividend received **(bal fig)**	(38)
Balance c/fwd	466

Instead of a schedule, a T-account could be used:

Associate

	$000		$000
Balance b/fwd	456	Dividend received (bal fig)	38
Share of profit of associate	48	Balance c/fwd	466
	504		504

Test your understanding 3 – The Z group

The following information is from the consolidated financial statements of Z:

Extract from consolidated statement of profit or loss for year ended 31 December 20X1

	$000
Profit from operations	900
Share of profit of associate	15
Profit before tax	915
Tax	(200)
Profit for the year	715

Extracts from consolidated statement of financial position as at 31 December 20X1 (with comparatives)

	20X1	20X0
	$000	$000
Non-current assets		
Investment in associate	600	580

During the year, Z received dividends from associates of $5,000.

Required:

Based on the above information, prepare extracts showing relevant figures to be included in the group statement of cash flows for the year ended 31 December 20X1.

6 Question practice

Test your understanding 4 – Consolidated extracts

Calculate the required cash flows in each of the following scenarios:

(1)

	20X1	20X0
	$	$
Non-controlling interest	840	440

The group statement of profit or loss and other comprehensive income reported total comprehensive income attributable to the non-controlling interest of $500.

Required:

How much was the cash dividend paid to the non-controlling interest?

(2)

	20X1	20X0
	$	$
Non-controlling interest	850	500

The group statement of profit or loss and other comprehensive income reported total comprehensive income attributable to the non-controlling interest of $600.

Required:

How much was the cash dividend paid to the non-controlling interest?

(3)

	20X1	20X0
	$	$
Investment in associate	500	200

The group statement of profit or loss reported 'share of profit of associates' of $750.

Required:

How much was the cash dividend received by the group?

(4)

	20X1	20X0
	$	$
Investment in associate	3,200	600

The group statement of profit or loss reported 'share of profit of associates' of $4,000.

In addition, the associate revalued its non-current assets during the period. The group share of this gain is $500.

Required:

How much was the cash dividend received by the group?

(5)

	20X1	20X0
	$	$
Property, plant and equipment (PPE)	500	150

During the year depreciation charged was $50, and the group acquired a subsidiary which held PPE of $200 at the acquisition date.

Required:

How much cash was spent on property, plant and equipment in the period?

Test your understanding 5 – AH Group

Extracts from the consolidated financial statements of the AH Group for the year ended 30 June 20X5 are given below:

Consolidated statement of profit or loss for the year ended 30 June 20X5

	$000
Revenue	85,000
Cost of sales	(60,750)
Gross profit	24,250
Operating expenses	(5,650)
Profit from operations	18,600
Finance cost	(1,400)
Profit before disposal of property	17,200
Disposal of property (note 2)	1,250
Profit before tax	18,450
Tax	(6,250)
Profit for the period	12,200
Attributable to:	
Non-controlling interest	405
Owners of the parent	11,795
	12,200

Note: There were no items of other comprehensive income.

Statement of financial position, with comparatives, at 30 June 20X5

		20X5		20X4
	$000	$000	$000	$000
Non-current assets				
Property, plant and equipment	50,600		44,050	
Goodwill (note 3)	5,910		4,160	
		56,510		48,210
Current assets				
Inventories	33,500		28,750	
Trade receivables	27,130		26,300	
Cash and cash equivalents	1,870		3,900	
		62,500		58,950
		119,010		107,160
Equity and liabilities	$000	$000	$000	$000
Equity shares	20,000		18,000	
Share premium	12,000		10,000	
Retained earnings	24,135		18,340	
		56,135		46,340
Non-controlling interest		3,875		1,920
Total equity		60,010		48,260
Non-current liabilities				
Interest-bearing borrowings		18,200		19,200
Current liabilities				
Trade payables	33,340		32,810	
Interest payables	1,360		1,440	
Tax	6,100		5,450	
		40,800		39,700
		119,010		107,160

Notes:

(1) Several years ago, AH acquired 80% of the issued equity shares of its subsidiary, BI. The NCI at the acquisition date was valued using the proportion of net assets method.

On 1 January 20X5, AH acquired 75% of the issued equity shares of CJ in exchange for a fresh issue of 2 million of its own $1 equity shares (issued at a premium of $1 each) and $2 million in cash. The net assets of CJ at the date of acquisition were assessed as having the following fair values:

	$000
Property, plant and equipment	4,200
Inventories	1,650
Trade receivables	1,300
Cash and cash equivalents	50
Trade payables	(1,950)
Tax	(250)
	5,000

Goodwill relating to the acquisition of entity CJ during the year was calculated on the full goodwill basis. On 1 January 20X5 when CJ was acquired, the fair value of the non-controlling interest was $1,750,000.

Any impairments of goodwill during the year have been accounted for within operating expenses.

(2) During the year, AH disposed of property, plant and equipment for proceeds of $2,250,000. The carrying value of the asset at the date of disposal was $1,000,000. There were no other disposals of property, plant and equipment. Depreciation of $7,950,000 was charged to the consolidated statement of profit or loss in the year.

Required:

Prepare the consolidated statement of cash flows of the AH Group for the year ended 30 June 20X5 using the indirect method.

Test your understanding 6 – Pearl

Below are the consolidated financial statements of the Pearl Group for the year ended 30 September 20X2:

Consolidated statements of financial position

	20X2	20X1
	$000	$000
Non-current assets		
Goodwill	1,930	1,850
Property, plant and equipment	2,545	1,625
Investment in associate	620	540
	5,095	4,015
Current assets		
Inventories	470	435
Trade receivables	390	330
Cash and cash equivalents	210	140
	6,165	4,920
Equity and liabilities		
Share capital ($1 shares)	1,500	1,500
Retained earnings	1,755	1,085
Other reserves	750	525
	4,005	3,110
Non-controlling interest	310	320
	4,315	3,430
Non-current liabilities:		
Loans	500	300
Deferred tax	150	105
Current liabilities:		
Trade payables	800	725
Tax payable	400	360
	6,165	4,920

Consolidated statement of profit or loss and other comprehensive income for the year ended 30 September 20X2

	$000
Revenue	2,090
Operating expenses	(1,155)
Profit from operations	935
Gain on disposal of subsidiary	100
Finance cost	(35)
Share of profit of associate	115
Profit before tax	1,115
Tax	(225)
Profit for the period	890
Other comprehensive income	200
Other comprehensive income from associate	50
Total comprehensive income	1,140
Profit for the year attributable to:	
Owners of the parent	795
Non-controlling interests	95
	890
Total comprehensive income for the year attributable to:	
Owners of the parent	1,020
Non-controlling interests	120
	1,140

Consolidated statement of changes in equity

	Attributable to owners of the parent	Attributable to the NCI
	$000	$000
Equity brought forward	3,110	320
Total comprehensive income	1,020	120
Acquisition of subsidiary	–	340
Disposal of subsidiary	–	(420)
Dividends	(125)	(50)
Equity carried forward	4,005	310

(1) Depreciation of $385,000 was charged during the year. Plant with a carrying amount of $250,000 was sold for $275,000. The gain on disposal was recognised in operating costs. Certain properties were revalued during the year resulting in a revaluation gain of $200,000 being recognised.

(2) During the year, Pearl acquired 80% of the equity share capital of Gem paying cash consideration of $1.5 million. The NCI holding was measured at its fair value of $340,000 at the date of acquisition. The fair value of Gem's net assets at acquisition was made up as follows:

	$000
Property, plant and equipment	1,280
Inventories	150
Trade receivables	240
Cash and cash equivalents	80
Trade payables	(220)
Tax payable	(40)
	1,490

(3) During the year, Pearl disposed of its 60% equity shareholding in Stone for cash proceeds of $850,000. The subsidiary has been acquired several years ago for cash consideration of $600,000. The NCI holding was measured at its fair value of $320,000 at acquisition and the fair value of Stone's net assets were $730,000. Goodwill had not suffered any impairment. At the date of disposal, the net assets of Stone had carrying values in the consolidated statement of financial position as follows:

	$000
Property, plant and equipment	725
Inventories	165
Trade receivables	120
Cash and cash equivalents	50
Trade payables	(80)
	980

Required:

Prepare the consolidated statement of cash flows for the Pearl group for the year ended 30 September 20X2.

7 Foreign exchange and cash flow statements

Exchange gains and losses

The values of assets and liabilities denominated in an overseas currency will increase or decrease partly due to movements in exchange rates. These movements must be factored into your workings in order to determine the actual cash payments and receipts during the year.

Dealing with foreign exchange issues

The loan balances of the Grey group as at 31 December 20X1 and 31 December 20X0 are presented below:

	20X1	20X0
	$m	$m
Loans	60	20

One of the subsidiaries of the Grey group prepares its financial statements in sterling (£). The exchange loss on the translation of the loans of this subsidiary was $10 million.

Remember that an exchange loss increases the value of a liability. This is not a cash flow. Therefore, the exchange loss must be factored into the cash flow workings as follows:

	$m
Bal b/fwd	20
Exchange loss	10
Cash received (bal. fig.)	30
Bal c/fwd	60

The cash received from new loans in the year is $30 million. This will be shown as an inflow within cash flows from financing activities.

Illustration – Cash flows and foreign exchange

A group had the following working capital as at 31 December 20X1 and 20X0:

	20X1	**20X0**
	$	$
Inventories	100	200
Trade receivables	300	200
Trade payables	500	200

During the period ended 31 December 20X1, the group acquired a subsidiary with the following working capital.

Inventories	50
Trade receivables	200
Trade payables	40

During this period the group disposed of a subsidiary with the following working capital.

Inventories	25
Trade receivables	45
Trade payables	20

During this period the group experienced the following exchange rate differences.

Inventories	11	Gain
Trade receivables	21	Gain
Trade payables	31	Loss

Required:

Calculate the movements in inventories, trade receivables and trade payables as they would appear in the indirect reconciliation between profit before tax and cash generated from operations for the period ended 31 December 20X1.

Solution

	Inventories	**Trade receivables**	**Trade payables**
	$000	**$000**	**$000**
Bal c/fwd	100	300	500
Bal b/fwd	(200)	(200)	(200)
	(100)	100	300
Less: Sub acquired in year	(50)	(200)	(40)
Add: Sub disposed in year	25	45	20
Adjustment for forex	(11)	(21)	(31)
Movement in the year	dec (136)	dec (76)	inc 249
Impact on cash flow	Inflow	Inflow	Inflow

Be careful with foreign exchange gains and losses:

- Assets are increased by a foreign exchange gain
- Liabilities are increased by a foreign exchange loss.

Overseas cash balances

If cash balances are partly denominated in a foreign currency, the effect of exchange rate movements must be reported in the statement of cash flows in order to reconcile the cash balances at the beginning and end of the period.

According to IAS 7, this reconciling item is presented separately from cash flows from operating, investing and financing activities.

Illustration – Overseas subsidiary

B Group recognised a gain of $160,000 on the translation of the financial statements of a 75% owned foreign subsidiary for the year ended 31 December 20X7. This gain is found to be made up as follows

	$
Gain on opening net assets:	
Non-current assets	90,000
Inventories	30,000
Receivables	50,000
Payables	(40,000)
Cash	30,000
	160,000

The overseas subsidiary made no profit or loss in the year. No goodwill arose on acquisition.

B Group recognised a loss of $70,000 on retranslating the parent entity's foreign currency loan. This loss has been recorded in the statement of profit or loss.

Consolidated statements of financial position as at 31 December

	20X7	20X6
	$000	$000
Non-current assets	2,100	1,700
Inventories	650	480
Receivables	990	800
Cash	500	160
	4,240	3,140
Share capital	1,000	1,000
Group reserves	1,600	770
	2,600	1,770
Non-controlling interest	520	370
Equity	3,120	2,140
Long-term loan	250	180
Payables	870	820
	4,240	3,140

There were no non-current asset disposals during the year.

Consolidated statement of profit or loss for the year ended 31 December 20X7

	$000
Profit before tax (after depreciation of $220,000)	2,100
Tax	(650)
Group profit for the year	1,450
Profit attributable to:	
Owners of the parent	1,190
Non-controlling interest	260
Net profit for the period	1,450

Note: The dividend paid by the parent company of the B group during the year was $480,000.

Prepare a statement of cash flows for the year ended 31 December 20X7.

Solution

Statement of cash flows for the year ended 31 December 20X7

Cash flows from operating activities

		$000
Profit before tax		2,100
Forex loss on loan		70
Depreciation charges		220
Increase in inventory (650 – 480 – 30)		(140)
Increase in receivables (990 – 800 – 50)		(140)
Increase in payables (870 – 820 – 40)		10
Cash generated from operations		2,120
Income taxes paid		(650)
Net cash from operating activities		1,470
Cash flows from investing activities		
Purchase of non-current assets (W1)	(530)	
		(530)
Cash flows from financing activities		
Dividends paid to non-controlling interests (W2)	(150)	
Dividends paid	(480)	
		(630)
Exchange gain on cash		30
Increase in cash and cash equivalents		340
Cash and cash equivalents at 1 Jan 20X7		160
Cash and cash equivalents at 31 Dec 20X7		500

Note: There have been no proceeds from loans during the year. The loan balance has increased by $70,000 ($250,000 – $180,000) as a result of the foreign exchange loss.

Workings

(W1) **Non-current assets**

	$000
Bal b/fwd	1,700
Exchange gain	90
Depreciation	(220)
Additions (bal. fig.)	530
Bal c/fwd	2,100

(W2) **Non-controlling interest**

	$000
Bal b/fwd	370
Total comprehensive income*	300
Dividend paid (bal. fig.)	(150)
Bal c/fwd	520

* This is the NCI share of the subsidiary's profit after tax ($260,000) as well as the NCI share of the foreign exchange gain (25% × $160,000)

Test your understanding 7 – Boardres

Set out below is a summary of the accounts of Boardres, a public limited company, for the year ended 31 December 20X7.

Consolidated statement of profit or loss and other comprehensive income for the year ended 31 December 20X7

	$000
Revenue	44,754
Cost of sales and other expenses	(39,613)
Profit from operations	5,141
Income from associates	30
Finance cost	(305)
Profit before tax	4,866
Tax:	(2,038)
Profit for the period	2,828
Other comprehensive income: Items that may be reclassified to profit or loss in future periods	
Total exchange difference on retranslation of foreign operations (note 5)	302
Total comprehensive income	3,130
Profit for the year attributable to:	
Owners of the parent	2,805
Non-controlling interests	23
	2,828
Total comprehensive income for the year attributable to:	
Owners of the parent (2,805 + 302)	3,107
Non-controlling interests	23
	3,130

Summary of changes in equity attributable to the owners of the parent for the year

	$000
Equity b/f	14,164
Profit for year	2,805
Dividends paid	(445)
Exchange differences	302
Equity c/f	16,826

Consolidated statements of financial position at 31 December

	Note	20X7	20X6
		$000	$000
Non-current assets			
Goodwill		500	–
Property, plant and equipment	(1)	11,157	8,985
Investment in associate		300	280
		11,957	9,265
Current assets			
Inventories		9,749	7,624
Receivables		5,354	4,420
Short-term investments	(2)	1,543	741
Cash		1,013	394
		29,616	22,444
Equity share capital		1,997	1,997
Share premium		5,808	5,808
Retained earnings		9,021	6,359
		16,826	14,164
Non-controlling interest		170	17
Total equity		16,996	14,181
Non-current liabilities			
Loans		2,102	1,682
Provisions	(4)	1,290	935
Current liabilities	(3)	9,228	5,646
		29,616	22,444

Notes to the accounts

(1) **Property, plant and equipment**

Property, plant and equipment movements include the following:

	$000
Carrying amount of disposals	305
Proceeds from disposals	854
Depreciation charge for the year	907

(2) **Short-term investments**

The short-term investments are readily convertible into cash and there is an insignificant risk that their value will change.

(3) **Current liabilities**

	20X7	**20X6**
	$000	$000
Bank overdrafts	1,228	91
Trade payables	4,278	2,989
Tax	3,722	2,566
	9,228	5,646

(4) **Provisions**

	Legal provision	**Deferred taxation**	**Total**
	$000	$000	$000
At 31 December 20X6	246	689	935
Exchange rate adjustment	29	–	29
Increase in provision	460	–	460
Decrease in provision	–	(134)	(134)
At 31 December 20X7	735	555	1,290

(5) **Liberated**

During the year, the company acquired 82% of the issued equity capital of Liberated for a cash consideration of $1,268,000. The fair values of the assets of Liberated were as follows:

	$000
Property, plant and equipment	208
Inventories	612
Trade receivables	500
Cash in hand	232
Trade payables	(407)
Debenture loans	(312)
	833

(6) **Exchange gains**

The net exchange gain on translating the financial statements of a wholly-owned subsidiary has been recorded in other comprehensive income and is held within retained earnings. The gain comprises differences on the retranslation of the following:

	$000
Property, plant and equipment	138
Legal provision	(29)
Inventories	116
Trade receivables	286
Trade payables	(209)
Net exchange gain	302

(7) **Non-controlling interest**

The non-controlling interest is valued using the proportion of net assets method.

Required:

Prepare a statement of cash flows for the year ended 31 December 20X7.

8 Evaluation of statements of cash flows

Usefulness and limitations

Usefulness of the statement of cash flows

A statement of cash flows can provide information that is not available from the statement of financial position or statement of profit or loss and other comprehensive income.

(a) It may assist users of financial statements in making judgements on the amount, timing and degree of certainty of future cash flows.

(b) It gives an indication of the relationship between profitability and cash generating ability, and thus of the quality of the profit earned.

(c) Analysts and other users of financial information often, formally or informally, develop models to assess and compare the present value of the future cash flow of entities. Historical cash flow information could be useful to check the accuracy of past assessments.

(d) A statement of cash flow in conjunction with a statement of financial position provides information on liquidity, solvency and adaptability. The statement of financial position is often used to obtain information on liquidity, but the information is incomplete for this purpose as the statement of financial position is drawn up at a particular point in time.

(e) Cash flows cannot easily be manipulated and are not affected by judgement or by accounting policies.

Limitations of the statement of cash flows

Statements of cash flows should normally be used in conjunction with statements of profit and loss and other comprehensive income and statements of financial position when making an assessment of future cash flows.

(a) Statements of cash flows are based on historical information and therefore do not provide complete information for assessing future cash flows.

(b) There is some scope to 'window dress' cash flows. For example, a business may delay paying suppliers until after the period-end, or it may sell assets before the period-end and then immediately repurchase them at the start of the next period.

(c) Cash flow is necessary for survival in the short term, but in order to survive in the long term a business must be profitable. It is often necessary to sacrifice cash flow in the short term in order to generate profits in the long term (e.g. by investment in non-current assets). A substantial cash balance is not a sign of good management if the cash could be invested elsewhere to generate profit.

Neither cash flow nor profit provides a complete picture of an entity's performance when looked at in isolation.

9 Other issues

Criticisms of IAS 7

The following criticisms have been made of IAS 7 Statement of Cash Flows

Direct and indirect method

Allowing entities to choose between using the direct or indirect method limits comparability.

Many users of the financial statements will not understand the adjustments made to profit when cash generated from operations is presented under the indirect method.

Lack of guidance and disagreements

There is insufficient guidance in IAS 7 as to how to classify cash flows. This can create the following problems:

- IAS 7 allows dividends and interest paid to be presented as cash flows from either operating or financing activities. This limits comparability between companies.
- Entities may classify cash flows related to the same transaction in different ways (a loan repayment might be split between interest paid within operating activities and the repayment of the principal in financing activities). This could hinder user understanding.

- There are disagreements about the presentation of payments related to leases. Some argue that they should be classified as a financing activity, whereas others argue that they are a form of investment activity.
- Expenditure on research is classified as an operating activity. Some argue that they should be included within investing activities, because it relates to items that are intended to generate future income and cash flows.

Disclosures

Current cash flow disclosures are deemed to be inadequate. In particular, there is a lack of disclosure about restrictions on an entity's ability to use their cash and cash equivalents (particularly if located overseas) and whether other sources of finance would be more economical.

10 Chapter summary

Objective of statements of cash flows

- To provide information on changes in cash and cash equivalents
- To enable users to assess the liquidity, solvency and financial adaptability of a business

Classifications of cash flows

- IAS 7 only requires 3 headings:
  - Operating activities
  - Investing activities
  - Financing activities

Preparation of group statements of cash flows

- Three additional elements:
  - Cash paid to non-controlling interest
  - Associates
  - Acquisition and disposal of subsidiaries/ associates

Foreign currency transactions

- Exchange gains must be taken out of the statement of financial position movements as they are not cash

Evaluation of statements of cash flows

- Proivdes information not available in the statement of financial position and the statement of profit or loss
- Shows relationship between profitability and cash generating ability

Test your understanding answers

Test your understanding 1 – Cash and cash equivalents

To qualify as a cash equivalent, an item must be readily convertible to cash and have an insignificant risk of a change in value. Furthermore, it should be held for the purpose of meeting short-term cash commitments.

Bank overdrafts are an integral part of most company's cash management. They are therefore generally treated as a component of cash.

The balance of $500,000 in a high interest account is readily available (only 28 days' notice is required to access it). This money is also held to meet short-term needs. Assuming that there is not a significant penalty for accessing this money, it should be included within cash equivalents.

The shares are not a cash equivalent. Shares are investments rather than a way of meeting short-term cash requirements. Moreover, there is a significant risk that the value of the shares will change. Any cash spent on shares in the period should be shown within cash flows from investing activities.

Test your understanding 2 – Extracts

(1) **Property, plant and equipment**

	$
Bal b/fwd	100
Revaluation	60
Leases	30
Depreciation	(20)
Disposals	(15)
Additions (bal. fig.)	95
Bal c/fwd	250

(2) **Tax**

	$
Bal b/fwd (50 + 100)	150
Profit or loss charge	180
Tax paid (bal. fig.)	(110)
Bal c/fwd (100 + 120)	220

(3) **Retained earnings**

	$
Bal b/fwd	200
Profit or loss	150
Dividend paid (bal. fig.)	(50)
Bal c/fwd	300

Test your understanding 3 – The Z group

Extracts from statement of cash flows

	$000
Cash flows from operating activities	
Profit before tax	915
Share of profit of associate	(15)
Cash flows from investing activities	
Dividend received from associate	5
Cash paid to acquire associates (W1)	(10)

(W1) **Associate**

	$000
Balance b/fwd	580
Share of profit of associate	15
Cash dividend received	(5)
Cash spent on investments in associates (bal. fig)	10
Balance c/fwd	600

Test your understanding 4 – Consolidated extracts

(1) **Non-controlling interest**

	$
Bal b/fwd	440
Total comprehensive income	500
Dividend paid (bal. fig.)	(100)
Bal c/fwd	840

(2) **Non-controlling interest**

	$
Bal b/fwd	500
Total comprehensive income	600
Dividend paid (bal. fig.)	(250)
Bal c/fwd	850

(3) **Associate**

	$
Bal b/fwd	200
Profit or loss	750
Dividend received (bal. fig.)	(450)
Bal c/fwd	500

(4) **Associate**

	$
Bal b/fwd	600
Profit or loss	4,000
Revaluation	500
Dividend received (bal. fig.)	(1,900)
Bal c/fwd	3,200

(5) **Property, plant and equipment**

	$
Bal b/fwd	150
New subsidiary	200
Depreciation	(50)
Additions (bal. fig.)	200
Bal c/fwd	500

Test your understanding 5 – AH Group

Consolidated statement of cash flows for the year ended 30 June 20X5

	$000	$000
Cash flows from operating activities		
Profit before tax	18,450	
Less: profit on disposal of property (2,250 – 1,000)	(1,250)	
Add: finance cost	1,400	
Adjustment for non-cash items dealt with in arriving at operating profit:		
Depreciation	7,950	
Decrease in trade receivables (27,130 – 26,300 – 1,300)	470	
Increase in inventories (33,500 – 28,750 – 1,650)	(3,100)	
Decrease in trade payables (33,340 – 32,810 – 1,950)	(1,420)	
Goodwill impaired (W5)	1,000	
Cash generated from operations	23,500	
Interest paid (W1)	(1,480)	
Income taxes paid (W2)	(5,850)	
Net cash from operating activities		16,170

Cash flows from investing activities		
Acquisition of subsidiary net of cash acquired (2,000 – 50)	(1,950)	
Purchase of property, plant, and equipment (W3)	(11,300)	
Proceeds from sale of property	2,250	
Net cash used in investing activities		(11,000)
Cash flows from financing activities		
Repayment of long-term borrowings (18,200 – 19,200)	(1,000)	
Dividend paid by parent (W7)	(6,000)	
Dividends paid to NCI (W6)	(200)	
Net cash used in financing activities		(7,200)
Net decrease in cash and cash equivalents		(2,030)
Cash and cash equivalents at 1 July 20X4		3,900
Cash and cash equivalents at 30 June 20X5		1,870

(W1) **Interest paid**

	$000
Bal b/fwd	1,440
Profit or loss	1,400
Interest paid (bal. fig.)	(1,480)
Bal c/fwd	1,360

(W2) **Income taxes paid**

	$000
Bal b/fwd	5,450
Profit or loss	6,250
New subsidiary	250
Tax paid (bal. fig.)	(5,850)
Bal c/fwd	6,100

(W3) **Property, plant and equipment**

	$000
Bal b/fwd	44,050
New subsidiary	4,200
Depreciation	(7,950)
Disposals	(1,000)
Additions (bal. fig.)	11,300
Bal c/fwd	50,600

(W4) **Goodwill arising on acquisition of subsidiary**

	$000
Fair value of shares issued (2m × $2)	4,000
Cash consideration	2,000
	6,000
Fair value of NCI at acquisition	1,750
	7,750
Fair value of net assets at acquisition	(5,000)
Goodwill at acquisition	2,750

(W5) **Goodwill**

	$000
Bal b/fwd	4,160
Goodwill on sub acquired (W4)	2,750
Impairment in year (bal. fig.)	(1,000)
Bal c/fwd	5,910

(W6) **Non-controlling interest**

	$000
Bal b/fwd	1,920
NCI arising on subsidiary acquired	1,750
Profit or loss	405
Dividend paid (bal. fig.)	(200)
Bal c/fwd	3,875

(W7) **Retained earnings**

	$000
Bal b/fwd	18,340
Profit or loss	11,795
Dividend paid (bal. fig.)	(6,000)
Bal c/fwd	24,135

Test your understanding 6 – Pearl

Consolidated statement of cash flows

	$000	$000
Cash flows from operating activities		
Profit before tax	1,115	
Finance cost	35	
Profit on sale of subsidiary	(100)	
Income from associates	(115)	
Depreciation	385	
Impairment (W1)	80	
Gain on disposal of PPE ($275 – $250)	(25)	
Increase in inventories ($470 – $435 – $150 + $165)	(50)	
Decrease in receivables ($390 – $330 – $240 + $120)	60	
Decrease in payables ($800 – $725 – $220 + $80)	(65)	
	1,320	
Interest paid	(35)	
Tax paid (W4)	(180)	
		1,105

Cash flows from investing activities		
Proceeds from sale of PPE	275	
Purchases of PPE (W5)	(800)	
Dividends received from associate (W6)	85	
Acquisition of subsidiary ($1,500 – $80)	(1,420)	
Disposal of subsidiary ($850 – $50)	800	
		(1,060)
Cash flows from financing activities		
Proceeds from loans ($500 – $300)	200	
Dividends paid to shareholders of the parent (per CSOCIE)	(125)	
Dividends paid to NCI (per CSOCIE)	(50)	
		25
Increase in cash and cash equivalents		70
Opening cash and cash equivalents		140
Closing cash and cash equivalents		210

Workings

(W1) **Goodwill**

	$000
Balance b/f	1,850
Acquisition of subsidiary (W2)	350
Disposal of subsidiary (W3)	(190)
Impairment (bal fig)	(80)
Balance c/f	1,930

(W2) **Goodwill on acquisition of subsidiary**

	$000
Cost of investment	1,500
Fair value of NCI at acquisition	340
Fair value of net assets at acquisition	(1,490)
	350

(W3) **Goodwill at disposal date**

	$000
Cost of investment	600
Fair value of NCI at acquisition	320
Fair value of net assets at acquisition	(730)
	190

(W4) **Tax**

	$000
Balance b/f ($360 + $105)	465
Acquisition of subsidiary	40
Disposal of subsidiary	–
Profit or loss	225
Cash paid (bal. fig.)	(180)
Balance c/f ($400 + $150)	550

(W5) **PPE**

	$000
Balance b/f	1,625
Depreciation	(385)
Revaluation gain	200
Disposal of plant	(250)
Acquisition of subsidiary	1,280
Disposal of subsidiary	(725)
Cash paid (bal. fig)	800
Balance c/f	2,545

(W6) **Dividend from associate**

	$000
Balance b/f	540
Share of profit of associate	115
OCI from associate	50
Dividend received (bal. fig)	(85)
Balance c/f	620

Test your understanding 7 – Boardres

Statement of cash flows for the year ended 31 December 20X7

	$000	$000
Cash flows from operating activities		
Profit before tax	4,866	
Finance cost	305	
Income from associates	(30)	
Depreciation	907	
Goodwill (W7)	85	
Profit on disposal of PPE (W1)	(549)	
Increase in legal provision	460	
	6,044	
Change in working capital		
Increase in inventory		
(9,749 – 7,624 – 612 acq – 116 ex diff)	(1,397)	
Increase in receivables		
(5,354 – 4,420 – 500 acq – 286 ex diff)	(148)	
Increase in payables		
(4,278 – 2,989 – 407 acq – 209 ex diff)	673	
	5,172	
Interest paid	(305)	
Tax paid (W2)	(1,016)	
Cash flows from investing activities		
Purchase of non-current assets (W3)	(3,038)	
Proceeds on disposal	854	
Cash consideration paid on acquisition of subsidiary, net of cash acquired (1,268 – 232)	(1,036)	
Dividend received from associate (W4)	10	
		(3,210)

Cash flows from financing activities		
Dividends paid	(445)	
Dividends paid to NCI (W6)	(20)	
Proceeds from debt issue (W5)	108	
		(357)
Change in cash and cash equivalents		284
Opening cash and cash equivalents (394 + 741 – 91)		1,044
Closing cash and cash equivalents (1,013 + 1,543 – 1,228)		1,328

Workings

(W1) **Profit on disposal of property, plant and equipment**

	$000
Sales proceeds	854
Carrying amount	(305)
Profit on disposal	549

(W2) **Tax paid**

	$000
Bal b/fwd (2,566 + 689)	3,255
Profit or loss	2,038
Tax paid (bal. fig.)	(1,016)
Bal c/fwd (3,722 + 555)	4,277

(W3) **Property, plant and equipment**

	$000
Bal b/fwd	8,985
Exchange gain	138
Acquisition of subsidiary	208
Depreciation	(907)
Disposal	(305)
Additions (bal. fig.)	3,038
Bal c/fwd	11,157

(W4) **Dividends from associates**

	$000
Bal b/fwd	280
Profit or loss	30
Dividend received (bal. fig.)	(10)
Bal c/fwd	300

(W5) **Debentures**

	$000
Bal b/fwd	1,682
Acquisition of subsidiary	312
Cash received (bal. fig.)	108
Bal c/fwd	2,102

(W6) **Non-controlling interest**

	$000
Bal b/fwd	17
Total comprehensive income	23
Acquisition of subsidiary (18% × 833)	150
Dividend paid (bal. fig.)	(20)
Bal c/fwd	170

(W7) **Goodwill**

	$000
Cost of investment	1,268
NCI at acquisition (18% × 833)	150
	1,418
FV of net assets at acquisition	(833)
Goodwill at acquisition	585

	$000
Goodwill b/fwd	nil
Goodwill acquired (above)	585
Goodwill impairment (bal. fig)	(85)
Goodwill c/fwd	500

chapter

25

UK GAAP

Chapter learning objectives

Upon completion of this chapter you will be able to:

- provide an overview of UK accounting standards
- discuss the key differences between the SMEs Standard and UK GAAP
- discuss basic Companies Act requirements in relation to the preparation of financial statements.

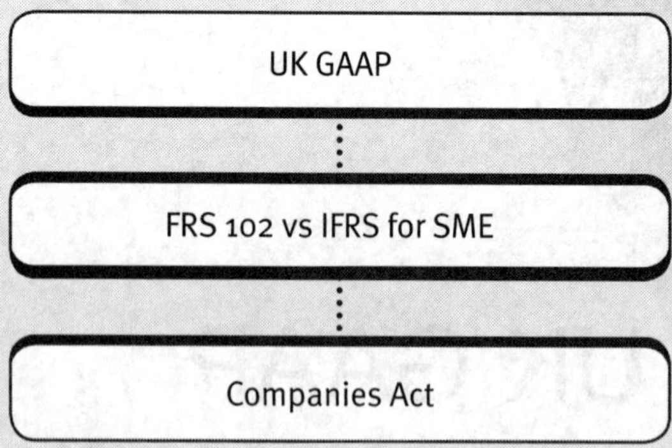

1 Purpose of chapter

The P2 UK paper

This chapter contains the additional syllabus content required for those who are sitting the P2 UK paper.

If you are sitting the P2 INT paper then you **do not** need to study this chapter.

2 UK GAAP

UK standards

Guidance about the accounting standards that UK companies should apply is found within FRS 100 Application of Financial Reporting Requirements. The rules are as follows:

- Listed groups must prepare their accounts under IFRS.
  - However, the companies within the group can take advantage of disclosure exemptions outlined in FRS 101 when preparing their individual (non-consolidated) financial statements.
- Other UK companies will apply FRS 102 The Financial Reporting Standard Applicable in the UK and the Republic of Ireland unless:
  - they voluntarily choose to apply IFRS, or
  - they are a micro-entity and choose to apply FRS 105 The Financial Reporting Standard Applicable to the Micro-Entities Regime.

- A small entity that applies FRS 102:
  - does not have to show other comprehensive income
  - does not have to produce a statement of cash flows
  - is exempt from many of the disclosure requirements of FRS 102.

FRS 101

FRS 101 Reduced Disclosure Framework applies to the individual financial statements of subsidiaries and ultimate parent companies. It provides exemptions from disclosure requirements that will result in cost savings when producing individual financial statements. FRS 101 does not apply to consolidated financial statements.

To apply FRS 101, the shareholders of a qualifying entity must have been notified about its use and they must not object.

FRS 102

FRS 102 is a single standard that is organised by topic.

Although FRS 102 is based on IFRS for Small and Medium Entities (the SMEs Standard), there are differences. The differences that are examinable in the P2 UK syllabus are outlined later in this chapter.

FRS 105

The Financial Reporting Council has withdrawn the Financial Reporting Standard for Smaller Entities (FRSSE). Micro-entities can now choose to prepare their financial statements in accordance with FRS 105 The Financial Reporting Standard Applicable to the Micro-entities Regime.

An entity qualifies as a micro-entity if it satisfies two of the following three requirements:

- Turnover of not more than £632,000 a year
- Gross assets of not more than £316,000
- An average number of employees of 10 or less.

FRS 105 is based on FRS 102 but with some amendments to satisfy legal requirements and to reflect the simpler nature of micro-entities. For example, FRS 105:

- Prohibits accounting for deferred tax
- Prohibits accounting for equity-settled share-based payments prior to the issue of the shares
- Prohibits the revaluation model for property, plant and equipment, intangible assets and investment properties
- Prohibits the capitalisation of borrowing costs
- Prohibits the capitalisation of development expenditure as an intangible asset
- Simplifies the rules around classifying a financial instrument as debt or equity
- Removes the distinction between functional and presentation currencies.

There are very few disclosure requirements in FRS 105.

3 Examinable differences between International and UK standards

Examinable differences between FRS 102 and the SMEs Standard

Although FRS 102 is based on IFRS for Small and Medium Entities (the SMEs Standard), there are differences. Some of these differences are included in the UK P2 syllabus.

Financial statement presentation

To comply with Companies Act, FRS 102 allows a 'true and fair override'. If compliance with FRS 102 is inconsistent with the requirement to give a true and fair view, the directors must depart from FRS 102 to the extent necessary to give a true and fair view. Particulars of any such departure, the reasons for it and its effect are disclosed.

Statement of cash flows

Under FRS 102, small entities, mutual life assurance companies, pension funds and certain investment funds are not required to produce a statement of cash flows. This exemption does not exist under the SMEs Standard.

Consolidated and separate financial statements

Under the SMEs Standard, a parent need not present consolidated financial statements if the parent is itself a subsidiary, and its ultimate parent (or any intermediate parent) produces consolidated general purpose financial statements that comply with full IFRS and IAS Standards or the SMEs Standard.

FRS 102 makes some slight amendments to the above to comply with Companies Act. In particular, consolidated financial statements do not need to be produced if the parent, and group headed by it, qualifies as small. The requirements of Companies Act are dealt with in more detail later in this chapter.

Inventories

FRS 102 specifies that the cost of inventories acquired through a non-exchange transaction (such as a donation or legacy) should be measured at the fair value of the inventories at the acquisition date. The SMEs Standard does not mention this issue.

Investments in associates

FRS 102 explicitly clarifies that an investment in an associate cannot be equity accounted in the individual financial statements of a company that is a parent. Instead, the investment in associate can be held at cost or fair value.

Under FRS 102, the cost of an associate should include transaction costs. These are excluded from the cost of the associate under the SMEs Standard.

Investments in joint ventures

FRS 102 explicitly clarifies that an investment in a jointly controlled entity cannot be equity accounted in the individual financial statements of a company that is a parent. Instead, the investment can be held at cost or fair value.

Under FRS 102, the cost of a joint venture should include transaction costs. These are excluded from the cost of the joint venture under the SMEs Standard.

Intangible assets

Under FRS 102, an intangible asset arising from development activity can be recognised if certain criteria are met. These criteria are broadly the same as under IAS 38. According to the SMEs Standard, research and development expenditure is always written off to profit or loss.

Under FRS 102, intangible assets can be held under the cost model or the revaluation model. The SMEs Standard does not permit the revaluation model.

Business combinations and goodwill

According to FRS 102:

- Negative goodwill (where the fair value of the net assets acquired exceeds the consideration) is recognised on the statement of financial position immediately below goodwill. It should be followed by a subtotal of the net amount of goodwill and the negative goodwill.
- The subsequent treatment of negative goodwill is that any amount up to the fair value of non-monetary assets acquired is recognised in profit or loss in the periods in which the non-monetary assets are recovered. Any amount exceeding the fair value of non-monetary assets acquired must be recognised in profit or loss in the periods expected to be benefited.

Under the SMEs Standard negative goodwill is recognised immediately in profit or loss.

Government grants

Under FRS 102, two methods of recognising government grants are allowed:

- The performance model
  - If no conditions are attached to the grant, it is recognised as income immediately.
  - If conditions are attached to the grant, it is only recognised as income when all conditions have been met.
- The accruals model
  - Grants are recognised as income on a systematic basis, either as costs are incurred (revenue grants) or over the asset's useful life (capital grants).

Under the SMEs Standard only the performance model for recognising government grants is allowed.

Borrowing costs

Under FRS 102, an entity may capitalise borrowing costs that are directly attributable to the construction, acquisition or production of a qualifying asset. Under the SMEs Standard all borrowing costs are recognised as an expense in profit or loss.

Employee benefits

Under FRS 102, the projected unit credit method must be used to estimate the defined benefit obligation.

In contrast, the SMEs Standard allows some simplified estimation techniques if an entity is not able, without undue cost or effort, to use the projected unit credit method to measure its obligation and cost under defined benefit plans. Entities are permitted to:

- **'ignore estimated future salary increases**
- **ignore future service of current employees**
- **ignore possible in-service mortality of current employees between the reporting date and the date employees are expected to begin receiving post-employment benefits'** (SMEs Standard, para 28.19).

Related parties

FRS 102 permits an additional exemption from the disclosure of related party transactions than the SMEs Standard. FRS 102 states that disclosures need not be given of transactions entered into between two or more members of a group, provided that any subsidiary which is a party to the transaction is wholly owned by such a member.

Income tax

The income tax section of FRS 102 differs significantly from the SMEs Standard.

- Profit or loss/statement of financial position:
  - FRS 102 adopts a profit or loss approach to the recognition of deferred tax. Timing differences are defined as differences between taxable profits and total comprehensive income as stated in the financial statements that arise from the inclusion of income and expenses in tax assessments in periods different from those in which they are recognised in financial statements.
    - FRS 102 makes an exception to this rule. It states that deferred tax should also be recognised based on the differences between the tax value and fair value of assets and liabilities acquired in a business combination.
  - In contrast, the SMEs Standard conceptualises deferred tax through the statement of financial position. The standard states that deferred tax should be accounted for based on differences **'between the amounts recognised for the entity's assets and liabilities in the statement of financial position and the recognition of those assets and liabilities by the tax authorities'** (SMEs Standard, para 29.9).
- Permanent differences:
  - FRS 102 uses the concept of permanent differences. Permanent differences arise because certain types of income and expenses are non-taxable or disallowable, or because certain tax charges or allowances are greater or smaller than the corresponding income or expense in the financial statements. Deferred tax is not recognised on permanent differences.
  - The SMEs Standard does not use the terminology 'permanent difference'. Instead, it says that deferred tax assets and liabilities are recognised for 'temporary differences'.

4 Companies Act

Examinable Companies Act requirements

The UK syllabus for P2 specifies that candidates must know the basic Companies Act requirements surrounding when single and group entity financial statements are required and when a subsidiary may be excluded from the group financial statements.

Single entity financial statements

A company is exempt from the requirement to prepare individual accounts for a financial year if:

- it is itself a subsidiary undertaking
- it has been dormant throughout the whole of that year, and
- its parent undertaking is established under the law of an EEA State.

Group financial statements

A company subject to the small companies regime **may** prepare group accounts for the year.

If not subject to the small companies regime, a parent company **must** prepare group accounts for the year unless one of the following applies:

- A company is exempt from the requirement to prepare group accounts if it is itself a wholly-owned subsidiary of a parent undertaking.
- A parent company is exempt from the requirement to prepare group accounts if, under section 405 of Companies Act, all of its subsidiary undertakings could be excluded from consolidation.

Exclusion of a subsidiary from consolidation

Where a parent company prepares Companies Act group accounts, all the subsidiary undertakings of the company must be included in the consolidation, subject to the following exceptions:

- A subsidiary undertaking may be excluded from consolidation if its inclusion is not material for the purpose of giving a true and fair view (but two or more undertakings may be excluded only if they are not material taken together).

- A subsidiary undertaking may be excluded from consolidation where:
  - severe long-term restrictions substantially hinder the exercise of the rights of the parent company over the assets or management of that undertaking
  - the information necessary for the preparation of group accounts cannot be obtained without disproportionate expense or undue delay
  - the interest of the parent company is held exclusively with a view to subsequent resale.

5 Question practice

UK focus question – Stream

Stream is a medium sized company which has invested in several smaller companies. The draft profit after tax in the consolidated statements for the year ended 31 December 20X1 is $5 million. However, advice is required about the following transactions:

(i) During 20X1, Stream spent $500,000 on development activities. These activities are still ongoing as at 31 December 20X1. However, the Directors of Stream firmly believe that this development will lead to future economic benefits. Stream has adequate resources to complete the development. The cash spent to date has been recognised as an intangible asset.

(ii) On 1 January 20X1, Stream took out a $10 million 6% bank loan to finance the construction of a new head office building. Construction commenced on 1 January 20X1 and was still ongoing at the year end. Interest on the loan for the year has been charged as an expense.

If a choice of accounting treatment exists, the Directors of Stream wish to select the policy that will maximise reported assets.

Required:

Calculate the revised consolidated profit after tax for the year ended 31 December 20X1 assuming that Stream prepares its accounts using:

(a) **The SMEs Standard**

(b) **FRS 102**

Solution

	(a) SMEs Standard	(b) FRS 102
	$000	$000
Draft profit	5,000	5,000
Issue (i)	(500)	–
Issue (ii)	–	600
Revised profit	4,500	5,600

Explanations

(i) According to the SMEs Standard, expenditure on development activity must be recognised as an expense. Therefore, if accounting under the SMEs Standard, the development asset currently recognised must be written off.

Expenditure on development can be capitalised under FRS 102 if relevant criteria are satisfied.

(ii) Borrowing costs must be expensed under the SMEs Standard.

According to FRS 102, borrowing costs can be included within the cost of a qualifying asset. Therefore, if Stream accounted under FRS 102, it would be able to reverse out the interest expense of $600,000 ($10m × 6%) and instead recognise it as part of the cost of its property, plant and equipment.

UK focus question – Sofa

Sofa is a company that has a number of investments. Sofa exercises control over some of these investments and significant influence over others.

Required:

Advise the Directors of Sofa as to the key differences between the SMEs Standard and FRS 102 that would impact the consolidated financial statements of the Sofa group. Where possible, discuss the potential impact that these differences would have on profit.

Solution

Under the SMEs Standard, negative goodwill is recognised immediately in profit or loss. According to FRS 102, negative goodwill is recognised on the statement of financial position as a deduction against goodwill.

- If a company acquires 'negative goodwill', the treatment under the SMEs Standard would lead to higher reported profits in the year of acquisition.

Under FRS 102, the cost of an associate should include transaction costs. These are excluded from the cost of the investment under the SMEs Standard and are instead written off to profit or loss.

- Under the SMEs Standard, profits will be lower in the year when an associate is acquired than under FRS 102.
- The lower carrying amount of the associate under the SMEs Standard may mean that impairments are less likely in the future.

UK focus question – FRS 105

You advise a client who is in the process of incorporating a new UK-based company. The company would qualify as a micro-entity and, as such, could apply FRS 105 The Financial Reporting Standard applicable to the Micro-entities Regime. Alternatively, it could apply FRS 102 The Financial Reporting Standard applicable in the UK and Republic of Ireland.

Required:

What factors should be considered when establishing whether the client should use FRS 105?

Solution

FRS 105 requires far fewer disclosures than FRS 102. This will reduce the time and cost burden of producing financial statements. However, consideration should be given to whether the users of the financial statements will find this lack of disclosure a hindrance to making economic decisions. This is unlikely in the case of such a small company.

FRS 105 does not permit property, plant and equipment, intangible assets or investment properties to be held at fair value. This will have a big impact on perception of the company's financial position.

Accounting policy choices allowed in FRS 102 have been removed in FRS 105. For instance, borrowing costs and development costs must be expensed. Profits reported under FRS 105 may be lower than if FRS 102 was applied.

If the company is expected to grow quickly, it might be easier to simply apply FRS 102 from the outset. That way, it will avoid the burden of transitioning from FRS 105 to FRS 102 at a later date.

6 Chapter summary

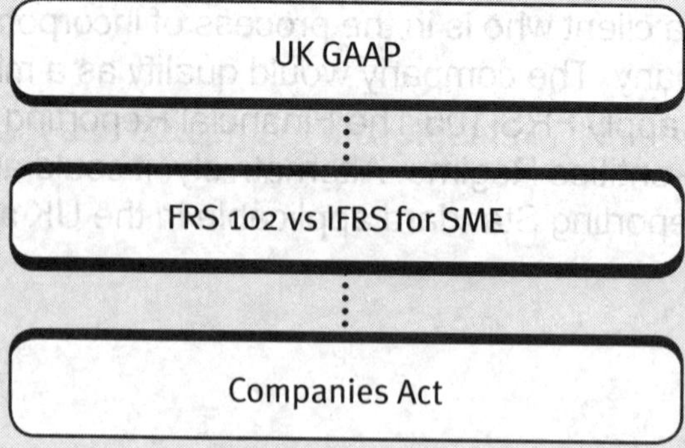

chapter

26

Questions & Answers

Test your understanding 1 – Cookie

Cookie, a company, prepares its financial statements in accordance with International Financial Reporting Standards. It has investments in two other companies, Biscuit and Cracker. The statements of financial position of all three companies as at 30 April 20X4 are presented below:

	Cookie	**Biscuit**	**Cracker**
	$m	$m	$m
Non-current assets			
Property, plant and equipment	80	85	67
Investments	101	10	–
	181	95	67
Current assets			
Inventories	19	6	25
Trade receivables	17	13	33
Cash and cash equivalents	22	3	14
Total assets	239	117	139
Equity and liabilities			
Share capital ($1)	21	10	20
Other components of equity	50	–	20
Retained earnings	105	79	43
Total equity	176	89	83
Non-current liabilities	40	10	18
Current liabilities	23	18	38
Total equity and liabilities	239	117	139

The following notes are relevant to the preparation of the consolidated financial statements:

(1) On 1 May 20X3, Cookie acquired 55% of the ordinary shares of Biscuit. Consideration was in the form of cash and shares. The cash consideration of $30 million has been recorded in the accounts of Cookie but no entries have been made for the 5 million shares issued. These had a fair value of $4.50 each on 1 May 20X3. The retained earnings of Biscuit at this date were $70 million.

(2) The fair value of the net assets of Biscuit at the acquisition date was $95 million. The difference between the fair value and carrying amount of the net assets was due to a brand that was not recognised by Biscuit. This brand was estimated to have a remaining useful economic life of 5 years. The fair value of the non-controlling interest in Biscuit at acquisition was $45 million.

(3) On 1 May 20X3, Cookie spent $56 million to acquire 70% of the ordinary shares of Cracker. On this date, Cracker had retained earnings of $30 million and other components of equity of $20 million. On 1 November 20X3, Cookie spent another $15 million in order to increase its holding to 90% of Cracker's ordinary shares. Cookie elected to measure the non-controlling interest in Cracker using the share of net assets method.

(4) During the year, Cookie sold goods to Biscuit for $4 million making a profit of $2 million. This sale was made on credit and the invoice has not yet been settled. One quarter of the goods remain in the inventory of Biscuit at the year end.

(5) There has been no impairment in respect of the goodwill arising on the acquisition of Cracker. At the year end, it was estimated that the recoverable amount of the net assets of Biscuit was $107 million.

(6) The investments held by Biscuit relate to equity shares that have been designated as fair value through profit and loss. They were purchased during the current year and are currently held at cost. At 30 April 20X4, these shares had a fair value of $15 million.

(7) Included in the non-current liabilities of Cookie is a loan denominated in another currency, the Dinar (DN). The loan, for DN10 million, was received on 1 August 20X3 and correctly recorded at the spot rate. No other entries have been posted. The following exchange rates are relevant:

	DN:$1
1 August 20X3	2.3:1
30 April 20X4	2.6:1

(8) Included in the property, plant and equipment of Cookie is an item of specialised plant which was constructed internally. Construction began on 1 May 20X3. The asset was recorded at a cost of $15 million and was attributed a useful economic life of five years. A breakdown of the cost is as follows:

	$m
Materials for construction	7.3
Directly attributable labour	2.9
Testing of machine	0.6
Training staff to use machine	0.5
Allocated general overheads	3.7
	15.0

The plant was available for use on 1 November 20X3 and was depreciated from this date.

(9) During the year, Cookie started selling goods under warranty. No warranty provision has been accounted for. Cookie will repair goods under warranty for any manufacturing defects that become apparent within a year of purchase. If all items under warranty at 30 April 20X4 developed minor defects, then the total cost of repairs would be approximately $6 million. If all items under warranty developed major defects, then the total cost of repairs would be approximately $14 million. The directors of Cookie estimate that 7% of items under warranty will develop minor defects within the warranty period and that 4% of items under warranty will develop major defects within the warranty period.

Required:

Prepare the consolidated statement of financial position for the Cookie Group as at 30 April 20X4.

Test your understanding 2 – Pineapple

Pineapple is a public limited company which has investments in a number of other companies. The draft statements of profit or loss for the year ended 30 September 20X3 are presented below:

	Pineapple	Strawberry	Satsuma	Apricot
	$000	$000	$000	$000
Revenue	9,854	3,562	2,435	6,434
Cost of sales	(5,432)	(2,139)	(945)	(3,534)
Gross profit	4,422	1,423	1,490	2,900
Administrative expenses	(1,432)	(400)	(523)	(600)
Distribution costs	(402)	(324)	(237)	(254)
Profit from operations	2,588	699	730	2,046
Investment income	386	15	34	135
Finance costs	(246)	–	(35)	–
Profit before taxation	2,728	714	729	2,181
Taxation	(486)	–	(161)	(432)
Profit after tax	2,242	714	568	1,749

Movements in the retained earnings of each company for the year ended 30 September 20X3 are presented below:

	Pineapple	Strawberry	Satsuma	Apricot
	$000	$000	$000	$000
1 October 20X2	5,645	1,325	2,342	3,243
Total comprehensive income for the period	2,242	714	568	1,749
Dividends	–	(400)	–	–
30 September 20X3	7,887	1,639	2,910	4,992

The following notes are relevant to the preparation of the group financial statements.

(1) On 1 October 20X2, Pineapple purchased 80% of Strawberry's 1 million $1 ordinary shares. It is the group's policy to measure the non-controlling interest at fair value at the date of acquisition. At 1 October 20X2, the balance on Strawberry's retained earnings was $1,325,000. The fair value of Strawberry's net assets was deemed to be $4,000,000. The excess in the fair value of the net assets over their carrying amounts is due to a factory building with a remaining useful life at the acquisition date of 40 years.

(2) Pineapple acquired 70% of Satsuma's 2 million $1 ordinary shares several years ago for cash consideration of $4,900,000. At the acquisition date, retained earnings of Satsuma were $2,045,000 and the fair value of the non-controlling interest was $1,600,000. On 31 March 20X3, Pineapple sold its entire shareholding in Satsuma for $5,600,000. Goodwill arising on the acquisition of Satsuma was impaired by 40% in the year ended 30 September 20X2. Satsuma is geographically distinct from the rest of the Pineapple group and therefore the disposal should be presented as a discontinued operation.

(3) On 30 June 20X3, Pineapple acquired 30% of the ordinary shares in Apricot. At 30 June 20X3, it was deemed that the fair value of a building owned by Apricot exceeded its carrying amount by $1,600,000. The remaining useful life of the building was 40 years at the acquisition date.

(4) On 1 October 20X2, Pineapple sold goods to Strawberry for $400,000. All of these had been sold to third parties by 30 September 20X3. On 1 August 20X3, Apricot sold inventory to Pineapple making a profit of $100,000. By 30 September 20X3, one fifth of these goods have been sold to third parties by Pineapple.

(5) Impairment testing on 30 September 20X3 revealed that goodwill arising of the acquisition of Strawberry was impaired by $300,000, and that the investment in Apricot was impaired by $50,000. Goodwill impairments should be presented in administrative expenses.

(6) On 1 October 20X2, Pineapple made an interest free loan of $1,500,000 to Blueberry, a key supplier, who was in financial difficulties. This loan is repayable on September 20X6. If the supplier had borrowed the money from a bank, they would have been charged annual interest of 12%. Pineapple has recorded the cash outflow and a corresponding financial asset at $1,500,000. No other accounting entries have been made, except to correctly record the required loss allowance.

(7) On 30 June 20X3, Pineapple sold a new product to a customer for $500,000 in cash and recognised the revenue in full. The terms of the sale indicate that Pineapple must offer technical support to the customer over the next 24 months. Pineapple usually charges $3,000 per month for technical support.

(8) Pineapple set up a defined contribution pension scheme on 1 October 20X2. Pineapple must make annual contributions into the scheme equivalent to 5% of employee salaries for that 12 month period. For the year ended 30 September 20X3, employee salaries were $900,000. Pineapple has paid $30,000 into the pension scheme in the current year and recognised this as an administrative expense.

(9) Strawberry has recently returned to profitability after several years of making losses. Strawberry correctly recognised no deferred tax in the prior year financial statements in respect of tax adjusted losses due to high levels of uncertainty in forecasting future profits. At 30 September 20X3, the tax allowable losses of Strawberry are $500,000 and it is firmly believed that these will be relieved against Strawberry's taxable profits in the next accounting period. No deferred tax entries have been posted in respect of these losses in the current year. Strawberry currently pays tax at 22% but, prior to the year end, the government announced that the tax rate will fall to 20% next year. All other deferred tax issues in the Pineapple group should be ignored.

Required:

Prepare the consolidated statement of profit or loss for the Pineapple Group for the year ended 30 September 20X3.

Test your understanding 3 – Vinyl

Vinyl has investments in CD and Tape. CD is located overseas and prepares its individual statements using the Mark (MK). The presentation currency of the Vinyl group is the dollar ($). The statements of financial position of Vinyl, CD and Tape as at 30 September 20X4 are presented below:

	Vinyl	CD	Tape
	$m	MKm	$m
Non-current assets			
Property, plant and equipment	350	290	160
Investment properties	10	–	–
Investments in subsidiaries	400	–	–
Financial assets	21	–	–
	781	290	160
Current assets			
Inventories	49	45	37
Trade receivables	76	46	49
Cash and cash equivalents	52	38	23
Total assets	958	419	269
Equity and liabilities			
Equity capital ($1/MK1 shares)	65	76	79
Retained earnings	501	275	101
Other components of equity	50	–	6
	616	351	186
Non-current liabilities			
Loans	200	15	24
Defined benefit deficit	50	–	–
Current liabilities	92	53	59
Total equity and liabilities	958	419	269

The following notes are relevant to the preparation of the consolidated financial statements:

(1) Vinyl acquired 75% of the ordinary shares in CD on 1 October 20X3 for MK360 million. The fair value of the non-controlling interest at the acquisition date was MK90 million and the retained earnings of CD were MK210 million. There were no other components of equity. The fair value of the net assets of CD approximated their carrying amounts with the exception of a brand. This brand was not recognised by CD but Vinyl estimates that it had a fair value of MK10 million at the acquisition date. The brand was deemed to have an indefinite useful economic life.

(2) Vinyl acquired 80% of the share capital of Tape on 1 October 20X0 for $100 million. At the acquisition date, the retained earnings of Tape were $19 million and other components of equity were $1 million. The non-controlling interest in Tape was measured using the share of net assets method. The fair value of the net assets of Tape at the acquisition date were $110 million. The excess of the fair value over the carrying amount of the net assets was attributable to non-depreciable land.

(3) The goodwill of CD and Tape was tested for impairment at 30 September 20X4. There was no impairment relating to CD. The recoverable amount of the net assets of Tape was $201 million. There have been no impairments before this date.

(4) It is the group's policy to measure investment properties at fair value. At 30 September 20X4, Vinyl's investment properties were valued at $14 million. This revaluation has not yet been accounted for.

(5) The only entry posted in the year for Vinyl's defined benefit pension scheme is the cash contributions paid into the scheme by Vinyl of $20 million. The following information relates to Vinyl's pension scheme for the current financial year:

Discount rate at 1 October 20X3	5%
Current and past service costs	$22m
Pension benefits paid during the year	$5m
Present value of the obligation at 30 September 20X4	$179m
Fair value of the plan assets at 30 September 20X4	$120m

(6) Included within Vinyl's loan balance are the proceeds from the issue of convertible bonds on 30 September 20X4. On this date, Vinyl issued 500,000 $100 4% convertible bonds at par. Interest is payable annually in arrears. These bonds will be redeemed at par for cash on 30 September 20X7, or are convertible into 75,000 ordinary shares. The interest rate on similar debt without a conversion option is 9%.

(7) The financial assets of Vinyl represent the amount paid on 1 October 20X3 to acquire redeemable preference shares in another company, which were classified to be measured at amortised cost. The effective rate of interest is 14.6%. Vinyl has received interest from these investments of $1.3 million, which has been recognised in profit or loss. Vinyl has not yet accounted for a loss allowance on these preference shares. It has calculated that the loss allowance required is $0.2 million.

(8) The following exchange rates are relevant:

	MK to $1
1 October 20X3	1.2
30 September 20X4	1.7
Average rate for the year to 30 September 20X4	1.4

Required:

Prepare the consolidated statement of financial position for the Vinyl Group as at 30 September 20X4.

Test your understanding 4 – Frank

The following financial statements relate to the Frank Group:

Consolidated statement of financial position as at 30 September 20X4 (with comparatives)

	20X4	20X3
	$m	$m
Non-current assets		
Property, plant and equipment	221	263
Goodwill	75	142
Investment in associates	204	103
Investment properties	82	60
	582	568
Current assets		
Inventories	256	201
Trade and other receivables	219	263
Cash and cash equivalents	103	42
Total assets	1,160	1,074

Equity and liabilities		
Share capital	122	102
Retained earnings	64	24
Other components of equity	59	30
	245	156
Non-controlling interest	104	87
	349	243
Non-current liabilities		
Loans	163	152
Deferred tax	44	33
Current liabilities		
Trade and other payables	524	486
Income tax payable	23	12
Overdraft	57	148
Total equity and liabilities	1,160	1,074

Consolidated statement of profit or loss and other comprehensive income for the year ended 30 September 20X4

	$m
Revenue	1,423
Cost of sales	(1,197)
Gross profit	226
Operating expenses	(150)
Profit from operations	76
Share of profit of associate	21
Profit on disposal of subsidiary	3
Finance cost	(12)
Profit before tax	88
Income tax expense	(19)
Profit for the period	69

Other comprehensive income – items that will not be reclassified to profit or loss	
Gain on revaluation of property, plant and equipment	50
Income tax on items that will not be reclassified	(10)
Total comprehensive income	109
Profit attributable to:	
Equity holders of the parent	43
Non-controlling interests	26
Profit for the period	69
Total comprehensive income attributable to:	
Equity holders of the parent	73
Non-controlling interests	36
Total comprehensive income for the period	109

The following information is relevant to the Frank group:

(1) Machinery with a carrying amount of $12m was disposed of for cash proceeds of $10m. Depreciation of $52m has been charged to operating expenses in the statement of profit or loss. As a result of a revaluation of Frank's factories during the year, a transfer has been made within equity for excess depreciation of $1m. Included in trade and other payables at the reporting date is $2m (20X3: $nil) that relates to property, plant and equipment purchased during the reporting period.

(2) Frank received a government grant of $3m in cash during the reporting period to help it fund the acquisition of a new piece of specialised machinery needed for its production process. The machinery was purchased during the year. Frank accounts for capital grants using the 'netting off' method.

(3) Investment properties are accounted for at fair value. New investment properties were purchased during the period for $14m in cash.

(4) During the reporting period, the Frank Group disposed of some of its shares in Chip. Frank held 90% of the ordinary shares in Chip before the disposal and 40% of the shares after the disposal (leaving it with significant influence). The Frank group received cash proceeds from the sale. The profit on disposal of $3m has been correctly calculated and credited to the statement of profit or loss. The fair value of the interest in Chip retained was $32m. Goodwill and the non-controlling interest at the disposal date were $40m and $4m respectively.

A breakdown of Chip's net assets at the date of the share disposal is provided below:

	$m
Property, plant and equipment	81
Trade and other receivables	32
Cash and cash equivalents	6
Loans	(30)
Trade and other payables	(55)
Net assets at disposal date	34

(5) During the period, $65m in cash was spent on investments in associates.

(6) Finance costs include a $2m loss on the retranslation of a loan that was denominated in sterling (£). All other finance costs were paid in cash.

Required:

Prepare a consolidated statement of cash flows using the indirect method for the Frank group for the year ended 30 September 20X4 in accordance with IAS 7 Statement of Cash flows.

Note: the notes to the statement of cash flows are not required.

Test your understanding 5 – Sunny Days

Sunny Days is an entity that breeds and matures beef cattle for sale. It prepares its financial statements in accordance with International Financial Reporting Standards and has a year end of 30 September 20X4. The directors need help with a number of unresolved accounting issues that are detailed below.

(a) In the financial statements for the year ended 30 September 20X3 Sunny Days reported biological assets of $1.8 million. Cattle with a carrying amount of $0.1 million died during the year ended 30 September 20X4 and Sunny Days sold cattle with a carrying amount of $0.4 million. During the current year, the company purchased new cattle and correctly recognised it at a value of $0.8 million. This was partly funded by an unconditional grant of $0.2 million from a local government agency.

Sunny Days does not have the information available to identify the principal market for its cattle. Details of the prices that Sunny Days could obtain for its entire herd at the two markets available to it at the reporting date are provided below:

	Market 1	**Market 2**
Estimated selling price ($m)	2.6	2.8
Cost of transporting cattle to market ($m)	0.1	0.4
Costs to sell (as % of selling price)	0.5%	0.5%

The farmland used by Sunny Days to rear its cattle was purchased for $3 million on 1 October 20X2 but was revalued to $3.2 million on 30 September 20X3. Due to declining property prices in the area, the land was deemed to have a fair value of $2.7 million as at 30 September 20X4.

(12 marks)

(b) On 1 January 20X4, the government announced new legislation which made some of Sunny Days' farming methods illegal. These laws became effective on 1 September 20X4. Due to short term cash flow difficulties, Sunny Days has not yet started to comply with the new legislation. It is estimated that the cost of compliance will be approximately $0.8 million. The government has said that fines for non-compliance are $0.1 million per month and will be strictly enforced.

The directors of Sunny Days wish to know how to account for the above costs as well as any resulting deferred tax impact. Fines are not a tax allowable expense. Sunny Days pays tax at a rate of 20%.

(5 marks)

(c) Sunny Days enters into a contract with a supplier to use a specific retail unit (Unit 5A) for a period of five years. Unit 5A is part of a larger retail space owned by the supplier. Sunny Days will use the retail unit to sell farm produce to the general public.

During the five year period, the supplier can force Sunny Days to relocate to one of the other retail units. The terms of the contract state that the supplier would have to pay all of Sunny Day's relocation costs, and make a payment to compensate for the inconvenience. The supplier would only benefit from moving Sunny Days if a larger retailer wished to move into Unit 5A and if they were willing to commit to using this space for more than five years. This is thought to be possible, but unlikely.

Sunny Days must open and operate Unit 5A during the hours when the larger retail space is open. However, Sunny Days can sell whatever products it wishes, at whatever prices it determines. The supplier will provide cleaning and security services.

Sunny Days will make fixed quarterly payments to the supplier. Sunny Days must also make an annual variable payment, calculated as a percentage of the revenue generated by Unit 5A.

The directors of Sunny Days require advice on whether this contract contains a lease.

(6 marks)

Required:

Discuss the accounting treatment of the above transactions in the financial statements of Sunny Days for the year ended 30 September 20X4.

Note: the mark allocation is shown against each of the three events above.

Professional marks will be awarded for the clarity and quality of presentation and discussion.

(2 marks)

(Total: 25 marks)

Test your understanding 6 – Coffee

Coffee is a company with a reporting date of 30 September 20X4. Its financial statements are prepared in accordance with International Financial Reporting Standards. There are a number of unresolved accounting issues, which are detailed below.

(a) The financial controller of Coffee was appointed during the current reporting period. She is concerned that some of the payments made this year are significantly larger than the amounts that were provided and accrued for. The two largest discrepancies are detailed below:

– Legal experts had previously advised Coffee that it would probably be found not liable in a court case concerning breaches in employee health and safety legislation. As such, a contingent liability was disclosed in the financial statements for the period ended 30 September 20X3. However, on 1 July 20X4, Coffee was found liable and was ordered to pay damages of $2 million.

– In its financial statements for the year ended 30 September 20X3, Coffee provided for income tax payable of $3 million. However, in January 20X4, Coffee's records were inspected by the tax authorities and a number of errors were discovered. The tax authorities recommended that Coffee improve its controls and training to prevent such mistakes from happening again. Coffee was not levied with any fines but the authorities deemed that the correct amount of tax payable on profits earned in the period ended 30 September 20X3 was $4 million. Coffee paid this in July 20X4.

Coffee requires advice as to the correct accounting treatment of these two events.

(6 marks)

(b) Coffee makes a number of loans to its customers. The interest rate on these loans is at a market rate. Within the first 12 months, Coffee sells these loan assets to another company called Tea. Tea, which is a subsidiary of Coffee, holds the loans until maturity.

At the period end, Coffee holds loan assets that it has yet to sell to Tea. Coffee wishes to know the accounting treatment of these loan assets in both its individual and group financial statements.

(8 marks)

(c) At the end of the reporting period, Coffee bought 200 kg of gold bullion for $4 million in cash. Gold bullion is traded on an active market and can be bought and sold instantly. The fair value of gold bullion changes erratically, and Coffee made the investment with the intention of trading it at a profit in the short-term.

Coffee is unsure whether the $4 million holding of gold bullion should be classified as cash and cash equivalents in its statement of cash flows.

(4 marks)

(d) On 1 October 20X3, Coffee spent $2 million on acquiring a customer list that would provide benefits to the business for 18 months. Coffee has used its own knowledge and expertise to enhance the customer list, and believes that this enhanced list will bring it benefits indefinitely. The directors estimate that, at the reporting date, the original list has a fair value of approximately $1.5 million and that the enhanced list has a fair value of approximately $5 million.

Coffee requires advice as to the correct accounting treatment of the customer list.

(5 marks)

Required:

Discuss the correct accounting treatment of the above transactions for the year ended 30 September 20X4.

Note: the mark allocation is shown against each of the four events above.

Professional marks will be awarded for the clarity and quality of presentation and discussion.

(2 marks)

(Total: 25 marks)

Test your understanding 7 – Bath

Bath is a public limited company with a reporting date of 30 September 20X4. Its financial statements are prepared in accordance with International Financial Reporting Standards. There are a number of unresolved accounting issues, which are detailed below.

(a) The directors of Bath have identified a number of operating segments. Details of these are provided below:

	Total revenue	External revenue	Total assets	Profit/ (loss)
	$m	$m	$m	$m
Delivery services	304	281	215	(10)
Vehicle hire	217	96	94	62
Removal services	51	46	173	14
Vehicle repairs	22	14	6	8
Road rescue	15	15	8	3
	609	452	496	77

The segments all earn different gross profit margins and, accordingly, Bath has concluded that they exhibit different economic characteristics.

Bath requires advice as to which of the segments are reportable in its operating segments disclosure note. For this purpose, information provided in parts (b), (c) and (d) should be ignored.

(6 marks)

(b) Bath's road rescue division was launched in the current financial year. Customers are charged an annual upfront fee. If the customer's vehicle breaks down during the following 12 months, Bath will send one of its mechanics out to fix or recover it.

The finance director of Bath has noticed that the vast majority of the road rescue customers did not require any breakdown assistance during the year. As such, he is proposing to recognise revenue upon receipt of the annual fee.

(5 marks)

(c) Bath purchased a new office building on 1 October 20W4 for $20 million and this was attributed a useful economic life of 50 years. On 30 September 20X4, the decision was made to sell the office building. At this date, the fair value was $17 million and costs to sell were estimated to be $0.1 million. The building was immediately marketed for sale at $17 million and it was expected that the sale would occur within 12 months.

In October 20X4, interest rates rose dramatically leading to a sharp decline in the property market. At 31 October 20X4, it was estimated that the fair value of the building was $13 million but Bath has not reduced the advertised sales price of the building.

Bath wishes to know the correct accounting treatment of the office building in the period ended 30 September 20X4.

(6 marks)

(d) During the reporting period, Bath purchased an investment in the shares of Bristol for $16 million and made a designation to measure them at fair value through other comprehensive income. Bath received dividends of $3 million during the reporting period. At the reporting date, the quoted price of the shares was $20 million and the present value of the estimated dividends that Bath will receive over the next 5 years was $18 million.

Bath pays income tax at a rate of 25%. The tax base of the investment in shares is based on historical cost. Since there are no plans to sell the shares, Bath believes that it would be misleading to account for any related deferred tax effects.

Bath requires advice about the accounting treatment of the investment in the shares of Bristol for the period ended 30 September 20X4.

(6 marks)

Required:

Discuss the correct accounting treatment of the above transactions for the year ended 30 September 20X4.

Note: the mark allocation is shown against each of the four events above.

Professional marks will be awarded for the clarity and quality of presentation and discussion.

(2 marks)

(Total: 25 marks)

Test your understanding 8 – Arc

Arc owns 100% of the ordinary share capital of Bend and Curve. All ordinary shares of all three entities are listed on a recognised exchange. The group operates in the engineering industry, and are currently struggling to survive in challenging economic conditions. Curve has made losses for the last three years and its liquidity is poor. The view of the directors is that Curve needs some cash investment. The directors have decided to put forward a restructuring plan as at 30 June 20X1. Under this plan:

(1) Bend is to purchase the whole of Arc's investment in Curve. The purchase consideration is to be $105 million payable in cash to Arc and this amount will then be loaned on a long-term unsecured basis to Curve; and

(2) Bend will purchase land and buildings with a carrying amount of $15 million from Curve for a total purchase consideration of $25 million. The land and buildings has a mortgage outstanding on it of $8 million. The total purchase consideration of $25 million comprises both ten million $1 nominal value non-voting shares issued by Bend to Curve and the $4 million mortgage liability which Bend will assume; and

(3) Curve had also entered into a lease obligation on 1 July 20X0 for an asset with a useful economic life of six years. The present value of the lease payments at that date was $3 million, and the implicit rate of interest associated with the lease obligation was 10.2%. The lease required that annual payments in arrears of $700,000 must be

made. No entries had been made in respect of the lease in the draft financial statements of Curve; and

(4) A dividend of $25 million will be paid from Bend to Arc to reduce the accumulated reserves of Bend.

The draft statements of financial position of Arc and its subsidiaries at 30 June 20X1 are summarised below:

	Arc	**Bend**	**Curve**
	$m	$m	$m
Non-current assets:			
Tangible non-current assets	500	200	55
Cost of investment in Bend	150		
Cost of investment in Curve	95		
Current assets	125	145	25
	870	345	80
Equity and liabilities			
Ordinary share capital	100	100	35
Share premium			8
Retained earnings	720	230	5
	820	330	48
Non-current liabilities:			
Long-term loan	5		12
Current liabilities:			
Trade payables	45	15	20
	870	345	80

As a result of the restructuring, some of Bend's employees will be made redundant. Based upon a detailed plan, the costs of redundancy will be spread over three years with $2.08 million being payable in one year's time, $3.245 million payable in two years' time and $53.375 million in three years' time. The market yield of high quality corporate bonds is 4%. The directors of Arc consider that, based upon quantification of relevant and reliable data at 30 June 20X1, it will incur additional restructuring obligations amounting to $3 million.

Required:

(a) **Prepare the individual entity statements of financial position after the proposed restructuring plan.**

(13 marks)

(b) **Discuss the key implications of the proposed plans, in particular whether the financial position of each company has been improved as a result of the reorganisation.**

(5 marks)

Professional marks will be awarded in part (b) for clarity and expression of your discussion.

(2 marks)

(Total: 20 marks)

Test your understanding answers

Test your understanding 1 – Cookie

Consolidated statement of financial position for the Cookie Group as at 30 April 20X4

	$m
Property, plant and equipment ($80 + $85 + $67 – $4.2 (W9) + $0.4 (W9))	228.2
Goodwill ($1 + $7) (W3)	8.0
Other intangible assets ($15 – $3) (W2)	12.0
Investments ($10 + ($15 – $10))	15.0
	263.2
Inventories ($19 + $6 + $25 – $0.5 (W7))	49.5
Trade receivables ($17 + $13 + $33 – $4 (W7))	59.0
Cash and cash equivalents ($22 + $3 + $14)	39.0
Total assets	410.7
Share capital ($21 + $5 (W3))	26.0
Other components of equity (W5)	67.8
Retained earnings (W5)	115.9
	209.7
Non-controlling interest (W4)	57.6
	267.3
Non-current liabilities ($40 + $10 + $18 – $0.5 (W8))	67.5
Current liabilities ($23 + $18 + $38 – $4 (W7) + $1 (W10))	76.0
	410.7

(W1) **Group structure**

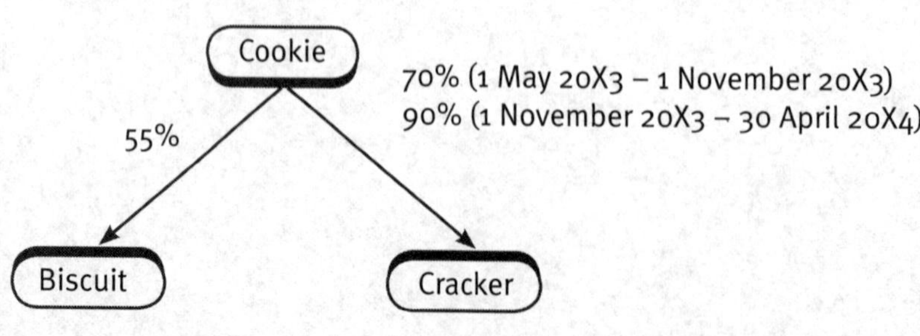

(W2) **Net assets**

	Acquisition	Reporting date
	$m	$m
Biscuit		
Share capital	10	10
Retained earnings	70	79
Investments ($15 – $10)	–	5
Brand (bal. fig)	15	15
Excess amortisation ((\$15/5) × 1 year)	–	(3)
	95	106

	Acquisition	Reporting date
	$m	$m
Cracker		
Share capital	20	20
Other components	20	20
Retained earnings	30	43
	70	83

(W3) **Goodwill**

Biscuit	$m
Cash consideration	30.0
Share consideration (5m × $4.5)	22.5
FV of NCI at acquisition	45.0
FV of net assets at acquisition (W2)	(95.0)
Goodwill at acquisition	2.5
Impairment (W6)	(1.5)
Goodwill at reporting date	1.0

The share consideration has not been accounted for. In the above calculation, $22.5m is being debited to goodwill. Adjustments will need to be made to share capital for $5m (5m shares × $1 nominal) and to other components of equity for $17.5m (5m shares × ($4.5 – $1.0)).

Cracker	$m
Consideration	56.0
NCI at acquisition (30% × $70) (W2)	21.0
FV of net assets at acquisition (W2)	(70.0)
Goodwill	7.0

Remember that goodwill is calculated on the date control is achieved. It is not recalculated if further shares are purchased.

(W4) **Non-controlling interest**

	$m
Biscuit NCI at acquisition (W3)	45.0
45% of Biscuit's post-acquisition net assets (45% × ($106 – $95)) (W2)	4.95
Cracker NCI at acquisition (W3)	21.0
30% of Cracker's post-acquisition net assets between 1 May 20X3 and 1 November 20X3 (30% × (($83 – $70) × 6/12)) (W2)	1.95
10% of Cracker's post-acquisition net assets between 1 November 20X3 and 30 April 20X4 (10% × (($83 – $70) × 6/12)) (W2)	0.65
Goodwill impairment (W6)	(0.7)
Increase in ownership (W11)	(15.3)
	57.6

(W5) **Group reserves**

Retained earnings

	$m
100% Cookie	105.0
55% of Biscuit's post acquisition profits (55% × ($106 – $95)) (W2)	6.05
70% of Cracker's post-acquisition retained earnings between 1 May 20X3 and 1 November 20X3 (70% × (($83 – $70) × 6/12)) (W2)	4.55
90% of Cracker's post-acquisition retained earnings between 1 November 20X3 and 30 April 20X4 (90% × (($83 – $70) × 6/12)) (W2)	5.85
Goodwill impairment (W6)	(0.8)
PURP (W7)	(0.5)
Loan retranslation gain (W8)	0.5
PPE capital expenditure error (W9)	(4.2)
PPE depreciation error (W9)	0.4
Provision (W10)	(1.0)
	115.9

Other components of equity

	$m
100% Cookie	50.0
Share issue (W3)	17.5
Increase in ownership (W11)	0.3
	67.8

(W6) **Goodwill impairment – Biscuit**

	$m
Year-end net assets (W2)	106.0
Goodwill (W3)	2.5
	108.5
Recoverable amount	(107.0)
Impairment	1.5

Under the full goodwill method, this impairment must be allocated between the group and the NCI based on their shareholdings.

Group share: 55% × $1.5m = $0.8m (W5)

NCI share: 45% × $1.5m = $0.7m (W4)

(W7) **Intra-group trading**

There has been trading between Cookie and Biscuit. The profit remaining in inventory of $0.5m ($2m × 25%) must be eliminated:

Dr Retained earnings (W5)	$0.5m
Cr Inventories	$0.5m

The invoice for the sales transaction remains outstanding. Therefore, the intra-group receivable and payable must be eliminated:

Dr Payables	$4.0m
Cr Receivables	$4.0m

(W8) **Loan**

The loan would have been initially recorded at $4.3m (DN10m/2.3).

As a monetary liability, it must be retranslated at the year end using the closing rate. This will result in a liability of $3.8m (DN10m/2.6).

The loan therefore needs to be reduced by $0.5m ($4.3m – $3.8m) with a gain of $0.5m being recorded in profit or loss.

Dr Non-current liabilities	$0.5m
Cr Retained earnings (W5)	$0.5m

(W9) **Plant**

Per IAS 16, general overheads and training are not allowed to be included within the cost of property, plant and equipment. Therefore $4.2m ($3.7m + $0.5m) should be written off to profit or loss.

Dr Retained earnings (W5)	$4.2m
Cr PPE	$4.2m

As a result of the error above, the depreciation charge for the year will be incorrect.

The depreciation charged on this asset will have been $1.5m ($15m/5 years × 6/12). The depreciation that should have been charged is $1.1m (($15m – $4.2m)/5 years × 6/12). Depreciation must therefore be reduced by $0.4m.

The correcting entry is:

Dr PPE	$0.4m
Cr Retained earnings (W5)	$0.4m

(W10) **Provision**

An obligation exists for Cookie to repair units that develop defects and that are still under warranty. Per IAS 37, where a provision involves a large population of items, the expected value of the outflow should be determined.

The expected value of the cost of the repairs is:

($6m × 7%) + ($14m × 4%) = $1.0m

The entry for this is:

Dr Retained earnings (W5)	$1.0m
Cr Provisions	$1.0m

(W11) **Increase in ownership**

Cookie obtained control over Cracker on 1 May 20X3.

On 1 November 20X3, Cookie increases its holding of shares. Goodwill is not recalculated and no gain or loss arises. Instead, this is deemed to be a transaction within equity.

There will be a decrease in the NCI. The difference between the consideration paid and the decrease in the NCI is taken to other components of equity.

	$m
Decrease in NCI (W12)	15.3
Cash paid	(15.0)
Increase in shareholders' equity	0.3

(W12) **Decrease in NCI**

The NCI in Cracker has decreased from 30% to 10%, a decline of two-thirds.

The NCI in Cracker before the share purchase was $22.95m ($21.0 m + $1.95m (W4)). The decrease in the NCI is therefore $15.3m (2/3 × $22.95m).

Test your understanding 2 – Pineapple

Consolidated statement of profit or loss for the year ended 30 September 20X3

	$000
Continuing operations	
Revenue ($9,854 + $3,562 – $400 (intra. co) – $63 (W1))	12,953
Cost of sales ($5,432 + $2,139 – $400 (intra. co) + $42 (W2))	(7,213)
Gross profit	5,740
Administrative expenses ($1,432 + $400 + $15 (W3) + $300 GW imp.)	(2,147)
Distribution costs ($402 + $324)	(726)
Profit from operations	2,867
Share of profit of associates (W4)	54
Investment income ($386 + $15 – $320 (W5) + $114 (W6))	195
Finance costs ($246 + $547 (W6))	(793)
Profit before taxation	2,323
Taxation ($486 – $100 (W7))	(386)
Profit for the period from continuing operations	1,937

Discontinued operations	
Profit for the period from discontinued operations (W8)	1,264
Total profit for the period	3,201
Profit attributable to:	
Equity holders of Pineapple (bal. fig.)	3,021
Non-controlling interest (W10)	180
	3,201

Group structure

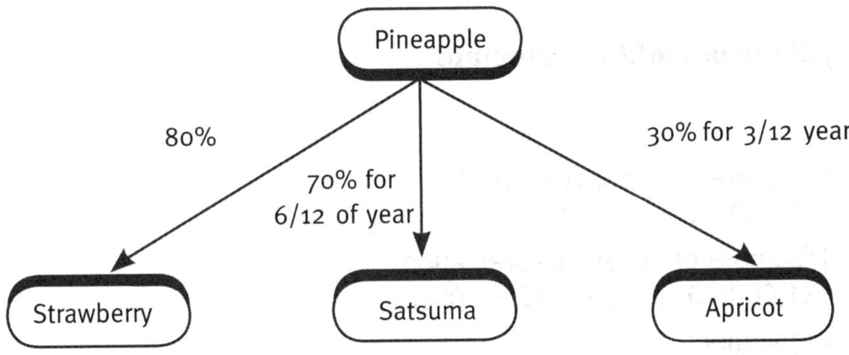

(W1) **Revenue**

A total price of $72,000 ($3,000 × 24) should be allocated to the performance obligation to provide technical support. This should be recognised as revenue over time.

Only 3 months of the service period have passed, therefore 21 months of service revenue must be removed from Pineapple's statement of profit or loss.

This amounts to $63,000 (21 months × $3,000 per month).

(W2) **Excess depreciation**

The carrying amount of the net assets acquired is $2,325,000 ($1,000,000 + $1,325,000).

The excess of the fair value over the carrying amount is therefore $1,675,000 ($4,000,000 – $2,325,000).

The extra depreciation required is $42,000 ($1,675,000/40 years).

(W3) **Pensions**

Pineapple is obliged to pay $45,000 ($900,000 × 5%) in the current year. It has currently paid $30,000. An accrual is required for $15,000 ($45,000 – $30,000).

(W4) **Share of profit of associate**

	$000
P's share of associate's profit ($1,749 × 3/12 × 30%)	131
P's share of excess depreciation ($1,600/40 years × 3/12 × 30%)	(3)
Impairment	(50)
PURP ($100 × 4/5 × 30%)	(24)
Share of profit of associate	54

(W5) **Dividends**

Strawberry paid a dividend in the year of $400,000 and therefore Pineapple would have received $320,000 ($400,000 × 80%). This should be removed from investment income.

(W6) **Financial assets**

The financial asset should have been initially recognised at its fair value of $953,000 ($1,500,000 × $(1/1.12^4)$).

The asset must be written down by $547,000 ($1,500,000 – $953,000), which will be charged to profit or loss.

The financial asset is measured at amortised cost. Investment income should be recognised at $114,000 ($953,000 × 12%).

(W7) **Deferred tax**

Strawberry should recognise a deferred tax asset for $100,000 ($500,000 × 20%) and should credit tax in profit or loss by the same amount.

(W8) **Profit from discontinued operations**

	$000
Profit to disposal date ($568 × 6/12)	284
Profit on disposal (W9)	980
	1,264

(W9) **Profit on disposal of Satsuma**

	$000	$000	$000
Proceeds from disposal			5,600
Carrying amount of subsidiary			
Goodwill at disposal			
Consideration	4,900		
NCI at acquisition	1,600		
FV of net assets at acquisition ($2,000 + $2,045)	(4,045)		
Goodwill at acquisition	2,455		
Impairment (40%)	(982)		
		1,473	
Net assets at disposal			
Share capital	2,000		
Retained earnings b/fwd	2,342		
Profit to disposal date (W8)	284		
		4,626	

NCI at disposal			
NCI at acquisition	1,600		
NCI share of post-acquisition net assets (30% × ($4,626 – $4,045))	174		
NCI share of impairment (30% × $982)	(295)		
		(1,479)	
Carrying amount of sub at disposal			(4,620)
Profit on disposal			980

(W10) **Non-controlling interest**

	$000
NCI % of Strawberry's profit (20% × ($714 + $100 (W7))	163
NCI % of Satsuma's profit to disposal (30% × $284 (W8))	85
NCI % of Strawberry's goodwill impairment (20% × $300)	(60)
NCI % of Strawberry's excess depreciation (20% × $42 (W2))	(8)
	180

Test your understanding 3 – Vinyl

Consolidated statement of financial position for the Vinyl Group as at 30 September 20X4

	$m
Property, plant and equipment ($350 + MK290/1.7 + $160 + $11 (W2))	691.6
Goodwill ($90.6 + $3.2 (W3))	93.8
Other intangible assets (MK10/1.7 (W2))	5.9
Investment properties ($10 + $4)	14.0
Financial assets ($21 + $3.1 – $1.3 – $0.2 (W11))	22.6
	827.9
Inventories ($49 + MK45/1.7 + $37)	112.5
Trade receivables ($76 + MK46/1.7 + $49)	152.05
Cash and cash equivalents ($52 + MK38/1.7 + $23)	97.35
Total assets	1,189.8
Share capital	65.0
Other components of equity (W5)	76.8
Retained earnings (W5)	572.7
Translation reserve (W6)	(88.8)
	625.7
Non-controlling interest (W4)	96.4
	722.1
Non-current liabilities	
Loans ($200 – $6.3 (W10) + MK15/1.7 + $24)	226.5
Defined benefit pension deficit (W9)	59.0
Current liabilities ($92 + MK53/1.7 + $59)	182.2
	1,189.8

Workings

(W1) **Group structure**

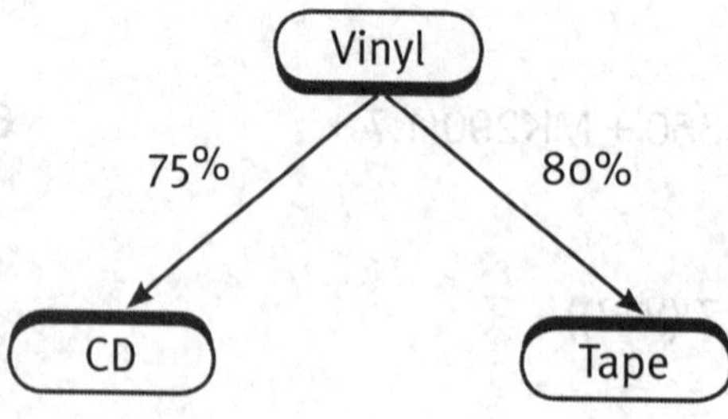

(W2) **Net assets**

	Acquisition MKm	**Reporting date** MKm
CD		
Share capital	76	76
Retained earnings	210	275
Brand (bal. fig)	10	10
	296	361

	Acquisition $m	**Reporting date** $m
Tape		
Share capital	79	79
Other components	1	6
Retained earnings	19	101
Land (bal. fig.)	11	11
	110	197

(W3) **Goodwill**

CD	MKm
Consideration	360.0
FV of NCI at acquisition	90.0
FV of net assets at acquisition (W2)	(296.0)
Goodwill	154.0

	MKm	Exchange Rate	$m
Opening goodwill	154.0	1.2	128.3
Exchange loss	–	**Bal fig.**	(37.7)
Closing goodwill	154.0	1.7	90.6

The total exchange loss of $37.7m will be allocated to the group and NCI based on their respective shareholdings:

Group: $37.7m × 75% = $28.3m
NCI: $37.7m × 25% = $9.4m

Tape	$m
Consideration	100.0
NCI at acquisition (20% × $110 (W2))	22.0
FV of net assets at acquisition (W2)	(110.0)
Goodwill at acquisition	12.0
Impairment (W7)	(8.8)
Goodwill at reporting date	3.2

(W4) **Non-controlling interest**

	$m
NCI in CD at acquisition (MK90/1.2 (W3))	75.0
NCI % of CD's post acquisition net assets 25% × (MK361 – MK296 (W2)/1.4)	11.6
NCI % of forex on CD's goodwill (W3)	(9.4)
NCI % of forex on CD's opening net assets and profit (W8)	(20.2)
NCI in Tape at acquisition (W3)	22.0
NCI % of Tape's post-acquisition net assets 20% × ($197 – $110) (W2)	17.4
	96.4

(W5) **Group reserves**

Retained earnings

	$m
100% Vinyl	501.0
Vinyl % of CD's post-acquisition retained earnings 75% × (MK361 – MK296 (W2)/1.4)	34.8
Vinyl % of Tape's post-acquisition retained earnings 80% × (($197 – $110) – ($6 – $1))	65.6
Goodwill impairment (W7)	(8.8)
Investment property gain ($14 – $10)	4.0
Net interest component (W9)	(3.5)
Service cost (W9)	(22.0)
Financial asset – effective interest (W11)	3.1
Financial asset – interest received (W11)	(1.3)
Loss allowance (W11)	(0.2)
	572.7

Other components of equity

	$m
100% Vinyl	50.0
Vinyl % of Tape's post-acquisition other components of equity 80% × ($6 – $1) (W2)	4.0
Remeasurement gain (W9)	16.5
Convertible bond (W10)	6.3
	76.8

(W6) **Translation reserve**

	$m
Vinyl % of forex on CD's goodwill (W3)	(28.3)
Vinyl % of forex on CD's opening net assets and profit (W8)	(60.5)
	(88.8)

(W7) **Goodwill impairment – Tape**

	$m
Year-end net assets (W2)	197.0
Goodwill (W3)	12.0
Notional NCI ($12 × 20/80)	3.0
	212.0
Recoverable amount	(201.0)
Impairment	11.0

The impairment loss is allocated to the group based on shareholding. The impairment loss attributable to the group is therefore $8.8m ($11m × 80%). The goodwill attributable to the NCI is not recognised under the share of net assets method. Therefore the NCI share of the impairment is not recognised.

(W8) **Forex on opening net assets and profit**

	MKm	Exchange Rate	$m
Opening net assets (W2)	296.0	1.2	246.7
Profit (W2)	65.0	1.4	46.4
Exchange loss	–	**Bal fig.**	(80.7)
Closing net assets	361.0	1.7	212.4

The forex loss is split between the group and the NCI based on their respective shareholdings:

Group: $80.7m × 75% = $60.5m
NCI: $80.7m × 25% = $20.2m

(W9) **Pension**

	$m
Net deficit b/fwd ($50 + $20)	70.0
Net interest component ($70 × 5%)	3.5
Cash contributions	(20.0)
Service cost	22.0
Benefits paid out	–
Remeasurement gain (bal. fig.)	(16.5)
Net deficit c/fwd ($179 – $120)	59.0

The cash contributions have already been accounted for. Therefore, the following adjustments are required:

Net interest

Dr profit or loss	$3.5m
Cr Net pension deficit	$3.5m

Service cost

Dr profit or loss	$22.0m
Cr Net pension deficit	$22.0m

Remeasurement gain

Dr Net pension deficit	$16.5m
Cr Other comprehensive income	$16.5m

(W10) **Convertible bond**

The convertible bond should have been split into a liability component and an equity component. The liability component is calculated as the present value of the repayments, discounted using the interest rate on a similar debt instrument without a conversion option. The equity component is the balance of the proceeds.

The repayments are interest of $2m (500,000 × $100 × 4%) per year, plus the repayment of $50m (500,000 × $100) on 30 September 20X7.

Date	**Cash flow**	**Discount rate**	**Present value**
	$m		$m
30/9/X5	2.0	1/1.09	1.8
30/9/X6	2.0	$1/1.09^2$	1.7
30/9/X7	52.0	$1/1.09^3$	40.2
Liability			43.7

The liability component is initially recognised at $43.7m so the equity component is recognised at $6.3m ($50m – $43.7).

The following adjustment is required:

Dr Loans	$6.3m
Cr Other components of equity	$6.3m

(W11) **Financial assets**

Interest should have been charged using the effective rate.

Investment income in profit or loss should be $3.1m ($21m × 14.6%). The interest received of $1.3m should be removed from profit or loss and deducted from the carrying amount of the financial asset.

The loss allowance will reduce the net carrying amount of financial assets and is charged to profit or loss.

The entries required are:

Effective interest

Dr Financial asset	$3.1m
Cr Profit or loss	$3.1m

Interest received

Dr Profit or loss	$1.3m
Cr Financial asset	$1.3m

Loss allowance

Dr Profit or loss	$0.2m
Cr Loss allowance	$0.2m

Test your understanding 4 – Frank

Consolidated statement of cash flows

	$m	$m
Cash flows from operating activities		
Profit before tax	88	
Finance cost	12	
Profit on disposal of subsidiary	(3)	
Share of profit of associates	(21)	
Depreciation	52	
Loss on disposal of PPE ($10 – $12)	2	
Impairment of goodwill (W1)	27	
Gain on investment properties (W2)	(8)	
Increase in inventories ($256 – $201)	(55)	
Reduction in receivables ($219 – $263 + $32)	12	
Increase in payables (($524 – $2 PPE accrual) – $486 + $55)	91	
Cash generated from operations	197	
Interest paid ($12 – $2 forex loss)	(10)	
Taxation paid (W3)	(7)	
Net cash from operating activities		180

Cash flows from investing activities

Purchase of PPE (W4)	(54)	
Proceeds from disposal of PPE	10	
Cash grant received	3	
Purchase of investment properties	(14)	
Dividends received from associate (W5)	17	
Purchase of associates	(65)	
Net cash impact of subsidiary disposal (W6)	35	
Net cash from investing activities		(68)

Cash flows from financing activities

Proceeds from share issue ($122 – $102)	20	
Proceeds from loan issue (W7)	39	
Dividends paid (W8)	(4)	
Dividends paid to NCI (W9)	(15)	
Net cash from financing activities		40
Increase in cash and cash equivalents		152
Opening cash and cash equivalents ($42 – $148)		(106)
Closing cash and cash equivalents ($103 – $57)		46

Workings

(W1) **Goodwill**

	$m
Bal b/fwd	142
Disposal of subsidiary	(40)
Impairment in year (bal. fig.)	(27)
Bal c/fwd	75

(W2) **Investment properties**

	$m
Bal b/fwd	60
Additions	14
Gain in P/L (bal. fig.)	8
Bal c/fwd	82

(W3) **Taxation**

	$m
Bal b/fwd ($33 + $12)	45
P/L	19
OCI	10
Cash paid (bal. fig)	(7)
Bal c/fwd ($44 + $23)	67

(W4) **Property, plant and equipment**

	$m
Bal b/fwd	263
Depreciation	(52)
Disposal of subsidiary	(81)
Disposal of PPE	(12)
Revaluation of PPE	50
Grant	(3)
Additions (bal. fig)	56
Bal c/fwd	221

Total PPE additions are $56m but $2m of this is included in payables and therefore has not been paid. This means that cash additions are $54m ($56m – $2m).

(W5) **Associates**

	$m
Bal b/fwd	103
Share of profit	21
Fair value of Chip retained	32
Additions	65
Dividends received (bal. fig)	(17)
Bal c/fwd	204

(W6) **Disposal of subsidiary**

	$m	$m
Cash proceeds (bal. fig.)		41
FV of interest retained		32
Goodwill at disposal	40	
Net assets at disposal	34	
NCI at disposal	(4)	
CA of subsidiary at disposal		(70)
Profit on disposal (per P/L)		3

At the disposal date, the subsidiary had cash and cash equivalents of $6m. The net cash impact of the disposal is therefore $35m ($41m – $6m).

(W7) **Loans**

	$m
Bal b/fwd	152
Disposal of subsidiary	(30)
Foreign exchange loss	2
Proceeds from loan issue (bal. fig.)	39
Bal c/fwd	163

(W8) **Retained earnings**

	$m
Bal b/fwd	24
Profit attributable to equity holders	43
Reserve transfer	1
Dividend paid (bal. fig.)	(4)
Bal c/fwd	64

(W9) **Non-controlling interest**

	$m
Bal b/fwd	87
Subsidiary disposal	(4)
Total comprehensive income	36
Dividend paid (bal. fig.)	(15)
Bal c/fwd	104

(W10) **Other components of equity (for proof only)**

	$m
Bal b/fwd	30
Group share of other comprehensive income ($73 TCI share – $43 profit share)	30
Reserve transfer	(1)
Bal c/fwd	59

Test your understanding 5 – Sunny Days

(a) **Biological assets**

Unconditional government grants related to biological assets are recognised in profit or loss when they become receivable. The government grant of $0.2 million will be recognised immediately in profit or loss because it was unconditional.

At the reporting date, biological assets are remeasured to fair value less costs to sell with gains or losses reported in profit or loss. Fair value is defined as the price that would be received from selling an asset in an orderly transaction amongst market participants at the measurement date. Fair value is determined by reference to the principal market or, in the absence of a principal market, the most advantageous market. The most advantageous market is the market which maximizes the net selling price that an entity will receive.

The principal market cannot be determined so the fair value of the biological assets at year end must be determined with reference to the most advantageous market. The net price received in market 1 is $2.49 million ($2.6m – $0.1m – ($2.6m × 0.5%)). The net price received in market 2 is $2.39 million ($2.8m – $0.4m – ($2.8m × 0.5%)). Market 1 is the most advantageous market and should be used to determine fair value.

The fair value of the herd is therefore $2.5 million ($2.6m – $0.1m) and the fair value less costs to sell is $2.49 million (see calculation above). The herd should be recognized at $2.49 million at the reporting date and a gain of $0.39 million (W1) will be recorded in profit or loss.

Land

The land is an item of property, plant and equipment. Revaluation losses on property, plant and equipment are recorded in profit or loss unless a revaluation surplus exists for that specific asset.

The revaluation on 30 September 20X3 of $0.2 million ($3.2m – $3.0m) would have been recorded in other comprehensive income and held within a revaluation reserve in equity. The downwards revaluation in the current reporting period is $0.5 million ($3.2m – $2.7m). Of this, $0.2 million will be charged to other comprehensive income and the remaining $0.3 million will be charged to profit or loss.

(W1) **Gain on revaluation of biological assets**

	$m
Bfd	1.8
Additions	0.8
Death and disposal	(0.5)
Gain	0.39
Cfd	2.49

(b) To recognise a provision, IAS 37 Provisions, Contingent Liabilities and Contingent Assets says that the following criteria must be satisfied:

- There must be a present obligation from a past event
- There must be a probable outflow of economic benefits
- The costs to settle the obligation must be capable of being estimated reliably.

No provision should be recognised for the $0.8 million costs of compliance because there is no obligation to pay (Sunny Days could simply change the nature of its business activities).

A provision should be made for the $0.1 million fine because there will be a probable outflow of resources from a past obligating event (breaking the law).

The fine is not an allowable expense for tax purposes and so the difference between accounting and tax treatments is not temporary. This means that no deferred tax balance is recognised.

(c) A contract contains a lease if it **'conveys the right to control the use of an identified asset for a period of time in exchange for consideration'** (IFRS 16, para 9).

To assess whether this is the case, IFRS 16 Leases requires entities to consider whether the customer has:

- the right to substantially all of the identified asset's economic benefits, and
- the right to direct the identified asset's use.

An asset – Unit 5A – is explicitly identified in the contract. Although Sunny Days can be relocated to a different unit, the supplier is unlikely to benefit from this. Therefore Sunny Days has the right to use an identified asset over the contract term.

Sunny Days has the right to substantially all of the economic benefits resulting from the use of the unit. This is because it has exclusive use of Unit 5A for five years, enabling it to make sales and to generate profits. The payments made to the supplier based on the revenue generated are a form of consideration that is transferred in exchange for the right to use the unit.

Sunny Days has the right to direct the use of the unit because it decides what products are sold, and the price at which they are sold. The restrictions on opening times outlined in the contract define the scope of a Sunny Day's right of use, rather than preventing Sunny Days from directing use. The supplier's provision of security and maintenance services have no impact on how Unit 5A is used.

Based on the above, it would seem that the contract between Sunny Days and its supplier contains a lease.

Test your understanding 6 – Coffee

(a) IAS 8 Accounting Policies, Changes in Accounting Estimates and Errors says that a prior period error is a misstatement in prior year financial statements resulting from the misuse of information which should have been taken into account. Prior period errors are adjusted for retrospectively, by restating comparative amounts. Changes in accounting estimates are accounted for prospectively by including the impact in profit or loss in the current period and, where relevant, future periods.

The court case

This is not a prior period error because Coffee had based its accounting treatment on the best information available. The payment of $2 million will be expensed to profit or loss in the year ended 30 September 20X4.

Tax

The mistakes made in the financial statements for the year ended 30 September 20X3 should not have been made based on the information available to Coffee. This therefore satisfies the definition of a prior period error. In the financial statements for the year ended 30 September 20X3 the current tax expense and the income tax payable should both be increased by $1 million.

(b) According to IFRS 9 Financial Instruments, an investment in debt should be held at amortised cost if it passes the 'contractual cash flows characteristics' test and if an entity's business model is to hold the asset until maturity. The contractual cash flows characteristics test is passed if the contractual terms of the financial asset give rise on specified dates to cash flows that are solely payments of principal and interest on the principal amount outstanding.

If an entity's business model is to both hold the assets to maturity and to sell the assets, and the asset passes the contractual cash flows characteristics test, then the debt instrument should be measured at fair value through other comprehensive income. All other investments in debt instruments should be measured at fair value through profit or loss.

Coffee's individual financial statements

Coffee regularly sells the financial assets, and therefore does not hold them in order to collect the contractual cash flows. In Coffee's individual financial statements, the financial assets should be measured at fair value at the reporting date with any gains or losses reported in profit or loss.

Consolidated financial statements

IFRS 10 Consolidated Financial Statements says that group accounts show the incomes, expenses, assets and liabilities of a parent and its subsidiaries as a single economic entity. Any profit or loss arising on the sale of the assets between Coffee and Tea must be eliminated when producing the consolidated financial statements.

Tea holds the financial assets until maturity. Therefore, the financial assets are held within the Coffee group in order to collect the contractual cash flows. In the consolidated financial statements of the Coffee group, the financial assets should be measured at amortised cost. Assuming that credit risk is low at the reporting date, a loss allowance must be created equal to 12-month expected credit losses.

The group could designate the financial assets to be measured at fair value through profit or loss if it reduces an accounting mismatch that arises from recognising gains or losses on different bases.

(c) IAS 7 Statement of Cash Flows defines 'cash equivalents' as **'short-term, highly liquid investments that are readily convertible to a known amount of cash and which are subject to an insignificant risk of a change in value'** (IAS 7, para 6).

The gold bullion is held for investment purposes, not for the purpose of meeting short-term cash commitments. There is also a substantial risk that the gold will go up or down in value and therefore it is not convertible to a known amount of cash. The gold bullion must therefore be excluded from cash and cash equivalents in the statement of cash flows. The money spent on the gold bullion would most likely be presented within cash flows from investing activities.

(d) Purchased intangible assets are initially measured at cost. The customer list will therefore be initially recognised at its cost of $2 million.

Expenditure on internally generated intangible assets (except those arising from development activities) cannot be distinguished from the cost of developing the business as a whole. Such items are not recognised as intangible assets. The enhancement to the list is internally generated and consequently cannot be recognised.

Intangible assets can only be held under a revaluation model if an active market exists. The customer list is bespoke and so no active market will exist. Therefore, it cannot be held at fair value.

The customer list should be amortised over its estimated useful life of 18 months. This is the period over which the benefits of the $2 million expenditure will be realised. The amortisation expense in profit or loss in the current period is $1.3 million ($2m × 12/18) and the carrying amount of the intangible at the reporting date is $0.7 million ($2m – $1.3m).

Test your understanding 7 – Bath

(a) According to IFRS 8 Operating Segments, an entity must report information about an operating segment if its:

- total revenue (internal and external) is 10% or more of the combined revenue of all segments
- reported profit or loss is more than 10% of the greater, in absolute amount, of (i) the combined reported profit of all operating segments that did not report a loss and (ii) the combined reported loss of all operating segments that reported a loss, or
- assets are 10% or more of the combined assets of all operating segments.

If total external revenue reported by operating segments is less than 75% of the entity's total revenue, additional operating segments must be identified as reportable.

Revenue

All segments with total revenue of greater than \$60.9 million (10% × \$609m) must be reported.

Delivery Services and Vehicle Hire pass this test.

Reported profit or loss

The total profit of the profit making segments is \$87 million (\$62m + \$14m + \$8m + \$3m). The total loss of the loss making segments is \$10 million. 10% of the greater is therefore \$8.7 million (10% × \$87m). This means that segments with a profit or loss of greater than \$8.7 million must be reported.

Delivery Services, Vehicle Hire and Removal Services pass this test.

Assets

All segments with total assets of greater than \$49.6 million (10% × \$496m) must be reported.

Delivery Services, Vehicle Hire and Removal Services pass this test.

75% test

Based on the above three tests, Delivery Services, Vehicle Hire and Removal Services are reportable. Together, their external revenue is \$423 million (\$281m + \$96m + \$46m). This amounts to 93.6% (\$423m/\$452m) of Bath's external revenue. Therefore, no other segments need to be reported.

(b) According to IFRS 15 Revenue from Contracts with Customers, an entity should recognise revenue when (or as) the entity satisfies a performance obligation by transferring a promised good or service to a customer. Entities must decide at the inception of a contract whether a performance obligation is satisfied over time or at a point in time.

An entity transfers control of a good or service over time and, therefore, satisfies a performance obligation and recognises revenue over time, if one of the following criteria is met:

- **'the customer simultaneously receives and consumes the benefits provided by the entity's performance as the entity performs**
- **the entity's performance creates or enhances an asset that the customer controls as the asset is created or enhanced, or**
- **the entity's performance does not create an asset with an alternative use to the entity and the entity has an enforceable right to payment for performance completed to date'** (IFRS 15, para 35).

The recovery service is consumed as time passes, since the service for a prior month cannot be re-performed again in the future. Revenue should therefore be recognised over time, rather than upfront.

An output method based on the time that has elapsed on the contract would probably provide the best estimate of the amount of revenue to recognise.

(c) Per IFRS 5 Non-current Assets Held for Sale and Discontinued Operations, an asset is classified as held for sale if it is available for immediate sale in its present condition and the sale is highly probable. To be highly probable, there must be an active plan to find a buyer, the asset must be being marketed at a price that is reasonable in relation to its fair value, and the sale should be expected within 12 months. An asset that is classified as held for sale should be measured at the lower of its carrying amount and fair value less costs to sell.

On 30 September 20X4 the sale appeared to be highly probable as the building was being marketed at its fair value. The carrying amount of the asset at 30 September 20X4 was $16 million ($20m × (40/50)). This is lower than the fair value less costs to sell of $16.9 million ($17m – $0.1m). Therefore, the asset should continue to be held at $16m.

The rise in interest rates occurs after the end of the reporting period. Therefore, the decline in the asset's fair value does not represent conditions that existed at the reporting date. This is a non-adjusting event. The asset will remain classified as held for sale in the financial statements for the period ended 30 September 20X4. The decline in the asset's value should, however, be described in a disclosure note.

(d) In accordance with IFRS 9 Financial Instruments, financial assets measured at fair value through other comprehensive income are remeasured to fair value each reporting date with the gain or loss recorded in other comprehensive income (OCI).

IFRS 13 Fair Value Measurement defines fair value as the price received when selling an asset in an orderly transaction amongst market participants at the measurement date. When determining fair value, priority is given to level 1 inputs, which are quoted prices for identical assets in active markets. Management's estimate of the dividends that will be received from the shares is a level 3 input to the fair value hierarchy. This should not be used to determine fair value because a level 1 input exists (a quoted price for an identical asset).

The shares should be revalued to $20 million and a gain of $4 million ($20m – $16m) recognised in OCI. The gain in OCI should be classified as an item that will not be recycled to profit or loss in future periods. The dividend received of $3 million is recognised in profit or loss.

According to IAS 12, deferred tax should be calculated on the difference between the carrying amount of a revalued asset and its tax base, even if there is no intention to dispose of the asset. The temporary difference of $4 million ($20m – $16m) will give rise to a deferred tax liability of $1 million ($4m × 25%). The gain on the investment was recognised in OCI and therefore the deferred tax charge will also be recognised in OCI.

Test your understanding 8 – Arc

(a) **Arc – restatement**

	Initial	**Adjusts**	**Notes**	**Final**
	$m	$m		$m
Non-current assets:				
Tangible non-current assets	500			500
Cost of investment in Bend	150			150
Cost of investment in Curve	95	(95)	(1)	
Loan to Curve		105	(2)	105
Current assets	125	105	(1)	150
		(105)	(2)	
		25	(3)	
	870	35		905
Equity and liabilities:				
Ordinary share capital	100			100
Retained earnings	720	10	(1)	755
		25	(3)	
	870	35		855
Non-current liabilities:				
Long-term loan	5			5
Current liabilities:				
Trade payables	45			45
	870	35		905

Notes:

(1) Disposal of investment in Curve for $105m, resulting in a profit of $10m.

(2) Long-term loan made to Curve.

(3) Dividend due from Bend.

(a) **Bend restatement**

	Initial	Adjusts	Notes	Final
	$m	$m		$m
Non-current assets:				
Tangible non-current assets	200	25	(3)	225
Cost of investment in Curve		105	(1)	105
Current assets	145	(105)	(1)	15
		(25)	(2)	
	345	–		345
Equity and liabilities:				
Ordinary share capital	100	10	(3)	110
Share premium		11	(3)	11
Retained earnings	230	(25)	(2)	205
	330	(4)		326
Non-current liabilities:				
Long-term loan		4	(3)	4
Current liabilities:				
Trade payables	15			15
	345	–		345

Notes:

(1) Purchase of investment in Curve for $105m.

(2) Dividend due to Arc.

(3) Purchase of land and buildings from Curve – comprising:

	$m
Non-voting shares of $1 each	10
Share premium (bal fig)	11
Mortgage liability taken over	4
	25

3 – Lease obligation as follows:

	Bal b/fwd	Int @ 10.2%	Cash paid	Bal c/fwd
	$000	$000	$000	$000
Y/end 30/06/X1	3,000	306	(700)	2,606
Y/end 30/06/X2	2,606	266	(700)	2,172

Current liability element = $2,606,000 – $2,172,000 = $434,000

(a) Curve – restatement

	Initial	Adjusts	Notes	Final
	$m	$m		$m
Non-current assets:				
Tangible non-current assets	55	(15.0)	(2)	40.0
Lease assets		3.0	(3)	2.5
		(0.5)	(3)	
Cost of investment in Bend		21.0		21.0
Current assets	25	105.0	(1)	129.3
		(0.7)	(3)	
	80	112.8		192.8
Equity and liabilities:				
Ordinary share capital	35			35.0
Share premium	8			8.0
Retained earnings	5	10.0	(2)	14.2
		(0.5)	(3)	
		(0.3)	(3)	
	48	9.2		57.2
Non-current liabilities:				
Long-term loan	12	(4.0)		8.0
Loan from Arc		105.0	(1)	105.0
Lease obligation		3.0	(3)	2.2
		0.3	(3)	
		(0.7)	(3)	
		(0.4)	(3)	
Current liabilities:				
Lease obligation		(0.4)	(3)	0.4
Trade payables	20			20.0
	80	112.8		192.8

Notes:

1 – Loan from Arc of $105m.

2 – Sale of land and buildings to Bend as follows:

	$m
Disposal proceeds (Mort tfr at + shares at FV $21m)	25
CV of land and buildings	15
Profit on disposal	10

(b) The plan has no impact on the group financial statements as all of the internal transactions will be eliminated on consolidation but does affect the individual accounts of the companies. The reconstruction only masks the problem facing Curve. It does not solve or alter the business risk currently being faced by the group.

A further issue is that such a reorganisation may result in further costs and expenses being incurred. Note that any proposed provision for restructuring must meet the requirements of IAS 37 Provisions, Contingent Liabilities and Contingent Assets before it can be included in the financial statements. A constructive obligation will arise if there is a detailed formal plan produced and a valid expectation in those affected that the plan will be carried out. This is normally crystallised at the point when there is communication by the company with those who are expected to be affected by the plan.

The transactions outlined in the plans are essentially under common control and must be viewed in this light. This plan overcomes the short-term cash flow problem of Curve and results in an increase in the accumulated reserves. The plan does show the financial statements of the individual entities in a better light except for the significant increase in long-term loans in Curve's statement of financial position. The profit on the sale of the land from Curve to Bend will be eliminated on consolidation.

In the financial statements of Curve, the investment in Bend should be accounted for under IFRS 9. There is now cash available for Curve and this may make the plan attractive. However, the dividend from Bend to Arc will reduce the accumulated reserves of Bend but if paid in cash will reduce the current assets of Bend to a critical level.

The purchase consideration relating to Curve may be a transaction at an overvalue in order to secure the financial stability of the former entity. A range of values are possible which are current value, carrying amount or possibly at zero value depending on the purpose of the reorganisation. Another question which arises is whether the sale of Curve gives rise to a realised profit. Further, there may be a question as to whether Bend has effectively made a distribution. This may arise where the purchase consideration was well in excess of the fair value of Curve. An alternative to a cash purchase would be a share exchange. In this case, local legislation would need to be reviewed in order to determine the requirements for the setting up of any share premium account.

The purchase consideration relating to Curve may be a transaction at an overvalue in order to secure the financial stability of the former entity. A range of values are possible which are current value, carrying amount or possibly at zero value depending on the purpose of the reorganisation. Another question which arises is whether the sale of Curve gives rise to a realised profit. Further, there may be a question as to whether Bond has effectively made a distribution. This may arise where the purchase consideration was well in excess of the fair value of Curve. An alternative to a cash purchase would be a share exchange. In this case, local legislation would need to be reviewed in order to determine the requirements for the setting up of any share premium account.

chapter

27

References

References

The Board (2016) *Conceptual Framework for Financial Reporting*. London: IFRS Foundation.

The Board (2014) *ED/2014/4: Measuring Quoted Investments in Subsidiaries, Associates and Joint Ventures at Fair Value.* London: IFRS Foundation.

The Board (2015) *ED/2015/1: Classification of Liabilities: Proposed Amendments to IAS 1.* London: IFRS Foundation.

The Board (2015) *ED/2015/3: Conceptual Framework for Financial Reporting*. London: IFRS Foundation.

The Board (2015) *ED/2015/8: IFRS Practice Statement: Application of Materiality to Financial Statements.* London: IFRS Foundation.

The Board (2016) *IAS 1 Presentation of Financial Statements*. London: IFRS Foundation.

The Board (2016) *IAS 2 Inventories*. London: IFRS Foundation.

The Board (2016) *IAS 7 Statement of Cash Flows*. London: IFRS Foundation.

The Board (2016) *IAS 8 Accounting Policies, Changes in Accounting Estimates and Errors*. London: IFRS Foundation.

The Board (2016) *IAS 10 Events after the Reporting Period*. London: IFRS Foundation.

The Board (2016) *IAS 12 Income Taxes*. London: IFRS Foundation.

The Board (2016) *IAS 16 Property, Plant and Equipment*. London: IFRS Foundation.

The Board (2016) *IAS 19 Employee Benefits*. London: IFRS Foundation.

The Board (2016) *IAS 20 Accounting for Government Grants and Disclosure of Government Assistance*. London: IFRS Foundation.

The Board (2016) *IAS 21 The Effects of Changes in Foreign Exchange Rates.* London: IFRS Foundation.

The Board (2016) *IAS 23 Borrowing Costs*. London: IFRS Foundation.

The Board (2016) *IAS 24 Related Party Disclosures*. London: IFRS Foundation.

The Board (2016) *IAS 27 Separate Financial Statements*. London: IFRS Foundation.

The Board (2016) *IAS 28 Investments in Associates and Joint Ventures*. London: IFRS Foundation.

The Board (2016) *IAS 32 Financial Instruments: Presentation*. London: IFRS Foundation.

The Board (2016) *IAS 33 Earnings per Share*. London: IFRS Foundation.

The Board (2016) *IAS 34 Interim Financial Reporting*. London: IFRS Foundation.

The Board (2016) *IAS 36 Impairment of Assets*. London: IFRS Foundation.

The Board (2016) *IAS 37 Provisions, Contingent Liabilities and Contingent Assets*. London: IFRS Foundation.

The Board (2016) *IAS 38 Intangible Assets*. London: IFRS Foundation.

The Board (2016) *IAS 40 Investment Property*. London: IFRS Foundation.

The Board (2016) *IAS 41 Agriculture*. London: IFRS Foundation.

The Board (2016) *IFRS 1 First-time Adoption of International Financial Reporting Standards*. London: IFRS Foundation.

The Board (2016) *IFRS 2 Share-based Payment*. London: IFRS Foundation.

The Board (2016) *IFRS 3 Business Combinations*. London: IFRS Foundation.

The Board (2016) *IFRS 5 Non-current Assets Held for Sale and Discontinued Operations*. London: IFRS Foundation.

References

The Board (2016) *IFRS 7 Financial Instruments: Disclosure*. London: IFRS Foundation.

The Board (2016) *IFRS 8 Operating Segments*. London: IFRS Foundation.

The Board (2016) *IFRS 9 Financial Instruments*. London: IFRS Foundation.

The Board (2016) *IFRS 10 Consolidated Financial Statements*. London: IFRS Foundation.

The Board (2016) *IFRS 11 Joint Arrangements*. London: IFRS Foundation.

The Board (2016) *IFRS 12 Disclosure of Interests in Other Entities*. London: IFRS Foundation.

The Board (2016) *IFRS 13 Fair Value Measurement*. London: IFRS Foundation.

The Board (2016) *IFRS 15 Revenue from Contracts with Customers*. London: IFRS Foundation.

The Board (2016) *IFRS 16 Leases*. London: IFRS Foundation.

The Board (2015) *IFRS for SMEs Standard*. London: IFRS Foundation.

The Board (2016) *IFRS Practice Statement: Management Commentary*. London: IFRS Foundation.

Index

Index

Index

Index